Unholy Trinity

Also by Mark Aarons
Sanctuary! Nazi Fugitives in Australia

Also by John Loftus
The Belarus Secret
Valhalla's Wake

MARK AARONS and JOHN LOFTUS

Unholy Trinity

HOW THE VATICAN'S NAZI NETWORKS BETRAYED WESTERN INTELLIGENCE TO THE SOVIETS

St. Martin's Press

New York

Library of Congress Cataloging-in-Publication Data

Aarons, Mark.
    Unholy trinity : the Vatican, the Nazis, and Soviet intelligence /
Mark Aarons and John Loftus.
        p.   cm.
    ISBN 0-312-07111-6
    1. World War, 1939–1945—Catholic Church.   2. Catholic Church—
Clergy—Political activity—History—20th century.   3. Fugitives
from justice—Germany—History—20th century.   4. National
socialists.   5. War criminals—Germany—History—20th century.
6. Soviet Union.   Komitet gosudarstvennoĭ bezopasnosti.   7. World
politics—1945–   I. Loftus, John.   II. Title.
    [D810.C6A23   1991]
    940.54′78—dc20   91-36181
                                                                             CIP

Photographs were drawn from the following sources: US National Archive (1, 2, 14, 15, 26, 28); Yugoslav National Archives (3, 12, 13, 16, 17, 18, 19); Tiskara Papinskog Sveučilista Gregoriane, Rome (5, 6, 7, 8, 9, 10, 11, 22); Ukrainian Archives (23, 24); ABN *Correspondence* (25; private collection of Pierre Vicary (20, 21)

First published in Great Britain by William Heineman Limited.

First U.S. Edition: January 1992
10 9 8 7 6 5 4 3 2 1

For Susan and Robyn

'In any case I long ago realized that it is almost
impossible for a layman and a non-Catholic, and
indeed for most Catholics and ecclesiastics outside
the Vatican City, to form a valid judgment or express
an authoritative opinion on Papal policy. The Pope's
decision may, or must be influenced by so many
imponderable or invisible elements. Moreover, not
only is the atmosphere of the Vatican supranational
and universal . . . but it is also fourth-dimensional
and, so to speak, outside of time . . . for example, they
can regard the Savoy dynasty as an interlude, and the
Fascist era as an incident, in the history of Rome and
Italy. They reckon in centuries and plan for eternity
and this inevitably renders their policy inscrutable,
confusing and, on occasion, reprehensible to practical
and time-conditioned minds.'[1]

– Sir D'Arcy Osborne,
British Ambassador to the Vatican,
March 1947.

'I gather that . . . some arrangement has been worked
out with Vatican and Argentina . . . protecting not
only Quislings but also (those) . . . guilty of terrible
crimes committed in Yugoslavia. I presume we must
protect our agents even though it disgusts me . . . we
are conniving with Vatican and Argentina to get
guilty people to haven in latter country.'[2]

– John Moors Cabot
American Ambassador to Belgrade
June 1947.

Contents

Preface

Unholy Trinity is the story of the Vatican's underground Nazi-smuggling networks, code-named 'Operation Ratline.' The first hints of the existence of the Vatican's Ratlines emerged in America. This was perhaps appropriate, as it was US intelligence which gave this name to the Holy See's escape networks. During World War II, the Office of Strategic Services coined the term 'Ratlines' for their escape and evasion networks used by US Air Force crews shot down in occupied Europe.

Ratline, in fact, did not refer to the Nazi vermin who were going out through the Vatican underground (although in hindsight it was an appropriate description). A ratline is the rope ladder reaching to the top of the mast, the last place of safety when the ship is going down. Thus Ratline became a generic intelligence term for an evacuation network.

Although OSS veterans like to boast about their Ratlines, the Vatican's were supposed to remain hidden forever. But beneath the sleepy town of Suitland, Maryland, there are twenty underground vaults, each an acre in size, crammed from floor to ceiling with classified documents from World War II and the Cold War. For nearly half a century they have been hidden from public scrutiny. As the decades passed, the successors to the original custodians had no idea what awful secrets lay buried in the vaults, until piece by piece they lifted the veil of Vatican secrecy.

By the time the intelligence chiefs read this book, it will be too late. It does not matter that these events are still highly classified or that the files were released by error; the fact remains that so many documents have been legally released that any further cover-up is pointless. The Vatican's Ratlines have passed from secrecy to history. It is an ugly legacy of spies, scandals, and Nazi smuggling. It is the sad history of the Vatican's intelligence service.

This book is not an attack on the institution of the Roman Catholic Church. Rather, it is an analysis of a tiny group of Vatican officials who secretly collaborated with the West in one of the most corrupt and immoral spy operations of the Cold War. The first half of this book documents the Church's War against Communism; the second half reveals Communism's war on the Church. What neither the Vatican nor the Western intelligence services realized until too late was that the Ratlines were really run from the Kremlin.

We have attempted to document three major scandals involving religion, espionage, and politics that have been withheld from Western audiences on dubious grounds of national security. It is rare to find a single volume that challenges so much conventionally accepted history, or exposes so much corruption. It is not a pretty story. It is, in large part, a modern American tragedy.

This will be a particularly difficult book for the twenty-six percent of the American public who are Roman Catholics. The first half of the book traces the flight of Nazi war criminals to America after World War II. The evidence confirms that a small cabal of Vatican officials coordinated the mass evacuation of Fascist fugitives to Argentina, Australia, Canada, and of course, the United States. Under the direction of Pope Pius XII, Vatican officials such as Monsignor Giovanni Montini (later Pope Paul VI) supervised one of the greatest obstructions of justice in modern history.

They did not act alone, however, and the religious scandal quickly became an intelligence scandal. For the next forty years, the American government kept the Popes' secret, but not merely to save the Vatican from embarrassment. There was more to it than that, much more. An international consortium of intelligence agencies was involved.

The Vatican's Ratlines had begun with the French Secret Service in 1945. Soon after, the British Secret Service elbowed its way into the French-Vatican Consortium, and when the Vatican began losing control, it turned to the Americans for help in 1947. President Truman did not want to recruit even Nazi scientists, let alone sanction wholesale smuggling of Eastern European Fascists. Behind the President's back a small coterie of right wing Americans committed mutiny. James Jesus Angleton told his old friend and informant, Montini, that he and Pius XII had nothing to fear. Everyone knew that Dewey would beat Truman in the 1948 elections. In the meantime, Angleton and his friend, Allen Dulles, would take care of everything.

They established a super-secret intelligence organization within the US State Department. While the CIA was hunting Nazis, the State Department was recruiting them with the secret help of the British, French, and the Vatican. Angleton and Dulles laundered millions through the Vatican to defeat the Italian Communists in the elections. In return, the Vatican facilitated the escape of tens of thousands of Nazis to the West where they were supposed to be trained as 'Freedom Fighters.'

When the Fascist recruits were sent back behind the Iron Curtain, everything went wrong. Arms laundered through the Vatican were promptly discovered and seized. The Nazi super-agents ended up betraying thousands of innocent anticommunists. In 1951 the British liaison, Kim Philby, was exposed as a Communist super-spy. Here was irony indeed: Through Philby, the Soviets had known all about the Nazi-smuggling, but had said nothing about the Vatican's Ratlines. It began to dawn on Dulles and Angleton that perhaps some of the Nazi nets taken over from Philby may have been riddled, in fact, with Communists disguised as Nazis.

Frantically, the State Department shifted its covert funding from those Nazi factions endorsed by Philby to the rival Fascist organizations which Philby had denounced. The emphasis shifted from Central European Fascists like the murderous Croatian Ustashi to Eastern European Fascists from Russia, Byelorussia, and the Ukraine. Our book reveals for the first time the incredible damage that was done to US security *after* Philby's Nazis had been quietly purged. Dulles had swapped Philby's KGB-controlled Nazis for an even deadlier group controlled by Soviet military intelligence.

The Russian People's Labor Alliance (the NTS) had been created by Stalin as a means to infiltrate Hitler's Nazi Party in Germany. During World War II, the NTS and the Nazis worked hand in hand. In fact, NTS was virtually the sole source of German intelligence inside the Soviet Union. Under the direction of Prince Anton Turkul, NTS passed on reams of misinformation that crippled the Nazi military offensive on the Eastern Front. Prince Turkul was perhaps the most extraordinary Communist double agent—far more valuable than Philby. There are indications that Philby's KGB network may have been deliberately discarded by the Politburo in order to pass the NTS on to the gullible State Department.

After Eisenhower was inaugurated in 1953, Dulles brought the NTS into the unwitting CIA. *Reader's Digest* and *Life* magazine praised the NTS 'Freedom Fighters', even donating money to Prince Turkul's organization without knowing that it was a Soviet scam. The Cold War turned into a disaster. Turkul's network betrayed every American strategy to the Communists. Turkul even instigated a premature rebellion in Hungary that was easily crushed by the Soviet military in 1956.

It was a humiliating debacle. By 1959, the United States had lost every courier, safehouse, and intelligence network behind the Iron Curtain. The intelligence scandal was swept quietly under the rug, just as the Vatican scandal before it. The Soviets kept quiet about the religious scandal because the Vatican's Nazi-smuggling provided a deadly method to infiltrate Western intelligence.

Why did the cover-up last so long, and who was behind it? We suspect that we have uncovered the tip of a third scandal, a political cover-up which continues to this day. The information we have discovered thus far may be of particular interest to an American audience.

Although our research is still under way for our sequel to *Unholy Trinity*, it may not be premature to give our readers a thumbnail sketch of the facts that support the following conclusion: The secret techniques used to launder money, guns, and smuggle Nazi 'Freedom Fighters' in the 1940s and 1950s were adopted by the Reagan/Bush Administration as the covert methodology to avoid Congressional review in the 1980s. In this history of the Cold War, American readers may recognize not only the blueprint for the Iran-Contra scandal, but also the names of many of its architects.

After World War II, when Allen Dulles was first establishing his networks of Fascist 'Freedom Fighters', he had a penchant for talent-spotting rising young Americans to help with the legwork. One of his first recruits was a young movie actor named Ronald Reagan. During the early 1950s, Reagan was a public spokesman for Dulles's front group, the Crusade for Freedom.

As Governor of California, Reagan knew so little about the Ustashi that he publicly proclaimed April 10 a Croatian ethnic holiday. When the incensed government of Yugoslavia pointed out that it was the day that Hitler created the Ustashi's Fascist puppet state, Reagan was forced to apologize. Yet as President, Reagan continued to invite former Fascists to the White House, even those whom the State Department previously admitted were notorious war criminals from the Kim Philby faction.

Another early Dulles protégé was William Casey. Casey was

stationed with US intelligence in London after World War II when the Vatican-British-American Intelligence Consortium was first getting under way. Dulles recruited Casey to oversee the 'International Rescue Committee' which facilitated the illegal emigration of Britain's Fascists to America during the 1950s. Casey was the American end of the Vatican Ratline, and learned how the game was played. In 1980, he became head of the CIA under Reagan.

Beyond doubt, Dulles's most important recruit was a young US Navy officer named Richard M. Nixon, who was plucked from the postwar obscurity of reviewing captured Nazi records to run for Congress, allegedly with right wing funding. To understand just how right wing, it should be noted that after his election, Nixon's former California law firm represented a prominent Fascist financier named Malaxa in his attempt to obtain American citizenship. Malaxa was later investigated for war crimes. During the late 1940s Dulles escorted young Nixon on a tour of Occupied Germany so that he could see the embattled 'Freedom Fighters' first hand.

Nixon's anticommunist credentials were so firmly established by 1951 that he was recruited to steer Senator Joe McCarthy from pursuing 'commie agents' inside Dulle's intelligence shop. In view of what Nixon and Dulles did later, perhaps it is a pity that McCarthy did not turn his venom on them. In 1953, Nixon was inaugurated as Eisenhower's Vice President and became the intelligence liaison to his old mentors—Allen Dulles, the new head of CIA, and John Foster Dulles, the new Secretary of State. As Vice President, Nixon warmly endorsed the 'Freedom Fighters' concept, and personally received prominent Fascist fugitives in the White House as potential 'liberators' of the captive nations behind the Iron Curtain.

By 1959, it was painfully clear to the intelligence chiefs of NATO that all of the Fascist emigré groups, including Turkul's NTS, had been hopelessly compromised by the Communists. Dulles was dismayed, but Nixon was frantic. He was about to begin his own Presidential campaign in 1960. It was not the time to admit that the Eisenhower administration had been duped by the Soviets into smuggling Nazis to America. It was worse than embarrassing; he had knowledge of a felony. Fortunately for Nixon, an orgy of secret record shredding took place inside the CIA and the Pentagon. Only the State Department knew what had happened, and they transferred their records to other agencies, but kept the indexes.

Lest we be thought unfair in ascribing knowledge of the Nazi movement to Richard Nixon, it should be noted that we uncovered a 'smoking gun' in the official Australian Parliamentary records. During the Nixon administration, the Australian Government asked the State Department for advice on how to handle problems with their Fascist Ustashi residents. In a lengthy briefing, a spokesman for State told his Australian counterpart that the Nixon administration had been quietly keeping track of these Croatian extremists, but did not do anything about them because they were important to 'get out the ethnic votes in five key states'. Apparently turning out the Nazi vote was deemed necessary to prevent Nixon from ever losing another close election.

During the 1970s the House Judiciary began investigating complaints from the Jewish community that there were Fascists living in America. The State Department committed outright perjury. Congress was told that State had no information when their own security computers had detailed information on war crimes committed by their Fascist employees.

The State Department's lies to Congress reached absurd proportions. They not only knew where the Nazis were in America, they knew why Nixon was still protecting them. The State Department was getting nervous: It was time for the Nazis to find a new home. The most sensitive war criminals were promptly transferred to the Pentagon as consultants on 'special operations.' Shortly afterward, Nixon was forced out of office in the Watergate scandal, but his Nazi secret was safe.

The Nixon Administration's lasting legacy to American politics was the Nazi cover-up. In 1977 Peter Rodino, Joshua Eilberg, and Elizabeth Holtzmann renewed the House Judiciary Committee's inquiry. Congressman Eilberg had come up with a potential list of forty-four Nazi suspects and sent the names around the government. One of the suspects was a known Byelorussian war criminal whose State Department dossier blatantly described how his illegal entry had been obtained. The suspect was also one of Philby's Nazis who was later denounced as a Soviet mole by a fellow Communist agent. Needless to say, the embarrassed intelligence community withheld the files from Congress.

But Congress did not give up. In 1978, the General Accounting Office sent an expanded list of all Nazi suspects to every government agency. The Nazi files were carefully reviewed by the intelligence community who added notes that the dossiers were not to be disclosed to the GAO. But the GAO knew of the existence of at least one Nazi who had been exposed by the press when he landed at Ellis Island. Without knowing they had struck a goldmine, the GAO asked for all dossiers on a Hungarian Fascist named Ferenc Vajta.

The problem was that Vajta was one of the key US informants inside the Vatican. Indeed, an entire chapter of this book is devoted to his activities. The Vajta dossiers spelled out the roles played by the State Department, British intelligence, and the Vatican. But in 1978, the government agencies could not risk a simple denial that they had any files: It was publicly known Vajta had been deported for his Fascist affiliations.

The solution was wickedly simple: The dossiers were sanitized with black magic markers to conceal the State Department's role and implicate the largely unwitting military. The GAO fell for it. They reported to Congress that only one unnamed Fascist had ever tried to emigrate, and he had been caught. The GAO concluded that there was no widespread conspiracy to assist Nazi immigration to America.

The equally unwitting CIA chimed in with testimony that 'no Nazis or war criminals or persons of that type' had ever been granted citizenship under the super-secret '100 Persons a Year' quota for recruiting foreign spies. The State Department, which knew better, issued the usual denials. Still, Congress was skeptical, and asked President Carter to establish an Office of Special Investigations within the US Justice Department to take over the war crimes inquiry.

One of the authors (John Loftus) joined OSI, and soon discovered the secret of Western recruitment of Nazis. Further cover-ups ensued after Reagan took up residence in the White House. The reason was very simple: The Fascists were being used in ongoing operations. Nixon-era Nazis were back on the payroll again, not as experts on anticommunism but as consultants on antiterrorism. They were working for the Special Operations Division, a covert unit to fight fire with fire, terrorism with terrorism.

The old spies claimed that SOD was running a secret war, no holds barred, declared, funded, and fought without the knowledge of Congress. Even the CIA did not know that it was their own director, William Casey, who had authorized SOD's operations. True, Casey hired a few old Nazis who had been recruited for SOD and for General John Singlaub's 'private' group, the World Anticommunist League. General Singlaub, however, maintains that he tried to purge the Nazis from WACL. There is no doubt that the Nazis were there.

Casey had revived the Ratlines with a vengeance. He copied Dulles's Cold War program down to the last detail.

By the early 1980s, there were reports of Central American death squads trained by Asian and European Fascists; reports that General Singlaub had created an enormous network of intergovernmental contributors to fund covert operations without the knowledge of Congress. Most alarming were tales of illegal US support for the Contras by laundering money through Israel, Taiwan, and South Korea.

In late 1986, the Iran-Contra Scandal became public knowledge, but the full truth did not emerge during the official investigations. Behind the back of Congress and the CIA, a new international intelligence consortium had been built in 1984. Guns, money, and agents were laundered through British intelligence to continue secret wars in Africa, Nicaragua, and the Middle East. There were whispers that the new operation was being run out of the White House itself. The British-American Ratline was back. Congress was conned again with stories that the Israelis invented the Iran-Contra connection in 1985.

The truth is that the Office of the Vice President started it in late 1983, when George Bush headed a planning group to reform Casey's SOD, which had been wound up amidst financial scandal in 1983. By April 1984, the new 'counterterrorism' scheme was authorized by National Security Decision Directive 138. Bush's National Security adviser, Donald Gregg, assembled the team that would liaise with British intelligence. At Casey's suggestion, a young colonel named Oliver North was borrowed from the National Security Council. Later, North's Annapolis classmate, a former Rhodes scholar who studied in Britain and later worked with Gregg in the CIA, was added to Bush's office. In public, their job was to draft the report of the Vice President's Task Force on Terrorism. In private, their mission was to coordinate the British takeover of Casey's secret wars. When these two men transferred back to the NSC in late 1985, they brought the secret warplan with them. Gregg maintains that he knew nothing of their activities.

In 1990, Mrs. Peggy Robohm sent John Loftus the files of a recently deceased British mercenary who had worked both for MI6 and the CIA. The British agent claimed to have worked with several of the Vice President's staff on the Iran-Contra effort during 1984. He even had joint BCCI bank accounts with North dating back to 1984, and

Swiss bank records of 43 million dollars of laundered money. He claimed that Senator Dan Quayle's assistant was the secret courier to Britain. The files were sent to the Special Prosecutor for Iran/Contra. Perhaps coincidentally, the Iran/Contra grand jury was reopened a few months later and began subpoenaing persons with knowledge of Casey's 'special operations.'

Ironically, the key evidence was made public when Oliver North's diaries were partially declassified in 1990. Among the earliest 1984 entries are notes of North's meetings to land NSDD 138. No one had bothered to match the names of North's acquaintances against the roster of the British Embassy.

Oliver North did not invent the money and gunrunning system used in Iran/Contra. He simply copied the one that Casey had used. There was one slight change. Instead of recruiting a Nazi, North hired a terrorist. In North's diary is a reference to 'M' who lives in a 'fortress-like residence in Marbella, Spain', heavily guarded by the local police. That is the address of Monzer Al-Kassar, chief money launderer for the PLO and a known international terrorist. Al-Kassar is a relative by marriage of Syria's chief of intelligence who directed most of the activities of the extremist wing of the PLO. It was Monzer ('M') who helped North bargain for the release of hostages.

There is no doubt that this leading PLO terrorist was on North's payroll. Buried in the Iran/Contra depositions are several payment references to Monzer Al-Kassar, including one for a million dollars. It is confirmed that Monzer supplied Communist weapons to the Contras, and suspected that he sold Contra secrets to the Communists. North never realized why the war in Nicaragua went so badly. If he had checked with any US intelligence agency, he would have been told that Monzer was not to be trusted. Those are the risks you take when you operate outside the law.

And Vice President Bush? What did he know of all this? Was he aware that his own staff were dabbling with Casey's Nazis and PLO terrorists? When a half dozen former Fascists were exposed on the Bush campaign staff in 1988, the roster of the 138 members of Bush's 'ethnic outreach' staff was quickly and permanently suppressed. What did Bush know and when did he know it? The President may have learned about the Ratlines when he was head of CIA. During his brief tenure, there was a nasty incident when Croatian Fascists hijacked an airliner. Yet, when Bush was running for President, his campaign staff listed April 10 as a Croatian holiday. The more things change, the more they stay the same. The same Fascist network introduced into American intelligence in the 1940s is still at work today, and Communist influence continues to affect these operations.

There are those who may wish to correct or criticize our work. You may reach us at PO Box 681, Rockland, Massachusetts 02370, USA.

July 1991

Unholy Trinity

PART ONE

The Church's War
Against Communism

1

A Spectre was Haunting Europe

No one can trace with precision the psychological roots of either heroic or tragic decisions, but the disasters that befell the Vatican after World War II may have sprung in part from one man's obsession. Thirty years before the Cold War, in May 1919, a Catholic priest was violently threatened in Germany. It happened on the last day of an abortive Communist uprising . . .

The fighting had raged all through the day as the remnants of the Red forces clung desperately to key positions around Munich's Palace of Justice and at the railway station. The ragged gunfire punctuated the death cries of the revolutionaries. The White troops, bearing their blue and white flag aloft and wearing fir twigs on their steel helmets, slowly but surely dislodged Munich's short-lived Soviet government.

May Day 1919 was a time of blood and madness. The anti-Communist troops wanted revenge for the ten hostages shot by the Communists the day before. The Whites took their vengeance in the brutal killing of some 300 Red Spartacists. In those chaotic last hours, another war – the long cold war of the Catholic Church – was perhaps also beginning.

As the Whites advanced into the city, the Papal Nuncio's residence was repeatedly raked in the crossfire. In the final spasm of massacre and retreat, the 'civilised' rules of war were abandoned as each side hunted for one last target of revenge. The priest could hear the mob coming; it was coming for him.

The Reds entered his extra-territorial compound and clattered up the stairs. The Nuncio 'insisted on facing them alone', dressed in his Bishop's robes. He coldly berated them, and in response they menacingly pointed their weapons at his head. It was one of those moments where history holds its breath.

The priest remained impassive and stared the mob down. With

a quiet smile he said, 'It's never wise to kill a diplomat'. The Spartacists were dumbstruck, and left soon after in the Nuncio's car. As one historian later recorded, by 'impressing them with his dignified, decisive and immovable protest he forced them to withdraw without daring to commit violence. It was a magnificent victory'.[1]

By mid-afternoon the victory was complete. The Pope's representative emerged from his bullet-scarred residence and angrily denounced the Reds' 'bestial hostage murder'. Despite his calm demeanour, the incident was a 'genuine shock to his system'.[2]

The Papal Nuncio was Eugenio Pacelli, who later became Pope Pius XII. For the rest of his life, he never forgot the moment that the Reds held a gun to his head. That memory became the Pope's recurring nightmare. Pacelli's 'private doctor recounted later that the Pope often relived it in his dreams even when he was nearly eighty'.[3] Some historians trace Pacelli's silence towards Hitler to that May Day in Munich:

> Pius XII's acquiescence in Nazi misdeeds during the Second World War ... can be traced back to that year when the Pope – as nuncio Pacelli – had an encounter with Soviet rule that turned him into an inflexible anti-Communist for the rest of his life.[4]

There is only circumstantial evidence to support the obsession theory. While publicly denouncing the Reds' murder of the ten hostages in 1919, the Nuncio ignored the 300 prisoners massacred by the Whites. A pattern of selective condemnation had begun that later appeared to many to be echoed by the Pope's silence concerning Hitler's atrocities and his strident denunciations of Stalin.

One historian maintains that Pius XII's vocal condemnation of Communist atrocities after the war can also be traced to Munich, claiming that 'it acted on him as a stimulant rather than a depressant, and many of his challenges to the Communists after the Second World War were inspired subconsciously by that remote incident'.[5]

Eugenio Pacelli was not the only priest to have experienced Bolshevik terror first-hand, nor was he the only future Pope who became an inflexible anti-Communist as a result. One year after the attack on Pacelli, the Papal Nuncio in Warsaw also witnessed Communist methods during the Russo-Polish war. Like Pacelli in

Munich, the Nuncio in Poland had personal experience of 'the anti-religious policy of the Moscow Government [which] inspired in him an abiding hatred of Bolshevism' and 'a conviction of its danger to a Christian Europe'.[6]

In 1922 the Papal Nuncio in Poland succeeded Pope Benedict XV, and took for himself the name of Pius XI. He was not a man to over-react to danger. The new Pope favoured a slow, balanced approach, 'patiently hoping to reach a practical understanding with the Bolshevik regime . . . to secure a measure of protection for Catholics in the exercise of their religion'.[7]

In October 1925 Pius XI sent a senior Jesuit to the Soviet Union to study the religious situation. His report 'was gloomy in the extreme', as he found the Orthodox Church 'hopelessly divided' and the Catholics 'suffering from a complete absence of bishops and acute shortage of priests'.[8]

But none the less Pius XI was still optimistic in 1925, and confident that Communism was corrupt and transitory. The inevitable collapse of Soviet rule in Russia would give the Vatican the long hoped for opportunity to bring the Orthodox schismatics back into Rome's fold. Therefore, 'quiet but thorough preparations [were] continually being made in Rome' for eventual missionary work in the East. The Pope himself had 'acquired a large piece of land in Rome in which [would] be erected a Russian seminary for the training of priests, chosen from the exiled clergy'.[9]

A few months later a British diplomat reported that while the Soviet situation 'filled him with despair', the Pope was certain that 'Providence' would soon provide a man 'capable of stirring the sluggish minds of the Russian peasants to action and with the capacity and courage to lead them to a better state of things'.[10] Providence had already delivered Lenin's death, but the outlook was far bleaker under Stalin.

Pius XI frequently preached of 'the licence and anarchy to which Liberalism and Socialism lead society', and of the need to resist 'the disruptive influences of Bolshevism'. As Stalin's campaign of religious persecution became more severe, he responded with explicit denunciations of 'a page of history dark with persecution and atrocities inconceivable in this 20th century'.[11]

The Pope frequently drew attention to the plight of the Church under Communism, where '[p]riests and nuns were daily facing death and worse than death in the territories of the Soviet Republic unobtrusively preaching the Word of God, ministering to the sick and dying, and bringing comfort to countless homes where all hope of better things had perished'.[12]

These denunciations remained in the background during the 1920s while Nuncio Pacelli negotiated with Soviet officials in Berlin, hoping for a Concordat, or at least a bilateral agreement. As the 1930s opened, Pius XI apparently concluded that there was no hope of an understanding and launched a strident public campaign against the atheistic foe.[13]

The bitter truth was that there was little Pius XI could do. As Stalin once asked with derision, 'how many divisions does the Pope have?' There was once a time when he could have answered, 'All the armies of Europe.' In its first thousand years, the Church grew from a tiny, underground cult into a vast, multinational power. As one Catholic historian has put it, the Pope 'examined the claims of candidates to the Imperial crown, organised the crusade against the Albigensian Heresy, deposed the King of England, John Lackland; he established around St Peter's throne a ring of vassal monarchies'.[14]

After the bloody Crusades of the Middle Ages, the Popes assumed many of the characteristics of Kings. Entire Italian provinces were politically incorporated into the Papal States. Citizens owed allegiance and paid taxes to the Bishop of Rome. But the traumas of the Reformation and the Napoleonic Wars signalled the gradual erosion of the Pope's earthly powers. By the middle of the nineteenth century, inexorable political, social and cultural processes sapped, and then overwhelmed, the Vatican's political power.

The unification of Italy, confiscation of Church lands, and the Pope's confinement to the few square miles of St Peter's symbolised the loss of temporal power. By the time of Pius XI's election, the world had long since outgrown its need for Emperor Popes. In many ways, this was the inevitable outcome of the onset of modernity and the consequent rise of democracy, anti-clericalism, liberalism, socialism and Communism. As a result, by the end of the nineteenth century it was widely believed to be 'anachronistic that the Popes should play a civil political role in the modern international community of Europe'.[15]

Instead of dealing with the changing times, the previous Popes had retreated inside the Vatican's walls. Catholicism began to stagnate under a heavy load of isolationism, conservatism and increasing rigidity. This was caused in no small part by a destructive election policy that excluded all but Italians from the Papacy by stacking the votes in the College of Cardinals. For several hundred years, the Universal Catholic Church had been virtually dominated by the Italian clergy.

The world was changing rapidly, and for the worse. Even in heavily Catholic Italy, old traditions of obedience to the clergy were gone and new doctrines were rising in their place. Mussolini's Fascist government had taken over Italy, and was enthusiastically welcomed by some rank and file Catholics. In addition to the growth of Fascism in Italy and the rise of Communism in Russia, the Holy See was concerned with the increasing influence of secularisation, materialism and even the spread of Democracy. Pius XI believed that this latter form of government, 'based on almost universal franchise, had grave defects' because it allowed even a common 'porter' to govern a democratic nation.[16]

These new doctrines were even more disturbing after the collapse of the old order in Central Europe. Traditionally, the Vatican had looked to the Habsburg rulers of the Austro-Hungarian Empire for the protection of Catholicism in Central Europe. The Habsburg dynasty was the Vatican's military bulwark between Protestant Prussia and Orthodox Russia.

The dismembering of the Austro-Hungarian Empire at the end of World War I was yet another major catastrophe for the Holy See. The long serving Secretary of State, Cardinal Pietro Gasparri, considered the resultant creation of a number of small, independent states to be 'extremely unfortunate'. In his view, 'the new Czecho-slovakia was so nationally heterogeneous and so geographically anomalous as to be unstable and likely to raise grave difficulties. His view of probable developments in a Serbian-dominated Yugo-slavia was the same.'[17]

The collapse of a stable Catholic Central European Empire was a major blow to the Vatican's historic conception of the proper order. The new nations emphasised secularisation, and rejected the ancient concept that their citizens owed a dual allegiance to Church and State. The Vatican viewed these changes with alarm:

With the break-down of this dual allegiance and the emergence of the omnicompetent secular State, tending in the direction of totalitarianism,

the Catholic Church held that disastrous results had followed. The secular-
ization of European society and its indifference to the Christian moral law
in politics and economics, had led to the *laisser faire* economy (the tyranny
of the astute); and that in turn to collectivist democracy (the tyranny of the
supposed will of the majority); that had then been followed by war
conducted between whole nations, which had given rise to totalitarianism
(the tyranny of armed and unscrupulous gangs).[18]

The greatest totalitarian threat the Vatican faced still came from
socialism, especially the brand advocated by the disciplined and
well organised international Communist movement. By the end of
the 1920s, the spread of 'atheistic Bolshevism' had made it even
more imperative for the Vatican to settle its political status and
stabilise its base of operations in Rome.

As a former diplomat, Pius XI understood the reality of modern
times, and opened discussions to resolve the Vatican's political
relationship with the Italian government. Since 1870, his predecessors had steadfastly refused to accept the loss of the Papal States
to Italy and had chosen to remain prisoners in the Vatican. Pius
XI offered to relinquish his claims to temporal power over the
former provinces in return for permanent recognition of the
sovereign status of Vatican City.

Pius XI never liked, let alone accepted, Fascism, declaring that
'no Catholic could be a genuine convinced Fascist'.[19] However, an
uncomfortable accommodation with Mussolini was reached to end
the Church's stagnation. In February 1929 the Lateran Treaty was
concluded, settling the so-called 'Roman Question'.

All that remained of the Papal States as a result were the few
square miles of Vatican City, together with some extra-territorial
colleges and institutes in Rome itself. In effect, Pius XI ruled a
tiny nation completely surrounded by Mussolini's Fascist state.
However small his kingdom, Vatican City was finally recognised
as the Pope's sovereign territory, complete with its own border
security (the medieval Swiss Guards), banks, postal service, diplomats and legal system.

The Lateran Treaty was a realistic admission that the twentieth
century had no place for the ancient status of the Popes as political
leaders. But the loss of the Papal States had brought about a major
change in the Holy See's orientation. From Leo XIII in the late
1870s, the Popes of Rome increasingly sought 'a supra-national
world moral authority'.

Taking a far greater interest in issues of social justice and the rights of workers (for example, Leo XIII's seminal 'Labour' Encyclical, *Rerum Novarum*), and in wider questions, like world peace, the Holy See tried to establish itself as a moral force against the iniquities of the modern world. The Popes were becoming diplomats for peace. The Lateran Treaty contained the essentials of this modern, supra-national moral position. In Article 24, the Vatican declared that

it desires to remain and will remain outside the temporal competitions between other States and international Congresses summoned for such an object, unless the contending parties make a unanimous appeal to its mission of peace, in all cases reserving to itself the right to assert its moral and spiritual power.[20]

After the 1929 Lateran Treaty with Mussolini and the 1933 Concordat with Hitler, Pius XI used the Church's enhanced diplomatic status as a springboard for its modern moral mission. Under the protection of sovereignty, condemnations of right-wing totalitarianism continued to issue from the Vatican. The strongest denunciations, however, were reserved for the left, particularly atheistic Communism.

As the 1930s opened, the Vatican began to come to terms with the fact that Bolshevik rule was proving more enduring than first expected. Pius XI's public statements on religious repression became more frequent and more strident, expressing 'horror and emotion over the acts of persecution and sacrilege that were being perpetrated in Russia', protesting at 'the ill-treatment and imprisonment of the Catholic clergy, including three bishops, two of Latin and one of Byzantine Rite, and against the activities of the anti-God League.'[21]

Increasingly the Church's pronouncements spoke of the 'Bolshevik Yoke' imposed by Stalin on his people. Communist principles were denounced by the Pope, effectively making it a practical impossibility for any Catholic to simultaneously be a Communist. At the same time, he condemned the increasing materialism of the age, exhorting his flock 'to return to a simpler and less ease-loving life'.[22]

At first the British Foreign Office perceived a definite lack of balance in Pius XI's concern with Communism's threat. They believed that his 'experience as Nuncio in Warsaw increased his natural hatred of Bolshevism to such an extent that it blinded him to the scarcely lesser dangers of Fascism and Nazism'. For much of the 1930s the British actually thought he was dangerously in Mussolini's pocket.[23]

But in March 1937, that view altered dramatically, when the Pope issued his famous Encyclical, *Mit brennender Sorge*, sharply attacking aspects of Nazi ideology and rule. It was smuggled into Germany and read from pulpits all over the country. In particular it denounced the many breaches of the 1933 Concordat negotiated by the Pope's Secretary of State, Cardinal Eugenio Pacelli. The Nazis' encouragement of anti-Christian doctrines, and their racist ideology and policies were also highlighted by Pius XI. 'Whoever gives the idea of race or people or state or form of government a value beyond that of the ordinary world and claims to make idols out of them, violates the divine order of things,' Pius XI declared, although he did not specifically mention Nazi attacks on Germany's Jews.[24]

The Pope had carefully prepared the ground for his anti-Nazi stand. Two weeks earlier he had issued another Encyclical, *Divini Redemptoris*, in which he declared that Communism 'is intrinsically wrong and no one who would save Christian civilization may collaborate with it in any field whatsoever'.[25] The British, though, believed that *Mit brennender Sorge* was an important turning point in Vatican policy. With almost none of its previous temporal might, the Vatican could do little but be a moral standard bearer, but Pius XI, unlike his successor, Pacelli, waved the banner well:

> Not only did His Holiness courageously assert the rights of catholicism against the attacks of international communism and German national socialism, but, in a world distracted by ideological controversies between dictatorships and democracies, capitalism and communism, abstract international ideals and concrete nationalist ambitions, he proclaimed the Church's neutrality as regards political systems and national differences, and reiterated and emphasised her unwavering support of the principles of social justice and international morality.[26]

As Pius XI edged towards death, his public statements became even more markedly anti-Nazi. One British diplomat noted that 'Nazi Germany has taken the place of Communism as the Church's most dangerous enemy'. A few days before he died in February 1939, Pius XI prepared a final speech to give to the Italian Bishops. In the most 'vigorous and caustic' language, he was ready to issue a stinging denunciation of Nazism and Fascism. The Pontiff, unfortunately, departed earth without ever delivering it.[27]

In his recent study of British–Vatican relations during this period, Owen Chadwick argues that in 'February 1939 it mattered more to the Powers who the new Pope was than at any election since the earlier nineteenth century'. The British and French hoped for a successor who would continue Pius XI's outspoken policies, especially his 'ideals of peace and justice, [and] his denunciation of racialism'. They wanted a Pope who would continue to preach with Pius XI's boldness against the Nazi menace.[28]

Naturally, Hitler and Mussolini hoped for the converse, for a Pope who would at least remain neutral in their struggle with Britain and France. Yet, as Chadwick shows in great detail, all sides supported Cardinal Eugenio Pacelli's elevation. Nearly every major player on the world stage, from very different perspectives and conflicting interests, saw Pacelli as the man most likely to serve their cause.[29]

Pacelli came from a prominent, aristocratic Roman family which had been influential in the Vatican since the early years of the nineteenth century. He could have chosen almost any career, but pursued the calling of the Church and was ordained in 1899. Although he wanted a pastoral career, he was rapidly inducted into the Holy See's Secretariat of State (the Vatican's Foreign Affairs Ministry) in 1901. He soon made a name for himself as a consummate Vatican diplomat, serving with such distinction that he was made titular Archbishop of Sardes. Prior to his posting in Munich, Pacelli had already risen to the senior levels of the Holy See's Secretariat of State, becoming Under Secretary for Extraordinary Affairs in 1914 at the age of thirty-eight.[30]

This section was in effect the Vatican's 'political organ' and administered the Holy See's relations with foreign governments, including negotiating Concordats. The Secretariat's other section, Ordinary Affairs, issued relief, alms and subsidies, and gave advice to Catholic Action throughout the world, thus influencing 'the internal politics of other countries'.[31]

After his heroic stand at Munich, Pacelli was appointed Papal Nuncio to Germany, and was responsible for negotiating Concordats with both Bavaria and Prussia. In 1929 he was made a Cardinal and the following year Pius XI appointed him Secretary of State. Described by a British diplomat as a 'man of impressively saintly character', a 'fine preacher, a man of great piety, intelligence and unusual personal charm', Eugenio Pacelli also played a major role in bringing about the Vatican's 1933 Concordat with Hitler's Germany.[32]

Two decades after his traumatic encounter in Munich, Cardinal Pacelli was lifted by his peers into the most exalted position of all, assuming the title of Pope just as the world was bracing itself for another World War. On 2 March 1939, his sixty-third birthday, Pacelli adopted the name of Pius XII. Some saw great significance in this, claiming that the new Pope thus declared his intention to continue his predecessor's anti-Nazi policies.

It is instructive to compare and contrast the decisions of Pius XI and Pius XII during their time on St Peter's Throne. The two former Nuncios had more in common than their Papal names. Both were diplomatic activists determined to resist the encroachments of Communism and re-unite the splintered Christian churches under the authority of the Vatican. In some ways, the Vatican's Cold War strategy evolved from the pre-war experiences of Pius XI. In other respects, Pius XII's policy was a radical departure from his predecessor.

In fairness, the differences between the two approaches arose less from their personalities than from the varying degree to which the Church itself was threatened by the evolution of Communism. Both were leaders of the Church in crisis, but their reactions were very different. For Pius XII, Communism was the all-consuming enemy because it posed a clear and immediate threat to the very survival of the Church. For Pius XI, Communism was but one of many pre-war threats. The danger was real, but still remote. Where Pius XI acted from a sense of immediacy about the Nazis, Pius XII adopted a more understated, diplomatic role. Certainly, Pius XI's outspokenness against Nazism's threat was all but absent from his successor's public stance. Following the outbreak of hostilities in September, Pius XII's policies, attitudes and actions pleased none of the combatants.

Pius XII's first decision was to consign his predecessor's undelivered denunciation of Nazism to the oblivion of the Vatican Secret Archives, where it remained for twenty years until John XXIII released extracts in 1959.[33] The controversy about Pius XII's policies during World War II is well known; readers may judge for themselves from the many scholarly texts which explore the evidence.[34]

On the one hand, the critics accuse Pius XII of having abrogated his moral and charitable roles during the war, of remaining silent when faced with the most urgent imperative to speak out against the massacre of millions of innocents. They believe that he should have spoken out with unequivocal moral force, instead of moderating and even masking his messages of sympathy and solidarity with the persecuted. Further, the Bishops of Europe could have been ordered to take more effective actions to discourage the atrocities, and provide greater moral and material assistance. Might not many of the dead have survived if the Pope had put the full weight of the Church's not inconsiderable resources into the anti-Nazi struggle?

On the other side, the Church has very ably defended itself from such attacks, arguing that the Pope did everything possible, under the prevailing conditions. Virtually surrounded by enemies in the tiny state of Vatican City, first by Mussolini's Fascists then by Hitler's Army, Pius XII could do little more than pursue a quiet, diplomatic approach to the great moral issues of the day. If he had done otherwise, the entire Church might well have been destroyed, and with it the last hope for the persecuted. All he could do was rescue as many potential victims as humanly possible, and this was done to the best of the Church's ability and means.

There is undoubted merit, and much substantial evidence, to support both these contending viewpoints. The truth is probably somewhere between the two extremes. In fairness to the Vatican, however, it should be recalled that none of the major powers emerged from the Holocaust with unstained records. The Western Allies, while willing to capitalise on 'atrocity stories' in their propaganda, did virtually nothing to help the victims; in some cases they actually refused Jews safe haven.

Since the end of the war, the Catholic Church has been singled out for turning its back on the Holocaust. With hindsight, one of the reasons for Pius XII's silence was his wish to secretly support the policies of the Western governments, particularly Great Britain.

In April 1943, a conference of British and American officials formally decided that nothing should be done about the Holocaust, and 'ruled out all plans for mass rescue'. The Foreign Office and

the State Department were both afraid that the Third Reich would
be quite willing, indeed eager, to stop the gas chambers, empty the
concentration camps, and let hundreds of thousands (if not millions) of Jewish survivors emigrate to freedom in the West. As late
as 1943 the British Foreign Office 'revealed in confidence' to the
State Department their fear that if approaches to Germany to
release Jews were 'pressed too much that that is exactly what
might happen'.[35]

The bigoted reality behind the Secret Report of the Easter 1943
Bermuda Conference was that not a single Allied nation wanted to
let the Jews settle in their country. The unspoken consensus was
that it was better to let Hitler handle them than arrange a mass
evacuation to America, Britain, or Canada. In short, the Jews were
expendable to the war effort. The Soviets, too, had a poor record
on this score and, of course, were busily carrying out their own
atrocities during and after the war.[36]

In fact, the Vatican's shocking silence towards the Jews was
fully in accord with Western policy. This is well illustrated by an
incident which occurred in 1944, just as Adolf Eichmann was
preparing his last major extermination operation. Most of Hungary's 800,000 Jews had survived until the Germans installed a
completely pro-Nazi government in March 1944.

An urgent plea was dispatched to the Vatican by an American
delegation. Acting on behalf of the War Refugee Board, they
requested Papal intervention to save the helpless victims. 'It is
both timely and fitting we believe that the moral values involved
and the spiritual consequences that must flow from indulgence in
the persecutions and mass murder of helpless men, women and
children be brought to the attention of the Hungarian authorities
and people'. They pleaded that 'His Holiness may find it appropriate to express Himself on this subject to the authorities and people
of Hungary, great numbers of whom profess spiritual adherence to
the Holy See.'[37]

Over the following months, Hungary's Jews were rounded up
and concentrated in hastily prepared ghettos, where they were
horrifically maltreated. Most were then shipped off to Auschwitz
and murdered. By October, their numbers had been drastically
reduced, but the Americans received information that up to
300,000 survivors were about to be deported to their certain deaths.
The Vatican was approached once more, and the Pope asked to

broadcast a public appeal to the people and clergy of Hungary, 'urging them to temporarily conceal Jews and oppose the deportation and extermination of these people to the full extent of their powers'.[38]

Rumours that the Pope might actually do this apparently reached the British, who were alarmed lest His Holiness go too far. They instructed their Ambassador to speak to Franklin Gowen, an American diplomat at the Holy See. Gowen reported that the Ambassador 'feared the Holy Father may make a Radio appeal on behalf of Jews in Hungary and that in his appeal he may also criticise what the Russians are doing in occupied territory. [He] said something should be done to prevail upon the Pope not to do this as it would have very serious political repercussions.'[39]

Gowen was not in the least perturbed, having already learned that Pius XII had decided against making the appeal, 'because if he did so he would in fairness to all have to criticise the Russians'. Without revealing this, the American quietly persuaded his British colleague to take no action to intervene with the Vatican.[40] Apparently the diplomats knew that their leaders wanted to avoid conflict with Stalin, so Hungary's Jews were abandoned.

It is ironic that Pius XII is condemned for following Western policy in public, while his private actions may have saved more Jewish lives than all the Allied governments put together. For example, the Vatican Nuncio in Berlin protected 28,000 Jews in the heart of the Third Reich itself by cleverly insisting that the Vatican would not allow German Catholics to divorce their Jewish spouses. As long as they were married to Catholics, the Jews were safe.[41] Using similar pretexts, the Vatican temporarily delayed deportation of Jews in the Balkans and slowed implementation of the racial laws for several years. Such efforts were ultimately ineffectual as most of the pro-Nazi clerics, such as Slovakia's Monsignor Tiso, ignored the Vatican.

In countries like Italy, where the Pope had some political influence, he used it well. Largely through his personal intercession, Mussolini's forces deliberately bungled the shipment of Jews from Italian-occupied areas. The Germans were so convinced of stereotypical Italian incompetence, that they did not realise the cleverness behind the botched shipment schedules:

> In Italy ... the deportation and murder of Jews began only after ... the Germans became masters of the country. There were Italian priests and

16

monks, who like those elsewhere, went out of their way to save Jewish lives. Several thousand Jews were at one time harbored within Vatican City. The sympathies of Pope Pius XII were not outspoken, though it was known that he condemned the barbarities which were being perpetrated against the Jews.[42]

Moreover, the Vatican bank was the conduit for secret bribes to save lives. The Israeli government publicly credits the Vatican for secretly negotiating payments that ransomed thousands of Jews from Nazi custody. Pius XII was not as evil as his critics claim, nor as righteous as his defenders hope. The record is mixed to say the least. The Pope was silent in public, but helped some Jews in secret. Churchill and Roosevelt made speeches in public, but their policy was to abandon the Jews. If the Pope was a hypocrite, he was not alone.

Far from being a covert supporter of Hitler, the Holy See's secret disgust with both Nazism and Communism was well known to Western diplomats. During the war, Monsignor Domenico Tardini, Under Secretary of State for Extraordinary Affairs, conveyed voluminous memoranda to Western diplomats. He emphasised that 'Europe is faced with two great dangers; Nazism and Communism. Both are opposed to religion, to Christian civilization, to personal liberty, to peace.' That the Vatican viewed Communism as the greater of the two evils is certain, as Tardini added that:

If even one of these evils – Communism, for example – were to remain an active force, Europe would, within a few years, be in a situation identical with that in which it finds itself today. In fact, Communism, once victorious, would find no further resistance in Continental Europe and would spread among the germanic peoples, the slav races and finally among the latins. In consequence, within the space of a few years there would be an enormous Communistic bloc, whose inevitable destiny it would be to provoke a war with England and America, regarded by the Communists as a Capitalistic bloc.[43]

In May 1943 Tardini openly predicted that 'there is ground for fearing (a) that the war will end in a preponderantly Russian victory in Europe and (b) that the result will be a rapid diffusion of Communism in a great part of continental Europe and the destruction there of European civilization and Christian culture.'[44]

Imminent Allied victory also realised Monsignor Tardini's worst fears – Soviet occupation of most of Central and Eastern Europe, and formation of a powerful Communist bloc. Previously there had even been talk of some sort of *rapprochement* between Moscow and the Vatican. However, as the Soviet Army advanced westwards, Moscow launched a vitriolic propaganda campaign, accusing the Holy Father of being 'pro-Fascist' and in favour of a German victory. Moscow had somehow learned of Pius XII's post-war plans for a Catholic buffer state in Central Europe, free of both German and Soviet influence. Hence their propaganda campaign to discredit the Vatican.

By February 1944, American intelligence had discovered the Soviets' purpose. They believed that the Soviets were very well informed of the Holy See's plans and activities, noting that the 'projects of the Vatican for the re-establishment of a Habsburg Monarchy in Central Europe and plans for the re-organization of a Catholic Federation to counteract the Soviets' religious policy, are no secret to Moscow'.[45]

US intelligence predicted that the Vatican would try to exclude America from Central Europe as well. Confirmation came from a senior SS intelligence officer debriefed by the Americans after the war. Albert Hartl left the Catholic priesthood in 1934, and the following year became Chief of Church Information in the notorious Reich Security Main Office (RSHA), with the rank of SS Major.

Hartl was, in fact, the Nazis' specialist in Catholic religious matters.[46] During the war he wrote numerous 'reports concerning political and religious trends outside Germany'. The SS officer was also sent to Rome on an especially sensitive mission in 1944 'to establish contact through the Vatican with the Western powers'. He was to convince the West to break with Stalin, 'and join with [Germany] against the Bolsheviks'. Hartl's senior position in German intelligence certainly gave him access to top secret information, as he told the Americans:

> When the Vatican realized that the United States and the Soviet Union would be victorious in the Second World War, it started immediately to form a bloc of Western European nations to effect a counter-balance to these two countries. France, 'the most beloved daughter of the Catholic Church', was to take the leading part ... Therefore, the Vatican turned its sympathies away from the Vichy government and toward the Free French under De Gaulle ...
>
> At the same time, the Vatican hopes to create a similar unity among the powers of Eastern Europe. This bloc was initiated by de Gasperi ... later Premier of Italy. De Gasperi, by means of this bloc, sought to increase not

only the influence of the Vatican, but also that of Italy. The plan was quickly supported by other Vatican dignitaries – among them were Archbishops Tardini and Montini, Bishop Hudal, and the Bishops of Gorizia and of Ljubljana.[47]

As we shall see, this tiny but highly influential cabal around Pius XII indeed favoured this secret policy. The two men most closely involved were Alcide de Gasperi, post-war leader of the Italian Christian Democrat party, and Monsignor Giovanni Montini, the Pope's Under Secretary of State for Ordinary Affairs since 1937.

Like Pius XII, Montini came from a well-to-do Catholic family with good connections to powerful figures at the Vatican. He, too, had pursued a brilliant career in the Secretariat of State, and established close relations with lay Italian Catholic political leaders. US intelligence described Montini as one of 'the most authoritative persons in the Vatican', who 'for many years has been among the important personalities in the Vatican Secretaryship of State'. It can hardly be alleged that Montini formulated policy without Pius XII's knowledge. Following Cardinal Maglione's death in August 1944, the Pope did not fill the Secretary of State position, effectively re-assuming the role himself.

Although the Pope formulated his own foreign policy, Montini and the other Under Secretary of State, Monsignor Tardini, were certainly among 'the most influential people of the Vatican'.[48] Both were in constant, daily personal contact with Pius XII, with whom Montini in particular enjoyed a 'special confidence' and 'a certain affinity of temperament'.

Their personal relationship was certainly close, but it extended into matters of high policy. In practice, Montini was Pius XII's personal assistant; he gave Montini 'particularly delicate and difficult tasks to perform'. During the war Pius asked Montini to organise the Vatican Information Service, whose ostensible task was to trace missing persons, refugees and prisoners of war. But US intelligence suspected that its role went far beyond humanitarian purposes.

Pius XII also asked Montini 'to supervise Vatican efforts for the resettlement of the millions of refugees and displaced persons who swarmed into Western Germany, Austria, Italy, and France' after the war. Further, as one of the Holy See's finest diplomats, Montini controlled foreign policy 'in regard to Italian politics'. As will be seen, each of these 'delicate and difficult tasks' brought Montini into the centre of the Pope's clandestine activities.[49]

Montini deservedly has a reputation as an anti-Fascist and Democrat. He had a close personal and political relationship with Alcide de Gasperi, who spearheaded the post war anti-Communist fight through the Christian Democrat party. The Vatican bureaucrat and the Italian Catholic politician had begun their close working relationship during the war. According to US intelligence they spent many weekends together discussing 'important political problems', particularly the Communist threat.[50] In fact they were working on active anti-Communist plans in Central and Eastern Europe. In the fearful days that followed Stalin's occupation of these regions, the two men forged even closer bonds.

It was probably not surprising, then, that the Americans concluded in 1944 that Moscow's anti-Vatican campaign 'should be considered as an attempt to serve as a serious warning to the Pope to refrain from any interference in problems affecting Catholic citizens' in areas occupied by the Red Army. Ominously, they also predicted that if Pius XII did not heed this threat, 'Moscow may have recourse to an anti-clerical movement among Soviet citizens of the Catholic creed'.[51]

The war had no sooner ended than this analysis was proved correct. New battle lines were immediately drawn, this time between the Soviets and their new satellites, and the Western democracies. It was a shattering blow to Pius XII, who became 'more than ever oppressed by the Communist menace in Europe i.e. [the] combination of atheistical materialism and Russian imperialism'.[52]

Where the Vatican was publicly silent towards Soviet and German atrocities during the war, Pius XII reversed his own policy in 1945 and decided that now the Church's voice had to be raised against Stalin's crimes. Montini was thrown into the fray, providing detailed reports to the Western powers on conditions in the Soviet zone of Berlin. They were replete with stories of confiscations, deportations, the proliferation of abortions as a result of widespread rape by Soviet troops, disease, deprivation and deliberate starvation.[53]

It was a scene of horror which the Vatican reported from every country under Soviet occupation. In Hungary, the Soviet troops under the eyes of their own officers and other civil authorities, who almost always remained passive, gave themselves over to unbridled sacking of private houses, sparing not even the Bishop's palace and the rectories, and putting to death not a few of the civil population. Even the Apostolic Nunciature was invaded and completely sacked, in spite of the protests of His Excellency the Nuncio. Women from ten years of age to seventy, not excluding religious women (about twenty) were raped . . . Bishop Apor of Györ was killed by a Russian soldier, while defending the honor and the life of the Faithful . . . Bishop de Mikes died from apoplexy, which was the effect of the sufferings inflicted on him by Russian soldiers. Many priests lost their lives while defending their people from similar outrages.[54]

By 1950 the Vatican had gathered enough intelligence to show that the same situation, to one degree or another, existed in all the other countries where the Communists had effective control – Albania, Czechoslovakia, Bulgaria, Romania, the Baltic States, Yugoslavia, eastern Germany and Poland. In newly acquired Catholic areas of the Ukraine, the hybrid Uniate Church was forcibly disbanded and united with the Communist-controlled Orthodox Church. Hundreds of priests were arrested or deported.[55]

As news from behind the 'Iron Curtain' filtered into the Holy See from 'reliable confidential channels',[56] the Vatican increased their criticism. In return, the Soviets stepped up their barrage against Pius XII. One British report summarised Moscow's propaganda thus:

The Pope is charged with being a reactionary, a supporter and protector of Hitler and the Nazis and of Mussolini and the Fascists . . . an enemy of democracy . . . an opponent of reforms benefiting the masses, but a champion of the vested interests of the privileged classes. He is accused of intervening in political life and, in general, of plotting to restore Fascist tyranny and to rob the progressive democracies of their newly-won . . . liberties. He is also denounced as an ally of Anglo-Saxon capitalistic imperialism.[57]

To bolster such claims, prominent clerics, including Cardinal Mindszenty of Hungary and Archbishop Stepinac of Croatia, were arrested, tried and imprisoned on basically trumped up charges. It was hardly surprising, then, that the British Ambassador's 1945 *Annual Report* noted that, with 'the eclipse of nazism and the passing of the persecution of the Church in Germany and German-occupied territory, bolshevism, with its worldwide Communist satellite organisation, automatically regained its former position as the Church's Enemy No 1'. The Vatican was 'engaged in a life-and-death struggle for survival'.[58]

The bureaucrats at the Foreign Office in London noted with satisfaction that the Vatican had apparently returned to form and was raising a long-term moral struggle against the evils of Stalinism. 'Believing that . . . the ultimate triumph of the Church is sure, the Vatican tends to take longer views than do secular governments . . . As is often said "The Church is eternal and can afford to wait".'[59]

There were clues that the Vatican was in fact pursuing a more immediate anti-Communist strategy. The British had discerned at least one unexpected post-war trend. They noted that Communist propaganda was increasingly linking the Vatican with Nazism and Fascism. The British admitted that it was 'a score on which the papacy is unfortunately slightly vulnerable in view of its attitude towards many men, who are or were virtually war criminals'.[60]

The Americans also received clues that the Church's strategy of patient resistance to Communism was being scrapped. In September 1946, Franklin Gowen reported that an extremely gloomy mood prevailed in the Vatican. According to Cardinal Tisserant, the 'outstanding Vatican authority on Russian affairs', a new war was imminent. 'Russia [was] now obviously in [a] favorable position to over-run Western Europe gearing Germany and Communist organizations to her war machine.'[61]

Between the Holy Years of 1925 and 1950, the enormous growth of Communism was threatening the survival of the Church. Persecution abounded in 1925, but a quarter of a century later had reached unparalleled levels. Pius XII must have reflected bitterly on the setbacks suffered by the Church over the previous century. First had come the rise of Italian nationalism, culminating in loss of the Church's lands. Then, in the aftermath of World War I, the Holy See had witnessed the destruction of the Catholic Central European Empire, and Bolshevism's first victory in Russia. Worse, Hitler's maniacal policies had awakened the Communist colossus which now controlled the beloved Catholic nations of Central Europe.

Which of the Pope's three crowns would Pius XII wear to meet the latest menace? At least the first crown remained undiminished. This signifies that the Pope is the spiritual head of the world wide Church, the 'Vicar of Christ' on earth and successor to St Peter.

In matters of theology, Pius's interpretations bound other priests as surely as his predecessors'. But after the war, millions of Pius XII's flock were forcibly separated from his theological leadership.

The second crown, too, remained undisturbed. Pius was the Bishop of Rome, titular head of the Roman Catholic Church with its vast administrative hierarchy of priests, nuns and lay people. They were, though, no match for Stalin's armies.

However, little was left of the third crown, representing the Pope's status as a sovereign head of state, equal in rank to Presidents and Prime Ministers. But Pius·XII's temporal crown was in fact a pale reflection of its once mighty self. He had no armies to command, only diplomats and their fellow travellers. In the Church's life and death struggle against Communism, the Pope opted for espionage and all that went with it. Before the end of World War II, the diplomatic cabal around the Pope had recruited agents for the next, and final war with Communism.

The genesis of these activities can probably be traced to the Pope's request to Montini to organise the Vatican Information Service. The American Army had observed the suspicious activities of this humanitarian agency as early as March 1944, noting that it had been 'organized for handling welfare messages by radio to and from prisoners of war in North Africa'. The Americans believed that some kind of clandestine activity was taking place and ordered that no 'extension of the Vatican Information Service can be contemplated, having due regard for security consideration'.[62] If later reports can be believed, the Vatican Information Service expanded after the war into a major intelligence force.

American intelligence had been taking an active interest in the Vatican's response to the 'Red Menace' for some time. Indeed, 'high ranking Allied intelligence officers' were reportedly in 'close relations with high Vatican dignitaries' well before the Nazi collapse.[63] In October 1945 the Americans noted 'the preponderant influence which the Jesuit fathers, who always present concrete and well-reasoned projects, tend to exercize at the Curia'. According to their source, the Jesuits were leading the Holy See's struggle with Moscow, and the

one positive step so far taken by the Vatican has been the organization of a penetration program; especially resourceful personnel is being sent into the area to lead the catholic elements and through their zeal and example keep these elements from wavering. Most of these agents are Jesuits.[64]

In late 1947, US intelligence received completely fantastic reports of Vatican involvement in clandestine anti-Communist operations. Jack Neal, head of the State Department's Division of Foreign Activity Correlation (a top secret intelligence group with the US Foreign Service), addressed a memo to FBI director J. Edgar Hoover, the chief of Naval intelligence and American diplomats at the Holy See:

> ... source which is considered most reliable has reported that the Vatican Information Service, with Headquarters in Vatican City, is the international espionage service of the Vatican.
>
> The same source reports that during and after the last war, Russian Army deserters organized clandestinely in Germany and Austria. Shortly after VE Day, this group was rumored to consist of several million people ... It seems, moreover, that the Vatican decided to make use of this clandestine organization, and reportedly has already spent millions of dollars toward this end, possibly through the above-mentioned Information Service.
>
> Most of the deserters are said to be Estonians, Lithuanians, Czechs, and other nationals of predominantly Catholic background, who were forcefully inducted into the Russian Army during the war.
>
> The Vatican is said to be presently organizing these men within the respective countries in which they are located, and reportedly is also planning to send to those countries in the future additional man-power, under the guise of displaced persons or immigrants. These groups allegedly are being organized in the various countries under the name of the Christian Front ... A primary prerequisite towards admission consists of each member taking an oath of allegiance to the Church, which entails loyalty to the latter over and above the prospective member's national allegiance. It is, of course, possible that individuals who join this organization are primarily interested in fighting Soviet Communism, and the Red Army in particular ...
>
> It is stated that since the Vatican is convinced that a Soviet invasion of Central and Western Europe is inevitable, it considers this recruiting and support of a clandestine buffer contingent a justifiable measure of self-defense and self-preservation.[68]

In hindsight, it is clear that few believed the Vatican had abandoned its patient resistance policy and launched a covert war. Such reports were promptly discarded as outlandish exaggeration. How could such a grand enterprise have hitherto gone undetected? Where would the Vatican find the resources for such an immense scheme, particularly as much of its wealth was in fixed assets?

An American diplomat at the Holy See cautioned that 'reports of the Vatican spending "millions of dollars," on para-military organizations should be treated with considerable reserve'. He outlined the moral and practical impediments to their involvement, citing the views of a 'highly placed Jesuit priest whose name has been linked with confidential information services'. His Jesuit informant knew nothing of the 'Christian Front', although on 'one occasion he professed to have a vague recollection of such anti-Communist groups in East Prussia and the Baltic countries. He believed, however, that they had been heavily penetrated by Russian agents.'[66]

Despite these overblown claims, there were grains of truth to some of the intelligence reaching Western agencies. As we shall see, the same group of senior Vatican officials who supported the Central European programme was also directing clandestine anti-Communist operations in this area. To say that its efforts led to disaster would be an understatement. The tiny cabal of right-wing officials around Pius XII was co-ordinating that most secret and most shameful operation in Vatican history: they were recruiting ex-Nazis to fight the Communists for control of Central and Eastern Europe.

Later, after American intelligence had staged a burglary at the centre of the Vatican's Nazi smuggling network, bugged its code room and recruited their own informants, it was discovered that many of the worst rumours were true. Some of the Vatican's anti-Communist recruits were notorious Nazi war criminals. A few Church officials were laundering stolen Nazi treasure to finance their 'freedom fighters'. Although it was not discovered until much, much later, Communist agents had in fact penetrated their command structure from top to bottom. The Vatican's 'anti-Communist' networks were secretly manipulated from Moscow. Some of the Vatican's Nazis were really spies for the Kremlin.

In the beginning, the Vatican's involvement with Nazi fugitives was disorganised, even amateurish. The first priest who ran the operation was Bishop Alois Hudal. As already seen, Hudal had been closely associated with Montini and de Gasperi in formulating the Holy See's response to the expected Allied victory. Now his job was to rescue as many Nazis as possible from what he believed was 'Allied vengeance', a task he grasped with considerable enthusiasm. Pius XII's nightmares were only beginning, as Hudal's wildly erratic operations led the Vatican on the first steps down the road to the Ratlines, and tragedy.

2

Bishop Hudal and the First Wave

The Vatican's road to disaster was paved with good intentions. The scandal of the Ratlines actually began innocently enough. At war's end the Western-occupied zones of Germany, Austria and Italy were teeming with millions of DPs – Displaced Persons from all parts of Europe. Most were legitimate victims of Nazism and Communism. They were the uprooted who had left their homes not through choice, but as a direct consequence of the war. Most could not return home because of Stalin's brutal occupation of Central and Eastern Europe.

Many were Catholics, and it was not surprising that the Vatican took up their cause with the Western military authorities. Months before the Third Reich disintegrated, the Holy See's Secretariat of State launched a concerted lobbying campaign. They wanted permission for selected priests to visit the civilian and prisoner of war camps. The aims of these missions were noble and humanitarian – to provide spiritual and material assistance, and to extend the hand of Christian Charity to the needy.

Among these largely innocent masses, however, were many Nazis who had the blood of millions of innocents on their hands. It was hard for the Church to know who was who. The Vatican has consistently claimed that they were unaware of the identity of those who were undeserving of their humanitarian assistance. But some influential priests not only knew who the Nazis were, they actively sought them out and provided extra-special treatment . . .

In 1948 Franz Stangl wearily trudged along the road to Rome. Three years earlier he had been an important man: Commandant of the Treblinka extermination camp. He was meticulous in his work. When the boxcars crammed full of deported men, women and children arrived, all they saw was an ordinary train station neatly decorated with flower boxes. In the distance were a few innocuous looking sheds. Franz Stangl insisted on order. The passengers were told to disembark for a routine rest stop and showers. As they disrobed, people were told to secure their valuables in numbered stalls so they could easily find them later.

It was all so swift, so organised, so deadly. The showers were actually a gas chamber where 900,000 people, mostly Jews, were murdered immediately upon arrival. Unlike Auschwitz, no work was done here. Treblinka existed for one purpose only: mass murder of human beings. Franz Stangl had commanded the Third Reich's most efficient death factory.

When it became clear the Nazis would lose the war, Treblinka was razed and efforts made to hide its traces. Poplar trees were planted over the site and a small farm built from the bricks of the dismantled gas chambers. A Ukrainian family was moved in, awaiting the arrival of the Red Army. Stangl would not be there: he had been transferred to fight Yugoslav partisans.

When the Third Reich collapsed, Stangl was captured by the American Army and interned at Bad Ischl, near Salzburg in Austria. In July 1945 he was transferred to the huge prisoner of war camp at Glasenbach, where he remained a virtually anonymous figure for over two years. Around Christmas 1947, the Americans handed Stangl over to the Austrians, who held him in the open prison at Linz. There were many Austrians willing to turn a blind eye towards a good comrade. The following May Stangl 'escaped' and travelled south. One of the most wanted war criminals had slipped the Allied net and was trudging slowly on his way to Rome.

After many days on dusty roads, he walked wearily across a bridge over the Tiber, looking for a priest whose name had been whispered back in the prison camps. Suddenly he found himself face to face with a former comrade, a security police officer who had served in Vichy France. 'Are you on your way to see Hulda?', the man asked. 'Yes,' Stangl replied, 'but I don't know where to find him.'[1] Years later, after he was re-arrested, Stangl's recollections of his escape were taped in a German prison by his noted biographer, Gitta Sereny. Stangl said that when he came to Rome he was in fact looking for Bishop Alois Hudal, Rector of the Pontificio Santa Maria dell'Anima, one of three seminaries for German priests in Rome. It was Hudal's name that had been whispered throughout the Nazi underground:

The Bishop came into the room where I was waiting and he held out both his hands and said 'You must be Franz Stangl. I was expecting you.'[2]

Stangl described the power and influence of Hudal's extensive smuggling network for fugitive Nazis. It was Hudal who arranged 'quarters in Rome where I was to stay till my papers came through. And he gave me a bit more money – I had almost nothing left.' After several weeks, Hudal 'called me in and gave me my new passport – a Red Cross Passport . . . [he] got me an entrance visa to Syria and a job in a textile mill in Damascus, and he gave me a ticket for the ship. So I went to Syria.'[3]

But when he was given his passport, the punctilious German noticed that his names had been reversed and said indignantly, 'They made a mistake, this is incorrect. My name is Franz D. Paul Stangl.' Hudal patted the naive Stangl on the shoulder and said in his fatherly way, 'Let's let sleeping dogs lie – never mind.'[4] Hudal knew that Stangl should never risk using his real name again. Like numerous fugitive Nazis, Stangl was very grateful to the charitable organisations of the Catholic Church which aided his escape.

Gitta Sereny asked Monsignor Karl Bayer for a comment. At the time, Bayer was the Rome Director of the Catholic relief organisation, Caritas International. He said that such mistakes were unfortunately commonplace in the post-war chaos. After all, the Church was dealing with enormous numbers of refugees. Stangl, he confirmed, probably 'would have received money – which came from the Vatican – or a ticket to Syria, but rarely both'. Bayer conceded that there were perhaps 'exceptional cases where "refugees" were given a ticket *and* money, but it didn't happen to anyone I helped.'[5]

Bayer initially played down Hudal's access to International Red Cross documents, but eventually admitted, 'Perhaps Hudal *did* get batches of passports for these particular people.' Finally he conceded that the money Hudal gave Stangl would certainly have come from Vatican funds. 'The Pope did provide money for this; in driblets sometimes, but it did come.'[6]

Was Stangl an isolated case, a regrettable but unavoidable accident by a legitimate Catholic charity? Or was he one of many who escaped via Hudal's secret Church connection? Simon Wiesenthal, who was responsible for Stangl's eventual recapture in Brazil in 1967, believes that a sophisticated Vatican network was involved.

Wiesenthal was in the courtroom when Stangl went on trial in Düsseldorf in West Germany, and heard him tell the judge that the Nazis had advance knowledge of the Vatican escape route. 'During the time we were in the internment camps we knew that we should go to Rome ... Catholics should go to Bishop Hudal [who would] give us an International Red Cross Identity card and then a visa.'[7]

The assistance Stangl received from Hudal is strikingly similar to that provided to other German war criminals. Gustav Wagner, one of Stangl's close friends, was also helped by Hudal. Wagner was the Commandant at Sobibor at the time Stangl was running Treblinka. These were the major Nazi extermination camps in occupied Poland. After their escape from Allied custody, they bumped into one another in Graz, Austria, and travelled together on the long road to Rome. They eventually ended up in Brazil, and both praised Bishop Hudal's help.[8]

Wiesenthal alleges that yet another Nazi, Alois Brunner, also escaped via Hudal's Vatican smuggling network. Brunner, one of the most brutal senior officials in the Jewish 'deportation' programme, escaped to Damascus in Syria where he still lives under the name of Dr Georg Fischer. By all accounts he remains totally unrepentant about the hundreds of thousands of victims he sent to be 'processed' by Stangl and Wagner.

Wiesenthal is convinced that Hudal was also responsible for smuggling the most infamous war criminal of them all: Adolf Eichmann, the chief architect of the Holocaust. As head of the SS Department for 'Jewish Affairs', Eichmann's careful supervision ensured that men like Brunner, Stangl and Wagner ran the machinery of death at peak capacity. Wiesenthal believes that Hudal equipped Eichmann with a new identity as a Croatian refugee called 'Richard Klement', and sent him to Genoa. There Eichmann was apparently hidden in a monastery under Archbishop Siri's charitable control, before finally being smuggled to South America.[9]

Someone so notorious could not be protected for ever. Eichmann was eventually tracked down in Argentina by Israeli intelligence, kidnapped, tried and executed in Jerusalem in 1962. What angers Wiesenthal is that a Catholic relief organisation, Caritas, 'paid all of the travelling expenses for Eichmann' to reach South America.[10]

Official Vatican historian, Father Robert Graham, admits that

Hudal might have helped 'a handful, a mere handful of Nazi war criminals to escape':

> When Eichmann was arrested it was alleged he passed through Rome and got some help from Bishop Hudal. Hudal was asked about this and said, 'I don't know, I helped a lot of people and Eichmann may have been among them. I don't know, he didn't use his own name'. Hudal did help Germans go off to Latin America, particularly Argentina, but that wasn't the Vatican, that wasn't Pius XII.[11]

If Eichmann was a case of unauthorised assistance, he was certainly not the only instance. Hudal seemed to make mistakes with frightening regularity. Wiesenthal recalls: 'During my search for Eichmann I found out that many [war criminals] were living in monasteries, equipped by Hudal with false documents', showing they were refugees. One point is certain: many war criminals who escaped to South America have gratefully acknowledged that they owed their freedom to the Austrian-born Bishop.

Hudal was certainly no stranger to the Nazis, having served during the war as Commissioner of the Episcopate for German-speaking Catholics in Italy, as well as Father Confessor to Rome's German community. Born on 31 May 1885, he became Professor of Old Testament Studies at the University of Graz in 1919. Four years later Hudal moved to Rome as Rector of the Pontificio Santa Maria dell'Anima, on the ironically named Via della Pace, the street of peace. If Wiesenthal was correct, it was anything but peaceful during Hudal's tenure. The Anima had been established in the sixteenth century for the theological education of German priests, but it was a hotbed of Nazi-smuggling in the post-war era.

It is not surprising that Wiesenthal accuses Hudal. The Bishop's pro-Nazi views were well known. Even Father Graham concedes the point: 'Hudal was rather notorious in Rome for being openly philo-Nazi. He had this idea that it was his divine call to settle relations between the Nazis and the Catholic Church.'[12] By the early 1930s, Hudal openly supported Hitler, travelling widely through Italy and Germany to address large crowds of German-speaking Catholics. From the very beginning of Nazi rule, he warmly embraced the new goverment as his own.[13]

Hudal was an ardent anti-Communist and convinced that the real threat in Europe was 'atheistic Bolshevism'. He therefore advocated reaching an understanding with the National Socialists, the only power strong enough to defeat Communism. Hudal believed that this was a life and death struggle for the Church, one that would decide whether Communism or Christianity would eventually survive.

His first contact with a senior Nazi was probably with Franz von Papen, Hitler's Vice Chancellor. Von Papen arrived in Rome in April 1933 to negotiate the Concordat between Berlin and the Holy See. A month later, Hudal gave a speech at the Anima in Rome. Among the invited guests were members of the German Diplomatic Corps, as well as local representatives of various Nazi organisations. The Bishop told his approving audience that 'in this hour of destiny all German Catholics living abroad welcome the new German Reich, whose philosophies accord both with Christian and National values'.[14]

There is no direct evidence that Hudal actually worked with von Papen on the 1933 Concordat, although he was closely connected with the Vatican's chief negotiator, Secretary of State Pacelli. However, by the following year Hudal had certainly become von Papen's political ally, and was consulted by him immediately following the unsuccessful Nazi *putsch* in Austria.[15]

Within a few years, Hudal's Nazi sentiments became public knowledge. In 1936 he published a 'philosophical' treatise, *The Foundations of National Socialism*. He later modestly claimed that his work examined trends in the Nazi Party, 'objectively as a scholar, not as a politician'. In fact, the book was fulsome in its praise for the ideas, programme and actions of the Nazis, although it did criticise anti-Christian elements in the Party. By this time many of the worst features of Nazi rule were already apparent. Yet Hudal argued that there were no philosophical reasons why 'good' Nazis and Catholics could not co-operate closely to build a Christian Europe.

Hudal was not the only cleric to hold these views. The Primate of the Austrian Church, Cardinal Theodore Innitzer, was at that time strongly pro-Nazi. It was natural, therefore, that he gave Hudal's book an 'imprimatur', or official Church permission for publication. The Cardinal glowingly endorsed it 'as a valuable attempt to pacify the German people's religious situation'.[16]

However, Hudal's book received a mixed reception from the Nazis. His friend and Vice Chancellor, Franz von Papen, was delighted 'that a Bishop of Hudal's rank so praised the positive achievements of National Socialism'. Nevertheless, Propaganda Minister Joseph Göbbels promptly banned it, reflecting the Nazis' hostility towards Vatican functionaries in general.

Leading Nazi ideologist, Alfred Rosenberg, justified the decision, declaring that 'we do not allow the fundaments of the Movement to be analyzed and criticized by a Roman Bishop'.[17] Despite the book's harsh treatment, Hudal was apparently well regarded by the Nazi hierarchy, for he held a Golden Nazi Party membership badge.[18]

Apparently Hudal's high Nazi profile did not harm his Vatican career. Since 1930 he had been a consultor in the Holy Office, a senior Vatican tribunal working 'in the most rigorous secrecy', as US intelligence reported. Founded in 1542 'to combat the Calvinist and Lutheran revolts', its role was basically ideological purity, 'to defend the faith, Catholic morals, and the unity of the Church against heresies, schisms' etc.

The Holy Office was 'concerned with the protection and surveillance' of religious doctrine. To put it bluntly, it was the section of the Vatican concerned with censoring books and educational materials. Hudal was no stranger to that. Today the Holy Office is the Congregation for the Doctrine of the Faith, and remains one of the most influential Vatican Ministries, the 'guardian of orthodoxy of doctrine' and enforcer of religious discipline.[19] The post of consultor is extremely important in this work, as these prelates 'have to examine, investigate, and prepare all the cases submitted to the Holy Office'.

Yet as Hudal's views grew more stridently and publicly pro-Nazi, nothing was done either to discipline or remove him from this powerful post. Instead the Vatican promoted him in June 1933 from priest to Titular Bishop, an extremely rare honour for a relatively lowly Rector of a teaching college.[20]

Despite this promotion, Father Graham distances Hudal's pro-Nazi political sentiments from the Vatican. They certainly had nothing to do with his choice Vatican assignments; he was merely 'a Catholic Bishop in good standing and among such people there's room for a lot of political opinions'.[21]

Father Burkhart Schneider, a German Jesuit, is also certain that 'Bishop Hudal was not at all close to the Vatican. And certainly not close to the Holy Father. He was . . . how shall I put it . . . even then slightly suspect – not taken seriously. He desperately *wanted* to be taken seriously.' Schneider, who worked with Graham preparing the Holy See's defence of Pius XII's wartime role, was adamant that Hudal 'was very much on the fringes'.[22]

By contrast, Father Jacob Weinbacher, who was in a better position to know, has no doubt that 'Hudal was very close to Pius XII . . . they were friends.' Weinbacher became Rector of the Anima in 1952, and clearly recalls several conversations in which his predecessor discussed his close personal relationship with the Pope. 'I talked a lot with him and this certainly emerged very clearly.'[23]

Weinbacher's account is not the only one which contradicts Graham's and Schneider's contention that Hudal had no influence with leading Vatican officials. One version alleges that Hudal and Pius XII had a longstanding friendship dating from 1924, when Pacelli was the Nuncio in Germany.[24]

Another more conspiratorial version is that Hudal followed in his patron's brilliant footsteps. Hudal's appointment to the Holy Office in 1930, and his elevation in 1933 to Titular Bishop of Ela, were due to Pacelli's growing influence at the Holy See. Certainly Hudal's promotions followed Pacelli's appointment as Secretary of State in 1930.

According to this theory, Hudal's close relationship with Pacelli is illustrated by the fact that 'Pacelli personally celebrated [Hudal's] mass of consecration' as a Bishop in the Anima. In fairness to Pacelli, it should be noted that he was by then the official Protector of the Anima. However, according to this version, their relationship was also very political, stemming from Hudal's role as Pacelli's adviser in the lengthy negotiations leading to the 1934 Concordat with Austria.[25]

Far from being just another anonymous cleric on the fringes of the Vatican, 'Hudal may well have been the sounding board for the Pope in the German speaking countries'.[26] The current Rector of the Anima, Monsignor Johannes Nedbal, is certain that Hudal was very close to Pius XI. Nedbal cites Hudal's part in the Austrian Concordat as the reason for his appointment as Bishop.

Nedbal admitted in a recent interview that Hudal's career was most exceptional. In his view, 'it's quite rare' that the head of a Roman college would be made a Bishop. Nedbal confirmed that Pacelli presided at Hudal's consecration as a Bishop, but insisted that this in no way recognised Hudal's pro-Nazi views. Rather, it was 'because Cardinal Pacelli was the protector of the Anima'.[27]

While conceding that Hudal worked directly with two Popes, Nedbal is rather scathing about his predecessor's rescue work for Nazi war criminals. 'It's quite possible that he helped individuals, a few people . . . He himself talks of helping several hundred but I think that's an exaggeration and he had a real propensity for exaggeration.'

Nedbal provided a fascinating insight into Hudal's character, emphasising that he 'was a man of very small stature and he was always trying to "big note" himself. You can see it in his photographs and if you knew him, you could see it as well.'[28] But for a man with an ego problem, Hudal certainly had unusual and powerful friends.

In 1943, for example, he met Walter Rauff, a major war criminal. Following Himmler's distress at witnessing a mass shooting of Jews at Minsk in 1941, Rauff had overseen the development of the programme for mobile gas vans. These 'Black Ravens' murdered Jews by pumping exhaust fumes from diesel engines into hermetically sealed chambers at the back.

Rauff's gas trucks were not without their macabre technical problems; in early tests the unfortunate victims died not from exhaust fumes, but from gradual asphyxiation. Instead of being quickly poisoned, the human cargo left claw marks on the metal walls as they slowly choked to death. Once Rauff's system was 'perfected', some 100,000 people, mostly Eastern European women and children, died in his mobile gas vans.[29]

Following the collapse of Mussolini's regime in September 1943, Rauff was dispatched to northern Italy where he served with the SS in the region around Genoa, Turin and Milan. Once again, his assignment was the extermination of the Jewish population. It was during this period that Hudal made contact with this notorious mass murderer.

The genesis of Hudal's and Rauff's friendship is something of a mystery. Alfred Jarschel, a former Nazi Youth leader, claims that Rauff first met Hudal in the spring of 1943, when Deputy Führer Martin Bormann sent him to Rome for six months without any apparent mission. This was at a time when the Reich desperately needed senior officers of Rauff's experience and calibre as the war's outcome still hung in the balance. Jarschel believes 'that the first contacts with the Vatican were established during those months, which were to lead eventually to the setting up of Hudal's escape network.'[30]

The time was fast approaching when it would be needed. By early 1944 when the Allies landed in Sicily, even Hudal could see that Hitler's 'Thousand Year Reich' was doomed. As long as the Nazi Armies were winning, he had proudly driven around Rome with a 'Greater Germany' flag on his car; but when the Allies arrived in the Italian capital in June 1944, Hudal 'was the first to change it – suddenly his flag was Austrian'.[31]

Like many Austrians in 1945, Hudal switched overnight from being a Fascist philosopher to demonstrating his new-found demo-cratic aspirations. Discarding his long held pro-German position, he rushed to join the Free Austrian Committee in Rome and even helped organise a 'symbolic' liberation of the Austrian legation, belatedly reclaiming his long lost national pride. Hudal was not alone in his hypocrisy. It is ironic that the people of Austria, who had a higher percentage of Nazi party members than Germany, immediately demanded special treatment as the first victims of Hitler's tyranny.[32]

There were many dramatic changes in the Vatican as well, one of which may have played a crucial role in the development of Hudal's escape network. In August 1944 Cardinal Maglione died. Pius XII decided not to appoint a new Secretary of State, reassuming personal responsibility for foreign policy. From that time, Monsignors Tardini and Montini worked directly for the Pope.

Ladislas Farago claimed in his controversial book, *Aftermath*, that this decision 'was Hudal's entrée to the highest echelon of the Holy See'. Farago argues that Hudal had been on the outer with Maglione, relying on infrequent contact with the Pope himself to influence Vatican policy. But now he 'acquired a friend in the Secretariat of State'.[33]

Maglione's death suddenly left Giovanni Montini in charge of Pontifical Assistance to refugees, opening the door for Hudal's plans. Farago claims that it was Montini who allowed Hudal access to Vatican passports and other identity and travel docu-ments, which he then used to aid his Nazi friends. At the same time Hudal allegedly developed good contacts with another important Vatican bureau under Montini's control. This was the

Pontifical Commission for Assistance, which was concerned with work among refugees. One of its major roles was issuing travel documents to legitimate refugees. Finally, Farago alleged that Montini gave Hudal access to Caritas International, a Catholic charity which paid living and travelling expenses to help genuine refugees.

One of the Vatican's official historians hotly disputes Farago's claims. While conceding that Hudal 'interested himself, by his own admission, with ex-Nazis', Father Robert Graham is certain that 'Bishop Hudal had *no* role' in the Pontifical Commission for Assistance. He was not 'even "close"' to its work.[34] However, Farago's claims, if true, would explain Wiesenthal's persistent allegations that Caritas and the Vatican refugee bureau were directly involved with Nazi-smuggling.

The Nazi connection may have been purely personal, through Hudal, rather than through the agency officials themselves. They insist their roles were purely humanitarian, claiming that they were entirely ignorant of any Nazi-smuggling operations. But if Farago's allegations are true, it is astounding that Montini would have allowed Hudal, a declared pro-Nazi, any access to these Vatican sections at a time when the Nazis were desperate to escape. Such a decision would have been seen by Hudal as an overt act of encouragement to aid his Nazi friends. If Farago is right, Montini apparently gave Hudal every opportunity to do so.

There is some circumstantial evidence in the American diplomatic records to support the claim that Montini was deliberately aiding Hudal's Nazi-smuggling. This came about in a fairly innocent way. Following the virtual collapse of the German Army in Italy, Pius XII began to campaign for the right to send his personal representatives to visit the tens of thousands of prisoners of war and civilian internees then held in Italian camps.

As previously discussed, the Pope wished to extend his 'mission of charity in favour of all the victims of war without national or religious distinction'. In taking up this case with the Allied authorities in August 1944, the Vatican Secretariat of State pointed out that the Holy See 'cannot fail to interest itself now in these German prisoners'.

Over the next few weeks, the British and American forces debated the Pope's request. They asked the Holy See to provide a detailed justification for the proposed visits, and received this reply:

> ... the Representative of His Holiness (usually an Archbishop), accompanied by a Secretary, acting if necessary as interpreter, visits the camp, bringing with him some small gifts (spiritual books, books of instruction or light literature, games etc.); makes a short discourse and spends some time with the prisoners or internees...
> ... the purpose of the visit of the Representative of the Holy See is to assure normal religious assistance to Catholic prisoners as well as to exercise that mission of charity proper to the Church by bringing some comfort to those in affliction.

It was a completely reasonable argument in favour of humanitarian and charitable works. On 10 November the US President's Personal Representative to the Pope conveyed the Allied decision to the Vatican Secretariat of State. These visits would be permitted, provided they were restricted to religious assistance, and each visit was requested individually.[35]

A very peculiar request followed a few weeks later. Having achieved their humanitarian goal, on 2 December the Vatican asked that a representative be permitted 'to visit the German-speaking civil internees in Italy'. The Bishop chosen to minister to the defeated enemy population was none other than Hudal, the Vatican's 'Spiritual Director of the German people resident in Italy'.

It is astonishing that the Holy See singled out the most notorious pro-Nazi Bishop in Rome for this extremely sensitive mission. It was well known that these 'civilian' camps were teeming with fugitive Nazis who had discarded their uniforms and were hiding among the legitimate refugees. The Americans were at least partly to blame for granting Hudal access to the internment camps. When a senior US diplomat at the Vatican forwarded the Secretariat of State's letter to Allied headquarters in Rome, he made no mention of Hudal's pro-Nazi sympathies. But the Americans at the Vatican knew all about Hudal's views. One diplomat had formed a bad opinion of him during the war, observing that he did not 'trust Bishop Hudal', as his 'reputation ... was not too good from an Allied point of view'.[36]

American intelligence were also aware of Hudal's views, and compiled an intelligence dossier on his pro-Nazi book.[37] Although Allied Headquarters had previously refused some Vatican requests for travel passes, the Security Division approved this one, 'provided the object of [Hudal's] visit is specifically limited to giving normal religious assistance to catholic internees'.[38] Still, for the Vatican to obtain an Allied travel pass for Hudal to visit the German internees was a bit like giving whisky to an alcoholic and telling him not to drink; the resulting corruption was inevitable.

Equipped with his special credentials, Hudal was free to spread the good news about the escape system to his German friends hiding in the camps. There was no need for wanted war criminals to visit Rome to obtain assistance; Hudal brought it to them. Many years later he wrote a frank confession about his travels:

> I thank God that He [allowed me] to visit and comfort many victims in their prisons and concentration camps and [to help] them escape with false identity papers.[39]

Hudal had nothing but contempt for the American victors who helped him:

> The Allies' war against Germany was not a crusade, but the rivalry of economic complexes for whose victory they had been fighting. This so-called business ... used catchwords like democracy, race, religious liberty and Christianity as a bait for the masses. All these experiences were the reason why I felt duty bound after 1945 to devote my whole charitable work mainly to former National Socialists and Fascists, especially to so called 'war criminals'.[40]

Hudal's self confessed activities are all the more controversial because he operated with the full authority of the Vatican. Far from being 'on the fringes' as Father Schneider argues, Hudal obtained the approval of high level officials. Without the Vatican's direct diplomatic intercession to obtain his Allied travel pass, he could never have succeeded in making contact with so many Nazi war criminals. Indeed, without such help, he would have been bottled up in Rome.

It appears that one of the first Nazis Hudal visited was his old friend, Walter Rauff, in Milan. Eighteen months earlier, Rauff had left Rome to become Head of the Milan SD. This made him the chief SS security officer for all of northwest Italy, including Turin and Genoa. By 1944, Pius XII was extremely concerned that Italy's major industrial region would be destroyed in the final Allied offensive.

With Rauff's assistance, the senior Wehrmacht commanders in

northern Italy began a series of secret surrender negotiations. Allen Dulles, the American intelligence chief in Switzerland, worked out the surrender of German forces with the help of Vatican intermediaries. These negotiations were codenamed Operation Sunrise, and although they were singularly unsuccessful in shortening the war, each of the Nazi officers involved escaped serious punishment.[41]

When the German Army in Italy surrendered on 29 April 1945, Rauff obtained a false passport in the name of Carlo Comte and rented a flat in Milan. He then took his copy of Mussolini's secret police archives, including the Fascist Party membership lists, and quietly buried them outside the city. He knew they would be very useful in the coming months and his judgement proved correct. The very next day, however, Rauff was arrested by the Americans and interned in Milan's San Vittore gaol. Within hours a priest arrived and arranged for Rauff to be transferred to an American Army Hospital.

According to Wiesenthal, Rauff's release was arranged by Monsignor Don Giuseppe Bicchierai, Secretary to Milan's Cardinal Schuster. Bicchierai was one of the Vatican intermediaries in the secret surrender negotiations, who sheltered Rauff after his release and arranged for him to stay covertly 'in the convents of the Holy See'.[42]

On the other hand, Alfred Jarschel believes that Rauff's release was engineered by the Milan branch of the Italian Communist Party. In exchange for Rauff's Fascist Party membership lists, the Communists allegedly turned a blind eye to the establishment of his escape organisation.[43] What neither Wiesenthal nor Jarschel realised was that Rauff was released to the custody of 'S Force Verona', an OSS unit working with the British-American 'Special Counter Intelligence' team in Italy (SCI-Z), headed by James Jesus Angleton.

The S Force was, among other things, the Western equivalent of Rauff's wartime anti-Communist section. Rauff was a valuable asset, and over the objections of the US Army's Counter Intelligence Corps, who called him 'an unrepentant Nazi' and recommended lifetime imprisonment if not elimination, S Force Verona took charge of the grateful Rauff. After an extensive debriefing on Communist activity in his sector, he was released. Perhaps this was because Rauff openly boasted of high level connections in the

Vatican negotiations, which he claimed could be 'confirmed by Hussman and Mr Dulles, allied agents in Switzerland'.[44]

It is no coincidence that Rauff's 'Mr Dulles' later became Director of the Central Intelligence Agency, or that James Jesus Angleton became head of CIA Counter Intelligence. Throughout Angleton's career he retained exclusive control over American intelligence liaison with the Vatican.[45] Whatever the American motive, it is incontestable that Rauff was released from custody and returned to his flat in Milan.

According to the French publication, *Cercle Noir*, Rauff made contact with Archbishop Siri of Genoa, and immediately went to work for the Vatican in establishing a Nazi-smuggling system. Apart from his high level American and Vatican contacts, Rauff's main contribution to Hudal's smuggling system may have been financial. The man who once ran the mobile gas truck programme now became a money launderer, with the help of Frederico Schwendt, Rauff's former SS colleague. Schwendt is considered among the greatest counterfeiters in history, having forged millions of banknotes during the war as part of an SS operation codenamed *Wendig*.[46]

The original intention was to undermine and possibly destroy the Allied economies, but, as the war was drawing to a close, Schwendt laundered the counterfeit money through various banks and obtained legitimate Western notes. This was the seed money for the first Nazi escape network. Wiesenthal claims that Schwendt turned the proceeds over to his old comrade, Walter Rauff.[47]

However, Jarschel has a slightly different version. He claims that Hudal contacted Rauff in July 1945, asking him to come to Rome for a secret meeting. This proved impossible, so Hudal suggested that Rauff travel instead to Genoa and contact the newly appointed and strongly anti-Communist Archbishop Siri, another key player in the Nazi-smuggling operation. Rauff went to Genoa and was received by one of Siri's private secretaries. Jarschel alleges that he was given a sizeable sum of money and a Red Cross passport with a valid visa for Syria. He then returned to Milan and established the escape network.[48]

Perhaps the truth is somewhere in between: Rauff probably used Siri's money to augment the proceeds from the counterfeit laundering operation. Jarschel and *Cercle Noir* both agree that over the next four years some of the most wanted Nazi war criminals passed from Rauff in Milan, to Bishop Hudal at the Anima in Rome and then on to Archbishop Siri in Genoa. Here they boarded ships and left for new lives in South America.

The Vatican has never opened its bank records to show what sums were allocated to refugee assistance. To this day the dossiers on Schwendt and the Nazi money laundering are among the most highly classified American intelligence documents. However, the one paragraph which was declassified contains an intriguing reference about Schwendt's connection to the Nazi underground:

> On the Brenner Pass route from Austria the first stop on the underground railroad in Italy is at a castle in Merano where German is the language of the directors. [It is owned by] an agent of the SS task force . . . sometimes called 'Group Wendig' under the command of Schwendt, Col. Frederick, who was responsible only to Kaltenbrunner and Himmler. One [agent] . . . claimed 5,000,000 Dollars from the US Government for property confiscated at Merano after the war's end. All this property was the loot of the SS group which had been stored in . . . Schwendt's HQ and other buildings in Merano. Included in this loot were large quantities of British Pound Notes.[49]

The report goes on to list banks in Britain, Palestine, Italy and Switzerland that were tied to Schwendt's network. But money alone was not enough. False papers were the most important requirement for escaping Nazis. Hudal could provide all of these: Italian identity papers, false birth certificates, even visas for their country of destination. The most necessary were International Red Cross Passports.

According to Madame Gertrude Dupuis, a senior official in the Rome branch of the Red Cross, it 'was comparatively simple for [Hudal] to achieve this; he was a Bishop don't forget – that did help . . . How could we refuse to accept the word of priests?' she asked.[50] Madame Dupuis explained that if Hudal had requested that Red Cross papers 'be made out according to his specifications' and sent to him at the Anima, 'they probably were'.[51]

The IRC in Rome was flooded with applications in the mass confusion at war's end. To be fair, millions of people were on the move throughout Europe, many had lost their homes and their identity papers; others with shady pasts preferred to 'lose' documents which might identify them to a War Crimes Tribunal.

Many relief organisations issued new identity documents to the refugees. Some were only valid in Italy. For example, the International Caritas and the Vatican Refugee Organisation (Commissione Pontificia d'Assistenza) both issued hundreds of local 'identity documents' each week at this time. Many refugees used these *unofficial* Vatican documents as the starting point for the long paper trail for emigration.

While a Vatican identity card could be used to apply for the many further documents needed for emigration, on its own it did not permit its holder to leave Rome, let alone Italy. There is therefore no truth to the oft-repeated allegation that the Vatican handed out thousands of passports to Nazis. Indeed, the only strictly Vatican passports were the official credentials for its accredited clerical diplomats and officials.

The Red Cross was a far more promising source for a fugitive Nazi. For those who could not risk a personal appearance at the refugee relief counters, there was a flourishing and lucrative black market in stolen and forged documents. Madame Dupuis had personal experience of this, angrily recalling seeing such papers in her superior's office at IRC's Rome Headquarters. 'I could see from several feet away that they were forged. Not only were they filled out differently from how we do it ordinarily, but my signature was obviously forged.'[52] While Madame Dupuis could do little about this situation, some IRC officials apparently turned a blind eye to these abuses.

The illicit trade in Red Cross documents was soon discovered by American intelligence. By late 1945 they were almost certain that fugitive Nazis were among the beneficiaries. This was confirmed in mid-1946, when there was a breakout of German prisoners from Rimini camp in northern Italy. Many escapees were subsequently apprehended with false IRC documents.

An investigation, codenamed Operation Circle, was launched by the American Army's Counter Intelligence Corps. They forwarded their early findings to Vincent La Vista, a senior Rome officer of the Division of Foreign Activity Correlation. La Vista had been involved in a number of top secret post-war intelligence operations, investigating Fascist espionage cells operating in America and commercial, financial and industrial dealings between Italy and Germany.

La Vista investigated and forwarded his report to Washington in May 1947. Since its release in 1984, it has become known simply as the 'La Vista Report'. Although the findings contain some significant errors, it is a fairly comprehensive analysis of illegal emigration through Italy. It should be noted that La Vista was himself a Catholic, but one of his main conclusions was that the Vatican was helping the escape of fugitive war criminals.[53] When his report eventually surfaced, this claim was strongly denied by the Church.

Official Vatican historian, Father Graham, argued that the report's real purpose had been 'completely misrepresented'. Its focus was not escaping Nazis, but 'Communist infiltration into Latin America. It isn't very honest or objective to pick out a page and a half where La Vista alludes to Nazis escaping, when the whole report wasn't about Nazis but Communists. The only real Nazi mentioned escaped with the help of the Jewish Zionist organisations.'[54]

However, much of La Vista's report is concerned with the role of Vatican institutions and officials in illegal Nazi emigration. The State Department officer listed nearly two dozen 'Vatican relief and welfare organizations engaged in or suspected of engaging in illegal emigration'. At the top of the list was the ubiquitous Bishop Hudal.[55] The US Army's CIC conducted extensive investigations into the black market in forged documents, and several reports were appended to La Vista's report.

Appendix B dealt extensively with the Rimini breakout the previous July. A reliable CIC informant reported that two of the escapees, Gianni and Vorkörper, 'had been instructed to proceed to Rome and contact' a CIC informant, who was supposed to help them emigrate to South America. The Germans were placed under surveillance and it emerged that Gianni's real name was Walter Fütling 'living in the apartment of a German woman who was formerly employed at the German Embassy in the Vatican'. The two escapees joined two other fugitives in Rome, who were in close contact with local priests.

One priest was reported to be 'aiding the escapees with food, lodging, and contacts with German and Vatican officials'. When two of the escapees went to Genoa to arrange transportation to South America, the CIC informant 'borrowed' their passports and discovered that they were 'issued by the International Red Cross'.[56] The CIC agent instructed his informant to attempt to obtain his own false passport. He did so 'by paying 20,000 lire to a person known to have contacts with the International Red Cross'.

The system for obtaining passports was simple. The informant was sent to a man who took down his personal details. The man had an inside contact who examined the IRC files, looking for 'the name of a missing or dead person who fitted the [informant's] description'. Two days later the CIC informant was told to apply for a Red Cross passport under the false name of Mirko Baucech. He also needed two letters of identification which his contact obtained from the Vatican and the Italian Red Cross.[57]

In August 1946 the CIC operation ceased when the men under surveillance were arrested; three were Rimini escapees and the fourth held 'false discharge permits'. The Germans admitted having contacts with people close to the Vatican. The CIC report also referred to another Vatican representative who had good connections with 'South American Consulates and business firms'. This Vatican contact was the last link in the 'German emigration chain which funnels all of its clients through the International Red Cross'.[58]

La Vista also confirmed that Milan was an important centre in the smuggling network. Although he does not mention Rauff, La Vista discovered a network run by his close friend, Frederico Schwendt:

> There is a general movement of Germans . . . who cross the border via Treviso and Milan for the sole purpose of obtaining . . . ficticious identity documents, passports and visas, and leave almost immediately via Genoa and Barcelona for South America.[59]

As a demonstration of how easily the Vatican could obtain false IRC documents, La Vista arranged for two 'Hungarian refugees' to visit Father Josef Gallov, who operated the Hungarian relief 'agency sponsored by the Vatican'. La Vista called Gallov 'an honest, conscientious Catholic Priest, but he is likewise a sentimental old man' who did not bother to ask too many questions of the 'refugees'.

The men had been chosen because they spoke Hungarian. They arrived at Father Gallov's office without any personal papers or documentation of any kind, saying they had just fled from the Soviets. 'Both men claimed to be natives of a small village in Hungary and to have lost their entire families in bombing raids during the war.' The second informant agreed to corroborate his friend's story under oath and Gallov prepared an affadavit. He then gave the man a letter to present to the Red Cross and, a few hours later, La Vista's informant obtained a perfectly valid passport. Shortly thereafter, the first informant simply reversed the procedure and obtained a passport for his 'Hungarian' friend. 'Needless to say,' La Vista commented, 'both men are Italian, neither ever having been outside Italy.'[60]

Yet another CIC officer concluded that IRC documents could be obtained without any identification through 'the assistance of persons operating under the protection of the Vatican'. Paul Lyon later became a key US liaison to the Vatican's Ratlines, but in 1946 he investigated their operations. He discovered that the Holy See was sponsoring the illicit trade in Red Cross papers, obtained either 'under an alias or with false nationality'.[61] Lyon also confirmed that Hungarian Catholic priest Father Gallov was central to this operation. He also identified some of those who obtained such false documents as 'known or wanted war criminals'.[62]

According to the CIC officer, the system for obtaining false papers was fairly straightforward. An applicant would be provided with a letter bearing 'an official stamp of the Vatican' to take to Gallov's 'personal contact in the International Red Cross . . . to secure a . . . Red Cross identity document'. This could then be used to obtain 'the necessary ration cards and temporary resident permit from the Italian police authorities to remain safely in Italy', while awaiting 'permission from the Consuls of Central and South American countries to immigrate'.[63]

La Vista's report initially caused a major upheaval in Washington. The State Department decided that the report 'required urgent attention'.[64] A top secret meeting was convened, but the Washington bureaucrats eventually decided to issue only a very discreet and informal protest.[65] La Vista was not even asked to follow up his investigation to establish the full ramifications of the Vatican smuggling network.

The Americans decided that good relations with the Holy See were more important than bringing mass murderers to justice. The State Department's orders to their representative at the Vatican were hardly a model of American outrage.[66] He was merely asked to 'approach the Vatican informally. I leave it to you to decide what, and how much, should be done in this regard'.[67] The diplomat took the hint, and decided that an oral message, or Note Verbale, would be sufficient. This is the lowest class of diplomatic communication, reserved for informal topics too insignificant to warrant an official Diplomatic Note.

Yet by the time the oral message was delivered, it had been watered down even further. Monsignor Walter Carroll of the Vatican Secretariat of State was only advised that 'unscrupulous persons, often engaged in illicit and clandestine activities' had somehow managed to obtain travel documents 'through the unwitting assistance of charitable organizations'. Although the message was somewhat ambiguous, there was apparently no mention whatsoever of La Vista's evidence that the Vatican was actively helping Nazis to escape.

The State Department seemed more concerned that the false documents might inadvertently assist Jews going to Palestine or 'secret [Communist] agents, many of them destined for the Western Hemisphere'. The bewildered Vatican official probably thought that the Americans were only concerned about sophisticated Jewish and Communist smuggling organisations. He hastened to assure the American diplomat that 'such agencies are not connected to the Vatican'.[68]

The American concluded his 'protest' by requesting the Vatican's assistance to ensure that all 'nations may be preserved from infiltration by unfriendly agents and that the charitable and benevolent work of assisting bonafide displaced persons . . . may not be prejudiced' by such illegal activities.[69] None of the priests named in the La Vista report was even mentioned.

If Father Graham only read the oral summary of this strange meeting, he would be quite right to assume that La Vista's report had nothing to do with smuggling Nazis. The American diplomat provided the lame excuse that it 'has not been possible to be more specific because of the need to protect our sources of information and our investigators who still have important work in progress. Also, I felt that my action should be tempered somewhat because officials in the Vatican have betrayed to me on several occasions their sensitiveness over the amount of private American capital which has gone into the financing of illegal migration.'

These may well have been the reasons for American indifference towards the Vatican's Ratlines. However, one researcher discovered a document in the US Archives which throws fascinating light on official US attitudes. According to Charles Allen, the very same day that this meeting with Monsignor Carroll was reported to Washington, another, *unsigned* letter was dispatched from Rome to Washington, warning that 'Monsignor Walter Carroll, Secretariat of State of the Holy See, had cautioned . . . in an "Oral Message" not to delve too deeply into the details of the financing of the Nazi escape routes'.[70]

Apparently the State Department was informed that the Vatican was, indeed, aware of the funding arrangements for the smuggling network.

While the diplomatic niceties were being observed, Hudal continued to send wanted fugitives down the escape route, until the Vatican itself came under concerted attack. A series of articles in the Italian press questioned the motives of Pius XII, who was by then widely labelled as the 'German Pope'. The entire Vatican–Nazi connection was threatened with exposure. For example, on 6 August 1947 the Milan based evening paper, *Milano Sera*, published an article headed 'Too many Germans around the Pope'. It claimed that within

> the Pontifical apartment in the Vatican, only German is spoken – a language in which the Pope is exceedingly well versed . . . The Pope lives on German cuisine . . . Pius XII's private secretary [Father Leiber] is a husky Bavarian . . . He is often seen about Rome in his car, from which he alights alone to stop at one of the typical German beer parlors . . . frequented by . . . SS war criminals who hide under assumed names.
>
> It is plain that the new myth, to which even the Vatican subscribes, of the 'poor German' who is paying the penalty for others' guilt and who has the right to assistance from the whole world, has arisen solely from this particular [pro-German] atmosphere which so tightly surrounds the Head of the Church.[71]

The Vatican realised that this form of publicity harmed its international reputation. They immediately knew who to blame. Pressure was applied to Hudal; he later wrote that Vatican diplomats began to shun him, some even calling him the 'Nazi, fascist Bishop – *troppo tedesco* [too much the German]'.[72] However, despite the fact that Hudal's Nazi-smuggling operation threatened to become a public scandal, it took nearly four years to replace him as Rector of the Anima. He finally bowed to the inevitable at

Christmas 1951, announcing that he would leave the Anima the following July.[73]

Convinced that his only sin was a bad press image, Hudal remained in Rome until his death, unrepentant for his work on behalf of Nazi war criminals:

> To help people, to save a few, without thinking of the consequences, working selflessly and with determination, was naturally what should have been expected of a true Christian. We do not believe in the eye for an eye of the Jew.[74]

Apparently Bishop Hudal believed that the Germans should be excused for their crimes in the name of Christian Charity while simple justice was a vengeful concept, at least when it applied to the killers of Jews. To his death, Hudal remained a convinced anti-Semite.

The press scandal that erupted in 1947 did not end the Nazi Ratlines. By the time Hudal's star was waning, more discreet priests had taken his place in the dark constellation of the smuggling system. There was one direct benefit from the threat of the press scandal. From that moment on, extraordinary measures were taken to conceal the existence of the Nazi escape routes. Their full extent would not be publicly discovered for another forty years.

Well before Bishop Hudal stepped off the stage, the scene was set for a more professional and clandestine smuggling operation that would assist war criminals and quislings from all the Catholic countries of Europe. Whether or not Hudal had acted alone, his successors were clearly authorised by senior Vatican officials. Like Hudal, his successors received their start in Nazi-smuggling as the result of official Vatican intervention to obtain Allied travel passes.[75] It is no coincidence that the Vatican selected Fascist priests from Central and Eastern Europe for this work. Hudal had already sent many Germans to South America, but now tens of thousands of non-German Nazi collaborators were clamouring for assistance.

As the Americans would soon discover, the Vatican was willing to smuggle Fascists of every stripe. What the Americans did not know was why the Holy See was involved.

3

A French Spy in the Vatican

Special Agent William Gowen was puzzled and frustrated. The American intelligence officer was increasingly despondent at his failure to trace the *émigré* Nazi underground in Rome and apprehend wanted war criminals who were thriving in the city. As soon as he discovered their whereabouts they disappeared from view, as if swallowed by a dark and unfathomable chasm. He was sure that a shadowy group called Intermarium was somehow involved, but lacked hard evidence to justify his suspicion.

A few months earlier, Gowen and his colleagues in the US Army Counter Intelligence Corps had seemed on the verge of a major breakthrough, but this was now further out of reach than ever. When the reports of Operation Circle had been assessed they thought they were close to solving the Vatican mystery. As previously discussed, this clandestine operation had been launched in July 1946 to discover how such fugitives were able to survive on the run, who was assisting them to hide in Rome and then leave for the safety of South America.

The American officers concluded that the Vatican was 'the largest single organization involved in the illegal movement of emigrants' in and through Italy, and that the Holy See's justification for 'its participation in this illegal traffic is simply the propagation of the Faith'. For it was

> the Vatican's desire to assist any person regardless of nationality or political beliefs, as long as that person can prove himself to be a Catholic ... The Vatican further justifies its participation by its desire to infiltrate, not only European countries but Latin American countries as well, with people of all political beliefs as long as they are anti-Communist and pro-Catholic Church.[1]

State Department intelligence officer, Vincent La Vista, reported that the Vatican had 'brought pressure to bear' on Catholic countries in South America, especially Argentina but also Mexico,

Cuba and others. This resulted 'in the foreign missions of those countries taking an attitude almost favouring the entry into their country of former Nazi (sic) and former Fascists or other political groups, so long as they are anti-Communist'.

During the investigations of this traffic, US intelligence had come across an array of Vatican-sponsored 'relief and welfare organizations in Rome engaging in or suspected of engaging in illegal emigration'. La Vista interviewed many Church officials involved, concluding that they were operating 'under the benevolent sponsorship of the Vatican':

> Needless to say, all of the Agencies operating in conjunction with or under the protection of the Vatican are financed by Vatican funds. No attempt was made to ascertain the amount of these funds, their origin, or their method of distribution, but it is the observation of this writer that substantial sums are being spent generously in the promotion of this work.[2]

La Vista was qualified to draw this conclusion, having investigated the web of illicit Nazi money laundering which occurred after World War II. Similar claims have been repeatedly made by other researchers. Austrian-based Nazi hunter, Simon Wiesenthal, has dubbed it the 'Roman Way'. He alleges that the Vatican ran a systematic smuggling system to spirit Nazi mass murderers out of Europe.[3]

The Vatican has consistently denied these claims. When La Vista's report surfaced in early 1984, it caused an international furore, forcing the Vatican to deny it. Their spokesperson, Reverend Romeo Panciroli, cited two of the Holy See's historians, Father Robert Graham and Reverend Pierre Blet. Graham claimed that La Vista's findings were 'propagandistic manoeuvres' by people who 'never lose the occasion to crucify' the Church. 'The accusations in the report are founded on nothing but air,' the American priest said.

Reverend Blet concurred that the report was 'artificial and false, unworthy of attention', and probably 'based on information furnished by questionable elements'. Reverend Antonio Weber, a German-born priest who ran a Vatican-sponsored relief organisation, went even further, stating categorically that 'the Vatican never hid or aided Nazis after the war'.[4]

Clearly there is little agreement between the Vatican and its critics. However, in mid-1947 William Gowen established that the truth lay somewhere in the middle. Gowen was in a good position to discover what was really happening. Not only was he a CIC agent, but his father, Franklin Gowen, was a senior State Department officer. In 1940 President Roosevelt had sent Myron Taylor to be his Personal Representative to Pius XII, and Gowen senior went to the Holy See as one of his assistants. He served there until 1947, when he returned to Washington. His son stayed in Rome and investigated the Vatican's Nazi connections.

Gowen junior was by then an up and coming young intelligence officer, ambitious for postings in the exciting world of European espionage. The shadowy Nazi diaspora seemed to have eluded his colleagues, but now Gowen was putting the pieces together. He had solved the puzzle that had frustrated him for so many months, going beyond Operation Circle's conclusions and getting right inside Intermarium. He discovered that the Vatican's total denials were not supported by the evidence; neither was the blanket claim that the Holy See *as an entity* was involved.

Rather, Gowen found that a well organised network of Central and Eastern European Nazi *émigrés* was operating on the Vatican's fringes, and receiving the secret support of a tiny but powerful cabal, of church and intelligence agents. These investigations took the best part of eighteen months and in the process the American officer also discovered that the Vatican cabal was only a small part of a mysterious spy organisation called Intermarium.

Gowen found that its roots went back to the early 1920s, to a so-called 'White' Russian *émigré* group which fled to Paris in the wake of the Bolshevik seizure of power. They were termed the 'Whites' to distinguish them from the Communist 'Reds' in the civil war. Once in Paris, a former Czarist general established a group to unite all nationalities subjugated by Communism.[5]

By the mid-1930s the Paris group had evolved into Intermarium, 'a secret international organization that desires as its members people whose homes are to be found in the "Intermare" – that part of Europe between the Baltic, the Black Sea, the Aegean, the Ionian Sea, and the Adriatic. Also included are the Caucasians.'

Intermarium grandly proclaimed the unity of sixteen nations 'inhabiting the territory between Germany and Russia proper . . . which are united in the effort of their struggle for liberation, as well as in their tendency to secure a peaceful existence and to participate in the construction of a new Europe and that of a world, free from tyranny, terror and famine'. Although the goal was to ensure the self-determination of all these disparate 'nations', it was almost completely impractical. Many of the countries supposedly united in these endeavours had long histories of bloody conflicts between themselves, in which ethnic, cultural and even religious differences played powerful roles.[6]

Nevertheless, Intermarium proclaimed the necessity for a powerful anti-Communist Pan-Danubian Confederation, comprised in the main of the Catholic nations of Central Europe. Before the war it had received strong support from both French and British intelligence for anti-Communist operations.[7]

Intermarium's goal was to create a *cordon sanitaire* against both the Russians and the Germans. This plan had received considerable support from France, Britain and the Vatican in the 1920s and 1930s. The Holy See looked with great fondness on France, proclaimed by Pius XI as 'the first-born of the great Catholic family'. The British Foreign Office had noted in October 1942 that the Vatican's post-war policy would 'favour the creation of a large Danubian federal State, if it gives promise of stability and is not controlled by Bolshevik Russia'.[8]

Gowen's CIC colleagues in Austria had found traces of this Pan-Danubian Confederation during their early investigations of the Ustashi's post-war revival. Formed in the late 1920s, this Fascist group had conducted a campaign of international terrorism in the 1930s. They were then placed in power in Croatia by the Nazis during the war, and proceeded to exterminate hundreds of thousands of innocent civilians. On 25 June 1945, only seven weeks after the war had concluded, the Ustashi had made contact with a Papal mission in Salzburg in the US zone of Austria. They asked for the Pope's assistance to create either another independent Croatian state, or at least 'a Danube-Adriatic union in which, according to all natural laws, Croatia would have its possibility for development'.[9]

Gowen had discovered the intricate connections between Intermarium, the Vatican, French and British intelligence by tracking down a young Hungarian he suspected was one of its key organisers. He hoped that Ferenc Vajta would provide valuable inside information on how Intermarium linked into the well organised and financed Nazi-smuggling network. He believed that Vajta could even confirm the Vatican's deep involvement in these activities, as he knew the Hungarian was well connected with Church leaders.

Vajta had proved an elusive quarry, well hidden in the *émigré* underground that had been built in Rome since war's end. Hints of his important role had emerged in late 1946, when the Hungarian government claimed that he was 'living in great state at the "Grand Hotel", Rome'. The CIC discovered this was untrue. Rather, 'according to fairly reliable sources', he was in fact living 'in one of the many monasteries in the Rome area'.[10] This chance discovery led Gowen to Vajta in the first half of 1947.

Gowen told Vajta's close friends that in return for information, he would assist the fugitive to regain possession of his identity papers, recently confiscated by the Italian police.[11] Vajta had a lot to tell. He said he had worked for over two years with both French and British intelligence, organising 'two clandestine movements against the Russians'. According to Vajta, the Vatican had supported these operations, informally working with the French and British to revive Intermarium after World War II.[12]

Vajta revealed that he had been Hungarian Consul General in Vienna at war's end, sent to organise the evacuation of Hungarian industry and establish escape routes for 'refugees'. He 'organised more than 7,000 train trucks of machinery and factories' to reach western Germany, and saved 'the great majority of Hungary's bourgeoisie and aristocracy' from the Soviets.[13]

The French soon discovered his key role as 'one of the few men who knew the location of this evacuated industry'. The French were desperately short of money to finance clandestine operations, and Vajta's stolen treasure became the main financial base for France's revival of Intermarium in 1945.[14] Vajta recalled that he had been easily located by French military intelligence in their occupation zone in Austria. He was recruited for special intelligence operations then taking shape at General Charles de Gaulle's Paris headquarters.

According to Vajta, the historical convergence of French and Vatican interests in Central Europe played a crucial role in de Gaulle's schemes 'to employ the factor of Catholicism'. Vajta told French intelligence of his pre-war role in their clandestine operations in Central Europe. While studying at the Sorbonne in the early 1930s, he joined the secretive *Grand Orient*, an organisation specialising in Central and Eastern European affairs which linked Francophiles from these regions to French activities.[15]

This was one of many reasons why Vajta was employed in 1945 and 1946 by the Deuxième Bureau and the French High Command in Austria. He claimed to be a personal favourite of de Gaulle himself, visiting Paris in late 1945 and gaining a first-hand impression of the President's aims. Gowen later noted that Vajta had not only helped to finance French operations, but also proved himself in various active anti-Communist operations. These included the 'arrest and expulsion of a Czechoslovakian Army search team, and the detection and courtmartial of Hungarian Soviet agent Galle'.[16]

Vajta explained that as soon as hostilities ceased, de Gaulle ordered an aggressive campaign 'to gain the sympathy of the peoples of Eastern Europe'. His aim was to create a counterweight to British plans and his conception was 'very simple' but, according to Vajta, very just. The French leader believed that it was necessary to prepare for a new war with Stalin to restore France's rightful role in the region.

De Gaulle told Vajta that France needed 'the friendship of those countries' *émigrés* who tomorrow, with discreet help, could become the rulers of Eastern Europe'.[17] Vajta claimed that he had received 'the authority of the French High Command in Austria to bring together in the French zone all the exiled politicians of South Eastern Europe'. He worked with two branches of French intelligence – État Majeur and the Deuxième Bureau – laying the foundation for Intermarium's resurrection. He categorically denied that former Nazis were involved.

Under French direction Vajta built intelligence centres in Innsbruck, Freiburg and Paris. 'The *émigrés* travelled with État Majeur papers', so that they could move about securely, and establish a sophisticated intelligence network. Vajta claimed that de Gaulle developed close relations with the Vatican. The French leader's plan 'was to collaborate with the Church and to be sustained by the Vatican in the struggle for the Europe of tomorrow. He knew too well that France alone was not strong enough to play the heavy cards.'

The French General staff were initially successful in gaining the Vatican's help, utilising 'Church personalities' to make contact with *émigré* leaders. One of the most important Vatican officials to take up their cause was French Cardinal Tisserant, the Holy See's leading Eastern European expert. Among other things, the French utilised Tisserant to approach the Vatican 'for a secret collaboration to "save European heritage"'.[18]

De Gaulle wanted the Pope's help to create a European Confederation, bringing together the Catholics of Spain, France, Italy, Austria, Germany, Poland, Hungary, Slovakia, Croatia, Slovenia and the Baltic states, among others. To realise this pipedream, de Gaulle knew that 'France would have to sign friendship treaties with Spain and Italy', establishing a powerful 'triangle' which would then be aided, 'under the Pope's influence', by the South American Catholic states. The success of this 'triangle' also depended on Vatican assistance 'to help French politics in Bavaria, Würtemberg and Baden-Baden for the creation of a federal state of Catholic Germany', detached from the Protestant majority.

The final link in de Gaulle's plan was a Central European Catholic Pan-Danubian Confederation, allied to Poland and the Baltic states. This would enable the detachment of Catholic Slavs from their Orthodox and Protestant countrymen, ensuring the collapse of Yugoslavia, Czechoslovakia and large parts of the Soviet Union itself, thus contributing greatly to rolling back the Bolshevik menace. De Gaulle's plan was the first formal step in Intermarium's revival.

Gowen later reported to his superiors that through 'the winter of 1945–46 the propaganda effort in Italy diminished . . . However, Vajta Ferenc . . . succeeded in establishing himself in "Intermarium". His reputation as a conceited adventurer true to only money did much to drive the Hungarians away from "Intermarium".'[19] Vajta became a senior Intermarium leader, writing two books and propaganda for the *Intermarium Bulletin*.[20] He later 'elaborated for État Majeur and the [French] Foreign Minster' a number of 'confidential plans' for organising clandestine Balkan activities.

After July 1946 Vajta lived briefly in Innsbruck with the local French intelligence chief, who proposed that Vajta should direct all *émigré* operations from Paris. However, he declined this invitation because of a major disagreement, left the French zone with his closest comrades and relocated to Italy. He soon re-established the close contacts he had built with the Vatican and Italian Catholic politicians during the late 1930s when he had been a journalist in Rome. Soon after, 'the Vatican retired from the circle of French interest'.[21]

American intelligence established that in Rome Vajta 'started to work with the Jesuits. This line of work took him to Spain and Switzerland.'[22] Gowen discovered the reason for his 'disagreement' with the French, who had demanded that Vajta sign over his rights in a Hungarian bauxite mine 'in return for financial and political backing'. Vajta severed most of his contacts, as he no longer wished to be branded as 'a French spy' by the Hungarian Communists.[23]

Vajta had filled in important gaps about France's role in Intermarium's post-war resurrection, but he also explained the British connection. The origin of post-war British activities was traced to the establishment of a 'Central European Committee' by Prime Minister Churchill in early 1944. His aim was to create a Confederation of Central European nations under London's influence.[24] As the war ended, the Secret Intelligence Service (MI6) launched a sophisticated intelligence operation to recruit Central and Eastern European émigrés.

Vajta explained that SIS aimed to establish 'a political league against Bolshevism', and provide material aid to draw the exiles into the 'British circle' for anti-Soviet counter-espionage and paramilitary operations. The British had also established Masonic Lodges among the exiles, thereby attracting 'the most eminent leaders of the Balkans'.[25] Then, using 'their very best teams', many of whom had worked with Intermarium in the 1930s, SIS took the initiative from the French. Although British and French operations were tentatively co-ordinated, the two European powers had very different plans: London wanted total domination of Central Europe.

'The first British intelligence experts and specialists were already working in Austria in June 1945', and Vajta's French bosses ordered him to liaise with the SIS teams. The SIS men were 'very clever and very hard, harder even than the French and better prepared'. Vajta knew that they had penetrated agents among the émigrés, establishing intelligence centres in Graz and Klagenfurt in the British zone of Austria. By July 1945, '215 British agents had begun the battle for the peace, among them some of the most important Balkan experts.'[26]

The British were convinced that war would soon break out with the Soviets, so they collected everybody, 'it didn't matter who they were, where they came from, what party they belonged to, what ideology they proclaimed'. According to Vajta, the British 'gave succour even to Nazis and the Ustashi', and from the first they 'built military and terrorist centres among all the Balkan refugees. They were in a hurry and didn't want to lose any time,' and soon they had 'a magnificent organisation' which reached into the most obscure parts of the Balkans.[27] A network of *émigré* centres was set up in Italy, Austria, Germany, London and even Paris.[28]

Gowen was finally putting together the pieces of the Intermarium puzzle. 'During the latter part of 1945,' he wrote, '"Intermarium" was in embryo form and by the summer of 1946, it was a well developed organization . . . British and French intelligence took considerable interest in the development of the organization.'[29]

By late summer 1946, British intelligence had achieved 'an undeniable predominance' over their French rivals. Vajta admitted his own contacts with the SIS men, especially after closer French–British co-operation was established in the second half of 1946. He told the Americans that ultimately his 'discussions with the British were not successful, because they asked for too much'. There was at least one major point of agreement between Paris and London: the United States should be excluded from these clandestine operations. They adopted the slogan of 'Europe for the Europeans, without Russians and Americans. Make the United States fight the Russians and exploit the victory'.[30]

Gowen noted that by mid-1946, Intermarium was sufficiently strong for British intelligence to launch 'a large-scale propaganda campaign' in the Italian Displaced Persons camps. 'Apparently the organization had considerable sums at its disposition, for it printed and distributed a 14 page charter of the "Free Intermare" and began printing a bulletin in Rome.'

Gowen also noted that 'the propaganda became so strong at Fermo camp', where many Croatian war criminals had settled, that Father Krunoslav Draganović, Secretary of the Confraternity of San Girolamo in Rome, 'became Croat representative to "Intermarium" in a quasi-official capacity'. The official representative was Croatian Peasant Party leader, Vlatko Maček, who was in fact residing in Washington. In Rome, the man who gave Intermarium its most powerful influence with the Vatican was Father Draganović.[31]

Described by CIC as a 'prominent member of Intermarium', Draganović was the most important figure in the clandestine network. San Girolamo was the centre of the operation, supported by powerful figures in the Holy See hierarchy. Founded in 1453 with the patronage of Pope Nicholas V, San Girolamo has produced some of the most outstanding Croatian scholars, scientists, writers and priests. Like France, Croatia is one of the Church's most beloved nations, a Catholic bulwark against the Orthodox schismatics.[32]

After World War II, Father Draganović skilfully used the benevolence with which the Vatican viewed San Girolamo, to build a thoroughly professional Nazi-smuggling system. With the help of other fanatic Croatian nationalist clerics, the Institute became the headquarters of the Ratlines. Born in 1903 in Brčko, Bosnia, Draganović had been brought up to be a fiercely proud Croatian Catholic. After completing his education in Sarajevo and Vienna he studied theology, taking his vows in 1928. In 1932, Draganović went to Rome to study at the Papal Oriental Institute and the Jesuit Gregorian University. He stayed there until 1935, working in the Vatican Archives. He then became secretary to Bishop Ivan Šarić of Sarajevo, who achieved notoriety in the war as the 'hangman' of the Serbs during the Ustashi's bloody massacres.[33]

Draganović had returned to Rome in August 1943, representing the Ustashi and the Croatian Red Cross. This allowed him to build his escape routes for Nazi war criminals. He was supported by Croatia's Archbishop, Aloyius Stepinac, who had provided Draganović with introductions to influential Vatican contacts. As a result, he could move in the highest circles, meeting regularly with Secretary of State Maglione, and even with Pope Pius XII. He also had close contacts with Axis diplomats at the Vatican, which would later prove invaluable.

Draganović began lobbying the British in favour of the Pan-Danubian Confederation in early 1944 when he delivered a lengthy memo to the British Ambassador to the Vatican. He passed on proposals made by senior Ustashi ministers in Zagreb, which were sent to London via the Vatican. Although nothing came of this early contact, Draganović's London connection blossomed after the war.

Draganović established very close relations with senior Vatican figures, especially Assistant Secretary of State Montini, who helped him gain access to the Pope's Refugee Assistance Commission. By 1944, he was ready to open his Ratline. He depended heavily on the Pontifical Assistance Commission, from which he obtained large numbers of identity papers. Although many, perhaps most, were given to legitimate refugees, thousands helped fugitives make good their escape from justice.[34]

One of Draganović's most important lay colleagues was Intermarium's President, Miha Krek. Leader of the Catholic Slovene People's Party, and a close friend of Vajta, Krek worked for British intelligence.[35] Gowen noted that Krek 'is known to have wide connections' and that one of his principal

> assistants is Kotnik Ciro, former Royal Yugoslav diplomat accredited to the Vatican. Kotnik who has been in Italy over twenty (20) years has built up a chain of useful contacts. Thus, in individual cases, Krek sends Kotnik to the Rome Questura [police] to 'fix up' the foreigners in Rome in whom Krek has an interest. This is relatively easy for Kotnik since he is the respected acquaintance of Dr Angelo de Fiore head of the Ufficio Stranieri [the Italian police section dealing with foreigners].[36]

Draganović's own contacts reached to the very top of the Italian Interior Ministry. The two men had another thing in common: high level Vatican contacts. Krek operated through the Slovene Assistant General of the Jesuits, Monsignor Anton Prešeren. The OSS reported that the Pope had received Krek and Prešeren 'in private audience' in November 1944. According to Italian intelligence, Prešeren was the leader of a powerful group of Slovenes inside the Vatican, which received 'a lot of help from the English'.[37]

Other British agents in Intermarium included the former Nazi Romanian Foreign Minister, Gregorij Gafençu; Casimir Papée, Poland's Ambassador to the Vatican; his fellow countryman, Myz-Mysin, who was the group's counter-espionage expert in Rome; Monsignor Ivan (John) Bučko, the 'spiritual leader of the Ukrainian resistance movement', who also had extremely good Vatican connections; and Ferdinand Durčansky, former Slovak Foreign and Interior Minister, and wanted war criminal. Even the Orthodox Serbs were represented at the Vatican by Dr Kosta Čukić, who was 'in charge of communications with the French', as the Italian secret service reported.[38]

The vast majority of Intermarium leaders were ex-Fascist leaders who worked either for British or French secret services, although there was also a fair sprinkling of Soviet agents. Needless to say, the CIC listed Ferenc Vajta as a senior Intermarium figure and its main propagandist in 1946 and 1947.[39]

Gowen was struck by the fact that many leading Intermarium figures also operated the Vatican-sponsored emigration bodies listed in La Vista's report. At the top of the list was Bishop Hudal of the Austrian committee, who ran the first crude escape networks while Intermarium was being organised: Father Draganović, Monsignor Prešeren, Bishop Bučko and Father Gallov were all active in Intermarium's Nazi-smuggling operations.[40]

William Gowen was reasonably sure that by developing his contacts with Vajta he would get to the bottom of the murky waters covering Intermarium. So he visited local police headquarters and 'arranged for the return of Vajta's documents from the Italians and continued the Intermarium investigation which led into a series of various channels'.[41]

Vajta explained that after arriving in Rome in September 1946, he quickly 'made contacts with various circles inside the Vatican', particularly with the Jesuits where fellow Intermarium leader, Monsignor Prešeren, was influential: they 'always supported my struggle'. As previously discussed, in October 1945 the OSS had identified the Jesuits as key Vatican agents involved in 'a penetration program' inside Communist-occupied areas.[42]

Vajta also 'worked especially closely with the Christian Democrats', and had 'lots of friends' in their top leadership.[43] On one occasion he negotiated a deal involving the Italian government and exiled Hungarian businessmen. Gowen reported that in 'the name of a group of businessmen in the French Zones of Austria and Germany, Vajta was responsible for negotiations with [the] Minister of Industry of the de Gasperi Italian Government. These negotiations were successfully concluded in August 1947.' The Hungarians re-established their industries in Italy, providing employment for a significant population, which might otherwise have looked to the Communists.[44]

After re-establishing his Church and Christian Democrat connections, Vajta extended his activities. In February 1947 he travelled to France and Spain where he obtained 'the help of the Archbishop of Toledo'. In Madrid he also contacted the local US Embassy, which discovered that Vajta was a friend of the former Polish Ambassador in Madrid, Marjan Szumlakowski, who assisted his work in Spain.

Vajta held discussions with Spanish Foreign Affairs officials which resulted in an agreement for the 'entry of Eastern Europeans into Spain'. The US Embassy commented that such people were 'not necessarily "pro-American" but favourable to Vajta's group'. In an obvious attempt to curry favour with US intelligence, Vajta also provided the Embassy with information on the Soviets' 'Tangiers network'.[45]

On his return to Rome, however, Vajta received a nasty shock: he was arrested 'as a war criminal'. Apparently the Hungarian government had organised this through Eugenio Reale, the Italian Communist Under Secretary of Foreign Affairs. 'At the time of my arrest, naturally the Church could do nothing for me,' Vajta said, emphasising that his close relations with them had 'remained intact'.[46]

After investigating the incident, Gowen reported that Vajta had taken up 'residence at the "Mediterranée" [hotel] on 10 April 1947 apparently after returning from Spain.' When he was arrested two days later he was 'interned in Regina Coeli jail', but on 26 April 'released despite the fact that he is on the official war criminal list and that Italy should automatically deliver him as such to the foreign authorities'.

Gowen reported that Vajta's release was 'believed to have been engineered by Pecorari, Secretary General of the Italian Demo-Christian Party, and Insabato, head of the Italian Agrarian Party. These two men are known to be in close contact with Vajta and to be in constant communication with him.'[47] Fausto Pecorari was also the Christian Democrat Vice-President of the Constituent Assembly.

Gowen further noted that Vajta had a close friend in the Pope's inner circle, one 'Padre Gallus of the Germanicum, the Pope's confessor'. The Germanicum is another of the colleges in Rome for German-speaking priests.[48]

Another example of Vajta's influence occurred soon after his release. About ten days before his arrest, one of his Hungarian friends had also been caught. Oliver Virtschologi-Rupprecht was the 'former editor of [the] Nazi daily *Magyarsar*', and 'one of the most notorious Nazi propagandists' in Hungary.[49]

Vajta arranged to save his friend through his influential Italian contacts. Gowen discovered this from Rupprecht himself, who later became one of his sources. The CIC Agent reported that Rupprecht had been

> arrested under his mother's name Marconnay in Bolzano for illegal entry. Prior to his entry to Italy he had been cleared by [the] French I[ntelligence] S[ervice] at Innsbruck which also recognized as legal his change in name . . . While in Austria he is known to have worked for the French and to have seen Vajta. Subsequent to his arrest he was transferred to Regina Coeli jail in Rome. There he met Vajta who had just been arrested. Vajta boasted that he would shortly be released and that . . . [Rupprecht] . . . would also be set free.

Gowen then reported a truly remarkable event. After Vajta was freed, Rupprecht was transferred to Farfa Concentration Camp for 'undesirable foreigners'. One day he was summoned by the Camp Director 'who informed him that a telegram had been received from the Ministry of Interior' ordering his 'escape':

> The next morning V[irtschologi]-R[upprecht] was placed on a bus and brought to the Salarian highway 30 kilometres from the camp and released. However, in the Farfa files he is listed as escaped. This man is now in Rome in contact with this Agent . . . [who] . . . presumes that it was through 'Intermarium' that this escape was organized.[50]

The tables were slowly but surely turning in William Gowen's relationship with Ferenc Vajta. At first the American believed himself master of the situation, bleeding his source dry and building a detailed picture of the intelligence, political and Church figures who had encouraged and organised Intermarium's clandestine activities. Now, though, it was Vajta's turn to use the Special Agent.

At some point in this process, Gowen completely altered his outlook. Previously he had diligently searched for wanted Nazis and refused all their offers of co-operation. He had initially believed that Vajta was a 'war criminal' and 'a conceited adventurer true to only money'. By early July 1947, Gowen was strongly advocating that American intelligence should take over Intermarium; before long, the CIC officer was no longer hunting for Nazis, but recruiting them.

One of his first Nazi recruits was Vajta himself. Hungary had requested his extradition in January 1946, but neither the French nor the British complied, although he was in their custody at various times.[51] Vajta complained to Gowen that, in comparison, the Americans took Nazi-hunting too seriously, failing to 'differentiate between Nazis, traitors and those forced to collaborate'.[52] Vajta recalled that immediately after the war the Office of Strategic Services had placed him on the 'Black List' of wanted Nazis, making him liable for 'automatic arrest'. As a result he was rounded up by the CIC and detained at Dachau. As luck would have it, one of his fellow prisoners was the Crown Prince of Siam, and a 'British officer came to release the latter and upon recognising Vajta's name, brought him out of the Center as well'.[53] Like many Nazi collaborators, Vajta was simply considered too valuable to French and British intelligence operations to be handed back.

Gowen discovered the reason for this: Vajta worked for the Hungarian secret service before the war, and had contacts with several Western intelligence services. He had also been a senior Nazi propagandist for German-sponsored newspapers which spewed out 'an incessant pro-Nazi and anti-Semitic barrage that poisoned Hungarian public opinion and prepared the ground for the anti-Jewish measures adopted during the German occupation in 1944'.[54]

Vajta justified his activities on the grounds that there was an anti-Soviet war being fought, telling Gowen he was 'pro-German, but anti-Nazi'.[55] His propaganda, intelligence and political work render this excuse totally hollow. But Vajta contended that he had been a victim of the Nazis, claiming they had savagely attacked him in the press.

However, when this was investigated, the Americans found no evidence that he had been persecuted because of his alleged anti-Nazi activities. Rather, they determined that he had been a member of a pro-Nazi party and had 'allegedly denounced numerous anti-Nazis. Reputation generally unsavoury,' the US Embassy in Budapest concluded.[56] Further, between 1941 and 1944, Hungary's pro-Nazi governments frequently sent Vajta on special missions, including to Berlin, Istanbul (then a centre of intense espionage by the major powers) and a number of Balkan countries then actively collaborating with the Germans. Clearly Vajta was a trusted and loyal agent of the pro-Nazi regimes in Budapest, as shown by his 1944 promotion to Consul General in Vienna.[57]

Vajta's account of his activities on behalf of the Nazis clarified other things that Gowen had discovered about Intermarium. He found that during the war 'it was believed to have been an instrument of the German intelligence'. In fact, even before the war, German Military Intelligence (the Abwehr) used Intermarium members as ' "agents of influence" abroad as well as reasonably reliable sources of information on the large *émigré* communities of Europe'.[58] It is an undisputed fact that by 1939, most Intermarium leaders had thrown in their lot with Hitler and the Nazis. After the war, they escaped punishment by helping British and French intelligence against the Soviets.

Vajta now wanted US support. 'You know, the United States was a horrible failure in Austria and Germany after the war. Our best experts put themselves at the disposal of the French and British services, seeing that in Salzburg and Frankfurt you Americans only wanted Jews, Sovietophiles and idiots. You believed that we were all Nazis, all collaborators, traitors and people with whom you couldn't work, whereas with the British and French we always found a very warm welcome.'

Gowen was hooked, wanting to know what could be done to rectify these past errors and establish an American presence in this vital field of intelligence and clandestine political work. 'The Vatican can and must play an historic role in this,' Vajta insisted

because it's also in its interests to win America for the real European reconstruction. The Vatican must assist us to come together, because even though the majority of Americans are Protestant, in the Danube's valleys there exists a dominant and traditional Catholicism, so America must look for the Holy See's help. From this collaboration a new and modern world can be born. We've had enough of small British and French intrigues. Now, at last, it's time to re-organise Eastern Europe in a way that the peace will be fruitful and we can return to some sort of equilibrium.

Gowen will still puzzled. What could America do? 'The British and French can't help us any longer economically, but the United States can,' Vajta said, pulling in his catch with some delight:

If you want peace in the world you must look to a Danubian Confederation in which the liberty of all people will be recognised, with a healthy and traditional democracy. The time has come to create the grand unity of Europe and a Pan-Danubian Confederation composed of peoples of the same culture, of the same traditions. It's simply necessary to help it for it to be born. It would be in America's own interest to work with us and accept our demands. You could ensure the collaboration in such a way that you could become very important.[59]

Little is known of what Gowen reported to his superiors following his meetings with Vajta. It is known that the Special Agent wrote a detailed five page report, but less than one page was declassified for release to the authors. Vajta's arguments certainly swayed the American, as demonstrated by the few uncensored paragraphs. Gowen reminded his superiors that he had previously concluded that only the discovery of Intermarium's true source of funding could 'lead to the full understanding' of its activities.[60]

The next four pages were totally blacked out by the censors at Fort Meade in Maryland, but something of its flavour can be judged from his conclusions:

The most outstanding feature of these complex activities is the inability of worthy anti-Communists to find a stable base of operations. No sooner do they start working in one direction than the government from which they have gotten backing changes policy.

The second outstanding feature is the lack of United States activity in this, the larger intelligence field. While the Russians, British, and French have to build up artificial societies to further their ends, it is the opinion of this Agent, that only the friendly coordination of worthy elements by the United States would be necessary to build a firm base for future healthy European political development.

Vajta now had an influential American agent supporting his world view, reporting on it in very similar tones to his own and recommending it wholeheartedly to 'higher commands so that its full international importance [can] be evaluated'.[61]

Gowen went even further in a later report: Vajta 'is a key man as he has been active in the *émigré* and clandestine political field since 1932 when he became so engaged as per instructions of the Hungarian Ministry of Foreign Affairs. He has excellent Vatican, British, French and Spanish contacts.'[62]

As far as the American was concerned, Ferenc Vajta was no longer a wanted war criminal. It seemed as though he had cemented his place with yet another Western intelligence agency.

Undoubtedly this was due largely to his successful discussions with Gowen. He later recalled that American policy had changed 'in the first months of 1947', as Washington became more interested 'in the problems of Eastern Europe'. After 'recognising the danger of Communism', Vajta said, the Americans adopted a more concrete policy.[63] A further rude shock, however, was in store for both the Hungarian fugitive and his new American friend.

Two months after Gowen recommended that the United States become involved with Intermarium, the Hungarian government renewed its efforts to bring about Vajta's extradition. Italian foreign affairs official, Reale, filed an extradition order against Vajta and on 1 September this reached Italian Police Chief, Ferrari, who automatically had to send out an arrest warrant.

The Interior Ministry Police Chief had previously told the Hungarians Vajta was not in Rome at all. Gowen later reported that Vajta returned to Rome on 3 September, from a secret trip with Casimir Papée. An 'outstanding Polish diplomat', Papée had been at the Holy See since 1939,[64] and was also a leading Intermarium member. He was also well connected with Western intelligence; Gowen reported that on their trip they met with British and French intelligence officers.

Gowen heard rumours that orders were to be issued for Vajta's extradition. On his return, friends met him and warned of his impending arrest. Instead of returning to the Pensione Patrizia, he went immediately to Castelgandolfo, about twenty kilometres outside Rome. This is the village where the Pope has his summer residence. Although it is not certain that Vajta was actually hidden on Vatican property, Castelgandolfo was a favourite hideout for fugitive Nazis at this time, as will be seen in the next chapter.

On the morning of 4 September 1947, Vajta left Castelgandolfo and returned to Rome, where he had many friends. Gowen noted that Vajta's connections reached to the very top of the Christian Democrat party. Its leader and Italian Premier, Alcide de Gasperi, had personally guaranteed Vajta's safety. Gowen also observed that the French had issued Vajta with false papers on which he still travelled around Europe in relative security.

The CIC officer then got to the heart of the matter, reporting what had occurred on 4 September:

> This Agent had an appointment with Vajta at 1400 at a bar in Piazza Venezia, Rome. Upon meeting, the information pertaining to the arrest

orders was immediately passed on and Vajta took refuge with an Hungarian Jesuit father in the nearby Jesuit Gregorian University. This Agent thereupon left for Castelgandolfo, fearing that the orders might have already reached the village and that it would be unsafe for Vajta himself to return. Orders from the Police were already on hand but this Agent stated that Vajta had gone to Rome to the Police. As a result, Vajta's effects were taken away by this Agent.

At 1730 this Agent picked up Vajta at the Gregorian University and left for Leghorn, arriving there that night. Vajta remained hidden in the Leghorn area the next day while this Agent returned to Rome. Vajta gave this Agent his false documents with which arrangements for flight from Italy would have to be made.

Upon the return of this Agent to Rome, he conferred with [censored]. The latter, asked where he thought Vajta should be sent, replied that Spain would probably be the best as far as [censored] was concerned. This Agent stated that Vajta himself apparently wanted to go to Spain where he knew General Franco, the Spanish Foreign Minister Artajo, and the Cardinal Primate of Spain personally.[65]

Gowen then made the necessary arrangements for Vajta to travel to Spain, promising that US funding would be made available if the Hungarian could organise a new movement. Once in Spain, the fugitive immediately linked up with his old friend, Marjan Szumlakowski. Vajta decided to establish a new anti-Communist group, which he called the Continental Union. His aim was to attract *émigré* leaders away from the British-controlled Intermarium, and take them into Washington's orbit. To achieve this, he and Szumlakowski held negotiations with senior officials of General Franco's government. As a result, a new *émigré* centre was established in Madrid.

They also received the assistance of a senior Hungarian Catholic priest, Monsignor Zoltán Nyísztor, 'formerly head of the Vatican Press Office in Rome'. This enabled them to enlist the support of the Papal Nuncio in Madrid, who came 'to their aid in a strongly-worded four-page letter to Foreign Minister Artajo', warning that Intermarium had been 'penetrated by French and British freemasonry'. Following the Vatican diplomat's intervention, Artajo ordered his officers to assist Vajta and his Continental Union.

Monsignor Nyísztor also introduced Vajta to one of Spain's leading Vatican experts, Joaquin Ruiz-Giménez, the president of the government-controlled Spanish Cultural Institute. Ruiz-Giménez's important role in Spanish–Vatican relations was demonstrated soon afterwards when he was appointed as General

Franco's Ambassador to the Holy See. Having secured the support of this senior Spanish official, Vajta launched a vitriolic campaign against Intermarium, alleging that many Soviet agents had penetrated the groups working for British and French intelligence. This resulted in a purge of Intermarium leaders from the Eastern European section of the Spanish Cultural Institute.[66]

Vajta and Szumlakowski then entered into an agreement with Ruiz-Giménez and senior Foreign Office officials for Spain to 'officially tolerate and silently aid' the Continental Union's activities. Intermarium was to be discouraged, and political and counterespionage contacts were established between the Spaniards and Vajta's group. The agreement provided for the free entry of Continental Union personnel into Spain, in exchange for intelligence on Soviet operations. The Cultural Institute provided 'silent' financial assistance for the Union to publish a cultural and information bulletin.

Vajta had succeeded yet again in establishing a powerful *émigré* centre, forcing former Intermarium figures to defect to the Continental Union. The Hungarian assured his American contacts that he did not want to 'get too close' to the Spaniards, as he was working towards firmer relations with US intelligence. To demonstrate his ability to provide good intelligence, he submitted a lengthy and detailed report on *émigré* affairs to the US Embassy, which stressed that Intermarium's British agents in Madrid were rapidly losing ground to his pro-US group.[67]

In pitching his line to the Americans, Vajta pointed out that 'the peoples of Europe are more favourable to American action than to Anglo-French action', especially after President Truman decided to take a strong anti-Communist line. However, he emphasised that the reaction in London and Paris to Washington's decision to 'put itself at the head of the anti-Communist campaign' had been to regroup, unifying their previously parallel campaigns to take 'united action not only against Communism but also against the U.S.' From intelligence he had gathered, he was certain that they planned for this 'silent struggle to become more spirited and stronger' by demonstrating that the most important *émigré* leaders were in their camp.[68]

Vajta's approach to the Americans was initially very successful, but soon he became a huge embarrassment to the US government. On 11 February 1948 the Army's Intelligence Division cabled the

US European Headquarters Command. They ordered an immediate investigation into Gowen's connections with his Hungarian Nazi contact. The message pointed out that there had been a great deal of publicity about Vajta's arrival in the United States 'on visa issued by American Consulate Madrid Spain marked "Diplomat" also has letter of commendation signed by Gowen . . . stating Vajta had been of great assistance to Counter Intelligence Corps in Rome giving information on immigrants from Russian satellite states'. The message also reported that Vajta had been identified 'as Hungarian war criminal, Nazi stooge and directly responsible for murder of American airmen downed in Hungary'.[69]

This had all come to light after Vajta arrived in New York on 16 December 1947. Apparently Gowen handed over his contact to State Department intelligence which brought Vajta to Washington. The Hungarian fugitive was issued with his visa in Madrid after presenting 'letters from William Gowen . . . indicating US interest in trip'.* The Embassy had passed the details of Vajta's trip to an intelligence agency official, together with a list of people he wished to meet in America. These included Cardinal Spellman, Jesuit leader Father La Farge and a host of *émigré* political leaders Vajta hoped to entice into the Continental Union.[70] Another contact Vajta wished to see was senior State Department official, Franklin Gowen, father of his CIC sponsor.[71]

The main purpose of Vajta's trip was to enlist support for the Continental Union. Although he had acquired influential backers in US intelligence and diplomatic circles, his mission turned into a disaster. News of his arrival rapidly reached two well known journalists, Drew Pearson and Walter Winchell. Soon the government was enveloped in adverse publicity, and someone had to be held responsible.

Vajta was immediately arrested and held on Ellis Island, and on 3 February 1948 the Hungarians requested his extradition. A secret Congressional enquiry was soon underway, but its results have never been released. Vajta himself became something of a media celebrity, boasting to the press, truthfully, that Italian

*In a recent discussion, Gowen insisted that neither he nor any other CIC agent played a role in bringing Vajta to the United States. It is very plausible that the State Department removed evidence of its recruitment of Vajta and falsely implicated the CIC by placing Gowen's letter of introduction in Vajta's visa file.

Christian Democrat leader, Fausto Pecorari, had requested Rome's Chief of Police to issue various permits to him. Predictably, however, democratic Hungarian groups publicly denounced Vajta as a 'Nazi', a view with which the American courts ultimately concurred.[72]

William Gowen's reports admitted not only his own involvement in Vajta's escape, but his close personal knowledge of the Vatican's role in hiding and assisting known Nazi fugitives. The special Agent's outlook was characterised by his belief that the storm then raging in Washington had been created by Hungarian Communists, who had somehow manipulated Drew Pearson into writing his article. In Gowen's view, the whole thing was a Communist provocation.[73]

Back in the United States, though, Vajta had become a public relations disaster for the government. The Immigration and Naturalization Service took action to have him summarily deported. Although he resisted through a series of legal appeals, he was finally thrown out in February 1950. Charles Ashman and Robert Wagman in their book, *The Nazi Hunters*, report that he went to Colombia after both Italy and Spain refused to have him back.

As the Americans did not want to return him to Hungary, which was still agitating for his surrender in 1950, it fell to the Holy See once more to extend its charitable hand to Vajta. According to Ashman and Wagman, 'the Vatican stepped in and arranged for Colombia to accept him, and for a small Catholic college there to employ him. He spent the rest of his life in Bogota as an economics professor.'[74]

By mid-1947, William Gowen had already recommended that America should ignore the Vatican's protection of an even more notorious Nazi mass murderer. As will be seen in the next chapter, he justified this because of the Holy see's contribution to the anti-Communist cause. After the publicity surrounding Hudal it may have been expected that the Vatican would become more circumspect. But Vajta was not the last of the Vatican's Nazi scandals. The worst was yet to come. For fugitive Nazis, all roads led to Rome.

4

A Staggering Blow to the Holy See

Ante Pavelić turned back to face the rising sun. Although the spring of 1945 was already some weeks old, the Slovene countryside was still cold and mist hung in the valleys and hollows. Despite the temperature, Pavelić wiped sweat from his brow. The fleeing dictator was now on foot, having abandoned his car on the clogged roads and joined the throng of refugees marching wearily towards Austria.

Pavelić reflected on the irony of his situation. A few days before he had been the Poglavnik of 'independent' Croatia, exercising comparable powers to the Führer in Germany. He had even managed to keep the death machine operating almost until the end, while the Germans were frantically dismantling theirs. Then, without warning the Nazis had capitulated. The Poglavnik was now just one of hundreds of thousands fleeing towards Austria to surrender to the British.

Pavelić recalled with bitterness his previous flight into exile in 1929. Then he had been a young man and an underground life – building his clandestine Ustashi terrorist network – had appealed to him. His twelve years abroad had seemed worthwhile, for in April 1941 he had assumed power in his beloved Croatia, even if the Italian Fascists and German Nazis exercised real authority behind the scenes.

The fugitive dictator had become used to power and wondered if he would ever taste it again. For Pavelić knew that if he fell into the wrong hands his future would be very short indeed. He hoped that his emissaries sent ahead into Austria had made the right contacts with British intelligence and the Catholic Church. If they had failed, only death awaited him.

Pavelić quivered, almost like a startled rabbit; he was sure he could see a motorised partisan unit in the distance. He turned again towards the Austrian frontier and broke into a desperate jog . . .

*

Such is the legend of Ante Pavelić's disappearance in May 1945, which has grown in the retelling over the years. Depending on which side is telling the story, his flight was either the end of the most glorious four years in Croatian history, or the country's liberation from a terrorist and mass murderer.[1]

It is impossible to know for sure the precise details of the Poglavnik's flight from his homeland. We do know that he fled from Zagreb to Austria via the Slovenian town of Maribor on the Yugoslav–Austrian frontier. However, both pro-Pavelić and pro-Tito accounts agree that panic was the predominant mood as the retreating Ustashi leadership fled for their lives ahead of the Communist forces.

Pavelić had many reasons for concern, among them the horrific massacres of Serbs, Jews and Gypsies over the previous four years; half a million innocent civilians slaughtered at his personal command. Many had been dispatched using extremely medieval methods; eyes had been gouged out, limbs severed, intestines and other internal organs ripped from the bodies of the living. Some were slaughtered like beasts, their throats cut from ear to ear with special knives. Others died from blows to their heads with sledge-hammers. Many more were simply burned alive.[2]

Even so, Pavelić hoped to be greeted in Austria by both Church and British leaders as a prominent Catholic leader in the struggle against 'atheistic Bolshevism'. After all, British intelligence had maintained close pre-war relations with his underground terrorist network, even after the 1934 assassination of Yugoslav King Alexander in Marseilles. Pavelić also knew that the Holy See looked on Croatia as 'the frontier of Christianity'; a special relationship between Croatia and the Pope extended back to 700 AD.[3]

Apart from this strong historical connection, Pavelić was also aware that Pius XII and his senior advisers held extremely charitable opinions of his militant Catholicism. During the war Pavelić had forcibly converted tens of thousands of Serbian Orthodox under penalty of death. In fact, the atrocities were already underway at the very moment Pius XII received the Poglavnik in private audience in late April 1941.

The bureaucrats at the British Foreign Office reacted with outrage at 'the reception by the Pope of a notorious terrorist and murderer', describing Pius XII as 'the greatest moral coward of our age'. When pressed to justify the reception, the Vatican explained lamely that Pavelić had only been received in his private capacity, not as head of the Croatian state. They could not ignore a Catholic 'statesman' such as Pavelić, the Vatican replied. But the Foreign Office 'was indeed astonished and pained that the Vatican should so consider him even for a moment'.[4]

The British Ambassador to the Holy See found it difficult when he took up the matter personally with the ever charming Pius XII:

> ... one approaches him with indignation in one's soul and protests on one's lips, [but] it is impossible not to be disarmed by his simplicity, humanity, friendliness and sincerity and by his devastating combination of saintliness and charm. One talks so easily to him, he listens so readily, responds so frankly and smiles so enchantingly and easily that one's carefully prepared attitude of dignified disapprobation just evaporates.[5]

The Pope called Pavelić 'a much maligned man'. Pius XII could not believe that he had been involved in the assassination at Marseilles, even though Pavelić had been convicted *in absentia* in a French court. The cynics back in the Foreign Office conceded that the Pope 'must indeed be a charmer', but told their Ambassador in no uncertain terms that his reception of Pavelić 'has done more to damage his reputation in this country than any other act since the war began'.[6]

It was hypocrisy of the most unbridled kind! Before the war, British intelligence had used Pavelić, despite his unsavoury reputation as a terrorist and murderer. Now, though, the Pope was to be thoroughly condemned merely for receiving him. Of course, times had changed, and Pavelić was massacring hundreds of thousands of innocents as part of Hitler's savage racial war. Surely the Holy Father would not stand aside and watch such ghastly deeds without raising the voice of Christian Charity?

A young Yugoslav by the name of Branko Bokun believed that the Pope could not. Bokun had been sent to Rome by one of Yugoslavia's intelligence chiefs to ask for the Vatican's intervention to stop the slaughter in Croatia. Armed with a large file of documents, eye witness accounts and even photographs of the massacres, Bokun finally gained entrance into the Vatican Secretariat of State in September 1941.

He wanted to deliver his file to Monsignor Giovanni Montini, Under Secretary of State for Ordinary Affairs, but could not gain an audience. Bokun was told to leave his file and come back a week later, with the promise that 'the Monsignor will give the matter careful consideration'.

This was at the height of the worst atrocities and Pavelić had taken steps of his own to influence Vatican opinion. He had dispatched Father Cherubino Seguić to Rome to counter the spreading horror with which the massacres were greeted in many Catholic circles. Seguić soon discovered that the Ustashi regime was viewed by many as 'a crowd of barbarians and cannibals'. He promply sought an audience with Montini, and recorded in his diary that the Vatican bureaucrat sought 'full information on the events in Croatia', also confirming that the 'calumnies' had reached the Monsignor's ears.[7]

Father Seguić seems to have had a persuasive effect on Montini. When Bokun returned to discuss his file detailing evidence of these 'calumnies', he received short shrift from Montini's secretary. Bokun was simply told that 'the atrocities described in your file are the work of the Communists, but maliciously attributed to the Catholics'. Bokun had the evidence but no access to Montini, while Seguić had no difficulty in presenting his side of the story.[8]

There is no doubt that Montini was well informed of the true situation, for on a number of occasions he castigated Croatia's representatives to the Holy See. While Montini would begin with harsh words, invariably these sessions concluded with assurances that the Holy Father would assist Catholic Croatia.[9]

The Pope's own attitude towards the murderous Ustashi leader was more than benign neglect. When Pavelić asked for another audience with the Holy Father in May 1943, he was assured by Secretary of State Maglione that 'there were no difficulties attached to the Poglavnik's visit to the Holy Father except that he could not be received as a sovereign'. Pius himself promised to give Pavelić his personal blessing again.[10] By this time, the Holy See possessed abundant evidence of the atrocities committed by his regime.

The Vatican has consistently defended its policy, pointing out that official Vatican recognition was denied Pavelić's state. However, senior Vatican officials, including Pius XII, regularly received his 'unofficial' diplomatic representative who called himself the 'Croatian Ambassador'. The Pope also continued to receive other senior officials and delegations, turning his face away from their countless victims.[11]

Pavelić's record was well known. On one occasion a visiting Italian Fascist journalist had been granted an interview with the Poglavnik. Noticing what appeared to be a large bowl of oysters, he had asked Pavelić whether they were from the Dalmatian coast. He was shocked when the dictator replied that they were forty pounds of Serbian eyes sent to him by his loyal Ustashi.[12]

On another occasion, Pavelić held discussions with Hitler in Berlin. In a strange reversal of roles, he castigated the Führer about the 'lenient' treatment of German Jews, boasting that in comparison he had completely solved the Jewish question in Croatia while some remained alive in the Third Reich.[13]

But when Hitler died, Pavelić could not be sure that even his staunchest Church supporters would offer him protection. He disappeared so completely that it was as though the Austrian countryside had suddenly opened up and swallowed him. In the following months, British and American intelligence combed the areas under their control. The Foreign Office and the State Department repeatedly told Tito's government that Pavelić would be returned to face trial as a war criminal, just as soon as he was found, but all they discovered were shadowy rumours.

The Communist government in Belgrade was sceptical of the West's repeated denials. Tito had a battle-hardened and extremely efficient intelligence network operating in Austria, tracking the Ustashi's movements. In July 1945 their Ambassador in London told the British that Pavelić had 'been made prisoner by the troops of Field Marshal Alexander, and . . . is now in the part of Austria under the control of the British Army'. In late August the Yugoslavs repeated their claim that Pavelić had 'been taken prisoner at Celovac (Klagenfurt), Austria, by British troops'.[14]

The Foreign Office was adamant that Pavelić had never been in their hands, and assured the cynical Yugoslavs that every 'effort is being made to discover the present whereabouts of Dr Pavelić'. Their 'energetic attempts' had 'produced no information except that Pavelić was still rumoured to be in the Saltzburg area on September 26th'.[15] Salzburg was not even in the British zone, having been occupied by the Americans.

There were still many leads for the British to follow. Serbian Četnik officers claimed that Pavelić was 'disguised as a monk in a monastery at Klagenfurt'; the Yugoslavs also alleged that he was in 'a villa not far from Klagenfurt'. The British conducted a 'thorough search' of the area 'without result' and finally decided that the fugitive must be in Soviet hands. They wrote to Foreign Minister Vyshinski, but received a negative reply.[16]

The Yugoslavs launched a vitriolic press campaign, claiming they had given the British 'precise information regarding the town and street' where Pavelić was living 'in complete freedom'. The Foreign Office decided that it was time for 'a little counter-battery work' and wrote to the Yugoslav Ambassador insisting that the Yugoslav press campaign 'was entirely without foundation'.[17]

The Yugoslav Ambassador persisted, telling the British in early January 1946 that Pavelić 'was disguised as a monk'. He asked if the British 'had no influence with the Vatican'. Tito was obviously convinced that the British were conniving with the Holy See to protect the Ustashi leader. The Foreign Office reacted with complete innocence, pointing everywhere else. They even asked their American ally if they perhaps had captured Pavelić, receiving yet another negative answer.[18]

Throughout 1946 the claims and denials went back and forth. The Yugoslav Communists sent diplomatic notes and directed their press to launch ever more hysterical campaigns. The message was always the same: the West could find Pavelić if they really wanted to, but refused because he and his supporters were being used in an anti-Tito crusade.[19]

The British response also became repetitive; 'especial efforts' had been made to trace Pavelić, who 'has at no time been in British custody, nor has his whereabouts ever been known to any British authority'. The Americans joined in these emphatic denials, stating that authorities 'in U.S. and British zones have searched diligently' for Pavelić 'without success'.[20]

As 1946 drew to a close, it had been eighteen months since Pavelić crossed the Austrian frontier and apparently disappeared into thin air. In examining the official files it is striking that they assume a significantly different tone in late November. Suddenly the Pavelić mystery was solved. A senior British Political Adviser reported that it was 'becoming increasingly clear that many of the more important quislings are taking refuge under the wing of the Church', pessimistically forecasting that little could be done 'unless the Vatican can be persuaded into active co-operation'.[21]

The British had found that five wanted Yugoslavs were 'at present in the Oriental Institution in Rome'. This was the Pope's institute specialising in Eastern European affairs, and enjoyed complete extraterritoriality. The Foreign Office feared that 'it would create a most unfortunate impression if the British authorities decided to arrest these men on Vatican property without any prior notice to the Vatican authorities'. They proposed to the Americans that they jointly tell Tito that 'since these traitors are resident on Vatican property, they are outside our jurisdiction, and that the Yugoslav Government should apply to the Vatican, to whom they have an accredited diplomatic representative'. The Americans were happy to go along with this cynical proposal.[22]

At last the British bureaucrats had someone to blame for Pavelić's disappearance. They noted on 18 December that it seemed 'more and more likely that Pavelić is in Italy and that his whereabouts may be known to Dr Draganović . . . and to no-one else'. The British had gathered detailed intelligence showing that Father Krunoslav Draganović, Secretary of the Croatian Institute of San Girolamo, was the main organiser of the Ratlines used by known war criminals to escape the Western dragnet. The Foreign Office believed the British Army's claim that it was 'unlikely that Pavelić has been in Austria since the British occupation, except possibly in transit'. They were certain that Draganović held the answer to the Poglavnik's disappearance.[23]

If Draganović's own version of his relationship with Pavelić can be believed, he thought the dictator was a brutal mass murderer, one of the 'most dangerous men' he had met in his whole life. Years later, Draganović maintained that he had repeatedly intervened with the Ustashi leadership during the war, begging for the lives of Jews, Serbs and even Communists.[24] The priest claimed that he had followed the commandments of Christian love, regardless of religion, politics or nationality. He bragged that this had endangered his own life, because the Ustashi strongly disapproved of his charitable work and forceful interventions. Draganović insisted that he took up his complaints with Pavelić himself.[25]

There is no independent corroboration of Draganović's account. If it is correct, it throws fascinating light on his post-war decision to aid this mass murderer, whom he rightly blamed for the extermination of innocent Serbs, Jews, Gypsies and others. Yet Western intelligence was certain that the two men were extremely close after the war, and that Pavelić could never have slipped through their dragnet without Draganović's charitable assistance.

Special Agent William Gowen and his colleagues in the Rome
detachment of the US Army's Counter Intelligence Corps found
out that their British ally had been lying all along: they knew a
great deal about Pavelić's whereabouts. This emerged in early
1947 when American intelligence launched its own intensive
operation in early 1947 to find Pavelić.[26] By the time the CIC
investigations were concluded, it was established that Yugoslav
intelligence had been right all along. According to 'reliable
sources', Pavelić had indeed made it across the Austrian frontier
and reached British lines, where he

> was protected by the British in British-guarded and requisitioned quarters
> for a two (2) week period. Due to the insecurity of his position and due to
> the inevitable embarrassment of the British Command, he then left these
> quarters but remained in the British Occupation Zone for at least two (2)
> or three (3) months more still in contact with the British I[ntelligence]
> S[ervice].[27]

This confirmed what Ferenc Vajta had told Gowen about SIS's
recruitment of the Ustashi immediately after hostilities had ceased.
Gowen's colleague, Special CIC Agent Robert Mudd, was also
working on the case, reporting on 30 January 1947 that the former
Poglavnik had fled from Yugoslavia and taken refuge at Klagenfurt, where he 'had an apartment and a villa', just as the Četniks
and Communists had previously claimed. This report provided
further evidence of the Catholic Church's involvement.

In 'April of 1946 Pavelić left Austria and came to Rome
accompanied only by an Ustashi lieutenant named Dochsen. Both
men were dressed as Roman Catholic priests. They took refuge in
a college there in Via Giacomo Belli, 3.' Pavelić's travelling
companion was in fact Dragutin Došen, a former senior officer in
the Poglavnik's Personal Body Guard. The British discovered that
Došen was 'a leading light of San Girolamo (Draganović's HQ)'.[28]

Mudd's informant believed that Pavelić had taken refuge in a
Vatican-protected college in Rome, although the authors could not
verify this claim. The informant also reported that Pavelić had
obtained a Spanish passport 'under the name of Don Pedro
Gonner', in preparation for his eventual escape, probably to Spain
or South America. However, in mid-1946 Pavelić was afraid that
he was too closely monitored and instead of leaving Europe, he
returned to Austria.

Mudd directed his informant 'to penetrate the Ustashi intelligence network', and report on their escape routes:

> ... the network runs from Grumo–Rome–Venice–Trieste–Ljubljana–Zagreb. The whole affair is run under the cover of the Roman Catholic clergy whose priests in these monasteries are nearly all of Croatian extraction ... The Ustashi organization in Italy is at present a tightly-knit group still maintaining its 'cell' organization, still publishing its papers, and still interested in the same aims that they professed before and during the war ... the focal point of all intelligence and activity is the Monastery of Saint Jerome (sic), Via Tomacelli, 132, Rome.[29]

From a very confidential source, American intelligence had discovered in May 1946 that the Poglavnik was living 'close to Rome in a building which is under the jurisdiction of the Vatican'.[30] This was soon after Pavelić had first arrived in Rome from Austria, and it is now known that the Poglavnik, like Ferenc Vajta, actually took refuge at Castelgandolfo, where the Pope's summer residence is located. It seems that many Nazis gravitated to Castelgandolfo, for Pavelić was housed with a former Minister in the Nazi Romanian government.[31]

US intelligence received even more sensational information from their confidential source, who claimed that 'Pavelić holds frequent secret meetings with Monsignor Montini, the Under Secretary of State of the Holy See'.[32] Gowen was just then starting to piece together the Intermarium jigsaw puzzle. From what he had learned from Vajta, he was convinced that the Vatican was deeply implicated in some very unsavoury business. Information received by the US Embassy in Rome in early January 1947 claimed that Pavelić had been in San Girolamo the previous month, and was travelling under several aliases.[33] Suddenly Gowen was on to a major case. By late January, the American intelligence officer had collected enough evidence from 'reliable informants' to report that Pavelić

> is at the present time in the extra-territorial walled-in compound on the left bank of the Tiber, at Lungo Tevere Aventino, Rome. This compound has within its walls five Catholic organizations ... 1) The Monastery of St. Sabina of the Dominican Order; 2) The St. Alessio School for Roman Studies; 3) The Cavaliers of the Sovereign Military Order of Malta; 4) The Benedictine Monastery of St. Anselmo; 5) A children's school run by Nuns. The compound is situated on top of the Aventine Hill which ... is reputedly honeycombed with subterranean tunnels which link the individual buildings.[34]

Having 'carefully checked' the compound, Gowen concluded that Pavelić was probably in the Monastery of St Sabina, reporting that other 'information from reliable informants tends to show that the tram line running beneath the Aventine Hill along the Tiber and thence to the Circus Maximus, the Colosseum and Via Cavour is the connecting link between Pavelić and Via Cavour, 210 int. 3, which is an Ustascia base well known in Rome'. Although we were unable to vertify the existence of an underground tunnel linking Pavelić with his loyal Ustashi supporters, Gowen attached a map to his report showing the route he believed it took to the tramline.[35]

Gowen seemed to have finally uncovered a concrete lead in the mysterious Pavelić case. He was still cautious, though, reporting that 'the information seems plausible and paints a plausible picture when it is taken as a whole'. However, he believed that only 'action against such known Pavelić contacts as Draganović, Krunoslav can ultimately reveal the hiding place of Pavelić and lead to his apprehension'.[36]

The net seemed to be finally closing and all fingers, from the British Foreign Office to the US Army's CIC, were now pointing at Father Draganović as the man who could lead to Pavelić's arrest and extradition. The focus of the Yugoslav press campaign now shifted to the Vatican. They claimed 'that a number of Yugoslav war criminals had been enabled to emigate from Italy under the protection of a Vatican institution'.[37]

US intelligence launched a comprehensive operation to establish the truth, quickly confirming that Draganović was in close contact with the former Croatian dictator all along. According to one report, Draganović was 'known as the "alter ego" of Ante Pavelić', with whom he maintained close relations. Indeed, Draganović operated a regular courier service between San Girolamo and the Poglavnik's Austrian hideout.[38]

After establishing the close relations between the two men, the Americans convened a top secret conference on 11 April 1947 to plan Pavelić's arrest. The US Army's senior Rome intelligence officers were all present to review the information available and put in motion a plan to penetrate Pavelić's Vatican network.[39]

Over the following weeks CIC officers received information that he was hiding in one Vatican-controlled institution or another. They also discovered more of the fugitive's aliases. The Jesuits were among his closest Church helpers at this time, assisting his plans to leave Italy by arranging for his passage to Spain under the alias of Padre Gomez, supposedly 'a Spanish Minister of Religion'.[40]

The barrage of reports that Pavelić had taken refuge under the wing of the Vatican forced a senior State Department official to ask the diplomats at the Vatican to make inquiries. He cynically pointed out:

> 'while I am aware of, and appreciate, the Vatican's humanitarian attitude towards criminals who may have shown any indication of repentance, it seems to me that Pavelić's peculiarly unsavory record would make it difficult for the Church to afford him protection.'

Washington was apparently in no hurry to receive a reply; there 'is no urgency about this case, but I should appreciate hearing anything you may be able to turn up'.[41] In Rome they evidently took this hint, taking over two months to report that they had not been able to confirm the wanted man's whereabouts; 'Pavelić, like Kilroy, seems to be everywhere. Or so the reports of dozens of sleuths would indicate.'[42]

By mid-June, the Foreign Office was also involved in the hunt, proposing that every effort be made to catch Pavelić. Apparently a huge chasm of mistrust existed between Washington and London. The British suspected that the Americans were deliberately sabotaging the plan, by insisting that the Italian police had to be involved in the operation, because 'from a practical point of view there is a far greater danger of a leakage or of inefficient handling'.[43] Ustashi intelligence was especially efficient in Rome, where they had extremely good connections with the Italian police, who had sponsored Pavelić during his exile in the 1930s.

This British position was cynically dishonest; while SIS protected Pavelić, the Foreign Office complained of US efforts to sabotage the plan to apprehend him. As we shall see, both governments were involved in devious and often conflicting machinations at higher policy making levels.

By mid-July the British had also received information that Pavelić was living 'within the Vatican city' and proposed a joint operation to arrest him.[44] The reluctant Americans agreed, but only if Pavelić's arrest was 'carried out to [the] greatest extent possible by [the] Italians'.[45] The British again warned against the risks of Italian involvement, insisting on 'the closest supervision of the whole operation by the Allied Security authorities'.[46]

On 28 July the State Department issued unenthusiastic instructions for American authorities to participate 'to [the] extent necessary and possible in [the] Pavelić case'.[47] The following day, the US Political Adviser in Rome passed this order on to the Supreme Allied Commander, still insisting that US forces would only 'assist the Italian authorities in endeavouring to arrest him at a suitable opportunity outside Vatican territory'. His British counterpart followed suit on 2 August.[48]

In fact, British and American officials were playing bureaucratic chess. The intelligence operatives on the scene were merely their pawns and really did not understand the game's rules. The British hoped to blame the Americans if the operation failed, while the Americans were desperate to force the British to make the arrest so they could claim that they were not responsible.

In this game, the British finally forced their ally to 'supervise the arrest' and it seemed that finally, after more than two years of prevarication, action was about to be taken.[49] On 7 August the US Deputy Chief of Staff at Allied Force Headquarters noted that it would 'be an extremely tricky operation requiring elaborate co-ordination between the U.S., British and Italian authorities and the maintenance of absolute secrecy'.[50]

Updated information was then collected on Pavelić's exact location, and it was discovered that he was 'hiding as an ex-Hungarian General under the name of "Giuseppe". He wears a small pointed beard and has his hair cut short'. Further, he

is living on Church property under the protection of the Vatican, at Via Giacoma Venezian No. 17-C, second floor. On entering the building you go along a long and dark corridor. At the end of the corridor there are two stairs, one to the left and one to the right. You must take the right. On the right the rooms are numbered 1, 2, 3 etc. If you knock once or twice at door No. 3 an unimportant person will come out. But if you knock three times at door No. 3, door *No. 2* will open. It leads to the room where Pavelić lives, together with the famous Bulgarian terrorist Vancia Mikoiloff (sic) and two other persons.

About twelve other men live in the building. They are all Ustasha and make up Pavelić's bodyguard.

When Pavelić goes out he uses a car with a Vatican (SCV) number-plate.[51]

News of the Poglavnik's hiding place in Via Giacoma Venezian belatedly reached the Italian public in September 1948, when the press published a sensational series of articles dealing with the

Vatican's role in the affair. By then, Pavelić was long gone, perhaps explaining why someone in Western intelligence leaked the story to the newspapers.[52]

Twelve months earlier, US intelligence had investigated Via Giacoma Venezian 17-C. They suspected that it was one of the Vatican's libraries, although we have not been able to confirm this. But they did confirm that some senior Vatican official was protecting Pavelić: he regularly travelled around in their official cars. As these bore the special number plates of the Diplomatic Corps, the Western authorities could not stop them, even when Pavelić left Vatican territory.

However, everything seemed in place; the joint intelligence team only had to quietly observe Pavelić, and when he left the Vatican's extraterritorial protection, follow him until he alighted from his Vatican car and arrest him. Three weeks went by and nothing happened, prompting London to ask Rome to 'report recent developments'. Another six weeks elapsed but still no answer was forthcoming; the Foreign Office grew agitated and again asked for a response.[53]

Eventually the operation was allowed to quietly die. The apparent determination to arrest this notorious Nazi mass murderer disappeared, just as Pavelić himself had seemingly done in May 1945. The answers to this further mystery are partially found in three key American intelligence documents. On 7 July 1947 Bernard Grennan, Chief of CIC Operations in Rome, directed his Supervising Agent, Gono Morena, to take Pavelić 'into custody on sight'. The order had come down the line from the Assistant Chief of Staff of Army Intelligence.

One week later, a handwritten note was added to Grennan's memo by Morena. He had received 'new instructions', which he summarised with a brief but all too obvious comment:

'Hands Off'

The order was passed to Morena by Grennan and Lieutenant Colonel Charles Hartman, the commander of Army Counter Intelligence in Rome. Grennan and Hartman were at the top level conference held on 11 April to plan the operation, and must have been astounded by this sudden change of direction.[54] Evidently someone much higher up the chain had already decided to sabotage the operation, even before it had been finalised. The senior American officers certainly passed the 'Hands Off' decision down their chain of command. From all the available evidence, however, it seems probable that the original decision was taken by British intelligence officers, who were the fugitive's real sponsors.

The American motive for quietly going along with London's decision to allow Pavelić's escape was really very simple. Senior US officials were then developing their own network of ex-Nazis, and were beginning to co-ordinate activities with both the Vatican and London.

The 'Hands Off' policy came into effect just eight days after Gowen completed his report on wanted Hungarian war criminal Ferenc Vajta and the Vatican connection. Gowen recommended on 6 July that American intelligence should take over Intermarium, passing his views up to 'higher commands so that its full international importance [can] be evaluated'.[55]

Gowen had certainly worked out which way the wind was blowing. No one cared about Nazis as long as they were anti-Communist. Nearly two months after the 'Hands Off' policy was decided, Gowen and another officer submitted a lengthy report on the Pavelić case. They noted, with a great deal of charity, that though 'fanatically anti-Serb and to a lesser degree anti-Orthodox, Pavelić is a cultured person and a social liberal'. They had to admit, though, that

> during the early months of the Pavelić regime about 150,000 persons of the Serb Orthodox faith were slaughtered – in many cases, it is a matter of record, they were offered salvation if they renounced their faith and became Catholics.
>
> Thus, today, in the eyes of the Vatican, Pavelić is a militant Catholic, a man who erred, but who erred fighting for Catholicism. It is for this reason that [Pavelić] now enjoys Vatican protection . . . Pavelić is known to be in contact with the Vatican which sees in him the militant Catholic who yesterday fought the Orthodox Church and today is fighting Communist atheism . . .
>
> For the reasons given above he is receiving the protection of the Vatican whose view of the entire 'Pavelić Question' is that, since the Croat State does not exist and, since the Tito regime cannot be expected to give anybody a fair trial, [Pavelić] should not be turned over to the present Yugoslav regime with the excuse of bringing him to justice. The extradition of Pavelić would only weaken the forces fighting atheism and aid Communism in its fight against the Church.[56]

The CIC agents were still a little uncomfortable with the Holy See's approach, so they went to some lengths to explain fully the Vatican's justification for its immoral policy:

Pavelić's crimes of the past cannot be forgotten, but he can only be tried by Croats representing a Christian and Democratic Government, the Vatican maintains. While Pavelić is allegedly responsible for the deaths of 150,000 persons, Tito is the agent of Stalin, who is responsible for the deaths of tens of millions of persons in the Ukraine, White Russia, Poland, the Baltic and the Balkan States over a period of twenty-five (25) years.[57]

Gowen and his colleague were also certain that Pavelić 'is today being supported and exploited by some power' other than the Vatican. As Pavelić had been 'protected by the British in British-guarded and requisitioned quarters' when he first arrived in Austria in May 1945, and knowing 'something of the British Intelligence system', the CIC officers were sure that this power was the United Kingdom.

They further pointed out that even Pavelić's arch enemies, the pro-Royalist Serbian Četniks, believed that 'he ought not to be turned over to Tito at the present time since his trial would be used as a basis for more anti-American and pro-Communist propaganda'. So the CIC officers recommended

that the Vatican and Chetnik views of Pavelić be appreciated and that no direct police action be taken against him on the part of the American Military Authorities. Such action would force his extradition to Tito and would bolster the present British anti-American campaign be (sic) waged among the political *émigrés* in Western Europe.[58]

The US intelligence officers were referring here to the long-standing British campaign to denigrate America in the eyes of the Nazi *émigrés*. They hoped to exclude the Americans from all aspects of the clandestine intelligence and military operations they had organised over the previous two years.

The CIC officers were aware that the British campaign included the claim that the Americans had returned many innocent anti-Communists to Yugoslavia. They commented that in 'the case of the Croats the British state that while they have only extradited seven (7) Croats from Italy the United States had extradited ninety-eight (98) from Austria'. It was completely false, but nonetheless a very effective propaganda tool in Britain's anti-American campaign. US intelligence was by then fully aware that SIS were recruiting ex-Nazis for their anti-Communist crusade.[59]

A *post facto* rationale was found to justify the 'Hands Off' policy. Neither the British nor the Americans were serious about apprehending Pavelić and sending him back to Tito's 'justice'. The bureaucrats in London and Washington formally favoured this course, while turning a blind eye to the activities of their intelligence services. SIS was then mounting major political, intelligence and military operations against Tito. Using Pavelić's followers, they wanted to overthrow the Communist government in Belgrade. Some sympathetic Americans were already working on these operations without official sanction. They, too, saw the Ustashi as useful weapons in the anti-Communist struggle.

Clearly, if the Americans handed over the head of the movement to the enemy, it would be impossible to expect loyalty from the Ustashi rank and file. The solution was clear: Britain must 'be forced to arrest and extradite him themselves. The ultimate disposal of Pavelić is necessary if the Croat democratic and resistance forces are to ever be recognized by the United States.'[60]

'Disposal', of course, meant escape, and the Holy See was the perfect 'fall guy' to shoulder the blame for smuggling Pavelić. The Vatican had the most to lose if he was handed over to the Communists. Soon after he helped Vajta to leave Rome, Gowen wrote a final report:

> Pavelić's contacts are so high and his present position is so compromising to the Vatican, that any extradition of [Pavelić] would deal a staggering blow to the Roman Catholic Church.[61]

Ante Pavelić was once again allowed to disappear into thin air. The names of his high level contacts inside the Holy See's bureaucracy are still highly classified. As seen earlier, at least one US intelligence source believed that it was Monsignor Giovanni Montini, the Pope's Under Secretary of State for Ordinary Affairs, and later Pope Paul VI. This is dismissed by present day senior Vatican bureaucrat, Monsignor Milan Simčić, who was Father Draganović's close colleague in Rome at that time.

Although Simčić rejected the claim that Montini was involved with the Poglavnik, he was absolutely certain that Pavelić was in close contact with Draganović. Simčić insisted that Draganović and Montini were also extremely close, suggesting the strong possibility that Montini, the future Pope, may have known of Pavelić's escape.[62]

A few months after Gowen's suggestion for the 'ultimate disposal' of Pavelić, the fugitive re-emerged in Argentina, where dictator

Juan Perón employed him as a 'security adviser'. There is considerable debate about exactly how the Poglavnik made good his final escape. What is known is that he departed Italy on 13 September 1947, arriving in Buenos Aires on 6 November aboard the Italian ship SS *Sestriere*, travelling under the name of Pablo Aranyos.

In the early 1950s, Avro Manhattan, a bitter critic of the Vatican and Catholicism, claimed that Father Draganović not only provided the Red Cross passport Pavelić used and arranged the shipping details, but actually accompanied the fugitive war criminal to Buenos Aires and stayed with him for twelve months. Despite Manhattan's religious bigotry, he was very well informed, having worked for British intelligence during the war.[63]

As late as 1986, this was still the 'semi-official' story peddled by the Yugoslav secret police, UDBA, in a series of articles in the Sarajevo-based *Svijet* magazine.[64] However, new evidence has recently emerged which suggests a different version. In early 1990 a secret Communist intelligence file was smuggled out of Eastern Europe to the authors. Although the identity of the Communists' source was not disclosed, whoever it was had intimate contact with the Poglavnik, his family and closest associates, as minute details of events and conversations were provided.[65]

The document confirms that Pavelić and Draganović met on numerous occasions, and the priest did in fact procure the Red Cross passport in the name of Pablo Aranyos, supposedly a Hungarian refugee. But according to this source, the two men had some kind of falling out. Draganović proposed that Pavelić leave Rome by air, and as this was thought too dangerous by the fugitive's closest advisers, the priest was cut out of the final preparations.

There is absolutely no mention in the Communist police file of Draganović accompanying the Poglavnik to Argentina. According to the source, the man who allegedly made the final arrangements was also a Croatian priest, by the name of Father Jole. His real identity is Father Josip Bujanović, another wanted war criminal now living peacefully in Australia.

This version of events is basically confirmed by Draganović's close colleague, Monsignor Simčić. In a taped interview, he freely admitted that Pavelić had asked Draganović to assist his escape. Simčić insisted that Draganović was working on smuggling the wanted man out of Italy. He was certain, though, that Pavelić eventually made other arrangements. This would seem to be the case, as the evidence points to Pavelić using his extremely influential contacts in the Italian secret service to make his escape. Whatever method Pavelić used, there is no doubt about Draganović's role in arranging the Vatican's protection prior to his embarkation, and providing him with the necessary travel documents.[66]

Further, Draganović had gone to considerable trouble to arrange to have Pavelić met when he reached Argentina. The ground had been very carefully prepared. According to US intelligence, one Daniel Crljen had been flown to Buenos Aires with Vatican assistance to 'confer with Gen[eral] Perón on the organization of an Ustasha "Elite" movement in the Argentine'.[67] Crljen was one of the movement's senior ideologues and propagandists, having played a key role in instigating the slaughter of Serbs during the war.

Crljen's mission had certainly been successful; Pavelić's arrival merely completed the transfer of almost his entire government to Argentina. Those veterans waiting to greet him included nearly every surviving cabinet minister, as well as many municipal officers, military and police commanders. Most were wanted war criminals, yet they too had evaded justice, using the same method as their Poglavnik.

Draganović's Ratline was a sophisticated and professional operation. It was extremely well organised and could handle hundreds of fugitives at one time. One of Draganović's key operatives estimates that as many as 30,000 people were funnelled from Austria to Rome, on to Genóa and new homes in North and South America and Australia.[68] Most of those running the Ratline had very shady pasts of their own. They were not part of some exotic SS 'brotherhood'. In fact, nearly all the personnel running the smuggling network were Croatian Catholic priests.

5
Ratline

It is absurd to believe that 30,000 fugitive Nazis escaped to South
America on the few U-Boats remaining at the end of the war, or
that they all made their own travel arrangements. Modern popular
culture has presented the escape of the Nazis in an adventurous,
almost romantic light. The most popular Nazi-smugglers are
ODESSA and Die Spinne, although other mysterious groups are
also mentioned from time to time. But in the main these stories
owe more to the fertile imagination of script writers and novelists
than to historical research and accuracy.

The truth is much more ordinary, almost mundane. It is all the
more shocking as a result. For whatever successes ODESSA
achieved, they were mere amateurs at Nazi-smuggling when
compared with the Vatican. Draganović's Ratline was truly professional, ensuring that many guilty war criminals reached safe
havens. Often they did not end up in the remote jungles of South
America, but settled instead in Britain, Canada, Australia and the
United States.

Most Nazi mass murderers were in fact not even German. At
the end of World War II, there were tens of thousands of Central
and Eastern European Nazi collaborators who were just as guilty
as their German sponsors. They were the leaders of Nazi puppet
governments, municipal officials, police chiefs and members of
local auxiliary police units which had carried out the Holocaust.
Many were on Allied 'Black Lists', either because they were
individually known to have ordered or committed war crimes, or
because they were members of units which had done the Nazis'
bloody work.

These were the people of most concern to Father Krunoslav
Draganović, Secretary of the Croatian Institute of San Girolamo
in Rome. Draganović was well known for his deep sympathy for
the Croatian Ustashi, even those who had committed war crimes.
Many relatively innocent Croatians had been cynically returned

by the British to certain death at the hands of Tito's Communist government in May 1945 But many horrendously guilty war criminals escaped, and were being hunted by Western intelligence. According to Draganović, their real crime was their anti-Communist nationalism.

The Ustashi were the first to be protected by Draganović. Britain and the United States decided after the war that Ustashi atrocities were so horrific that all proven members would be handed over to the Communist government, a policy never actually implemented due to a dramatic change of heart in Washington.[1]

Official Vatican historian, Father Robert Graham, admits Draganović's role. Graham initially described those helped by Draganović as 'Croatian refugees', but then conceded that many were Ustashi members. 'I've no doubt that Draganović was extremely active in syphoning off his Croatian Ustashi friends.' But Father Draganović, like Bishop Hudal, was not the Vatican. 'Just because he's a priest doesn't mean he represents the Vatican. It was his *own* operation. He's not the Vatican.'[2]

However, this explanation is not supported by the facts. As recounted earlier, Draganović had been in Rome since August 1943, negotiating for Pavelić at the Vatican and working for the Croatian Red Cross. Pavelić's plans for a smuggling network were already well advanced. US intelligence reported a few months later 'that the Pavelić Government has purchased sixty Argentine passports for evacuation purposes. Funds have been transferred to Argentina.'[3]

Draganović was the key man in setting up this Ratline. He established contacts with Pius XII, as well as senior officials of the Vatican Secretariat of State and Italian intelligence. His most important connection was with Monsignor Montini, Under Secretary of State for Ordinary Affairs, and the man responsible for the Pope's charitable work for refugees.

Like Bishop Hudal, Draganović also received very favourable treatment from the Allied authorities. In late 1944 the Vatican requested that he be permitted to visit the camps where his fellow countrymen were housed. Although Draganović was well known to Western diplomats as a fanatic Ustashi, Allied intelligence gave him *carte blanche*. Using American travel papers, he then ventured out from Rome in May 1945. Travelling in an American car, he visited northern Italy and the regions around Klagenfurt and

Villach on the Austrian–Yugoslav border. Here he made contact with senior Ustashi leaders, and also with other Fascist priests who worked on the Ratline.[4]

Draganović's smuggling network was organised around the Brotherhood of San Girolamo, which took its name from the Institute at Via Tomacelli 132. This was the central base for the operation. The Brotherhood's Committee consisted of Monsignor Juraj Magjerec, President and Rector of the Institute; Deputy President and Treasurer, Father Dominik Mandić, assisted by Vitomir Naletilić; and Secretary, Father Krunoslav Draganović. The Brotherhood was soon recognised as the official Croatian Committee of the Pontifical Welfare Commission, the Pope's own refugee assistance body.[5]

This was a powerful base on which to build the network's ever expanding operation. Ostensibly the Croatian Committee offered moral and material assistance to refugees. But, through the Pontifical Commission, they also maintained close connections with the International Red Cross and the Allied authorities in Italy. Draganović had especially close relations with two Western intelligence officers, Colonel C. Findlay, the Director of the Displaced Persons and Repatriation section of the occupation force, and his assistant, Major Simcock. This proved invaluable, for these officers were only too willing to assist the priest's clandestine activities.

Draganović also had close relations with important Italian officials, especially the Minister of Internal Affairs, Dr Migliore, who directed the Italian secret service and the police section dealing with refugees in Italy. Draganović reached an agreement with Migliore to gain unofficial Italian support for his Ratline, especially from the foreigners section of the Questura.[6]

Through this web of influential contacts, Draganović built a sophisticated network, stretching through Italy, Austria and Germany. The official Croatian Committee of the Pope's Refugee Commission was able to send its agents out to visit the numerous camps where the fugitive Nazi war criminals had taken refuge. Most of these agents were Croatian Catholic priests, and while much of their spiritual and material work consisted of helping the sick, invalids, widows and genuine refugees, there was plenty of time to assist the fugitives.[7]

In the course of researching this book a number of visits were made to the Institute of San Girolamo in Rome, searching for eye witnesses to Draganović's activities. The current Rector, Ratko Perić, was initially cool, absurdly claiming that Draganović had never been an important figure. However, Perić suggested we talk with a priest who was actually there. Monsignor Milan Simčić was one of Draganović's closest colleagues in the smuggling network. Through Simčić, contact was established with Father Vilim Cecelja and Monsignor Karlo Petranović, also close colleagues in the Ratline. Each of these Croatian priests spoke freely about their important roles in the smuggling network.

The First Priest

The smuggling operation started in Austria, where Father Cecelja was the link to Rome. Cecelja died a few months after he gave a taped interview in which he vividly recalled his work on the Ratline. His last years were spent in a picturesque village just outside Salzburg where he was cared for by the nuns of the Maria Pline convent. By then in his eighties, Cecelja was a small man with a pronounced stoop, and in obvious poor health. He was still immensely proud of his important role for his beloved Croatia. Although critical of the Ustashi for giving Croatians 'a bad name', he showed neither guilt nor remorse for his own important post in the Ustashi.

Cecelja freely admitted his senior post of military chaplain in the wartime Ustashi forces.[8] In fact, he was Deputy Military Vicar to the Ustashi militia (as opposed to the ordinary Croatian Army, which took little part in the atrocities) with the rank of Lieutenant Colonel. He was appointed by Pavelić himself in October 1941 and later confirmed by his close friend, Archbishop (later Cardinal) Aloyius Stepinac.

Cecelja was unashamed about being listed by Tito's government as 'war criminal number 7103'. While he criticised the Ustashi in 1989, he had previously been extremely proud of his membership. Ten days after Pavelić was put into power by the Nazis, the official Ustashi newspaper, *Hrvatski Narod* (*Croatian Nation*), published a lengthy interview with Cecelja. Headlined 'The Ustashi Priest Cecelja', it was a contemporary account of his true attitudes.

Cecelja boasted of his important role in the movement's illegal pre-war activities in Zagreb, where many underground Ustashi leaders had secretly met at his vicarage. He admitted his secret

Ustashi membership, proudly describing the ritual oath he had taken before two candles, a crucifix and crossed dagger and revolver. This entitled him to the revered title of 'Sworn Ustasha', which only pre-war veterans were allowed to use. The Fascist priest later presented Pavelić with his crucifix and candles as a sign of devotion. Cecelja also spoke with pride of his leading role in organising 800 peasants to fight alongside the Nazi invaders.

When a priest was required to officiate at Pavelić's swearing in ceremony, Cecelja was only too pleased to do the job. He administered the oath to his Poglavnik, giving the Church's blessing to the Nazi puppet regime. Shortly after, Cecelja publicly 'greeted the moment of freedom with delight', openly proclaiming his close connections with senior Ustashi cabinet ministers, like Mile Budak. A few weeks later, Budak publicly announced the fate of the two million Serbs in Croatia: one third were to be killed, another deported and the rest forcibly converted to Catholicism. Cecelja, however, did not amend his benign attitude towards Budak.[9]

Cecelja's subsequent attitude toward the Ustashi is very puzzling. From the safety of half a century, he criticised his old comrades. But during the vital period when they were carrying out some of the worst massacres of World War II, he was a loyal adherent. This is shown by his inclusion in Pavelić's official delegation to Rome in 1941, which was blessed by Pius XII at the Vatican on 17 May. By then the dictator's anti-Serbian and anti-Jewish laws had already been proclaimed and the genocide was underway. The delegation's main 'achievement' was to cede the Dalmatian coast to Italy, hardly an act of Croatian patriotism.[10]

In view of prevailing conditions in Croatia during the war, it is impossible that Lieutenant Colonel Father Cecelja could have been unaware of the murder of hundreds of thousands of Serbs, Jews and Gypsies. Yet he admits to remaining at his post until the worst excesses had been perpetrated, although he did not mention the high decoration bestowed on him by his beloved Poglavnik.[11] It was only in May 1944 that he finally abandoned his post to go to Vienna, allegedly to care for wounded Croatian troops. His real task was to prepare the Austrian end of the escape network, for he also founded the local branch of the Croatian Red Cross, which provided ideal cover for his illegal work.

In his interview, Cecelja claimed that he was 'a member of the Central Headquarters of the International Red Cross during the war'.[12] In fact, the IRC refused officially to recognise the Croatian Red Cross, although it did provide a great deal of unofficial assistance. Cecelja's control of the Austrian section of this body proved vitally important to Draganović's Ratline operation.[13]

An American diplomat subsequently exonerated Cecelja of all charges of Nazi collaboration. The US Consul in Zagreb claimed that he had been banished by Pavelić to Vienna for his role in an anti-Ustashi plot. However, this seems unlikely, as Cecelja continued to travel regularly on official Ustashi planes between Vienna, Zagreb, Prague and Berlin, laying the groundwork of the Nazi escape network. Further, in 1944 Cecelja received orders from Zagreb to conduct an intensive propaganda campaign among the Ustashi in Austria, especially at the officer training schools. Instead of being one of Pavelić's enemies, as the American claimed, he was actively bolstering Pavelić's flagging cause until the very end.[14]

By Easter 1945, it was obvious that the 'independent' Croatian state was doomed. With the Red Army on the march, this 'Sworn Ustashi' priest left Vienna and shifted his base to Alt Aussee near Salzburg, where many fugitive Nazis gathered at the end of the war. The area around Salzburg was in fact one of the major destinations of his Ustashi comrades, who were forced to flee a few weeks later. He was well positioned to assist them to avoid repatriation by the Allies.

Cecelja was supplied with Red Cross and American papers which enabled him to travel freely through the US occupation zone. It was yet another example of the Allies supplying a Fascist priest with travel papers, which he promptly used to help notorious mass murderers evade justice. Cecelja declared proudly: 'As I travelled in the American zone, I used to leave these small Red Cross identity papers in all the camps . . . I was in charge of organising papers for people who had lost theirs.' He made no secret of having helped fugitives to change their identities – 'I had blocks of Red Cross application forms', with which he provided new identities to anyone who wanted to change their names and personal histories.[15]

Then, on 19 October 1945, he was arrested by the 430th CIC Detachment of the US Army. He remained in gaol for the next eighteen months, because the CIC had discovered that Father Cecelja was allegedly 'the Ustashi head in this region'. They knew he was using the Croatian Red Cross as a cover for his real activities: to 'protect Ustashi members at Salzburg' who were 'wanted war criminals'. According to the Assistant Chief of Staff of US Army Intelligence in Austria, Cecelja endangered 'the security of the occupational forces as well as the objectives of Military Government'.[16]

Ten months later, the Yugoslav government requested his extradition as a traitor, accurately outlining his activities on behalf of the Ustashi during the war.[17] The Foreign Office noted that the 'fact that he was a chaplain in the Ustaši Armed Forces may be sufficiently incriminating for him to be handed over'. Eventually, the British decided that 'most of his works seem to have been humanitarian and non-political'. The Americans interrogated him in December 1945, and over the following eighteen months strenuous efforts were made to exonerate this 'Sworn Ustashi'.[18]

One of those who spoke in his favour was his old friend, Archbishop Stepinac. During his 'show' trial in Zagreb in October 1946, Stepinac described Cecelja as 'an honourable man, against whom I cannot utter even a single word of reproach . . . if everyone were like Cecelja not a hair would fall from any head'.[19] Another senior prelate who took up his case was American Bishop Joseph Patrick Hurley, who was in Yugoslavia as the Pope's representative. Hurley believed that the Yugoslav motive was 'purely political', merely part of their campaign against the Church.[20]

On the basis of a quite inadequate investigation, the US Consul in Zagreb recommended that Cecelja 'not be surrendered to [the] Yugoslavians', as he was a 'priest of high standards'.[21] This intensive campaign followed the decision of the US Extradition Board in Austria to approve the 'Yugoslav request for extradition as collaborator of Vilim Cecelja'. Previously, the Americans had found that there was insufficient evidence to justify his extradition, asking the Yugoslavs to provide further substantiation.

By 4 April 1947, the Board considered the Yugoslav charges were confirmed by their own intelligence reports which 'reasonably establish Cecelja's participation in collaborationist activities'.[22] Ultimately, however, this finding was ignored and US Secretary of State, George Marshall, ordered that he was not to be surrendered. He was too late. The Ustashi priest had been released seventeen days before.[23]

After his release, Cecelja spent some time in hospital and then returned to smuggling wanted Nazis. When he applied for a visa to visit America in 1957, his official security check declared that the allegation that Cecelja was 'purposely harbouring and hiding ex-Ustasha members was never substantiated'. However, US intelligence had gathered a great deal of information linking Cecelja to militant Ustashi activities.

Four years before the Fascist priest was granted a US visa, American officers in Austria had noted that Cecelja's Croatian Red Cross branch was in fact controlled by the Ustashi. They were using its various offices as an 'information collecting agency' for clandestine operations in Yugoslavia and Austria. Further, Cecelja was known to be one of the key Ustashi organisers in Austria, where he regularly attended militant gatherings and delivered fiery speeches to the assembled faithful. Later, he was directly implicated by Australian security authorities in a series of terrorist actions launched by Ustashi cells operating in Sydney and Melbourne.[24]

In fact, the Americans had ample evidence that Cecelja was directly involved in a range of clandestine Nazi activities. In his 1989 interview, he freely admitted his role in Draganović's Ratline. He was proud of assisting these fugitives 'with food and accommodation, registering them and providing them with immigrant papers, giving them the opportunity to move around the world to Argentina, Australia and South America. I got the papers from the Red Cross.'[25]

Cecelja was well informed about those he sent down the Ratline to Rome and on to their new homes. 'Some of them were high ranking ministers and civil servants,' he admitted. Further, he was certain that Draganović had the approval of the Vatican for his work, claiming that the Holy See had asked him to take care of a broad based emigration of Central European 'refugees'. Draganović 'was fully empowered by the Holy See and was in charge not only for Croatians, but for everybody', he emphatically declared in his taped interview.[26]

Although fast approaching death, Cecelja vividly recalled how the smuggling system worked. Up in Austria the fugitives would be cared for by his section of the organisation, which provided them with money, food, accommodation and the false papers they needed to travel from Austria to Italy. Down in Rome, Draganović was at the operation's nerve centre. He arranged the international travel documents and through his high level contacts with South American consulates, organised the necessary visas, especially to Argentina. Once a week Cecelja called Draganović who told him how many places were available that week. Cecelja then sent exactly that number to Rome.[27]

This interview with an unabashedly Fascist priest had been truly astounding. His testimony was a vital link in the chain of evidence about the Ratline and its connection with the Vatican hierarchy. Western intelligence files fully confirm Cecelja's recollections. The British established that the 'nucleus around which all Ustaš activity in Italy takes place . . . [is] . . . the Confraternity of S[an] Girolamo in Rome'. They discovered that not only was Draganović 'the brains behind the Ustaš movement in Italy,' but he had a remarkably similar history to Cecelja's.[28]

The Second Priest

Like his close friend in Austria, Father Draganović was also a wanted war criminal. The Yugoslav War Crimes Commission recorded that he had been a senior official of the committee dealing with the forced conversion of Orthodox Serbs to Catholicism. Further, they had discovered his leading role in the forced requisitioning of food during the Nazis' bloody anti-partisan offensive on Kozara mountain in western Bosnia in the summer of 1942. This was the same offensive in which Austrian President Kurt Waldheim played a leading role as a Nazi officer.[29] Pavelić awarded Waldheim a major decoration for his services, and then followed him to Austria at war's end.

In July 1947 the Yugoslavs requested Draganović's extradition, especially citing his role in the Kozara offensive, which was carried out in his capacity as Vice President of the Ustashi's 'Office for Colonisation'. This office was an integral part of the Nazi genocide machine, preparing the Serbs and Jews for extermination or, if they were extremely lucky, deportation.[30] Although Draganović claimed to have taken a strong stand against the Ustashi's massacres, allegedly even complaining to Pavelić himself, he did not deny the substance of the Communist charges. When the Nazis occupied Zagreb in April 1941, he was Professor of Theology at the local University. He later recounted that when the 'independent' Croatian state was proclaimed, 'I was waiting in Zagreb with tears in my eyes. I thought that the Croatian nation, after eight centuries, had created their most deep wishes for independence and autonomy.'[31]

Draganović fully accepted Pavelić's state. He felt that he had gained his freedom when the Ustashi came to power, and co-operated with them 'as a citizen according to the laws of the Lord'. One of the tasks he admitted performing with great energy was overseeing the conversion of Orthodox Serbs to Catholicism, as a member of the special committee established for this purpose.[32]

He claimed he had never actually been present in the Serbian villages where the forced conversions took place. These were 'celebrated' by Catholic priests under the close scrutiny of heavily armed Ustashi police units. The threat of death hung over these ceremonies, as the Serbian peasants were fully aware that these same units had been conducting massacres in the neighbouring areas. However, there was at least one occasion when Father Draganović ventured out of his comfortable office in Zagreb. He did not hide the fact that he had held the senior position of Vice President of the Ustashi's Committee for Colonisation. Two witnesses confirmed that the priest had been present at the bloody Kozara offensive, when the Colonisation Committee had played a key part in the assault on the population.[33]

In another striking parallel with Cecelja's career, Draganović also worked on Croatian Red Cross matters. In August 1943 Pavelić and Archbishop Stepinac dispatched him to Rome. American intelligence observed that it was 'a classic example of "kicking a man upstairs" inasmuch as it is fairly well established that the leaders of the Independent State of Croatia expected the prelate, through his good connections in the Vatican, to be instrumental in working out the orientation of Croatia towards the West rather than the East'.[34]

Although Draganović was supposedly sent to Rome because of his defiance of Pavelić, he also admitted accepting appointment as the Ustashi's representative to the Vatican. Perhaps this explains why he continued to have access to senior members of Pavelić's regime on his regular visits to Croatia. Like Cecelja, Draganović travelled on several occasions to and from Zagreb, consulting with his Ustashi superiors. Apparently there was a concerted campaign to provide these Fascist priests with good cover stories, enabling them to present themselves as victims of the Ustashi, while they quietly got on with the task of building the underground escape network.[35]

Draganović also received a 'large subsidy' from the Ustashi government, much of which remained in his hands at the end of the war. American intelligence further established that as 'he was a trusted follower of Ante Pavelić . . . he was entrusted with . . . all valuables smuggled by the Ustacha'. These funds were the financial base on which his Ratline was initially built.[36]

According to British intelligence, at the end of the war San Girolamo assumed the 'role of granting asylum' to the Ustashi *émigrés*:

> In the summer of 1945 Draganović made a personal tour of the camps where ex-members of the Ustaš armed forces and political organisations were being accommodated. He soon developed an intensified political activity and made contact with the chief Ustaš representatives. In this he was assisted by other Croat priests and close liaison was maintained between S. Girolamo and the Ustaš groups throughout Italy and also in Austria. This led to the formation of a political intelligence service enabling S. Girolamo to collect reports and data on political trends among the *émigrés*. It is also probable that the information received from these reports was then passed on to the Vatican.[37]

The Third Priest

The distinctive characteristic of the Ratline was that most of its operatives were Croatian priests, many of them unashamed Fascists. Cecelja and Draganović had murky pasts, but Father Dragutin Kamber was a bloody mass murderer. Like so many of the priests involved in the smuggling network, Kamber had a longstanding connection with San Girolamo, studying there in the late 1920s and early 1930s.

The Yugoslav government requested Father Kamber's extradition in April 1947, claiming he had been a Ustashi member since 1936. After the Axis invasion, he was appointed head of the Ustashi administration at the town of Doboj, 'and one of his first acts was to set up a concentration camp, which he himself headed as camp commandant. He introduced in the district the Nazi racial rules and accordingly issued orders for the Jews to wear yellow arm-bands and for the Serbs to wear white bands.'

Later, 'he proclaimed that the Serbs and Jews were to be exterminated as harmful to the *ustasha* State. In Doboj he carried out mass arrests and internment of Serbs. Many of the victims were first brought for interrogation to Kamber's house and, on his orders, were subsequently killed in the cellars of that house. The first to be killed in this way were the Serbian teachers and priests.'[38]

These were fantastic charges against a Roman Catholic priest. Surely they were just Communist propaganda? However, the British Consul in Zagreb made enquiries and found that Kamber was 'responsible, to some extent, for the massacres at Doboj'. Further investigation established that he had also been an officer in Pavelić's notorious Personal Body Guard, and had definitely 'incited [the] wholesale massacre of Serbs at Doboj in Bosnia'. The British further noted that Kamber was 'in close contact' with San Girolamo.[39]

Despite Draganović's close relations with Fascist priests like Cecelja and Kamber, he repeatedly lied to Western intelligence officers, claiming that he had no connection with the movement at all.[40] Both British and American intelligence found this to be untrue. One US report concluded that 'his task [is] to co-ordinate and direct Ustacha activity in Italy. He provides them with moral and material help', arranging to send them to South America:

> He is helped in this activity by his numerous contacts with the Embassies and Legations of South America in Italy and with the International Red Cross and by the fact that the Croatian Confraternity of the College of S. Girolamo degli Illirici, where he has his office, issues false identity cards to the Ustacha. With such documents and with the approval of the Pontifical Welfare Commission for Refugees, located in Via Piave 41, Rome, which is controlled almost exclusively by Ustacha, passports can be obtained from the International Red Cross, where Draganović has some way of ensuring their issue.[41]

The Fourth Priest

Is it possible that a Fascist priest could have had access to the Pope's charitable welfare organisation without anyone in the Vatican hierarchy knowing? The 'Pontifical Welfare Commission', after all, was an official Vatican body which the Pope had established to assist genuine refugees. Draganović's abuses must have been known in senior Vatican circles, since the false identity cards he issued to fugitive war criminals were 'printed at the Franciscan printing press'. US intelligence discovered that this had been arranged by Father Dominik Mandić, the official Vatican representative at San Girolamo.[42]

Mandić, it will be recalled, was a senior member of San Girolamo's Brotherhood, which was the official Croatian section of the Pope's Refugee Assistance Commission. He was also a senior official in the Franciscan order, holding the position of General Economist, or treasurer. Not only did he arrange to print San Girolamo's false identity papers, he also put the Franciscan press at the disposal of the Ustashi propaganda machine. Much of the British-sponsored campaign waged in DP camps like Fermo, Modena and Bagnoli owed its success to the Franciscan printers. Mandić himself regularly visited the camps to deliver rousing speeches to the assembled Ustashi militants.[43]

Father Mandić was a crucial link in the Ratline. Using his connections with the Italian secret police, Draganović got the Franciscan's identity cards accepted 'as official documents on the basis of which Italian identity cards and residence permits were issued'. The Italians closely monitored Draganović's activities. They launched a top secret intelligence operation, and soon discovered that numerous Ustashi fugitives were using the false identity cards printed by the Franciscans. The Italians found that many wanted criminals were housed at San Girolamo, including senior members of Pavelić's government, but no action was taken against Draganović or the Italian officials who assisted him.[44]

British intelligence also monitored this development closely, although they decided to hide their information from the Italians:

> There is incontrovertible evidence that some of the most notorious war criminals were issued in this way with the S. Girolamo identity card under an entirely false name and thus were enabled to obtain Italian residence permits, visas and other documents allowing them to emigrate.[45]

CIC Agent Robert Mudd certainly procured 'incontrovertible evidence' about Draganović's activities. He penetrated his own spy into San Girolamo, and his reports confirmed the Italian intelligence reports. Italian agents described San Girolamo as 'a den of Croatian nationalists and Ustashi. It is said that the walls of the college are covered in pictures of Pavelić.'[46]

Monsignor Milan Simčić worked in San Girolamo at this time, assisting Draganović in his 'rescue' operations. He indignantly denied that Pavelić's photo was displayed in San Girolamo, because photos of civilian authorities were not permitted in 'a Church institution'. Simčić conceded that some Ustashi were allowed to sleep in the Institute, 'but this was only for a few months in 1945'.[47]

But in February 1947 Mudd's spy found very different conditions inside the Institute. He confirmed the Italian secret service's information, reporting that San Girolamo 'was honeycombed with cells of Ustashi operatives':

> In order to enter this Monastery one must submit to a personal search for weapons and identification documents, must answer questions as to where he is from, who he is, whom he knows, what his purpose is in the visit, and how he heard about the fact that there were Croats in the Monastery. All doors from one room to another are locked and those that are not have an armed guard in front of them and a pass-word is necessary to go from one room to another. The whole area is guarded by armed Ustashi youths in civilian clothes and the Ustashi salute is exchanged continually.[48]

Simčić agreed in a taped interview that there was extremely tight security at San Girolamo at this time. Although he denied that the young men employed to guard the building were armed, he claimed that precautions were necessary due to the ever present threat of attack from the Communists. 'I was in danger and no one could just enter San Girolamo, because people there were extremely scared. The Communists attacked us a few times, as is well known.'[49]

Mudd's spy obtained a great deal of information which explained the Communists' intense interest in what was going on at San Girolamo. He gained a first-hand insight into the calibre of those either living in San Girolamo or 'in the Vatican'. The spy had wormed his way into a position of some trust, for he knew the identities of those attending Draganović's regular clandestine meetings. Far from being religious occasions, these gatherings were all politics. Rather than bringing the faithful together, those in attendance were more like a who's who of the most wanted and notorious Croatian war criminals:

1. Ivan Devčić, Lt. Colonel.
2. Vrančić, Dr Vjekoslav, Deputy Minister of Foreign Affairs.
3. Toth, Dr Dragutin, Minister of Croat State Treasury.
4. Sušić, Lovro, Minister of Corporations in Croatian Quisling Government.
5. Starčević, Dr Mile, Croat Minister of Education.

6. Rupčić, General Dragutin, General of Ustashi Air Force . . .
8. Pečnikar, Vilko – Ustasha General and C[ommanding] O[fficer] of Ustashi Gendarmerie.
9. Marković, Josip, Minister of Transport in Pavelić Government.
10. Kren, Vladimir – Commander-in-Chief of the Croat Air Force.[50]

By September 1947, US intelligence had established that several of these senior Ustashi leaders were living with their Poglavnik in what was believed to be one of the Vatican's libraries at Via Giacoma Venezian 17-C.[51] Among them were Lovro Sušić, Pavelić's Minister of National Economy. He had worked closely with the Nazis on the deportation of Croatian workers for forced labour in Germany, later serving with the bloody SS Division Prince Eugen. Sušić's surrender to Tito's government had been agreed in August 1946.[52]

Dragutin Toth was another senior figure on Mudd's list. He had been Pavelić's Minister of Trade and Industry, president of the Croatian National Bank and, finally, Minister of Finance.[53] John Colville of the British Foreign Office, who later admitted that he had deliberately allowed many 'fanatic' Ustashi to escape justice, thought that Toth 'sounds, and looks, a bad hat'. Both London and Washington agreed to Toth's surrender to the Yugoslavs, but he also went down Draganović's Ratline and made his way to Argentina in mid-1947.[54]

Vjekoslav Vrančić was another senior war criminal to benefit from Vatican protection. Vrančić's key role in the extermination programme is clearly demonstrated by his appointment as Under Secretary of the Ustashi Interior Ministry. This was the body directly responsible for the concentration camps and repressive police apparatus. Vrančić was supposed to be handed over to the Yugoslavs, but three days after this decision was taken he mysteriously 'escaped' from British custody. He then made his way to the safety of San Girolamo and was sent down the Ratline by Father Draganović. In November 1947 US intelligence reported that he had arrived in Argentina under the name Ivo Rajičević, where he became a major figure in the revival of the Ustashi's terrorist apparatus.[55]

One further case is that of Vilko Pečnikar, a veteran of the movement and organiser of Pavelić's pre-war terrorist groups. During the war he rose to be a General in Pavelić's Personal Body Guard, also commanding the brutal Gendarmerie which worked in close collaboration with the Gestapo. Both Britain and America agreed to hand him over to Tito.[56]

US intelligence described Pečnikar as 'anti-Hebrew, anti-Serb, pro-Austrian, living in a monastery'. According to this report, Draganović and Pečnikar worked closely together on re-organising the Ustashi movement. The Fascist priest allowed Pečnikar to have access to the treasure he had collected for his Ratline. As will be seen, some of this also financed a new Western-backed terrorist campaign inside Yugoslavia.[57]

All these war criminals were on the list supplied by Mudd's spy in San Girolamo. But the clandestine operation 'stopped abruptly when it became too dangerous for the counter-intelligence agent in the Monastery'. The US officers wanted further proof, so Gowen arranged for a daring burglary of Draganović's office, the centre of the Vatican's smuggling operation. It is not known how this was achieved, but the results were spectacular, for Gowen was able to photograph many of Draganović's top secret records.[58]

The documents procured from Draganović's office were handed on to Mudd for assessment. One of the most important documents was a list of the nominal roll of Croatians who 'are fed, clothed, housed and otherwise provided for by the Monastery of San Girolamo'. By comparing this roll with the West's lists of wanted war criminals, Mudd established that it also included 'the names of several long sought after Jugoslav War Criminals whose presence in the Monastery and whose sponsorship by the Vatican Draganović has consistently denied'.

In fact, at least twenty of those housed at the Institute were on the West's 'Black Lists'. Details about these fugitives were obtained from one of the most significant files photographed during the burglary. It disclosed not only their true identities, but also the aliases Draganović had given them.[59] Other documents contained detailed information on Draganović's system of procuring Central and South American visas.

Mudd reported the results of Gowen's burglary of San Girolamo in September 1947. He noted that the 'photostats of personal files and documents of the Croat Nationalist priest Draganović, Krunoslav procured in Rome indicate clearly his involvement in aiding and abetting the Ustashi to escape into South America. The documents also indicate his connections with Ustasha personnel, a fact which Draganović has formally denied personally to this

Agent'.[60] Mudd further reported that 'all this activity seems to stem from the Vatican, through the Monastery of San Geronimo to Fermo, the chief Croat Camp in Italy. Chief among the intelligence operatives in the Monastery of San Geronimo appear to be Dr Draganović and Monsignor Madjarac.'[61]

Mudd concluded by describing how those Ustashi living in the Vatican travelled between their lodgings and San Girolamo:

> ... these Croats travel back and forth from the Vatican several times a week in a car with a chauffeur whose licence plate bears the two initials CD, 'Corps Diplomatic'. It issues forth from the Vatican and discharges its passengers inside the Monastery of San Geronimo. Subject to diplomatic immunity it is impossible to stop the car and discover who are its passengers.
>
> Draganović's sponsorship of these Croat Quislings definitely links him up with the plans of the Vatican to shield these ex-Ustashi nationalists until such time as they are able to procure for them the proper documents to enable them to go to South America.

The Fifth Priest

The next and final stop on the Vatican's sophisticated Ratline was Genoa, where yet another Croatian priest took charge of the passengers. Monsignor Karlo Petranović is now almost eighty years old and has lived in Niagara Falls, Canada, for the past three decades. Although he complains of a few ailments and has had heart bypass surgery, he is in remarkably good health and still very active. When interviewed in 1989, he seemed a generous and kind-hearted man, but after the war he was Draganović's operative in Genoa, shipping out hundreds of fugitive war criminals.

In a taped interview, Monsignor Petranović was adamant that he had never been a member of the Ustashi. When the Nazis invaded Yugoslavia in April 1941, Petranović was a chaplain in the Army. The day the 'independent' Croatian state was proclaimed he was stationed at Topuško, south of Zagreb. After hearing of this development, he returned to Ogulin where he had been the parish priest since 1934. Ogulin is a mixed Croatian and Serbian district, and during the war was the scene of some of the most brutal and widespead Ustashi massacres of Serbs. Petranović stayed there throughout the war, but only heard vague rumours of these atrocities.[62]

When asked about his attitude to Pavelić's 'independent' Croatia he said, 'I was very happy when it was created', but as for masacres, 'I saw nothing'. When pressed further, he recalled that he 'heard rumours that people were dying, and there were one or two Jews in Ogulin, but I don't know what happened to them, they just disappeared'. According to Petranović, his superior ordered him to stay away from politics and although he welcomed and recognised the new Croatian state, he claims to have obeyed this order.[63]

In the Public Record Office in London we discovered documents that directly contradict the Monsignor's version. When the Yugoslavs wrote to the British in July 1947 requesting Petranović's extradition, they categorically stated that he was a Ustashi member. They claimed he had joined the movement immediately after the invasion, whereupon he was appointed to a number of very senior and influential official positions. In fact, he had been given the rank of captain in the Ustashi army, also accepting the position of deputy to the local Ogulin Ustashi leader. Contrary to Petranović's claim that he was not involved in politics, the Yugoslavs maintained that 'he became a very important factor in the policy of the local Ustaši regime which decided on the life and death of the Serbs of Ogulin and the surrounding district. As evidence shows, this policy consisted of terror against the entirely innocent Serbian population, resulting in the extermination of about 2,000 local Serbs.'[64]

The Yugoslavs went even further, alleging that Petranović had organised and instigated a number of very serious war crimes. On one occasion, they claimed, he had directed the arrest and execution of seventy prominent Serbs. Another time the priest was allegedly responsible for the removal of five or six Serbian patients from Ogulin's hospital, who were killed 'in the most brutal circumstances'. A further incident was the murder of Dr Branko Živanović on 31 July 1941, 'on the basis of a false statement made by Petranović'.

This was in the summer of 1941 at the height of the Ustashi's first assault on the Serbs. During this period, the Yugoslavs said, Petranović had helped organise 'the mass arrest of [the] Serbs of Ogulin and district' who were robbed and killed, 'some at Brežno, the others near the village of [St] Petar'. Another allegation concerned Petranović's role in the death of about one hundred Serbs at the end of July, a massacre carried out 'in accordance with a decision made by the Ogulin Ustaši committee' of which Petranović was a senior and influential member. The Yugoslav extradition request ended by claiming that, in 'addition to these crimes, the Ustaši committee at Ogulin, of which Petranović was an active functionary, is responsible for sending hundreds of local Serbs and Croats to the Ustaši concentration camps, which resulted in the extermination of the majority of them'.[65]

Despite his denial of any connection with the Ustashi during the war, there is independent evidence which supports the Yugoslav charges. For example, on 1 July 1941, the official Ustashi newspaper, *Novi List*, announced Petranović's appointment 'to the post of *pobočnik* in the camp for the district of Ogulin'.[66] This was precisely the position which the Yugoslavs claimed Petranović had held: he was indeed second-in-command to the Ogulin Ustashi leader.

When asked about his post-war activities, Monsignor Petranović cheerfully admitted that he helped 'a couple of thousand people' leave Italy via Genoa. When the war ended, he says he witnessed the Communist massacres of captured Ustashi. After a brief stay in Zagreb, he was dispatched to the Yugoslav-Austrian border, where he moved freely among the fleeing Ustashi. He settled for a time in Graz where many notorious war criminals were hiding. His work there was aided by Bishop Ferdinand Pawlikowski, who obtained clearance from the local police chief to allow Petranović to stay in Graz.

From there he made his way down to Trieste, where the local Bishop arranged his accommodation, and then on to Milan where he was helped by Cardinal Schuster, finally arriving in Genoa towards the end of 1945. He wanted to go to San Girolamo in Rome, but as it was full remained in Genoa and became Draganović's local operative.

Petranović's first contact with the smuggling network was through fellow wanted war criminal, Father Kamber, who took Petranović for a long walk down by Genoa's harbour and suggested that he could assist. Soon afterwards Dragnović himself visited Genoa and recruited Petranović to the Ratline. He desperately needed a reliable link in this key Italian port city, someone who could be counted on to procure plenty of berths on ships for South America. Petranović agreed to carry out the work on one condition:

he insisted that San Girolamo pay his phone bills. According to Petranović, he received no other assistance for his work in Genoa.[67]

When asked about his role in the Ratline, Petranović explained that it was really quite straightforward. Draganović would regularly ring to tell him how many places he required. Petranović would already have visited the local shipping offices and obtained guaranteed berths. He would tell Draganović how many berths were available, and that number of people were sent to Genoa a couple of days before embarkation. Draganović had already provided the passengers with the requisite travel documents and visas, so Petranović only needed to find them lodgings for a few days and then conduct them to the ship.[68]

Some of those he assisted were undoubtedly genuine refugees. He is particularly proud of having helped Hungarian-born actress Zsa Zsa Gabor to travel to America where she launched her famous career. However, Western intelligence knew that most of Petranović's passengers were not aspiring film stars. They were fully aware that many senior war criminals were escaping via Genoa with his aid. For example, in Feburary 1947 a list of wanted Croatians was sent from Rome to London. British intelligence had also penetrated San Girolamo, for they knew that the fugitives were soon to be sent down the Ratline to Genoa, where accommodation and other assistance 'will probably be arranged by the Croat priest Father Petranović'.[69]

The British then made Petranović a major surveillance target, noting that he was 'helping Croat *émigrés*, and in particular, Ustaši, escape to the Argentine'. Over the following months they confirmed that those assisted by Petranović were mainly 'listed war criminals', also noting that the Croatian priest was 'probably identical with the wanted Croat quisling'. Three who had recently departed with the priest's help were the Pavelić government ministers Stjepan Hefer, Mile Starčević and Vjekoslav Vrančić. They had all been hidden in Rome by Draganović, who had also obtained their false travel documents and sent them to Petranović's charitable arms in Genoa.[70]

Monsignor Petranović now shrugs off the important work he did for Draganović, saying that it really was not well organised and certainly not political, merely 'God's Providence'. However, he had very good connections in the Church hierarchy, especially

Genoa's Bishop Siri, yet another senior prelate involved in smuggling fugitive Nazis. US intelligence discovered that Siri was one of the main organisers of 'an international organization whose purpose is to arrange for the emigration of anti-Communist Europeans to South America . . . This general classification of anti-Communists would obviously cover all persons politically compromised with the Communists, namely Fascists and Ustaschi and other similar groups.'[71]

Siri was the same senior prelate who was allegedly Walter Rauff's contact in setting up Bishop Hudal's escape network to smuggle wanted Germans out of Europe. Not surprisingly, his operation was mainly concerned with assisting German fugitives, including Adolf Eichmann. But he also helped Petranović, lending a hand whenever he could.

Although Siri maintained his own organisation, he was fully informed of the Croatian network. Petranović recalled one example of the close relationship he enjoyed with Genoa's Bishop. The Croatian was caring for a number of fugitives who urgently needed to leave for Argentina, but he could not procure enough berths. So he sent a telegram in Siri's name to the shipping office in Buenos Aires, requesting that places be made available for his passengers. This had the desired result, and they were allowed to embark. Petranović later informed Siri of this forgery, but instead of being angry, the Bishop was delighted at the Croatian's initiative.[72]

Petranović also vividly recalled one of the few occasions when Western intelligence took effective action against his operation. This occurred in early March 1947, when Major Stephen Clissold visited Genoa. Clissold had been a British diplomat in Zagreb before the war, then he served as a liaison officer to Tito's partisans. His mission in Genoa was to arrest suspected Ustashi war criminals before they set sail on the SS *Philippa*, one of the ships which regularly plied between Genoa and Buenos Aires with its cargo of fugitives.

Clissold worked for the British Special Screening Mission, tracking down fugitive Nazis. He had received reliable information that a group of wanted war criminals, travelling under false names, would embark on the *Philippa* on 4 March. He knew that Vladimir Kren would be among this group, travelling under the alias of Marko Rubini. In his memoirs, Clissold recalled that the wanted men were 'sponsored by the Pontifical Commissione de Assistenza', and 'were being looked after in Genoa by Father Petranović, a trusted collaborator of Draganović'.[73]

The day the ship was to leave port Clissold's men intercepted sixteen of Petranović's passengers as they tried to board. One man, 'of thick-set and distinctly non-Semitic aspect', gave his name as Marko Rubini. Clissold recalled that his 'manner, at first truculent, turned ingratiating and finally servile as he admitted that he was General Vladimir Kren, the former Yugoslav airforce officer who had organised notable defections to the Germans in April 1941 and been rewarded with the command of Pavelić's airforce'.[74] US intelligence had previously discovered Kren's name among those senior Ustashi officials under Draganović's care. Eventually he was one of the unlucky few to be handed over to the Yugoslavs.

When Petranović heard that Kren and nine others had been detained by Clissold, he went to see the British officer, urging him to 'let these people go'. He remembers that Clissold only smiled, but said nothing. The next day Petranović again intervened with the British officer, saying that 'Croatians were very unhappy with Yugoslavia and therefore joyful when the Independent State of Croatia was proclaimed'. This, apparently, was supposed to mitigate in favour of those who had loyally served the Nazi cause.[75]

This was one of the very few occasions when Western intelligence triumphed over the very well organised and successful Ratline run by Father Krunoslav Draganović and an array of Croatian clerics. A few weeks later the British arranged an ambush at San Girolamo itself, arresting about one hundred men as they left a meeting.[76]

Mostly, however, the Western operations were spectacularly unsuccessful. The reason for this was very simple. Sections of the Allied authorities were in fact co-operating with the Vatican to ensure that many fugitives were allowed to slip quietly out of Genoa. One US diplomat discovered that the Western powers were 'apparently conniving with [the] Vatican and Argentina to get guilty people to haven in latter country'. This was indeed the case. Both Washington and London had entered into arrangements with the Holy See to assist many Nazi collaborators to emigrate via Draganović's smuggling system. The Vatican was cynically being used as a respectable cover for the West's own immoral conduct.[77]

The successful operation at Genoa was the exception to an

otherwise shoddy Western effort. Gowen's burglary at San Girolamo had probably disclosed Kren's alias, making him one of the
handful who did not benefit from the Allies' policy of amnesty.

The Priests' Passengers

There is no doubt that Draganović and his colleagues organised
their network because of their ardent, even fanatical, Croatian
nationalism. Nor can there be any debate that most were Fascist
priests and committed Ustashi militants, sharing Pavelić's hysterical hatred for the Serbs. What, though, was their justification as
Christians for shielding mass murderers from justice? A unique
insight into their mentality is provided in a lengthy memo Draganović sent in May 1947 to the American Ambassador to Italy.[78]

Draganović argued persuasively that justice under the Communists in Yugoslavia was virtually non-existent. He unequivocally
declared that those 'who have committed war crimes', especially
'crimes against humanity . . . must be punished'. However, he then
cleverly argued that the most culpable should not be classified as
war criminals, by distinguishing between those who had personally
perpetrated such crimes and the *political leaders* of Pavelić's government. His view was that 'to be a state official, even with a high
function, or member of the Ustasha Movement does not need
signify that the persons in question are war criminals'.[79]

Such a statement, of course, could be seen as completely
unexceptional. War criminality should be judged by the evidence
in each case, not merely established by general allegations of
political misconduct. However, the only people condemned by
Draganović as war criminals were the rank and file who actually
bloodied their hands in the villages and concentration camps.

He excluded those politicians who actually enacted the racial
laws which legalised mass slaughter. These were the senior ministers and functionaries of Pavelić's 'independent' Croatia, who in
their statements and propaganda openly instigated mass murder,
thus creating a vicious climate. Some uneducated Croatian peasants therefore came to believe that mass extermination was an
acceptable, even desirable, form of behaviour. Yet Draganović
defended the former and condemned the latter.

This, then, was his justification for assisting Pavelić and his
closest colleagues. However, even this was a lie, for he also

knowingly helped many common murderers. Ljubo Miloš, for example, had been a senior official at the Jasenovac concentration camp. One of his notable acts was the 'ritual killing' of Jews. After a transport had arrived in the camp, Miloš 'would put on a physician's gown, send the guard to bring him all those who had applied for hospital, take them to the "ambulance", put them along the wall and with a strike of the knife cut the victim's throat, shear his ribs and slit open his belly'.[80]

Miloš also supervised other brutal methods of extermination. Naked prisoners were thrown alive into the raging furnace of the brick factory attached to the camp, while others were bludgeoned to death with clubs and hammers. Miloš was definitely not an 'innocent' Croatian patriot who had merely served in Pavelić's government out of a sense of 'duty' to his nation. He was a common sadist and murderer, guilty of exactly the types of crimes Draganović believed deserved punishment.[81]

Yet Draganović extended his 'Christian Charity' to this man. There is no doubt that he knew of Miloš's terrible crimes, for he later condemned Jasenovac as 'the most horrible bloodbath that Croatia has ever known'. According to Draganović, Miloš was 'a monster, a slaughterer of innocent people and a coward'. He had first met this 'monster' in Austria in mid-1945, where he was hiding under a false name and later saw him in Rome. The priest admitted that he gave Miloš a great deal of money, but only because he feared that Miloš would kill him.[82]

However, Western intelligence established that Draganović was lying. They discovered that Miloš was living in an Italian camp and were about to apprehend him. Draganović was tipped off by someone in British intelligence, and used his sophisticated network to spirit Miloš away to safety.[83]

This was a fairly common occurrence. Western intelligence repeatedly observed that Draganović had advance warning of their operations to arrest war criminals. They even discovered that he had obtained the lists of those to be arrested, indicating his influence with senior levels of Western intelligence. In fact, many key Allied officers were very co-operative. Draganović regularly visited the military and intelligence headquarters in Rome, where Major Simcock would tell him the details of impending operations to apprehend fugitives.[84]

One of the most intriguing aspects is that so many of the war criminals assisted in this way, including Miloš, were later captured on terrorist missions inside Yugoslavia. Perhaps the real reason for Draganović's benevolence related to Pavelić's need for men to serve in his secret anti-Tito army then being organised with Western help.

What kind of priest would extend his protection to a killer like Ljubo Miloš? The Italian press investigated Father Draganović in 1948, describing him as 'robust and slender, dressed impeccably as a priest'. They reported 'that this priest, undoubtedly a complex and ambiguous figure, proposes to justify the criminal Ustashi with evangelical reasons'.[85] At this time the Ratline was operating at maximum capacity, but Draganović was surrounded in mystery and intrigue. Legends grew around the Vatican's 'eminence grise', but few really knew, let alone understood, the real man.

Three of his closest colleagues recently provided fascinating insights into his character. Each had been an important figure in the Ratline, working with amazing dedication to rescue his comrades. Draganović's superb intellect left an indelible impression on both Monsignor Petranović and Father Cecelja. Petranović recalled him as 'reserved, distant and very serious', not someone who often shared a joke or engaged in light hearted banter.[86]

Monsignor Simčić gave the most intimate account. Of the three priests, he was the closest to Draganović, working on the Ratline in Rome for several years. He was 'an amazing person, a great activist and a superb organiser, a man of great ideas. Like all such people he tended to be interested in the big projects and leave the details to others. Perhaps he relied too much on his intuition.'

Simčić was fulsome in his praise of Draganović's intelligence, and certain of his greatness. He was 'one of the most important men in Europe, a great scholar with an excellent knowledge of history'. Draganović had a 'big heart, big horizons, and was far sighted but naive like some great people are'. His naivety did not stop Draganović from also being a great conspirator. 'He had a great love of conspiracy', and thrived on code words and clandestine meetings. He frequently took elaborate precautions to avoid surveillance when he ventured out from San Girolamo. But Simčić was sure that Draganović was not 'careful in many matters. A true conspirator would not have made the mistakes he did.'[87]

Not many of the eye witnesses with whom we spoke agreed with this last point. However, nearly everyone who knew Draganović agreed that he was one of the most conspiratorial men they had ever met. One British intelligence officer remembered him being like 'all Croats, very conspiratorial'. This officer was well acquainted with Balkan intrigues. He had served in Greece, Yugoslavia and Albania during the war, and was then active in anti-Tito operations in post-war Italy. On several occasions he had lengthy discussions with Draganović, finding him rather unapproachable 'from a human point of view. I think he was very cold, very much a realist . . . He was not expansive, flamboyant or outgoing, but very closed and conspiratorial.'[88]

Was it possible, we asked this British officer, that Pius XII did not know of Draganović's conspiracy to smuggle Nazis? In a taped interview, he told us that Western intelligence was fully informed of the Vatican's intrigues, including the racket to supply Nazis with false documents. Draganović was definitely the key figure, he insisted, adding that Pius XII 'knew everything about Father Draganović's activities, otherwise he would never have stayed in his position'.

From the intelligence available to him, this officer was certain that Draganović's real status in the Vatican was 'head of the Balkan desk of the Secretariat of State'. Father Draganović was 'very close, for example, to Monsignor Angelo dell'Acqua', then a very senior Vatican intelligence officer. Later dell'Acqua became an Archbishop, but according to the British officer at that time he was really Draganović's superior in the Vatican intelligence hierarchy. He further confirmed Draganović's close links with Italian intelligence, which were well known in the small circle of Western intelligence agents in Rome. There were close social connections between these officers, and gossip was very common.

In his experience, nearly everyone in Western ingelligence knew that Draganović was protecting Ante Pavelić, who was hiding in the Vatican. Further, Draganović's Ratline was an open secret in the intelligence community at the time. The priest was notorious for helping war criminals to escape. He mentioned other Ustashi figures who he knew had been protected by the Church. One was former Colonel, Jozo Rukavina, who 'was working as a gardener in Vatican City'.

In fact, Draganović was widely known among Western intelligence operatives at the 'Balkan grey eminence'. This was a standing joke among both American and British officers, in whose circles Draganović moved freely. This was also confirmed by Simčić, who was certain that Draganović had direct contact with British, American and Italian intelligence.[89] The former British officer was also emphatic that 'you can almost talk about interlocking directorships between Western intelligence and the Vatican at this period'.[90]

If this allegation is true, Pius XII is deeply implicated in a much wider conspiracy than merely Draganović's smuggling network. The Vatican has persistently denied claims about the involvement of its own senior officials in Draganović's network, let alone with Western intelligence operations.

There is at least some evidence to support this view. For example, one British diplomat at the Vatican came to their defence in November 1947, claiming that it was 'unlikely that the Vatican approve the political, as opposed to the religious activities of Father Draganović & Company'. However, the Foreign Office totally rejected this:

> We fully understand the views of the Vatican authorities and subscribe to some of them ourselves. While we cannot condemn the charitable attitude of the Church towards sinful individuals we feel, however, that there has been much evidence to show that the Vatican has permitted the encouragement both covert, and overt, of the Ustaši. This wholly undesirable organisation has not only been collectively responsible for vile atrocities on an immense scale during the war but has ever since its inception made use of murder as a normal political weapon. There is surely all the difference between giving shelter to let us say dissident Slovene priests, and giving positive aid to a creature like Pavelić?[91]

For its part, the Holy See has gone to considerable lengths to discredit and cast doubt on the reliability of Western intelligence reports which implicate the Church. For example, when we were researching this book, Vatican official historian, Father Graham, warned us not to rely on the veracity of US intelligence reports. Yet the British consistently confirmed the American information. So did the Italian secret police, who also closely monitored the conspiracy. It seems very difficult to believe that Western intelligence was wrong so regularly, in both its information and general analysis. After all, they had penetrated agents into the Ratline's headquarters. The Americans went one better, and actually broke into San Girolamo and photographed Draganović's files.

Further, two key witnesses *inside the Church* confirmed the Vatican's involvement. Monsignor Milan Simčić and Father Vilim Cecelja, both close confidants of Father Draganović, were certain that senior Vatican officials knew about Draganović's work and approved of it.

Today Simčić is a senior Vatican official, who freely admits that San Girolamo protected senior Ustashi fugitives and helped them to escape. He knew this first-hand, not from hearsay. In two taped interviews, Simčić recalled that many fugitives had been housed, fed and clothed by the Institute. He was absolutely clear that the 'most important people', including 'former government ministers, heads of army formations and former police chiefs were handled separately by Dr Draganović'. Simčić claimed that Draganović had a sophisticated underground network to deal with these people, utilising radio communications and intelligence contacts.[92] These were precisely the Ustashi fugitives identified by Western intelligence as taking shelter in San Girolamo and the Vatican.

Those mentioned by Simčić could not be called 'refugees' by any stretch of the imagination. By his own admission they were the senior politicians and officials of one of the most infamous Nazi puppet governments. Simčić merely commented, with an apparent easy conscience, that San Girolamo's role was not 'to make any moral judgements about the people we were helping. Our job was to make it possible for them to escape and history could judge them later.'

Father Graham, though, emphatically insisted that Draganović 'was not the Vatican'. He was running his own *independent* operation, and Pius XII and Assistant Secretary of State Montini had not known about it, let alone approved.

The Sixth Priest

Simčić now dropped his bombshell. According to his first-hand account, 'Dr Draganović and Montini were together very many times', discussing San Girolamo's work. Simčić is certain that the Vatican Assistant Secretary of State knew exactly what this work entailed, for Draganović frequently sought his advice and assistance in specific cases. Often he would ask Montini to 'obtain more visas' from countries that were not issuing an adequate number and the Vatican bureaucrat would intercede with the relevant diplomats.[93]

Simčić was just as certain that this relationship worked both ways, and that Draganović frequently returned Montini's favours. He insisted that:

> Montini got in touch with Draganović many times, asking him to help people on his behalf.

Not only was Montini aware of Draganović's Ratline, but Simčić is certain that he actually utilised it himself. When asked what this meant, Simčić claimed still to possess copies of letters from Montini to Draganović in which the senior Vatican official asked for assistance to smuggle certain people. Although Simčić would not produce these documents, he insisted that Montini had asked Draganović to act on the Holy See's behalf on several occasions.

In fact, there 'were excellent relations between us and the hierarchy'. While Simčić carefully avoided implicating Pius XII there is no doubt that the Pope was fully aware of Draganović's work. As already discussed, Montini was the Pope's favourite at this time, and directly supervised the Holy See's charitable work for refugees. As the two prelates met daily and discussed the Secretariat of State's work, it is inconceivable that Pius XII was left in the dark. In other words, two senior Vatican officials were informed. Both the reigning and future Popes (Montini later became Paul VI) approved of Father Draganović's Ratline.[94]

Father Cecelja went even further than Simčić, claiming that Draganović was the Holy See's official representative for the emigration of all Nazi groups, not just Croatians. Although Simčić disagreed on this point, it is independently confirmed by other sources. Božidar Kavran, a senior member of Pavelić's post-war underground network, has testified that Draganović boasted in his presence that he was the Vatican's official representative for all Eastern European nations. Finally, US intelligence identified Draganović as the Vatican's 'DP Resettlement Chief'. They knew this because they were utilising his Ratline to smuggle their own agents out of Europe.[95]

Apart from eye witnesses and the unanimous opinion of Western intelligence, there is other evidence that clearly demonstrates Draganović's influence with both the Secretariat of State and the

Pope himself. For example, on many occasions the Vatican intervened on behalf of interned Ustashi prisoners in Allied camps.
Nearly always these intercessions were engineered by Draganović.
On one occasion, in early March 1946, Draganović appealed to
leading Church figures around the world, including Cardinals
Griffin and Gilroy in Britain and Australia, requesting their
assistance. He then actively lobbied the Secretariat of State to
intervene formally.[96] Finally, Draganović went directly to Pius
XII.

The object of his appeal was two hundred former Ustashi militia
men, and numerous members of the infamous SS Divisions Prince
Eugen and Handžar. The former was composed of Yugoslav
Germans, while the latter was raised from the significant Moslem
population of Bosnia. Both had committed atrocities against
innocent civilians. Others whose cases were advocated by Draganović included former Ustashi government ministers, Dragutin
Toth, Vjekoslav Vrančić, Mile Starčević and Stjepo Perić, as well
as former air force chief, Vladimir Kren. Several of these men later
turned out to be hiding in San Girolamo or the Vatican, as
discovered by Mudd's spy.

The Vatican soon acted, taking up these cases with American
and British diplomats and recommending their 'kind attention and
consideration' of Father Draganović's appeal.[97] Many more diplomatic interventions by the Vatican followed, most on behalf of men
who had so recently perpetrated the Nazi Holocaust.

Draganović had many opportunities to pass his message to Pius
XII. For example, in June 1946 San Girolamo's Executive Committee appointed a 'special delegation' to attend a personal audience with the Pope. Draganović was a senior member of this
committee, so it was not surprising that his 'close friends', Dr Ivo
Omrčanin and Professor Nikolić, a well known Ustashi propagandist, were chosen to attend the meeting. The Italian government
had complained to the Western powers about Omrčanin's activities
twelve months before, noting that he had been an official of the
Ustashi Foreign Ministry.[98]

US intelligence determined that Omrčanin had 'worked closely
with Draganović . . . to assist Croatian refugees emigration matters'. Simčić recalled Omrčanin as a man full of his own self-
importance, always boasting of his central role. Nonetheless,
Simčić confirmed that Omrčanin 'was very close to Draganović

and they co-operated during that period'.[99] Omrčanin had in fact worked directly under Draganović in the Croatian Committee of Pontifical Assistance between 1948 and 1953, touring the DP camps and sending thousands of fugitives down the Ratline.

Omrčanin now lives in Washington, from where he publishes a stream of pro-Ustashi propaganda tracts. He confirms Simčić's and Cecelja's views. For instance, in a 1986 interview he claimed that Assistant Secretary of State Montini was aware of the full dimensions of Draganović's smuggling network. Omrčanin also boasted that they had sent 30,000 people down the Ratline, including many German scientists and technicians.[100]

Finally, there is the issue of the Vatican's involvement in San Girolamo's finances. British intelligence discovered that Father Dominik Mandić controlled San Girolamo's finances 'with considerable dexterity'. He was the treasurer of the official Croatian section of the Pope's Assistance Commission for Refugees. The British established that one of his principal tasks was to 'arrange the placing against Italian currency of the gold, jewellery and foreign exchange deposited by high-ranking Ustaš officials', in reality the valuables of Pavelić's murdered victims, stolen by the fleeing Ustashi.[101]

Mandić was the senior Franciscan official who placed the order's printing press at San Girolamo's disposal so that false identity cards could be provided to the fugitives. American intelligence discovered that he was in fact 'a representative from the Vatican' at San Girolamo. It is not without coincidence that Father Mandić was the treasurer of Draganović's smuggling operation.[102]

Is it possible that all the eye witnesses who worked on this network are lying, perhaps to serve their own political ends? Or that all the Western intelligence officers got the facts completely wrong? According to Father Graham, the Holy See did not even know about, let alone endorse, what Draganović and his fellow Fascist priests were doing.

This seems highly implausible. The declassified Western intelligence and diplomatic records totally support the eye witnesses. American officers like William Gowen and Robert Mudd employed extraordinary means to find out the truth. They infiltrated spies into San Girolamo, penetrated the Ustashi intelligence network and even illegally photographed Draganović's files. Their findings were unambiguous: the Vatican was behind this Fascist priest's activities. Gowen came to believe that the Vatican's attitude, although perhaps unsavoury, was entirely justified by the exigencies of the Cold War. This makes his conclusions about the Vatican's involvement all the more powerful.

British SIS files on this subject (as in nearly all cases) are completely closed. However, there are several key diplomatic and military intelligence reports publicly available that completely support the American findings. It is impossible to believe that all these reports were written by incompetent or prejudiced officials. After all, both the British and later the Americans had recruited the very same Nazis who were being protected by the Church. Their information actually came from within the very bowels of the machine. Further, it is clear that Western intelligence was both co-operating with and cynically manipulating the Vatican for its own ends.

In summary, it is virtually inconceivable that the *key* officials in the Vatican hierarchy were ignorant of Draganović's Nazi-smuggling network. It is true that these prelates were only a tiny cabal, but they numbered among them the most influential officials, including the Pope and at least one Assistant Secretary of State. They were the men with access to real power and resources.

There was a reason for their protection of Nazis. Britain's SIS had not helped the Vatican save Ante Pavelić through misguided notions of benevolence and charity. They wanted a great deal in return. They wanted agents to infiltrate Communist Yugoslavia, to gather intelligence and conduct terrorist strikes on strategic targets and Communist personnel, especially the feared secret police.

These agents were drawn from the ranks of Pavelić's defeated Ustashi. Harking back to the militant days of Christendom, the Poglavnik dubbed these Catholic warriors the Križari – his Crusaders. The Vatican scandal was only beginning.

6

The Golden Priest

The main hall of the old Zagreb Fair was packed with a carefully picked crowd of 1500 Communist stalwarts. The fifty-seven defendants of the 'show trial' nervously awaited the inevitable verdicts with an air of resignation. Throughout July and August 1948 a farcical judicial process had been conducted in the close, hot summer. An almost carnival atmosphere had prevailed, as the unruly spectators alternately applauded the prosecution with great enthusiasm, then cat-called, jeered, booed and laughed at the unfortunate Ustashi militants brought to account for their crimes.

The proceedings had been broadcast live over the local radio station, a tightly controlled Communist propaganda outlet. Whenever there was an embarrassing departure from the carefully prepared script, the crowded court room would shout 'Long Live Comrade Tito', and the radio station would switch to repetitious slogans glorifying the dictator's regime.

No one was surprised at the guilty verdicts, or the death sentences and long terms of imprisonment. But despite the crudeness of the trial, none except diehard Ustashi supporters believed that the outcome was not justified. Among the defendants were some of Ante Pavelić's most brutal mass murderers, men who had implemented their Poglavnik's bloody racial and political policies with unbelievable relish.[1]

Their war crimes, though, had merely been a backdrop to the trial's real purpose: to crush the morale of the largely anti-Communist populace. The defendants were the cream of Pavelić's Crusaders, or Križari, the underground resistance movement left behind to raise an insurrection against the Communists. Most of those on trial had infiltrated into Croatia from the Križari's bases in Austria over the previous two years.

Their orders were to strengthen the underground and launch a violent campaign of assassination, sabotage and disruption, preparing for the moment when they would finally settle scores with their old enemies. Their aim was to link up with powerful units operating in the rugged terrain, destroy telegraph, telephone and railway communications, attack industry and murder 'more prominent political and military representatives'. Instead of finding a well organised underground of over 300,000 men, they soon encountered Tito's efficient and ruthless secret police. Most were in Communist hands within a few days of crossing the border, many within hours.

Although the whole Križari affair was obviously manipulated, the prosecutors and judges cleverly turned it into an effective propaganda exercise, linking notorious war criminals with both the West and the Catholic Church. Most of the defendants admitted their murderous roles for Pavelić. Many implicated unspecified Western intelligence services, said to have provided logistical support, training and equipment for the terrorist operations inside their homeland.

Not surprisingly, in light of the powerful position of the Croatian Catholic Church, special attention was reserved for the sinister machinations of the Vatican, which allegedly had been plotting Tito's downfall in league with Archbishop Stepinac and the local clergy. Tito had begun his campaign against the Church in November 1945, announcing that 'terrorist organisations had been discovered which were led by priests and made up of Ustaše, who had now changed their names to Crusaders'.[2]

Trials of Križari members began the following month, when Father Ivan Condrić and four other priests were found guilty of organising Križari terrorist actions. The man behind these schemes was said to be Father Krunoslav Draganović, Secretary of the Confraternity of San Girolamo in Rome and the 'Ustashi representative at [the] Vatican'.[3]

Many of the defendants in the 1948 trial admitted taking refuge at San Girolamo, where Draganović recruited them to the Križari. They outlined his central role in directing the underground network, even claiming that the Pope himself had blessed the work during a meeting with Draganović. According to one defendant, Draganović was the Križari's 'grey eminence', the 'chief person who perhaps acts stronger behind the scenes than publicly. He was the main leader, because he had behind him all forces, both [the] Vatican and the foreign powers.'[4]

In a typical rhetorical flourish, the Communist prosecutor claimed that an 'especially shameful role' had been played by 'Vatican circles'. Father Draganović had 'established contact between the Ustashi terrorist groups', the Vatican had financed them and Draganović had set up a 'spy centre' in Trieste in 1945 and sent in the first group of terrorists.

Draganović had also maintained close contact with British and American intelligence, who had directed and assisted the Križari's military preparations. Ljubo Miloš told the court that Pavelić and Draganović had closely collaborated, jointly issuing orders to the terrorist groups. Miloš knew what he was talking about, having been saved from Allied arrest by Father Draganović, despite his bloody record as a Ustashi war criminal.[5]

These charges were fantastic. If true, the Vatican had actually supported wanted war criminals to launch a terrorist campaign against the 'atheistic Bolshevik' foe. Back at the Foreign Office in London, the bureaucrats dismissed the claims, noting that much of 'the "evidence" produced to this effect was of course puerile'. Still, they had to admit that Brigadier Fitzroy Maclean's Mission in Italy had stumbled across substantial evidence implicating US intelligence in aiding the Ustashi's activities. There was no doubt, the British further noted, that San Girolamo 'was the centre of much suspicious activity'.[6]

Having decided that their American ally was the most plausible guilty party, the Foreign Office happily washed its hands of any responsibility for the disastrous collapse of the anti-Communist cause in Yugoslavia. The reality was very different . . .

William Gowen and his CIC colleagues had started to unravel Britain's role in the Križari's operations during their hunt for Ante Pavelić in 1947. As already discussed, they soon discovered that the Vatican was sheltering Pavelić, with the connivance of the British Secret Intelligence Service. In the course of establishing this, Gowen also confirmed sensational claims made by Ferenc Vajta. It will be recalled that the American's Hungarian Nazi contact had told him that SIS was behind the military and political revival of the Ustashi.

Gowen investigated the Križari's finances and soon uncovered the unsavoury truth: their money came partly from the 'treasure' which 'Pavelić's henchmen' had carried out of Croatia. According to Gowen, the Ustashi had fled with a large number of truckloads of this stolen booty. When the British SIS apprehended Pavelić in Austria in May 1945, they also picked up some of his loot. Gowen believed that the following story of what really happened was 'closest to the truth':

> British Lt Colonel Jonson was placed in charge of two (2) trucks laden with the supposed property of the Catholic Church in the British Zone of Austria. These two (2) trucks, accompanied by a number of priests and the British officer, then entered Italy and went to an unknown destination.[7]

Major Stephen Clissold confirmed that two such Ustashi 'treasure trucks' had indeed reached Austria. Not surprisingly, Clissold did not mention the British role in removing them to Italy, claiming instead that they 'were deposited in the safe-keeping of a monastery'.[8] Perhaps the 'treasure' had been in a monastery, but Gowen was certain that the British were now using it to finance

> the Croat resistance movement in Yugoslavia. The resistance forces . . . go by the name of Križari (Crusaders) . . . Radio contact is maintained by means of a field radio operated by Vrančić, a former Pavelić minister, located in the British Zone of Austria. The Ustascia courier service within the Austrian Zones is believed aided by the Roman Catholic Church in Austria. The Cardinal of Graz is known to be on close terms with . . . Professor Draganović, Krunoslav, known Pavelić contact in Rome.[9]

Yet again, Western intelligence found that Father Draganović was at the centre of the Ustashi's clandestine activities. Indeed, he was widely known in Western intelligence and *émigré* circles as 'the golden priest' because he controlled a large part of the stolen treasure.[10] Although Colonel Jonson had taken away two truck-loads in 1945, this was only a fraction of Pavelić's loot.

Four hundred kilos of gold, worth millions of dollars, and a considerable amount of foreign currency had been secreted at Wolfsberg, where it was under the control of former Ustashi Minister, Lovro Sušić. Draganović discovered this from senior Ustashi officials during his visit to Austria in mid-1945. They were apparently determined to maintain some independence from the British, who they feared would seize the gold, so they asked Draganović to save it. The priest was only too willing to oblige, for he contacted Sušić and with his agreement took forty kilos of gold bars to Rome, concealed in two packing cases.[11]

There is no doubt about Draganović's close connections with the Ustashi hierarchy in this money laundering scheme. Sušić appointed Draganović to a three person committee to control the treasure. His colleagues, former Ustashi Minister Stjepan Hefer, and Gendarmerie General Vilko Pečnikar, were also senior Križari officers. Pečnikar was Pavelić's son-in-law and played a particularly important role in the terrorist network. US intelligence discovered that he 'maintained contact with several clandestine Nazi organizations' and operated a sophisticated intelligence service which liaised between the Austrian and Italian groups. All of these men were wanted war criminals, but evaded the Western dragnet with Draganović's help. At one time or another, they each had taken shelter under his wing, either at San Girolamo or in some other Vatican-protected haven.[12]

Draganović's close colleague on the Ratline, Monsignor Milan Simčić, is certain that his conspiratorial friend was not involved in the Križari's operations. Simčić recalled the mood which prevailed among the Ustashi at the end of the war. There was widespread optimism, he said, and a firm belief that the Western powers would soon launch a new war against Communism, and topple Tito's regime. The Ustashi high command thought that their exile would end almost as soon as it had begun, and with Western help they would return to create another 'independent' Croatian state.

According to Simčić, the Križari were 'idealists', who organised the terrorist network without any assistance from either Draganović or Western intelligence, although he conceded that many were also 'fanatics'.[13] However, Draganović admitted at least some involvement with the Križari high command, although he tried to minimise his role.[14]

Draganović sought desperately to place the whole blame for the Križari on Pavelić, who, he said, had organised the terrorists while hiding in the British zone of Austria. The man entrusted to command the operation was one of the Poglavnik's most faithful servants, Božidar Kavran, assisted by Lovro Sušić, Draganović's partner in saving the stolen treasure hidden in Austria. Although the priest did admit to discussing the Križari with Kavran at a meeting in Rome, he insisted that he was not the Križari's Church contact.[15]

He claimed that this was another Croatian Fascist priest, Father Josip Bujanović, who had been the Ustashi leader at the town of Gospić during the war. A young British captain by the name of Evelyn Waugh had investigated Father Bujanović's activities in Gospić, and concluded that 'he is credibly reported to have taken a hand in the massacre of Orthodox peasants'.[16] Like his fellow priests running the Ratline, Bujanović fled Croatia in front of the Communists and became a senior Križari officer working directly under Kavran and Sušić. As previously discussed, Bujanović arranged for Pavelić's trip to Argentina, and then followed him to South America, before finally settling in Australia.

Having confirmed that Father Bujanović was a senior officer in the terrorist network, Draganović denied his own involvement. Indeed, he 'was certain that a priest should not be part of such a revolutionary organisation', and unequivocal that he remained aside from the Križari. In fact, he claimed actively to have discouraged participation in such dangerous operations. His old friend, Monsignor Simčić, fully supported Draganović on this point.[17]

However, in tracking down Pavelić's treasure, Gowen found that the Church's involvement with the Križari went much deeper than Father Bujanović. In fact, the CIC officer finally pieced together yet another jigsaw puzzle which had confused US intelligence over the previous two years. His CIC colleagues in Austria had placed the Križari under close surveillance immediately war ended, arresting some of its senior leaders. They quickly established that the retreating Ustashi had enlisted 'the Roman Catholic Church in their struggle'. As outlined earlier, this was achieved on 25 June 1945 when a meeting was held with a 'papal mission in Salzburg'.

A letter was addressed to the Pope, elaborating the Ustashi's plan to create either a new Croatian state or some form of the Pan-Danubian Confederation. In support of their request for assistance, they argued that Croatia was a bastion in the fight against the large 'Serbian state' (i.e. Yugoslavia), which was 'a tool of Russia for the conquest of the Balkans'.[18] There is a great deal of evidence that the Vatican responded positively to these approaches. One British intelligence officer recently confirmed that the Križari had extremely strong links with the Vatican.

This officer worked on anti-Communist operations in Italy after the war and was certain that the Church had also been a link to senior Italian politicians and bureaucrats who assisted the Križari's terrorist operations. In the hysterical mood of the early Cold War years, Croatia was seen by the Vatican as its stronghold in the Balkans.[19]

American intelligence recorded that the Ustashi have 'received much assistance from the Catholic Church since the end of the war'.[20] One of their principal Church helpers was Archbishop Andreas Rohracher of Salzburg. According to Ljubo Miloš's testimony at the Križari 'show trial', Rohracher put the Church at the disposal of Intermarium's Pan-Danubian Confederation.

At Rohracher's initiative, a meeting was called by the Bishop of Klagenfurt to discuss bringing the Catholic nations of Central Europe into this Confederation. Apart from Rohracher and the Bishop of Klagenfurt, Bishops Gregory Rožman of Ljubljana and Ivan Šarić of Sarajevo attended the meeting. The last two prelates had been enthusiastic Nazi collaborators, US intelligence noting that Bishop Šarić was a '"hangman" known to Croatian Serbs, and those in Bosnia and Herzegovinia under the regime of the Ustachis during the war'.[21]

Archbishop Rohracher had also interceded on behalf of the Ustashi with the Allied authorities in Austria, 'to create a favorable impression' in preparation for their offer to 'put themselves at the disposal of Anglo-American leadership'. The Italians obtained reliable information in June 1945 that the British had immediately accepted this offer. It came from no less a source than Father Draganović's close colleague in the Ratlines, Ivo Omrčanin. According to the Italian report, Omrčanin told them that Pavelić and his closest comrades were meeting regularly with 'sympathetic elements of the British forces, who have been paying for the reorganisation of a united Ustashi for eventual use against Tito'.[22]

Another Italian report noted that these activities aimed 'to overthrow Tito's regime in Yugoslavia'. American intelligence agreed that their British ally was co-ordinating the operations in Austria. Gowen established that in August 1946 a 'considerable number of pamphlets were dropped in Croat territory by planes, apparently from the British Zone of Austria. These pamphlets, signed by Pavelić . . . declared that ceaseless warfare would continue until such time as either Tito or Pavelić was permanently eliminated.' The latter would be the victor in 'this death struggle'.[23]

Further, the US officers received information that the Križari's military supplies were almost completely British, including 'mortars, machine guns, sub-machine guns, two-way field radios and uniforms of British manufacture. The condition of the weapons is good and each man is furnished with a firearm. Nearly all the arms are of British types.'[24]

The Ustashi's approaches to the Catholic Church were apparently equally successful. US intelligence received information that the Križari's 'organization has extended to the Vatican, where the center of the Command is currently located. From the Vatican, help is delivered by underground methods, such as delivery of arms and other vital supplies . . . Arms arriving in Croatia are said to come from Switzerland.'[25]

The outlandish charges made by the Yugoslavs during the Križari 'show trial' may have had more than a little substance after all. Twelve months before the trial had even commenced, the CIC in Salzburg had learned from a reliable source that Draganović was not only the head of the 'Croatian Clerical Party', but also a senior leader of the Križari. He maintained excellent contact with his forces inside Croatia and received 'the backing of the Catholic Church'.[26]

The Salzburg CIC detachment later reported that this so-called 'Clerical Party' was 'under the direct leadership of the Pope', who wanted to create the Catholic Pan-Danubian Confederation.[27] It was further established that Draganović was working 'hand-in-hand' with the Slovene Clerical Party.[28]

The two most important members of this group in Rome were both senior Intermarium figures – Miha Krek, political leader of the Slovene Catholics and Monsignor Anton Prešeren, the Assistant General of the powerful Jesuit order. The Italian secret service noted the influence exercised by the Slovenes at the Vatican as early as August 1944. The Italians observed that the Slovene clericals were actively collaborating with the Nazis, and already working closely with Draganović in providing welfare and assistance to 'refugees'. At that time, Reverend Ahčin was the 'go-between' for this group and the Vatican, the Italians noted.[29]

From their contacts in Italian intelligence, the Americans discovered in July 1945 that Krek, Prešeren and Ahčin were really British agents.[30] By that time, Prešeren was the main contact with the Holy See. Under cover of the Church, and in close co-operation with Draganović, the Slovenes had established their own section of the Križari.[31]

The Slovenes did not make exaggerated claims like their Croatian comrades, who falsely boasted of having between 40,000 and 300,000 Križari in the Papuk mountains and other rugged areas. The Slovenes, however, kept up a constant stream of propaganda to convince the Allies that they, too, had major forces in the field.[32] Interrogation of Slovene leaders indicated that their guerrilla units were operating mainly in the Gorensko region and Pohorje mountains, maintaining a high level of co-operation with the Ustashi groups. They 'are clothed in American and British combat dresses, and armed by subguns. Their ranks consist of deserters and farmers, mostly.'[33]

The spiritual leader of the Slovenian Križari forces was Bishop Gregory Rožman, whose pastoral centre was in the capital, Ljubljana. This very political Bishop had not set foot there since early May 1945, when together with other Nazi collaborators he had fled to Austria. Here he found a warm welcome from the Bishop of Klagenfurt in the British occupation zone. Rožman desperately needed his protection, for he was one of the most wanted Nazi collaborators. In Krek's absence during the war, Rožman took charge of the Slovene Clerical Party, establishing close ties with both the Italian Fascists and the Nazis.

Rožman was more than a mere figurehead, taking an active part in organising the quisling forces. In mid-1942, he went on a secret mission to the Vatican, asking Pius XII to obtain weapons, food, uniforms and other essential equipment for his Catholic anti-Communist army. As a result, the Italians supplied Rožman's forces. At his suggestion, a number of priests also assumed key military and intelligence roles for the Axis powers.[34]

When the Italians capitulated in September 1943, Rožman organised the smooth transition to Nazi rule, suggesting the formation of the Slovenian Homeguard to Hitler's Gauleiter. This Homeguard was completely under German control, serving directly under the command of the local SS and Higher Police chief. It was infamous for its massacres of civilians, especially supporters of the Communist-led partisans, while its secret police conducted a campaign of terror and murder under the Gestapo's direction.[35]

While these atrocities were taking place, Rožman gave enthusiastic support to the Nazi cause, issuing numerous appeals for Slovenes to 'fight on the side of Germany'. His Pastoral Letter of 30 November 1943 was typical of the stridently pro-Nazi tone of the Bishop's 'spiritual work'. Having urged his faithful to fight for Germany, he pointed out that only 'by this courageous fighting and industrious work for God, for the people and Fatherland will we, under the leadership of Germany, assure our existence and better future, in the fight against [the] Jewish conspiracy'.[36]

There was little doubt in London that Bishop Rožman was a notorious Nazi quisling who deserved extradition to Tito's Yugoslavia. The evidence against him was overwhelming. In addition to his anti-Semitic Pastoral Letter, Rožman was photographed on the dais with the local SS commander during an official ceremony. The Homeguard had just sworn to serve under Hitler's command and were marching past their commanding officer. The SS General stood rigidly to attention, giving the Nazi salute, while the Bishop gave pious approval to his quisling army.

By late 1945, the Foreign Office concluded that Rožman had clearly 'collaborated with the enemy' and was no less guilty than others who had been turned over to the Communists.[37] However, Rožman had powerful friends at the Vatican, and this ultimately explains why the British allowed him to 'escape' and play a major role for the Križari.

Six months before the war ended, Krek and Monsignor Prešeren took up Rožman's cause with the Pope. At a meeting with Pius XII on 26 November 1944, they delivered the Bishop's personal letter to the Pontiff. Rožman outlined his plan for a Western-backed effort to defeat Tito's partisans and install a pro-Western government.[38] As soon as hostilities ceased, the Vatican launched a concerted campaign to secure their Bishop's freedom, repeatedly asking that he be given safe conduct from Austria to find refuge at the Holy See.[39]

They even offered to send a specially selected priest to travel to Klagenfurt to collect Rožman. The man chosen for this task was none other than Father Draganović, who later recalled that rescuing Rožman was one of the most important tasks given him by the Vatican. Draganović was ordered to locate the Bishop on his visit to Austria in May 1945 and bring him back to Rome. He worked hard to carry out his mission, attempting to procure the necessary travel papers for Rožman to make the journey. However, he encountered serious difficulties with the British. Although they permitted him to visit the Bishop, they refused to provide the travel pass and Rožman was forced to remain in Austria. Draganović was disgusted, complaining bitterly that politics had intruded into the Church's charitable work.[40]

Indeed they had, for in response to the Holy See's interventions, the Foreign Office noted that Rožman was 'a quisling'. This explained why they refused Draganović's entreaties, for they had decided that Rožman could on no account be permitted to 'find sanctuary at the Vatican'. Officially, the British favoured his surrender to the Communists. But with typical cynicism, they blamed their American ally for their failure to carry out this decision. Their Embassy in Washington reported in January 1946 that on 'account of the probable repercussions amongst Catholics in this country and elsewhere [the] State Department want to be quite sure of their ground before agreeing to the surrender of Bishop Rožman'. Senior US bureaucrats, however, had unofficially indicated that they would probably ultimately agree to hand him over to Tito.[41]

In fact, senior State Department officials concluded that the 'case as presented by the Yugoslav Ambassador is sufficient to justify handing the Bishop over to Yugoslavia'. However, the Secretary of State simply decided that the Vatican's interest in the case overrode the evidence. America refused to agree with London's proposal for Rožman's extradition.[42]

British intelligence were delighted. The attitudes of the Americans and the Holy See were perfect smokescreens for their real plan. Over the following twenty months the British maintained some nominal supervision of Rožman at his relatively luxurious residence at the Bishop of Klagenfurt's Palace. As the Cold War threatened to 'hot up', they decided unofficially to release the Bishop, despite their previous decision to deliver him up to the Yugoslavs.

This followed yet another intervention by Intermarium President Krek, who exerted considerable pressure on the Foreign Office through the good offices of a Labour Member of Parliament. Krek's entreaties on Rožman's behalf were laced with numerous fabrications and lies, among other things asserting that the 'Holy Father approved all deeds of Mnsgr. Dr Gregorius Rožman' during

the war. According to Krek, Rožman had really been a courageous
anti-Nazi. The real reason for Tito's extradition request was that
Rožman had also been 'a vigorous, active, unyielding adversary of
the Communists'.[43]

The British knew Krek's version was completely inaccurate, but
nonetheless the campaign then being waged in parliament coin-
cided with their own plan. This involved doing a deal with the
Vatican to bring about the very solution they had been requesting
for the previous two years. The British proposed quietly to allow
the Bishop to 'escape', travel from Klagenfurt to Salzburg, and
thence to the safety of Italy and finally the Vatican. Once he had
'escaped', Rožman would be under the care of the Catholic Church
and no longer the Foreign Office's concern.

So in November 1947 a British Diplomat visited Monsignor
Tardini, head of the Extraordinary Affairs Department in the
Vatican's Secretariat of State. He explained the scheme to Tardini,
who 'was very relieved to hear of H. M. Government's proposal,
and he immediately suggested that the best thing' would be to
send Rožman to the United States, where he felt sure that the
American Catholic Bishops 'would, if requested by the Pope, be
glad to look after' him.[44]

Tardini also mounted a spirited defence of Rožman, saying that
he was 'an excellent bishop'. His only offence was 'that he had
done everything to organise an anti-Tito Government, in the
expectation that the British and American troops, who, in his view,
stood for order and civilisation, would get to his part of the world
before Tito's troops, who were only a "Godless and shirtless
crowd"'.[45]

Tardini did not mention that Rožman's anti-Communist government was in fact completely under Nazi control, although he
'added that it was true the Vatican laid down as a general maxim
that the clergy should not interfere in politics, but they left it to the
bishops to decide how to interpret this in the light of local
conditions and their effect on the faithful. Bishop Rožman had
acted for the best according to his conscience, and the Vatican
could not disown him.'[46]

Back in London they were very pleased at Tardini's response,
and immediately asked the Americans if they would go along with
the scheme. However, even as the final arrangements for the
Bishop's 'escape' were being made, Rožman quietly slipped away

without warning. This prompted the British bureaucrats to observe hypocritically: 'It seems curious that a Paladin of the Roman church should have failed to keep his word.' Rožman was by then fully aware of the deal struck with the Vatican. Nonetheless, the Foreign Office feigned shock that a senior prelate, who was merely 'on parole', could have acted dishonestly.[47]

In fact, Rožman's escape was part of a wider plan. The Bishop had quietly slipped away following a message from American Cardinal Spellman to Archbishop Rohracher of Salzburg, telling him that Rožman 'could find sanctuary in the United States'. Soon after, on 11 November 1947, Rožman quietly disappeared from the Bishop of Klagenfurt's palace and made straight for the protection of Archbishop Rohracher in Salzburg. The Foreign Office noted that the story doing the rounds in Vienna was that Rožman had 'left Klagenfurt in an American army staff car, driven by an American driver!'[48]

This may explain why US intelligence soon discovered the real reason for Rožman's disappearance. They traced him to his hideout in Salzburg, and put him under close surveillance. They reported that Rožman enthusiastically resumed his work for the Nazi underground immediately he fled from Klagenfurt. The quisling Bishop had linked up with the Križari command and undertaken an extremely important assignment on their behalf.

According to the Americans, Rožman intended to visit Berne in Switzerland, where US intelligence officers had recently discovered the whereabouts of much of the Ustashi treasure Pavelić had sent abroad. With the help of Catholic priests, Pavelić had begun to transfer large quantities of gold and currency to Switzerland in early 1944. Some of the treasure had been taken to Italy by British Lieutenant Colonel Jonson to finance the Križari forces. Another portion went to Rome with Draganović and also ended up financing the terrorist network.[49]

But over 2,400 kilos of gold and other valuables still remained secreted in Berne. It was supposed to be used to 'aid refugees of the Catholic religion', but was really earmarked for the Ustashi's clandestine operations. Although the Allies had temporarily prevented them from gaining access to these funds, by early 1948 the time had come to use the Church to retrieve the loot.

In Berne, Rožman's Ustashi friends were engaged in wholesale fraud, using the black market to convert the gold into dollars, and later, into Austrian schillings. '[A]id to the refugees is accounted for at the official rate of exchange for dollars,' the American officers noted, adding that 'malpractices have been carried on (officially, the dollar is worth 10 schillings; on the black market, 100 to 150).' According to reliable information:

> Rožman is going to Berne to take care of these finances. The money is in a Swiss bank, and he plans to have most of it sent through to Italy and from there to the Ustashis in [the] Argentine.[50]

A short time later Rožman duly arrived in Berne, accompanied by Bishop Ivan Šarić, the 'hangman' of Sarajevo. By the end of May 1948, Rožman had apparently carried out this money laundering operation for the Ustashi, for he visited the US Consulate in Zurich and was given a 'non-quota immigration visa as a minister of religion'. He then travelled to the United States and settled in Cleveland, Ohio.[51]

The circle was now almost complete. Pavelić's stolen 'treasure' had been tracked down through close monitoring of the movements and activities of the quisling Bishop of Ljubljana. But this was only the beginning of the Križari's money laundering schemes. Through high level Church figures, the Križari command actually received Vatican funds. Some was used to induce the Italian government of Alcide de Gasperi to provide the weapons they required for their anti-Tito crusade . . .

Hints of this were first picked up in the Allied zone of Trieste by Special CIC Agent, Willard Thomas. In May 1947 one of his informants came into close contact with Križari 'Colonel', Drago Marinković. According to Thomas's source, Marinković had 'the responsibility for securing arms and funds from Italian sources', travelling widely on these missions between Trieste, Venice and Rome. Further, Marinković had 'contacted the Vatican in Rome where he recently was successful in securing a large sum of money, although whether this was received from the Vatican or from some other party through the facilities of the Vatican is not known'.[52]

Thomas noted that this money had been used successfully to procure weapons, 'as during the past week a truck and trailer carrying Sub Machine Guns camouflaged with furniture . . . was met by a group of people who were waiting to carry the arms into

Yugoslavia'. The US officer commented that while the West was apparently not helping the Križari in Italy, 'they are supposed to be furnishing aid across the Austrian border'.[53]

The source of these arms shipments was determined a few weeks later when the Americans investigated Slovenian Križari leader, Franjo Lipovec. According to their information, Lipovec had been one of the first Križari leaders recruited by British intelligence after the war. In 1945 he was picked up by the SIS in Trieste, where he was later 'employed on a salary basis' by a British Army intelligence unit.

The CIC officers established that Lipovec was the main liaison between the Križari and the Italian government. In August 1946 he met senior Italian military intelligence officers who 'proposed that some degree of cooperation should be established'.[54] Lipovec accepted their offer and 'sold himself and his plans completely' to the Italians. His plans were in turn furnished to de Gasperi's *chef de cabinet*, and the Italian Premier subsequently 'assured Lipovec that ... his government would *unofficially* do everything within their means to strengthen the Tito opposition.' Unconditional public support was promised when the situation was more favourable.

With the financial support of Italian intelligence, Lipovec and his comrades then launched a propaganda campaign to make new recruits among the *émigrés* in Trieste. The next step was to arm the Križari units there, and after several meetings with Italian intelligence, Lipovec reached an agreement 'whereby weapons from Italian Army supply depots would be made available to Lipovec for his onward forwarding to Križari elements' in Trieste.

In February and March 1947, eight arms shipments were delivered under this agreement, including over 500 automatic weapons, some 4,000 hand grenades, 100 pistols and over 30 time bombs. Italian intelligence paid the transportation expenses to take the weapons into Yugoslavia from the Allied zone of Trieste.[55]

A former British intelligence officer, who served in Trieste at this time, confirms these American reports. In a taped interview, he recalled that his orders were to establish a special anti-Communist security office in Trieste. Most of his team were British officers, but they co-ordinated their operations with both American intelligence and local Italian police. The latter were in effect Trieste's

Special Branch, or 'political police', but were really under Allied command.[56]

Their main task was to control Yugoslav subversive activities, including infiltrations into the so-called Free Territory of Trieste, which was under British military rule. In investigating Communist intelligence operations, this British officer came into contact with anti-Communist Yugoslav terrorists, who were smuggling weapons into their homeland, helped by Italian Fascists.

According to this officer, Trieste was the 'meeting point for the resistance forces inside Yugoslavia and the forces who were financing, controlling and directing them in Italy'. The main liaison was Professor Ivan Protulipac, described by the British officer as 'Father Draganović's man in Trieste'. In the 1930s, Protulipac was the leader of an official Church group, ironically also called the Križari. After the war, he took a leading role in the terrorist Križari, until Communist agents assassinated him in Trieste in late 1946.[57]

The British officer also confirms that Draganović was working closely with Italian intelligence, smuggling arms into Yugoslavia under cover of the Italian Red Cross. These were the same Italian intelligence officers described in the American reports as Lipovec's link to de Gasperi. The British officer was also aware of the West's role in the Križari's operations, although he had no personal involvement.

He told us that common criminals, especially drug smugglers and black marketeers, were frequently utilised to assist the Križari to cross the Yugoslav border. In his view, this was one reason why the West's political and military operations were a disaster. 'We always used the wrong elements. We took any crook, any compromised person', including Nazis and murderers.[58]

Although the British dominated the joint intelligence operation in Trieste, close liaison was maintained with the Americans. The Trieste CIC detachment received information about joint British–American operations involving

an Allied sponsored recruiting campaign ... for volunteers for the Križari Movement. Many of these volunteers have already been taken to an American training camp in or near Udine, where they receive training. They are furnished with American Army rations and uniforms, plus 700 lire pay daily ... On completion of their training the men are furnished with American arms and taken into Austria, from which they enter Jugoslav territory. They have use of British camps in Austria . . . to which they retire for periodic rests.[59]

The Americans believed this story was possibly Communist-inspired propaganda, 'circulated in an attempt to discredit the Americans, and as such, is not true at all'.[60] However, there certainly were Americans working in Trieste and Udine on joint Allied Križari operations.

For example, according to our former British intelligence contact, Colonel Lewis Perry was ostensibly with the US CIC detachment in Trieste during 1946 and 1947, although he did not wear any distinguishing military insignia on his uniform. 'I know he used to regularly go to Rome, and I'm absolutely sure he must have known Draganović'. As will be seen, Perry later became one of the key US links in Father Draganović's Ratline.

Perry was one of the few Western officers identified by name at the Križari 'show trial' in Zagreb in 1948, specifically accused of being the head of the 'spy centre in Trieste'.[61] The Yugoslavs found out a great deal about Perry from the defendants. For example, the most senior Križari on trial, Božidar Kavran, provided many details about the American's contacts with the terrorist network.

Kavran was the wartime commander of Ustashi headquarters, and then after the war was in charge of the Križari's Austrian base at Trofaiach. He worked directly under Pavelić and Draganović on Križari terrorist and intelligence operations. Nearly forty years later, his interrogation reports were smuggled out of Eastern Europe to the authors. These revealed many aspects of Perry's work in Trieste, especially his close relationship with Srečko Rover, one of the younger rising stars of the terrorist network. Kavran and Rover worked closely even before the war, when they were both underground Ustashi members in Bosnia, involved in a plot to assassinate King Peter.

When the Nazis arrived in 1941, Rover became a member of one of Pavelić's murderous Mobile Courts Martial, summarily executing the Ustashi's racial and political enemies. After serving on this roving extermination squad, Rover was sent to Austria for special officer training, and then promoted to serve in Pavelić's Personal Bodyguard, a repressive police unit similar to the Gestapo.[62]

After the war, Rover joined the throng of wanted war criminals hiding out in the Italian countryside, and soon enrolled in the

Križari underground. He got his false identity papers from Draganović at San Girolamo, allowing him to obtain official documents, especially Italian residency papers. Rover worked closely with Draganović, undertaking numerous missions on behalf of the Ustashi's 'grey eminence', and eventually rising to the very top of the Križari command.[63]

Early in 1946 Rover was dispatched to Trieste to work with Draganović's intelligence network. He contacted Colonel Perry and established close working relations with the American intelligence officer. Apparently Perry was impressed with Rover's proposals, for he recruited the Križari 'captain' and supplied him with travel and identity documents. The American then sent him into Yugoslavia to establish a clandestine route for infiltrating agents into Yugoslavia. It was the start of a very profitable relationship for the 'little wolf', the nickname fondly given to Rover by his Križari comrades.

Nearly every time Rover was in trouble with Western authorities, Perry came to his assistance. The Allied Nazi hunting units arrested Rover on many occasions, but Perry's interventions ensured his release. Rover's relationship with the American also gave the 'little wolf' access to resources and information which assured his rapid promotion through the Križari ranks, finally becoming Kavran's second-in-command at the Trofaiach base in Austria.

As the clandestine network expanded, Rover undertook many important assignments. At first he was a courier, carrying top secret instructions between Križari leaders. He also became skilled at procuring and forging sophisticated travel and identity documents, allowing him and his comrades to travel freely, even in Communist Yugoslavia. Then he recruited volunteers for the terrorist and intelligence missions.

After returning from his clandestine mission for Perry, Rover travelled to Rome and met with Draganović to report directly on his recent successes. He was soon working closely with other senior members of Draganović's network, including many who later turned up on trial in Zagreb.

From the very beginning of his relationship with Perry things seemed to go wrong. For example, Rover's first mission for the American had taken him to Rijeka and Zagreb. Although he returned safely, the very next person Rover sent in via this route was immediately captured. Despite this, the 'little wolf' told his closest comrades that he believed the route he had established through Trieste was perfectly safe, and should be used for further operations.

Perhaps it is only coincidental, but nearly every Križari operation on which Rover worked was a complete disaster. Pavelić himself came to suspect that Rover may have been a Communist double agent, or at least some sort of *provocateur*. Among the senior Križari leaders, Rover seems to have been one of the few who repeatedly entered Yugoslavia and avoided detection and arrest by Tito's secret police. Apparently Rover was extremely lucky, unlike the many Križari he recruited in Italy, Germany and Austria.

Under orders from Draganović and Kavran, he travelled through the numerous camps in the Western zones, persuading many Ustashi to enlist in the Križari. When he became Kavran's deputy at Trofaiach, he was in charge of the underground's radio communications. He was well acquainted with the secret codes used to communicate between the Austrian headquarters and the Križari units inside Yugoslavia.

When the last disastrous operations were launched in mid-1948, Rover was placed in charge of guiding the terrorist groups into the country. Coincidentally, all the men he took across the border were either killed or captured, most within hours, the stragglers within days. The survivors found themselves before Tito's court in Zagreb in 1948. It seems that Srečko Rover was one of a handful of senior Križari operatives not amongst their ranks. Later Rover ran similar fiascos from Australia.

In retrospect, it is clear that the Communist secret police were well informed about all major aspects of the Križari's plans. Some US intelligence officers in Salzburg had suspected this since late 1947, when Dr Petar Prokop approached them asking for 'active financial and moral support'. Prokop promised to carry out acts of terrorism inside Yugoslavia as proof of the Križari's 'ability and organization'. The Americans commented that 'Prokop may be an Agent Provocateur used by [the] Tito authorities in an attempt to compromise US Agencies'.[64]

The evidence presented at the Križari 'show trial' in 1948 left little doubt that the Communist secret police had used double agents to run a very sophisticated counter operation. Somehow they had obtained the secret radio codes used by the Križari, and were informed well in advance of the precise details of their operations. They knew the exact routes used by the groups, as well as the dates and times of their entry into the country. With these advantages, it was easy for the secret police to lure the unsuspecting Križari into their hands using their own radio codes. Once inside the country, they were picked up at will.

It was a pattern that was eerily repeated over the coming years. Despite these terrible setbacks the operations were continued, and even extended into other Communist countries. Throughout the 1950s and into the 1960s the Yugoslav government held trials of captured agents, many allegedly financed by and operating under the orders of Father Draganović. One US intelligence report detailed massive illegal currency dealings in Austria, noting that these financed 'sending couriers and agents into Yugoslavia'. The counter-intelligence officer concluded that 'these present and past activities are being carried out by high-ranking Ustasha adherents, in conjunction with the Austrian government and the Catholic Church, which are attempting to establish the "Intermarium" or "Inter-Danube" state, composed of all the Catholic nations in Southeast Europe.'[65]

Pavelić's Križari were just a part of a wider effort launched by the Vatican in co-operation with Western intelligence. Other underground Catholic armies had been raised to disrupt, and if possible overthrow, the Communist regimes of Central and Eastern Europe. In Czechoslovakia, Poland, the Baltic states and the Ukraine, clandestine Nazi groups were operating in close liaison with the Križari.

US intelligence initially thought that these operations went under the codename 'Integral'. They soon discovered that the Križari's partners were notorious Fascists, operating under the leadership of Ukrainian Nazi Stepan Bandera to build yet another powerful Catholic-dominated alliance – the Anti-Bolshevik Bloc of Nations. They were soon working for the West on operations similar to the Križari, which ended in the same disastrous way.[66]

Long before British and American intelligence officers enticed the Vatican into these operations, the Communist secret police had taken action to frustrate and destroy the Western-backed *émigrés*. It would be years before the true story of Communist penetration and manipulation of the Catholic Nazis emerged from the classified intelligence files.

PART TWO

Communism's War Against the Church

7
The Vatican's Black Orchestra

The first public hint that Communist agents had deeply penetrated the Holy See came in 1967, when Father Krunoslav Draganović suddenly disappeared behind the 'Iron Curtain'. The one man who knew every detail of the Ratlines, including the role of two Popes, was about to call a press conference inside Communist Yugoslavia. Previously it had been Pacelli's recurring nightmare about Munich which had dominated. Now it was Montini's turn to have nightmares.

Tito must have been delighted. It quickly turned into a spectacular propaganda coup. Draganović had been at the centre of the Vatican's intelligence network for over three decades, and been on the closest terms with both Pius XII and Paul VI, the reigning Pope. He had also collaborated with Western intelligence on a variety of sensitive operations.

Even better for Tito, Draganović was prepared to do the unthinkable, and openly heap praise on Communist Yugoslavia. By the time Father Draganović met with local and foreign journalists on 15 November 1967, he had actually been in Yugoslav hands for over two months. The Vatican's 'grey eminence' confidently addressed the assembled press corps before he would permit questions, and most accounts agree that he seemed to be completely in control.

Draganović's Ustashi friends were certainly unprepared for his performance. His previously bitter denunciations of Serbian and Communist domination of Croatia had completely disappeared, replaced with glowing praise for the 'democratisation and humanising of life' in Tito's Yugoslavia, and its commitment to de-Stalinisation.[1] A few days earlier, the Yugoslav press had published Draganović's letter to the District Attorney in Sarajevo, where he was living freely. He had nothing but praise for Tito's Yugoslavia, which 'with its independent ways and internal and international politics has so far been an example and guide to many nations'.[2]

To the undoubted consternation of many local Catholics, Draganović stated that religious freedom and the Church's mission were flourishing in Communist Yugoslavia. He also emphasised that he had returned to the country 'deliberately and freely' and not as the result of 'kidnapping, trickery, entrapment or police manoeuvres', as the *émigré* Ustashi press had claimed.[3]

However, Draganović's close confidant and co-worker on the Ratlines, Monsignor Milan Simčić, strongly disputed this. Father Draganović did not freely return to Yugoslavia, 'he was arrested by UDBA [the Yugoslav secret police]', he insisted in early 1990. According to Simčić, UDBA had laid an elaborate entrapment plan to lure Draganović to a meeting on the Yugoslav–Italian frontier, where he was kidnapped in mid-September 1967.[4]

Simčić claimed that the bait was laid by an UDBA officer, who happened to be distantly related to Draganović. Claiming to be disillusioned with Communism, he offered 'to confidentially inform the Americans about what the Yugoslav army was doing against the Atlantic Treaty [NATO]. Therefore UDBA arrested him through a trick.'[5]

Numerous versions soon gained currency among *émigré* Ustashi around the world. One popular story was that the priest had been an UDBA agent all along. It was even claimed that he had fled with San Girolamo's entire archives, which he promptly turned over to UDBA. Others speculated that Draganović had submitted to the wishes of Pope Paul VI, who asked him to return to his country for the good of the Church.[6]

Draganović's return also fascinated the Yugoslav media, but the semi-official 'inside' story was not published for nearly twenty years. In 1986 the Sarajevo-based *Svijet* (*The World*) magazine published a fifteen part series by a former UDBA officer and a journalist based on official documents. According to their version, an UDBA agent had indeed been involved, but not in the manner claimed by Simčić and the *émigré* Ustashi.

The articles disclosed that an UDBA officer by the name of 'Zlatko' had befriended Father Draganović in the early 1960s, maintaining close connections first in Rome and then later, in Vienna and Pressbaum in Austria. Draganović was apparently aware of Zlatko's mission, but nevertheless he allowed himself to be drawn into the UDBA trap. Finally, in late August 1967, he supposedly agreed to return.

On 10 September he met Zlatko at a hotel above Trieste and departed in a Yugoslav-registered Mercedes. A short time later they crossed into Yugoslavia and Draganović was taken first to Belgrade, and a few days later, to Sarajevo, where he was held by UDBA for a short time.[7] The senior Croatian prelate, Cardinal Šeper, hinted at foul play, claiming that UDBA had planted an agent in Draganović's inner circle.[8]

However, as Western intelligence desperately scrambled to re-evaluate the Vatican's Ratlines, many fingers pointed directly at Draganović. The old hands were horrified at the possibility that he had really worked for the Communists all along. The reaction of one former British intelligence officer was typical. As previously discussed, this intelligence specialist found Father Draganović a cold and unapproachable character. With the benefit of hindsight, he believed that the priest must have worked for the Communists at some time:

> I think he was very much a realist, and I'm not certain to this day whether he was not a double agent . . . it's impossible that Draganović, having been . . . the 'grey eminence' of Balkan intelligence in the Vatican, particularly from a Croatian point of view . . . [would] go back and end his life . . . [there] . . . on a voluntary basis. I just don't believe it. He went on a voluntary basis, he was never kidnapped . . . if they didn't kill him, it means he was a double agent. There's no two ways about it, in my opinion.[9]

When confronted with this claim, Monsignor Simčić expressed complete amazement:

> This is beyond logic, beyond everything. I knew him in the very depths of his soul . . . he was a great Croatian who could not even conceive of Yugoslavia. He fought all his life for a free Croatia. He was against any Yugoslavia, regardless of the politics of the regime . . . Draganović was religiously anti-Communist. Now, you tell me, how could he be a Yugoslav spy, especially for Communist Yugoslavia?[10]

Far from being a cold realist, as claimed by the British officer, 'Draganović was very naive', and had been completely fooled by a very effective Communist spy. According to Simčić, 'a man of ill repute . . . a notorious spy', had indeed infiltrated Father Draganović's headquarters at San Girolamo in Rome. His name was Miroslav Varoš.[11]

Varoš's career closely tracked Draganović's. They both came from Sarajevo, and soon after Draganović went to Rome in 1943,

Varoš followed. He, too, became active in Ustashi *émigré* politics, quickly establishing close relations with San Girolamo, where he worked for Draganović as a typist. He wrote prolifically for various *émigré* papers and, according to the Communists, worked for a number of Western intelligence agencies.[12]

Simčić, however, was certain that it was Varoš who lured Draganović into UDBA's hands. It was also Varoš who had organised the guerrilla operations in Yugoslavia. He surely was a double agent, for after Draganović's arrest, he returned to Yugoslavia and continued his work for UDBA.[13] If Monsignor Simčić's version is correct, the priest who smuggled thousands of fugitive Nazis to freedom with the support of Pius XII, Montini and powerful sections of Allied intelligence, was simply tricked and kidnapped because of his naivety.

The British officer could not recall this naive streak in Draganović's character.[14] In some ways it does not matter who is correct. For both Simčić and the British officer agree that the Communists had successfully penetrated the Vatican's Ratline. Whether it was Draganović or Varoš is really academic; either way, Tito knew everything about the Holy See's activities, and Pope Paul VI's key role.

In a taped interview, Milan Simčić was adamant that the Communists did not obtain their information from Draganović. 'He was also a great man in tragedy,' he said proudly. 'When they caught him and forced him to give certain statements, even then he was great in saving others – he accepted the responsibility . . . UDBA didn't get anything important.' Draganović later smuggled a letter to Simčić, telling him: 'Be at peace, no one is in danger as a result of my words.'[15]

Certainly, the Yugoslav public would not have known that Draganović had been at the centre of the Vatican's most remarkable operation of this century. Instead of re-running the 1940s propaganda line against the Holy See, virtually no details of the Church's involvement were publicly disclosed. The Communist-controlled press merely reported that Draganović had 'skilfully avoided giving direct answers to some "delicate questions"'. However, it is certain that UDBA had forbidden Draganović to tell the world what he knew. Instead, he was ordered to bitterly denounce the Ustashi's international terrorist network and, at every appropriate opportunity, to praise Tito's regime.[16]

It should be recalled that this regime had consistently labelled Draganović as a war criminal, the organiser of an elaborate Nazi-smuggling system, and the brains behind the Križari terrorist operations. Yet when they finally had him in their hands, they did nothing to punish him.[17] Instead, he was permitted to shelter behind an amnesty passed by Tito's government in 1962. Obviously a deal had been done, for Draganović assured the Yugoslav public that 'the organs of the state authorities behaved towards me correctly, what is more, humanely and with consideration as towards a human being and priest, for which I sincerely and publicly thank them'.[18]

Eventually, although they kept a close eye on him, the secret police allowed him to settle quietly in Sarajevo. He promptly went back to work for his beloved Church, and spent the rest of his days updating the general register of the Catholic Church in Yugoslavia, which he had published in 1939.[19] He died peacefully in June 1982, and although UDBA immediately confiscated a large collection of his papers, no plausible official explanation of his 'defection' has been forthcoming.

Despite the extraordinary propaganda coup which the *public* revelations had handed the Communists, Monsignor Simčić was certain that they had not successfully blackmailed Draganović:

'Noooo', he said emphatically, 'Draganović was not a man who could be blackmailed ... I'm 100% sure that they could not have blackmailed him ... Nor did they get anything significant from him.'[20]

Perhaps, in the end, Father Draganović was sent home as a sacrificial lamb – part of a sophisticated deal struck between Tito and the Vatican. The roots of his ultimate demise can probably be traced to 1960 when another series of "show trials" occurred in Yugoslavia. Draganović was again said to be the organiser of an underground network of Ustashi priests, operating in widely dispersed areas of the country. Apparently, his money laundering days had continued unabated, for he had allegedly laundered millions of dinars to support the network's subversive activities.[21]

Soon after these further sensational allegations, Draganović 'removed himself' from San Girolamo, heralding a marked improvement in Vatican–Yugoslav relations.[22] His old friend Vilim Cecelja, who had run the Austrian end of the Ratline so efficiently, lamented that Draganović 'was not accepted any more' in senior

Vatican circles. In fact, he was distinctly on the outer from that moment on, and as 'he was in the top leadership, he was the one decapitated'.[23] According to the Yugoslavs, Draganović was actually removed from San Girolamo, and assaulted by powerful factions within the Vatican. It was shortly after this that the mysterious UDBA officer 'Zlatko' contacted Draganović and supposedly began the long process of 'bringing him home'.[24]

Over the next few years a remarkable thaw took place between the Holy See and Communist Yugoslavia, culminating in a series of top level talks and ultimately a protocol which virtually normalised relations in June 1966.[25] Fourteen months later, Father Draganović was back home, praising the protocol and denouncing the 'direct political activities of priests' which had 'in the past brought [the Church] so much ill fortune'.[26]

Perhaps Krunoslav Draganović was a victim of the new mood sweeping the Catholic Church in the wake of Pius XII's death, the ascension of John XXIII and the radical departures of the Second Vatican Council. But it seems much more likely that the deal that had been struck between Tito and the Vatican included a provision requiring Draganović to retire behind the 'Iron Curtain' and quietly co-operate with UDBA. The Communist secret police knew almost everything anyway, and this was probably the reason why the Vatican was forced to yield. This may have been the price that Father Draganović paid – even willingly – for the dreadful errors the Vatican had made in establishing the Ratlines.

Strangely enough, both Monsignor Simčić and the semi-official UDBA version agree on at least one important point: Draganović performed extremely well under interrogation. According to *Svijet*, he was extremely cunning, defeating at least one senior UDBA officer entirely and pushing another to the point of total exasperation. The Communists admitted that Draganović cleverly evaded their probing when he believed they did not know the answer to their questions. But when he was certain they were well informed, he co-operated.[27]

However, new evidence has recently emerged that he in fact admitted a great deal to UDBA. In 1990 a copy of one of Draganović's most revealing statements was smuggled out from an Eastern European Communist source to the authors. This is the first time that Father Draganović's confession to UDBA has been in Western hands. The document is dated 26 September 1967 and is undoubtedly the first comprehensive statement made by the priest after his mysterious return. It described in great detail how the Vatican built the San Girolamo Ratline, and the close connections maintained by the Pope's Refugee Commission with the Red Cross and Italian and Western intelligence.[28]

Draganović also disclosed many details of the Vatican's role in saving Pavelić's war booty, and the operation of the Križari's underground terrorist network. Perhaps UDBA already knew most of these details from Varoš and other sources. A considerable amount could only have been provided by Draganović personally. Even *Svijet* admitted that his information had enabled UDBA to piece together the labyrinth of the *émigré* underground, and its connections to Western intelligence. UDBA interrogated Draganović almost non-stop for two weeks on these matters, revealing everything about the Ustashi diaspora, and corroborating UDBA's own voluminous files.[29]

However, even after his death, the Communists did not publish the whole story. Although *Svijet* obviously based their 1986 articles on Draganović's interrogation reports, no mention was made of the key issues canvassed in this first document. In fact, Draganović's confession gave the Communists a unique insight into the secrets of the Vatican's Ratlines. They were secrets which Tito chose to bury very securely, for they have never been publicly disclosed before, even in Yugoslavia. They included:

★ an intimate description of his high level contacts with the Vatican Secretariat of State

★ a detailed outline of San Girolamo's smuggling system, including the names of the priests who held key positions, and the formal connections they maintained with the Pope's Welfare Commission

★ the names of the Allied officers with whom he had worked closely

★ the names of his Christian Democrat contacts inside the Italian Ministry of Internal Affairs

★ a complete overview of his senior role in co-ordinating the Vatican's Ratlines for all Central and Eastern European nationalities

★ minute descriptions of secret missions he had undertaken on behalf of the Vatican

★ an account of his own role in saving and smuggling the Ustashi's stolen treasure

★ details of the Ustashi's money laundering operation in Switzerland

★ descriptions of the leading personalities, command structure and operations of the Križari[30]

The version so carefully contrived by UDBA in *Svijet* ignores these aspects. They did let slip at least one very interesting fact: Father Draganović had also been working for West German security chief, Reinhard Gehlen, the former Nazi intelligence General on the Eastern front.[31]

It seems that Draganović had penetrated all the major Western security services. Yet if Milan Simčić is correct and Miroslav Varoš, not Krunoslav Draganović, was the UDBA spy in San Girolamo, then the Communists knew nearly every detail of the Ratlines before Draganović returned home. The Vatican had probably long since realised this, for it turned out that the Soviets had penetrated the *émigré* Nazi groups long before the Pope had decided to use them. Like Draganović, their agent had penetrated most Western intelligence services, and a few more besides . . .

While Eugenio Pacelli was still a Papal Nuncio in Munich, and before Pius XI had become Pope, Soviet military intelligence had already recruited an agent who would wreck the Vatican's anti-Bolshevik schemes for the next half century. Ironically, the Communists utilised the same tactics and methods used by the Czarist secret police over the previous few centuries. The Empire had always been paranoid about the numerous ethnic groups which sought independence from the Russian centre.

Decades before Felix Dzerzhinsky organised the fearsome Cheka, the Czar's secret police had become skilled manipulators of these dissident nationalists. Whenever and wherever Ukrainian, Byelorussian or Baltic separatist movements grew up, the Czar's police were busily penetrating them with moles. Their tasks included creating intense factionalism and personality splits, dividing the movements and shattering their nationalist dreams. One of the goals of the *agents provocateurs* was to provoke the would-be revolutionaries into taking premature action which could easily be defeated by the Czar's men.

The Bolsheviks were mindful of the Czar's successes. After all, they had themselves fallen victim to exactly this tactic. It was hardly surprising that the Communists decided to employ the same methods against their anti-Communist opponents, who fled in the wake of the Red Army's victory in the civil war. In fact, some of the police officials who had run these operations under the Czar were recruited into the Cheka, where they faithfully passed their secrets to the Bolsheviks. Soviet intelligence evolved into two rival agencies, the civilian KGB and the military GRU. For the last seventy years they have faithfully copied the Czar's *agents provocateurs* tactics.[32]

In each generation, Soviet intelligence created 'anti-Communist' *émigré* front groups, ostensibly to foment revolution and topple Bolshevism. The front groups attracted support from the West. Considerable financial assistance was supplied and close ties forged with various Western intelligence services. This enabled the Communist double agents running the front groups to co-opt the legitimate *émigré* opposition, splinter their leadership and provoke them into premature and poorly organised rebellions which were easily defeated. More importantly, the false front groups were a vehicle for long-term Soviet penetration of Western society.

The first and classic example was *The Trust*, organised by Felix Dzerzhinsky himself. It was supposedly an organisation of dissident monarchists and generals, plotting to overthrow Lenin. British intelligence poured huge sums of money into *The Trust* without realising they were subsidising the Communists. This is the famous spy scandal that enabled the Soviets to capture Sidney Reilly, the much renowned 'ace of spies'.[33] During the 1950s the CIA fell for a similar trap and poured millions into Operation WIN in Poland, only to discover to their horror that their anti-Communist forces were largely a figment of Soviet imagination. For seventy years *émigré* agents were a critical factor in ensuring Communism's survival.[34]

What no one ever realised was that there was yet another *émigré* group headed by a long term Communist agent which had an equally disastrous effect on the Holy See. The Vatican's nemesis was a member of the Czar's nobility, Prince Anton Vasilevich Turkul, arguably the greatest professional spy of the twentieth century. During Turkul's extraordinary career he penetrated the Imperial Russian Army, the French Deuxième Bureau, the Japanese General Staff, Mussolini's headquarters, both British Secret Services (MI5 and MI6), Ribbentrop's personal intelligence service (Bureau Jahnke), Admiral Canaris's Abwehr, Wehrmacht Intelligence on the Eastern front (the Fremde Heere Ost or Foreign Armies East, headed by General Reinhard Gehlen), the SS Security Service (SD) and passed Soviet disinformation to virtually every nation in both the Axis and Allied camps.

After World War II, Turkul worked for West German intelligence (the Gehlen Org), collaborated with many of the spy services of NATO, including the American Military Intelligence Service (MIS – for offensive intelligence), the US Army Counter Intelligence Corps (CIC – for defensive purposes), the ultra-secret State Department Office of Policy Co-ordination and the Central Intelligence Agency. Unlike Kim Philby, Turkul was not exposed during his lifetime. He died in 1959, without anyone proving that his exclusive loyalty lay with Soviet Military Intelligence, the GRU.

It appears that not even senior officers of the KGB knew that the GRU had placed an agent right inside Vatican intelligence. Turkul was the double agent who wrecked all of Pius XI's hopes to overthrow the Bolsheviks, and later sabotaged Pius XII's plans to mediate an Anglo-German alliance against the Soviets. Prince Turkul was at once the Vatican's best secret agent, and its greatest secret enemy. Until now, his story has never been fully told.

No one knows when Prince Turkul was first recruited by the Bolsheviks. Much of his early history is shrouded in mystery. Even his birthdate is uncertain. One intelligence report says that he was born on 12 November 1892 in Odessa.[35] Another states that he was born exactly nine months earlier in Bessarabia.[36]

When he was in his early twenties, Prince Turkul served the Czar as an officer in the Don River Legion. After the Revolution, he joined the White counter-revolutionary army, was promoted to Colonel and at some later time to Brigadier General. Turkul's command of his White division was not without controversy, for US intelligence recorded that it was 'alleged that while in this position, shipments received by him of British arms were actually turned over to the Red Forces'.[37]

One of the keys to Communist victory in the Russian civil war was that several of the opposing White generals were really working for Lenin and Trotsky. In addition to Prince Turkul, Generals Skoblin, Voss and the son of General Abramow were also double agents. Perhaps the Bolshevik triumph was due less to Trotsky's military genius and more to the brilliance of his intelligence service. After the civil war, the Communist double agents had still not been discovered. Turkul and the other White Russian officers were evacuated to Paris by the sympathetic French Government, which, along with the British, had financed much of the anti-Bolshevik effort.[38]

In 1925 British intelligence sent Commander Dunderdale to liaise with the White *émigrés* in Paris. The older generals, led by Baron Wrangel and Aleksander Kutepov, had established a White Russian veterans' corps known by its cyrillic acronym, ROWS.[39] ROWS supervised a secret 'Combat Organisation' as well as a counter-intelligence service, the Inner Line, to concoct schemes for restoring the Czarist monarchy in Russia.[40] The recently released intelligence files explain why their plans met with little success.

Soon after ROWS was created, the double agents went to work to sabotage the *émigré* resistance. ROWS was to be discredited as ineffective or exposed as totally penetrated by the Communists. A number of new front groups (even more dominated by the Bolshevik clique) were to be established in its place. Over the next ten years, the older generals of ROWS were kidnapped, murdered or assassinated. Turkul's fellow agent, General Skoblin, would emerge as head of the ROWS Inner Line by climbing over the bodies of his victims.[41]

Turkul was among the original group of double agents who came to Paris from Gallipoli in 1920, and was later suspected of involvement in the plots against the ROWS leaders, Wrangel and Kutepov.[42] However, Turkul was spared much of the ensuing scandal in Paris as he was quickly re-assigned to the Balkan section of ROWS. He was in fact being prepared for the second phase of the Bolshevik strategy.

According to top secret information of the 'utmost discretion to British intelligence', Turkul's new superior was Claudius Voss, alias Alexandrov. Voss was regarded as one of Britain's leading agents inside the Inner Line during the 1920s. This key agent was in charge of counter-intelligence for Slovakia. As was later discovered, Voss was loyal to the Bolsheviks, not to ROWS or the British.[43]

Voss's direct superior in the Inner Line was General Abramow, chief of the Balkan section in Sofia, where Turkul had also conveniently settled. Voss pushed General Abramow out of the way by exposing his son as an agent of Soviet civilian intelligence. This was a cynical example of how the GRU sacrificed agents from a rival Communist organisation (the predecessor of the civilian KGB), in order to advance their own men.[44]

Predictably, the Abramow scandal, coming on the heels of the series of assassinations and kidnappings in Paris, substantially discredited ROWS in the eyes of the White Russian *émigré* community.[45] Another front group was waiting in the wings to replace it. Since 1924, Voss had actively participated in the founding of the Narodny Trudovoi Soyuz (NTS), or People's Labour Alliance, and had talent-spotted young Prince Turkul as NTS's future star. Originally dependent on ROWS, the stepchild NTS lost no time in denouncing the old Monarchist organisations.[46]

Turkul emerged as a leader of the 'new generation' of NTS anti-Communist *émigrés* and a variety of other front groups, all untainted by the mud that clung to the old ROWS leadership. Between 1927 and 1931 Turkul shuttled between Sofia and Paris, ostensibly keeping himself above the fray, but always making new contacts. According to US intelligence, his 'enemies considered him the ruiner of ROWS and an opportunist'.[47]

When NTS went to work for Menzies of British intelligence, the Soviet agents, including Turkul, were already in place.[48] By 1930 Turkul's cover as an anti-Communist organiser was impeccable and for the next several decades he and the NTS remained at the forefront of Menzies's anti-Communist intrigues:

> The main group used by MI6 for operations inside the Soviet Union until the end of the 1960's was the People's Labor Alliance (NTS) founded in 1930 in Belgrade by social democratic Russian *émigrés* who sought the overthrow of the Communist regime from within and its replacement with a parliamentary democracy.[49]

American intelligence had a rather different view of NTS ideology, calling it Fascist, anti-democratic and violently anti-Semitic.[50] It should be noted that such attitudes did not prevent the Americans from taking over NTS from the British in the 1950s, not realising that this right-wing group had been thoroughly infiltrated by Soviet intelligence since the 1920s.

By 1930, the Soviet spy services had completely polarised the *émigré* community in Paris. The military branch, later the GRU, focused mainly on the ethnic Russian exiles. NTS with its pro-Russian orientation attracted those exiles who favoured the restoration of the geographical borders of the Czarist empire, including the ethnic minorities of the Baltic provinces, the Ukraine, Byelorussia and the Slavic regions of the Balkans. The NTS insisted on retaining these non-Russian minorities as subordinate parts of Greater Russia once the Bolsheviks were overthrown.

The Soviet civilian espionage branch, later the KGB, generally concentrated on the non-Russian ethnic minorities which had organised separatist groups to break away from Great Russian domination. These rival *émigré* organisations – Intermarium, Prometheus and the Abramtchik Faction etc. – had an anti-Russian orientation. Unlike the GRU's recruits, these exiles from the minority populations hated Russian imperialism and favoured splintering the Soviet Union into a loose confederation.

Instead of unifying Russian and non-Russian *émigrés* around their common hatred of Bolshevism, *agents provocateurs* ensured that the dissidents spent more time fighting each other than their common enemy. The pattern of division and competition, so skilfully employed by Czarist police and taken over by the Cheka after World War I, lasted well into the Cold War. No matter which way the anti-Bolshevik *émigrés* turned, Soviet double agents were waiting to co-opt their strategies.

As Menzies's biographer confirms, His Majesty's Secret Service recruited *émigré* cadres for 'terrorism and sabotage' against the Soviets. Britain was not alone in employing terrorists before World War II. Few Western intelligence services had scruples when it came to dealing with extremist groups, even those with Fascist tendencies like NTS, as long as they professed anti-Communism.[51]

The truth is that during the 1920s and 1930s a little dose of right-wing extremism was perfectly acceptable to several intelligence services. Turkul always claimed to oppose the anti-Russian philosophies espoused by groups such as the Ukrainian-dominated Anti-Bolshevik Bloc of Nations (ABN). However, he never let his affiliation with NTS prevent him from occasional collaboration with the minority separatists who also worked for the British and the French. He was hired by the Deuxième Bureau in Paris just as the Vatican and the French General Staff were recruiting White Russian supporters for Intermarium.[52]

Since Intermarium was dedicated to independence for non-Russian minorities, it may seem contradictory to have included ethnic Russians as members. But, as William Gowen reported, everyone was welcome in Intermarium as long as they were anti-Soviet, and 'it is supposedly for this reason that the "White" Russians are included as the first victims of Communism'.[53]

Indeed, there is evidence that factional groups like Intermarium were formed out of the disintegration of ROWS. According to

Gowen, Intermarium was 'an outgrowth of a "White" Russian society organised in Paris before World War II by a former Czarist General ... of the old Paris group'.[54] In view of the recently discovered evidence that White Russian double agents deliberately arranged the disintegration of ROWS, there is ample reason to suspect that Intermarium inherited the same group of Red agents who had infiltrated ROWS in the early 1920s.[55]

To illustrate the confusion of the times, some intelligence services used the term 'White Russian' to refer to anti-Communist ethnic Russians, while other agencies called the Byelorussians 'White Russians', although they were a separate ethnic minority opposed to both Red and White Russians. Although Byelorussia literally means 'White Russia' in English, the term is similar to but not the same as, the Russian word for the anti-Communist White forces. To compound the confusion, some Byelorussians were Reds as well, working with NTS's White Russian network for the Soviets.[56] The ethnographic lines were further blurred by frequent inter-changes between the various Soviet and Western intelligence services and their various front groups.

One wonders how the Soviets could keep it all straight, but it should be recalled that confusion was part of their game plan. Indeed, the Abramtchik Faction illustrates the complex intelligence cross-overs between the NTS and the separatists. The British-sponsored Prometheus network supposedly controlled the Abramtchik Faction in Paris which in turn controlled another Byelorussian sub-group which was part of NTS at the same time they were receiving funds from the Vatican through a Baltic Bishop. The head of this Byelorussian hodge-podge was Mikolai Abramtchik, yet another Communist agent in pre-war Paris.[57] Abramtchik was a Byelorussian (White Russian) separatist working for the anti-Communist Great Russians while secretly working for the Reds. If such devious complexities gave headaches to the Communists, it was nothing compared to the pain they inflicted on the West and the Vatican. A disgruntled American agent simply threw up his hands and privately referred to all the *émigrés* as 'lower slobbovians' after the Al Capp comic strip. It really was not funny in view of what happened.

The one thing that is clear is that back in the 1920s, before Western intelligence groups like Intermarium and Prometheus were even formed, the Soviets had infiltrated each new organisation that popped up in Paris. Control of counter-intelligence screening for the Parisian *émigrés* had already been taken over by the Communists. The trusted Inner Line security apparatus was riddled with agents like Skoblin and Voss who could supply false vetting for double agents. Moreover, Turkul himself was well placed to infiltrate agents into every faction under the guise of NTS's broad-minded collaboration.

Since Turkul was supported by both British and French intelligence, it is not surprising that NTS eventually developed networks among the traditionally pro-Russian Serbs in Yugoslavia (the Mihailović Faction which was later dropped by Britain in favour of Tito). Turkul also had contacts inside the traditional anti-Russian Ukrainian separatist movement (the Melnyk Faction which was later dropped by British intelligence in favour of Stephen Bandera's group). Turkul even had contacts with the Abramtchik Faction of the Byelorussians who supported anyone who was in power at any particular moment. Abramtchik in fact worked for both the Poles and the Soviets, collaborated with the Nazis and was later passed on to the CIA by the British.[58]

In view of the tendency of the exiles to work simultaneously for anyone who paid them, Anthony Cave Brown is probably correct to list the Abramtchik Faction and other pre-war groups as working for the British, while acknowledging the CIA's estimate that the *émigrés* took 'handouts' from more than one Western intelligence service.[59] Soviet intelligence must have been amused as one spy service after the other swallowed the *émigré* bait.

The anti-Communist networks in Paris soon attracted the attention of the infant German intelligence service, which opened a file on General Turkul in 1927.[60] One German officer in particular, Wilhelm Canaris, wanted to join the *émigré* game, and offered to pool German support for the common cause:

> During this same period ... Canaris also had some part in founding an embryonic intelligence network in Central Europe and the Balkans, and co-operated with at least one Entente agency – most probably the British – against Communist agents who had begun to flood into Western Europe to provoke revolutions in support of the Kremlin.[61]

A few years later, on 1 January 1934, Admiral Canaris became Chief of the German Military Intelligence Service, the Abwehr.[62]

As we shall see, there can be little doubt that Turkul was the go-between for joint Anglo-German co-operation against the Communists. During the 1930s Menzies's representative to the *émigré* groups in Paris was Charles Howard Ellis, Dick or Dickie to his friends, of whom he had many among the Russian exile community:

> Dick Ellis dealt with anti-Communist exiles in Europe. He was the SIS expert on what Stalin called the nationalities question – the euphemism for unrest among non-Russians making up half the population of the USSR. Stalin regarded White Russians as potential leaders of revolt. Ellis dealt with the best known of the White Russian leaders in Paris, General Andrei Turkul – and encouraged him to keep up his powerful Nazi connections. The Nazi Germans had secret plans for using White Russians and Ukrainians to overthrow Stalin.[63]

Perhaps Ellis thought he was doing the right thing in helping Admiral Canaris prepare for war against the hated Communists. To this day, there is some question whether Ellis aided the Nazis on his own or under instructions from Menzies. Before 1939 it made sense to share British networks with the Germans in the common anti-Soviet struggle.[64] Unfortunately, Ellis was also using Turkul's German connections for personal gain, augmenting his meagre salary by working on the side for Admiral Canaris. Even after Hitler came to power, he was a paid Nazi agent and later admitted selling the rosters of British intelligence agents.[65]

In 1936 General Turkul was doing a little selling of his own: behind Menzies's back he had peddled NTS to the Japanese. According to his recently declassified intelligence file, Anton Turkul is listed as an agent who 'worked for the Japanese in Russia, head of [the] Russian fascist party in Japan, speaks fluent Japanese'.[66] The Japanese paid Turkul through a bank account in New York right up until Pearl Harbor. Turkul later bragged that his organisation had been subsidised by the Japanese General Staff which regarded NTS as an excellent method of keeping an eye on Soviet intentions.[67]

The Japanese did not realise that the Soviet GRU was keeping an eye on them. Turkul's GRU contact in Japan was one Richard Sorge, a German journalist who had infiltrated the Japanese Army for the GRU.[68] After the ring had worked successfully for a few years, Turkul decided in 1938 to sell his own 'Japanese' net to the

Germans. Turkul used as his go-between a German Jew, code-named MAX KLATT, whose real name was Richard Kauder. 'Klatt' claimed to have a spy ring inside the top levels of the Soviet military which was willing to sell documents to the Abwehr.

General Turkul wrapped such a shroud of secrecy around himself and Klatt that, as late as 1961, 'Herr Klatt' was described by Ladislav Farago as the most effective (and mysterious) of all the Nazi spies:

This inscrutable man (whose real name and true identity were never established) was *the* Secret Agent Extraordinary of the Abwehr against the Soviet Union. Who he was, how he looked, and what made him work for the Abwehr, aside from purely mercenary considerations, I do not know ... suddenly he blossomed out as a secret agent on a massive scale...

In August, 1938, Klatt arrived in Vienna and was taken by a mutual friend to the colonel [of the Abwehr] ... He came to the meeting with a startling amount of intelligence, especially about the innards of the Soviet Air Force. He claimed to have a link to the Soviet Legation in Sofia and said he was receiving the bulk of his information from the Soviet Union via short-wave radio. Although he was extremely accommodating, he steadfastly refused to reveal anything more about his sources, but he did volunteer to leave his material with the Abwehr so that it might be examined closely before a deal was made ...

His material stood the test of the most painstaking checking. The discovery of this remarkable agent was considered so important that it was reported directly to the Chief of the General Staff, an unusual step, and, from then on, the Klatt material was handled with top priority by special officers in Berlin. His data became the basis of German planning against the USSR on the highest echelon, something few spies in history could claim.

When the deal was made (and it was fantastic in terms of money; Klatt was extremely expensive), the new master spy returned to Sofia to become the top secret agent – and virtually the only direct-action spy – the Abwehr had working full-time in this important sector of the secret war. This phenomenal spy never disappointed his employers. And he never ceased to intrigue them ... All efforts over the years to disclose anything at all about Klatt personally, and about his sources, proved in vain.[69]

But who were the 'special officers in Berlin ... at the highest echelon' who put this mysterious Jew in charge of Nazi espionage against the Soviets? US intelligence identified Admiral Canaris as one of Klatt's superiors.[70] But the Turkul/Klatt team had another contact whose name has been kept secret for the last fifty years.

General Turkul and his Jewish assistant 'Klatt' worked directly for
Oberst (Colonel) Kurt Jahnke, Chief of the Jahnkebureau, Ribbentrop's personal intelligence service. Jahnke was also a trusted
adviser to Rudolf Hess and Hitler himself. During World War II
all of Jahnke's records for the years 1933 to 1938 were confiscated
by the SS.[71]

However, one senior SS officer read the Jahnke dossiers before
they vanished. Eleven years after World War II, Walter Schellenberg wrote his memoirs, in which he vividly recalled how Jahnke
had developed 'excellent connections with Japan' through unusual
channels, involving a former Czarist officer and a German Jew.[72]

General Turkul was not mentioned by name, an understandable
precaution since both of them were still working for the British SIS
at the time the memoirs were published.[73] Still, Schellenberg left
substantial clues, confirmed by recently declassified American
intelligence files, which clearly identify Turkul as the Czarist
officer who worked for the Nazi intelligence hierarchy.

For example, Schellenberg boasts that this agent ran a spy ring
inside Stalin's General Staff at Marshal Rokossovsky's Soviet
military headquarters.[74] American intelligence files list Rokossovsky's General Staff as one of Turkul's sources.[75] Similarly, Schellenberg states that one of Jahnke's contacts in Japan was Richard
Sorge.[76] American intelligence files state that Sorge passed information to Berlin through Turkul's assistant, Klatt.[77]

The recently declassified files also confirm that Schellenberg's
unnamed German Jew was Max Klatt, Turkul's Jewish intelligence chief who worked for Jahnke and Admiral Canaris before
being taken over by the SS. Schellenberg's memoirs detail how the
SS helped Jahnke protect his German Jew from the Gestapo
because he was such an invaluable intelligence source on Japan.
Schellenberg further identifies the rescued German Jew as the chief
of a world-wide 'information network [which] went through various countries and penetrated every stratum of society. He furnished
quick and exact reports from the senior staffs of the Russian
Army.'[78]

There was only one team of a Czarist officer and a German Jew
with 'excellent Japanese connections' who spied on the Soviets for
the Abwehr and were later protected by the SS from the Gestapo.
Schellenberg's account is confirmed in all important details by the
secret post-war interviews of Turkul and Klatt. But there was

something which Schellenberg mentioned which the earlier investigations had missed, something that only Schellenberg had seen: the files on Kurt Jahnke's secret connection to Turkul. Schellenberg's recollection of these long destroyed documents is of more than academic interest. As we shall see, the evidence shows that Turkul became Jahnke's courier to the Vatican.

On 26 August 1939 Hitler shocked his General Staff with news of the Ribbentrop–Molotov pact. It was now safe, he told them, to attack Poland. The war would go well, he predicted. 'I am only afraid that at the last minute some *Schweinhund* will produce a plan of mediation.'[79]

Kurt Jahnke tried to do just that the following day. On 27 August he 'used every conceivable means to bring an English intelligence man to Hitler' for eleventh-hour peace negotiations. Much to Jahnke's dismay the British agent was turned away when he arrived in Berlin. Jahnke knew that an alliance with the Soviets would mean war with Britain, but Hitler's mind was made up. So was Jahnke's. If Hitler could not understand that Germany must ally itself with Britain against the Soviet Union, then Hitler must be removed.

On 29 August, Jahnke's British agent returned to London and reported that the German General Staff were plotting to depose the Nazi regime. Word leaked back to the Gestapo who wanted to arrest Jahnke for high treason, but Admiral Canaris stopped the indictment.[80]

For years Canaris and Jahnke had been secretly plotting to overthrow Hitler and form an Anglo-German alliance against Stalin. There is evidence of careful pre-arrangement with the Vatican to pass the plotters' messages in the event of hostilities. On 3 September 1939, the same day that Britain and France declared war on Germany, Admiral Canaris made contact with British intelligence through the Vatican. One week later, Canaris passed the Vatican news of Nazi atrocities against Catholic priests and Jews in Poland. The Vatican gave the information to French and British intelligence.[81]

The Vatican's plan to help Canaris and Jahnke replace Hitler did not sit well with the Soviets in 1939. Stalin wanted Germany, France and Britain to fight a long and bloody war until the Red Army could move in and take over Central Europe. If this plan were to succeed, the Vatican had to be prevented from helping the

German opposition to negotiate peace with Britain. Apparently the GRU (and Jahnke) sent their best agent. Sometime before the outbreak of war, Prince Turkul moved from Berlin to Rome.[82]

On the eve of war, the anti-Hitler group made contact with Pius XII, who had just assumed St Peter's throne. In October the Pope was asked to play the part of intermediary between Germany and Britain. Canaris had selected Dr Joseph Müller, a Catholic lawyer from Munich, as his first courier to the Vatican. In October, Müller arrived in Rome and met his old friend, Monsignor Kaas, near the Quo Vadis Chapel off the Appian Way. The Jahnke–Canaris group of conspirators was soon given the code name *Schwarze Kapelle* after the Black Chapel in Rome. But the anti-Hitler group is better known as the Black Orchestra; apparently *Schwarze Kapelle* is a German pun on the *Rote Kapelle*, the famous Soviet spy ring known as the Red Orchestra. Subsequent developments in the Vatican revealed that there was more than irony involved in the similarity of names:

> By the first fortnight of October 1939, Müller was able to report to Canaris and [his deputy] Oster that the Pope had consented to serve the *Schwarze Kapelle* as intermediary with the British government in the person of Sir D'Arcy Osborne, the British ambassador at the Holy See. His Holiness, Müller reported, had accepted with the words: 'The German Opposition must be heard in Britain,' and he [the Pope] would be its voice. The objective of the Pope's intercession would be a peace based upon the proposition that Britain and France would not attempt to take advantage of the disturbance that would follow the deposition of Hitler to invade and occupy Germany.[83]

Pius XII wanted to tread a careful path. If he succeeded, Hitler would be overthrown and the West would join in a common war against Stalin. If he failed, Hitler would wreak vengeance on the Catholic Church. For security reasons, Pius XII stated that he would not meet with Müller directly, but would receive his communications through a Jesuit priest, Father Leiber, a Vatican Archivist, whom the Pope trusted absolutely. Leiber would pass Müller's messages to the Pope, who would pass them on to the British Ambassador personally, because it would be perfectly normal for the Pope to meet him regularly. On 27 October Müller was summoned to meet Father Leiber at the Jesuit Gregorian University. The Foreign Office had given Osborne permission to conduct armistice negotiations with Canaris's *Schwarze Kapelle*.[84]

Word of the Vatican negotiations quickly reached Heydrich of SS intelligence. The source of the original leak has never been determined, but in hindsight it may have been a Soviet agent who wished to sabotage peace talks with the West.[85] In any event, it was Heydrich who gave the code name Red Orchestra to the Soviet file and Black Orchestra to the Vatican file.[86] Perhaps he suspected (correctly) that a common bond existed. But in 1939 the SS were unaware that the *Kapellmeisters*, or orchestra leaders for the *Schwarze Kapelle* were Canaris and Jahnke, the chiefs of the rival German intelligence agencies.

As the SS surveillance around the Black Orchestra tightened, Canaris had to move quickly to convince Hitler that Müller was not a traitor, but the Abwehr's best double agent inside the Vatican. Much to Heydrich's chagrin, Hitler believed the story, and the SS had to put the Black Orchestra file on hold.[87] At first Canaris believed that a Fascist Benedictine monk named Keller had betrayed the Black Orchestra negotiations, but it seems unlikely for soon another more dangerous leak appeared.

A Swiss newspaper published a report that 'high officers of the German general staff' were involved in a plot against Hitler.[88] That information could not have come from a lowly Benedictine monk. In fact, only a handful of people inside the *Schwarze Kapelle* knew of the difficulty Canaris was having recruiting allies from the skittish General Staff. Someone on the inside had leaked the story.

The Swiss newspaper leak threw the plotters into uproar and made the General Staff even more nervous. One historian records that

> someone in the German group asked what guarantees could be got that if the Germans overthrew Hitler the western allies would not force a Carthaginian peace like Versailles upon Germany. From the widow of one of the conspirators, von Dohnanyi, we have evidence that her husband suggested a secret guarantee of the proposed conditions of peace by the Pope. The guarantee was to be got through Müller.
>
> Early in November 1939, Müller came again to Monsignor Kaas, who put him in touch with Father Leiber the Pope's secretary. Not without doubts whether he was doing what was right, Father Leiber put the plan personally to the Pope ... The Pope was being invited to engage in a conspiracy to overthrow a tyrant, and incidentally to put himself and his aides into those dire risks which attend conspirators ... On 6 November 1939 Father Leiber assured Josef Müller that the Pope was ready to do 'all he can' for peace.[89]

Unfortunately, the SS was by then increasing its efforts to find out what the Vatican was doing. They had already sent a phony 'peace offer' to British intelligence. Menzies warned his agents that the terms of the new offer did not correspond to the other Vatican messages, but it was too late. The two British agents who had gone to Venlo to negotiate were kidnapped by Schellenberg and taken back to Germany.[90]

The Foreign Office suspected further treachery and broke off all peace negotiations, although Menzies tried to keep the lines to Canaris open:

> The Vatican talks hung fire for over a month, and were only resumed when the Pope vouched for the bona fides and honesty of Müller. With that assurance, made personally by Pius XII in a communication to Lord Halifax, the conversation reopened with a meeting between the Pope and Sir D'Arcy Osborne, which took place – according to the British Cabinet Minutes – at the Vatican on January 12, 1940.[91]

The peace talks dragged on through February, March and April of 1940 with both the Pope and the British getting ever more impatient with the delays and increasingly dubious about the Black Orchestra's chances of success. According to several eye witnesses, explicit terms for an Anglo-German peace treaty had actually been concluded, but Canaris found that no one in the Germany Army was willing to overthrow Hitler. On 3 April 1940 the Pope told Osborne that he feared their efforts had come to an end.[92]

In an act of desperation, Canaris sent Müller back to the Vatican in May to warn the Pope about Hitler's plans for a sneak attack on Belgium and the Netherlands. Not only were the warnings disbelieved by the Allies, but Belgian telegrams incriminating the Vatican were intercepted by the Nazis *before the invasion was launched*. Hitler was furious at the security leak, and ordered the SS to investigate. This time Canaris barely managed to talk his way out. His cover-up succeeded only with the help of some 'elfin mischief' in the form of an alibi from the good Jesuit Father Leiber, but the Müller link to the *Schwarze Kapelle* had to be closed down.[93]

Despite the *débâcle*, the *Schwarze Kapelle* decided to put forth new peace proposals 'through other secret channels'.[94]

It did not take the SS long to find out what they were. There is only a hint in the American files of Turkul's pre-war service to the Vatican; a brief notation that he was supplied with false passports by the Abwehr and money from the Japanese to send 'apostles' into the Soviet Union for propaganda. This may have been Turkul's first espionage work for the Jesuits who, as mentioned in Chapter One, had been trying with limited success to infiltrate their own agents into Soviet territory. It is perhaps only a coincidence that Turkul was running his own early Japanese Ratline into the Soviet Union for the Abwehr at the same time as the Jesuits. Even if Turkul had no direct Jesuit connection in 1938, his Abwehr boss certainly did.

It was probably Canaris himself who asked Turkul in 1938 to do for the Black Orchestra what he was already doing for the Japanese; spy on both the Nazis and the Soviets. Admiral Canaris, the 'Jesuitical Russophobe' had a direct liaison with Father Leiber of the Jesuits, the Pope's confidant. According to American intelligence, Turkul suddenly left Paris and moved to Berlin to form 'his own White Russian Army which succeeded in smuggling people in and out of Russia'.[95] Turkul later claimed that it was the Hitler–Stalin Pact that drove him to quit Berlin, but it is possible he had already moved to Rome at the end of 1938.[96]

On the other hand, the move to Rome may have been ordered by the Black Orchestra after Dr Müller was 'anonymously' exposed. Turkul pretended to share Canaris's belief that any pact with Stalin was a betrayal of the White Russian cause. Turkul certainly had a plausible motive for wanting to overthrow Hitler and had the right connections to the Black Orchestra through Jahnke. But after Müller was exposed, the Black Orchestra had to shift to a more secure method of communication. It must have seemed logical to use Turkul's NTS network as back up couriers to the Vatican and the British.

NTS had longstanding relations with British intelligence. Several of Turkul's close associates were Uniate and Orthodox clergymen who were well known to the Jesuits. Indeed, the Jesuits had built an entire college in Rome to train Uniate seminarians.[97] Moreover, Turkul had something invaluable to offer the Jesuits who were worried about security. What could be more secure than diplomatic immunity? The Japanese Secret Service was already funding Turkul's NTS network. By giving NTS couriers diplomatic passports from Japanese-controlled Manchuria, they could travel freely across Europe without embarrassing questions from the Germans, or so they thought. There is evidence that the Jesuits fell for it completely.

In the spring and summer of 1940, the SS began receiving tips about a Japanese spy ring with connections to the Vatican. Two envoys with Japanese-controlled diplomatic credentials were intercepted carrying sensitive documents on the German war effort. The envoys were not orientals at all. One was a White Russian who belonged to the Melnyk faction of the Ukrainian nationalists and the other was a Slav whose last name was given by Schellenberg simply as K.[98]

K was found to be carrying detailed high level information on German military strength and future plans. Under interrogation, K admitted that the plans were to be taken to Rome where 'the material was transmitted by the Japanese Embassy to a trusted agent of the General of the Jesuit Order, Ledochovski'. K could not tell the SS how the Japanese–Jesuit collaboration began, but it appeared to have been a systematic arrangement.[99] According to Owen Chadwick:

> The Jesuit general Ledochowski was a Pole, deeply pro-British, passionately anti-Nazi, a strong and courageous man. In August 1939 the Italian ambassador at the Vatican, Pignatti, told his government that under Ledochowski the whole Jesuit order was 'drawn up, with extreme decision' against Nazi Germany.[100]

Through K, the SS had stumbled across the alternative route for the Vatican's communications with Jahnke and the *Schwarze Kapelle*. Cave Brown believes that K was a man named Kunzcewincz.[101] However, he may have been another member of Turkul's net, Dr Tuan Kowalewsky, a Polish-Ukrainian separatist who obtained his information from another Japanese spy, Omida, who lived in Sofia. Turkul's intelligence chief, the German Jew Klatt/ Kauder/Max also lived in Sofia. He too had a Japanese connection:

> The spy's actual source was neither the Soviet Legation in Sofia nor some mysterious informants on the Red Army General Staff, but solely the obscure correspondent of a Tokyo newspaper, Isono Kiyosho by name, who had his headquarters in the Rumanian capital. From the correspondent the lines led directly to the residence of Dr Richard Sorge, the Soviet's own master spy.[102]

In fact, everywhere the SS investigators turned, Japanese spies with connections to Turkul's network kept turning up. Schellenberg leaves enough references in his memoirs to clearly connect Turkul's Japanese network to the Vatican in the summer of 1940. According to Schellenberg, when the SS checked further they found that the Vatican information was being passed to British intelligence through a Japanese journalist in Stockholm. Turkul's organisation did have a Japanese contact in Stockholm, a journalist named Enomoto who knew Turkul personally.[103]

From Stockholm to Switzerland to the Vatican, all the signs led back to Turkul's work for Canaris and the Jahnkebureau. Yet the SS did nothing to smash the Black Orchestra. There were rumours that Canaris had evidence of Heydrich's homosexuality and Jewish antecedents locked in a safety deposit box in Switzerland, with instructions to send the documents to the *New York Times* if he was ever arrested. Schellenberg believed that Canaris had a similar file on Himmler.[104]

The actual reason for SS inaction in 1940–41 may be more mundane. The Jahnke–Turkul channel was the only one capable of providing reliable intelligence on both Japanese and Soviet intentions at a critical period in German history: it was the time that Hitler was considering war against the Soviet Union. In April 1941 Tokyo and Moscow had signed a neutrality pact. But Japan had also signed a treaty with the Third Reich. If Hitler attacked Stalin, which pact would the Japanese honour?[105]

Like Leopold Trepper's Red Orchestra network in Western Europe, both the Turkul and Sorge networks were fully informed of Hitler's war plans against the Soviet Union, but Stalin refused to believe his own spies. When Operation Barbarossa was launched in June 1941, it came as a complete surprise. Stalin waited with bated breath to see if the Japanese, like Hitler, would betray their pact and launch an attack from the east. In the autumn of 1941, with winter approaching, even Hitler had become anxious about Japanese intentions. This was the moment the GRU had been waiting for. The Third Reich was in a panic for information in the Orient: they could turn to only one reliable source.

The Gestapo grumbled, Heydrich fumed, but in 1941, Schellenberg swallowed his suspicions and asked Jahnke to use his excellent channels, the mysterious team of the Czarist officer and the German Jew, to carry a message to the Japanese Secret Service. By October 1941, the Germans had received their response: the Japanese would not attack the Soviet Union, but they would support the Axis war effort by attacking the Americans at Pearl Harbor.[106]

If Hitler was less than thrilled by the Japanese response, the Soviets were ecstatic. They frantically stripped their Mongolian divisions from the Soviet eastern borders and shipped them west to Moscow.[107] On 2 December 1941 a German reconnaissance unit reported that they could see the gleaming towers of the Kremlin in their binoculars. Four days later the Soviets threw their newly arrived divisions against the Nazis. Hitler did not know it, but the tide of war was turning against him for ever. The Turkul network was a cancer from which the Third Reich would never recover. Canaris and Jahnke were using the Black Orchestra channels to inform the Vatican (and Turkul) in advance of all of Hitler's moves.[108] As US intelligence discovered too late, the Vatican's Black Orchestra and Moscow's Red Orchestra were one and the same:

> ... the Schwarze Kapelle was formerly comprised of high ranking Wehrmacht officers and had at one time been directed by Admiral Canaris. [Source] stated that the Schwarze Kapelle had been activated between the years 1930 and 1934, at which time the Rote Kapelle, an organization comprised mainly of MVD [Communist intelligence] members and sympathizers, was active as a resistance organization. Initially the two organizations were coordinated to form a united front, however, the Schwarze Kapelle activities subsided to the extent that those individuals who remained active looked to the Rote Kapelle for guidance.[109]

Even after the Red Orchestra's Japanese connection, Richard Sorge, was exposed as a Soviet agent by the Japanese and Jahnke was exposed as a British agent by the SS, Turkul continued to be trusted by the Germans because of his service to the Black Orchestra. Even in 1942, when Heydrich denounced Canaris's Abwehr for political unreliability, Turkul and his Jewish spy chief survived, but under new masters. Since the Third Reich had virtually no other source for Soviet war plans, Turkul's organisation was ordered to share its precious MAX reports on Soviet troop movements with other German agencies. Canaris ordered the transfer of Turkul's organisation to General Gehlen of the Fremde Heere Ost (FHO – Foreign Armies East), the intelligence headquarters of the German Wehrmacht on the Eastern front.

Klatt's MAX material was so invaluable to the German High command that in the summer of 1942 the Abwehr organisation physically moved to Gehlen's headquarters in Vinnitsa in the Ukraine. On paper, Klatt still reported to the Abwehr, but in practice the MAX reports on the Soviet order of battle were flowing directly to Gehlen's headquarters.[110] Turkul's intelligence production was important enough to force a *de facto* merger between two rival branches of German intelligence. Heinz Höhne, the noted German historian, aptly described the network's value to the Third Reich:

> The most sensational information on the Red Army, however, came from a mysterious figure . . . a Jewish trader named Klatt, whose code-name was 'Max'. His information was so accurate that the sceptics in FHO often wondered whether Max was not a double agent feeding fake Russian material back to the Germans. No one in FHO knew the truth, which was that, via Isono Kiyosho, a journalist living in Sofia, Max had tapped the Japanese Secret Service, which was better informed than any other about the Soviet Union.[111]

Gehlen needed Klatt's help, but apparently did not realise that while he was reading Klatt's information on the Soviets, Klatt was probably reading every file he could in Gehlen's intelligence headquarters.[112] It probably seemed necessary for Klatt to be briefed on German battle plans so that he would know where Gehlen needed the most information. In any event a great deal of gossip can be picked up inside any intelligence office. One thing is certain: whatever Klatt learned from Gehlen he was passing on to the Kremlin.[113]

American intelligence analysts tried for years to discover what Turkul was doing in Rome during the war, but were sent on a wild goose chase by Turkul's British employers and his fellow NTS conspirators. The Americans were led to believe that Turkul's Roman activities were insignificant, that he was out of the German intelligence loop completely, a '*quantité negligible*'. One German officer remembered differently. He recalled that during the week that Klatt's assistant, Lang, went to visit Turkul in Rome, the MAX reports from the Soviet Union stopped completely. But when Lang came back from his Roman holiday with Turkul, he brought the backlog of MAX reports for the entire week.[114]

But apart from this single visit, how was Turkul able to smuggle the voluminous MAX information in and out of Rome? He knew that the Japanese–Vatican courier system was exposed, that the

Nazis had previously intercepted and decoded the Vatican's warning of the Belgian invasion and that Klatt was under near constant surveillance by the Gestapo. Schellenberg let the cat out of the bag when he casually admitted that the SS had a German agent in Rome who was 'closely connected to the Vatican'. The agent refused to use couriers, wireless, or travel to Germany, but he had very important information about the Soviet Union. Schellenberg solved the communication problem by giving the Roman source a new secret invention, the burst transmitter. 'The rapidity of the transmission made it impossible for any direction-finder to establish the location of the transmitter.'[115]

The recently declassified intelligence files show that Klatt commanded an extensive radio network across the continent, but that his post-war American interrogators never discovered the central burst transmitter in the Vatican (which Schellenberg revealed only much later). Schellenberg was not the only one to hire the Jahnke–Turkul network. Far from being an insignificant figure in Rome, Turkul was 'allegedly on excellent terms with Mussolini who often asked for [Turkul's] opinions on Russian matters. He was supposedly a frequent guest of Mussolini's; however some people state that Mussolini asked Germany to suppress [Turkul] when he left Italy.'[116]

Mussolini had good reason to be angry. Just as Turkul had sold the phony MAX reports to the Germans, he had convinced the Italians to purchase an equally false MORITZ network that fed Mussolini reams of Soviet disinformation. With the help of his undetectable SS transmitter, Turkul was perfectly placed in Rome to monitor the Axis war effort and report to his Soviet masters. After all, in the summer of 1942, his agents were operating right inside the German intelligence headquarters for the Eastern front.[117]

Although it is beyond the scope of this book, there is reason to believe that Turkul was the mysterious 'Source Werthe' who supplied the Soviet Lucy ring in Switzerland with daily German battle plans long after other members of the Red Orchestra had been captured. The Black Orchestra provided perfect cover for Soviet Military Intelligence: no matter how much evidence the Gestapo gathered against Turkul and Klatt, the heavyweight team of Jahnke and Canaris would intervene to protect them.

Even the Japanese Secret Service provided unwitting assistance as they continued the Jahnke connection in an effort to mediate peace between Stalin and Hitler. As Schellenberg himself admits, Jahnke was a critical player in these efforts. After Sorge's capture in 1942, Turkul had the only secret channel open to Japan.[118]

As Turkul's network had access to German military intelligence on a daily basis, and in view of the widely acknowledged admission that the MAX information shaped much of the German war plans on the Eastern front, the entire history of the Red Orchestra (and much of World War II) may have to be rewritten. The Turkul files have confirmed that the Supreme Command of the German Army received only that information which was approved by the Soviets. Turkul's network may have been the decisive factor behind many Soviet victories during World War II.[119]

Two decades later, American intelligence still had no idea how the MAX system worked, although they knew it was somehow run by the Soviets. The missing link for the American interrogators was the Vatican–Japanese connection. We can reconstruct the system by speculating on how the pieces which are now known to exist fitted together in the Soviet scheme. From Moscow, the Soviet disinformation went to their net in Japan, which couriered it to the Vatican (probably by diplomatic pouch after the K incident). After Sorge was arrested, the MAX reports were probably shipped through one of Turkul's Japanese journalists directly to Rome through a Vatican pouch.

From Rome they probably went by burst message to one of Klatt's listening posts, and then via a secure wire link to Gehlen's headquarters. Klatt's liaison to Gehlen copied down the German battle response and sent it back down the channel to the Soviets, who always had the last move on the chessboard. Thanks to Schellenberg's unwitting technical assistance with the burst transmitter, couriers were no longer needed. The MAX system became so highly automated (and untraceable) that by 1943, Turkul could step out of the loop entirely.[120]

Only a month after the Klatt operation was transferred to Gehlen's headquarters in the Ukraine, Turkul received an alarming message. The Germans were proposing to reverse Hitler's brutal anti-Slavic policies and recruit Ukrainian, Byelorussian and Russian soldiers to fight for the Third Reich. If the plan were ever approved, millions of Central and Eastern Europeans might volunteer to fight the Soviet Army. The Ukrainians alone could provide enough manpower to turn the tide for the Nazis.[121]

As soon as the burst transmitter replaced the MAX courier system, Turkul's new assignment for the Soviets was clear:

1. Monitor anti-Communist activities through his White Russian network
2. Hamstring the German anti-Communist effort by setting the factions against each other
3. Keep the Soviets informed of all new developments[122]

There were new developments indeed. In 1942 some Vatican officials were rumoured to support the new German policy of using Slavic volunteers against the Communists. There was talk of greater religious freedom and an end to racial persecution of the Slavs. There were even reports that high level negotiations with the Nazis over the Church's position in the Ukraine were already underway.

If the Pope endorsed a German crusade, the Catholics of Central Europe might join with the White Russians and Soviet prisoners of war in the common cause of liberation. The Red Army would be overwhelmed. At all costs, any Vatican initiative in the Ukraine must be stopped before it ever got off the ground. In 1942 Soviet military intelligence turned its attention to Rome. Turkul's assault on the Vatican had begun in earnest. What the Pope did not know was that many Ukrainian priests were already working for Turkul's 'anti-Soviet' network.

8

The Catholic Army of the Ukraine

The lights burned late in the Pope's private quarters in September 1942. It was not a time for peaceful rest. The Nazis wanted Pius XII to make a deal: endorse the Third Reich or face the destruction of the Catholic Church. Throughout the summer, the pressure on the Pope had increased. Despite intervention by his old German friend, Franz von Papen, the Nazis kept turning the screws tighter and tighter. Harassment of Catholics in Europe increased.[1]

The Ukrainian Catholics had been among the hardest hit. On 26 August 1942 the Pope had written to his old friend, Metropolitan Szepticky, Archbishop of the Uniate Catholic See of Lvov in the Polish province of Galicia.[2] It was a hard letter to write. The Uniate Catholics had endured so much. They were a religious hybrid, the result of being the last outpost of the old Austro-Hungarian empire. Ukrainian in nationality, Orthodox in Slavic liturgy, but obedient to the Pope of Rome, Archbishop Szepticky and his stubborn flock had endured hatred and persecution at the hands of Czarist Russia, the Poles and then the Bolsheviks.[3]

Now it was Szepticky's golden jubilee and the Nazis had arrived. The fiftieth anniversary of a priest's ordination is usually cause for special rejoicing. But on this occasion, Pius XII could only commiserate with the old Archbishop, now approaching his eightieth birthday. Szepticky's fellow priests and pastors were suffering terribly at the hands of the Germans. In his letter the Pope sympathised with their plight.[4]

The reply was even more disturbing. Archbishop Szepticky reminded the Pope that three years earlier, he had asked the Pope's permission to commit suicide as a protest against the Communist takeover of Galicia. Stalin had persecuted the Uniate Catholics even more savagely than the previous Polish occupation. Death would have ended the old Archbishop's agony, but on that occasion the Pope had been firm and refused Szepticky leave to die.[5]

However, Szepticky's 1942 letter was not a further request to commit suicide: 'The last three years have persuaded me that I am not worthy of this death which would have had less meaning before God than a prayer spoken by a child.' Now he wrote of the horrors of the new masters of the Ukraine, the Nazis. 'Liberated by the German army from the Bolshevik Yoke, we originally felt a certain relief, which however lasted no more than one or two months.'[6]

Indeed, Szepticky himself had blessed the Nazi 'liberators', and welcomed the 'independent' government of the Ukraine proclaimed by Jaroslav Stetsko of the OUN. The Organisation of Ukrainian Nationalists was a Fascist revolutionary sect under the leadership of Stephen Bandera and his deputy, Jaroslav Stetsko. They had previously served German intelligence in organising pogroms in the East. The fanatical Fascists of the OUN had long awaited the day when Hitler would break his pact with Stalin and place them in power in the Ukraine.[7]

On the heels of the invading German Army in 1941, the OUN returned to Galicia. The biographer of a young Jewish eyewitness named Simon Wiesenthal recounted what they did next:

> They celebrated their return to Lwow by starting a pogrom that lasted three days and three nights. When the massacre was over, 6,000 Jews had been killed ... The Jews were ordered to form a long row, face the wall and cross their arms behind their necks. A Ukrainian began to shoot ... The shots and shouts of the dying men were getting closer to Wiesenthal. He remembers that he stood looking at the grey wall without really seeing it. Suddenly he heard the sound of church bells, and a Ukrainian voice shouted 'Enough! Evening mass!'[8]

Although devout in their loyalty to Church and Reich, the Ukrainian collaborators were treated with disdain by the Germans. At that time, the Nazis thought they had no use for an OUN puppet government. Within a month, Stetsko and the other OUN leaders were thrown out or imprisoned under house arrest in Germany.[9] The true face of the Nazi administration was revealed to Archbishop Szepticky. 'Little by little, the government has instituted a truly unbelievable regime of terror and corruption ... Today, the whole country feels that the German regime is if anything worse, almost diabolically worse, than the Bolshevists.'[10]

It was not only the 200,000 Jews who had already been killed who troubled the Archbishop; 'hundreds of thousands of Christians' were being systematically slaughtered by the Nazis and their local Ukrainian henchmen. The survival of the Ukrainian Catholic

Church was threatened: Archbishop Szepticky was writing to tell the Pope that soon the clergy in the Ukraine would be extinct.[11]

Of course that need never happen if the Pope would consider the Nazis' alternative: he could help them resolve a difficult problem. Stalin had been turning people against the Nazis by reviving the Orthodox Church as a potent propaganda force against the Nazi occupation. What the Nazis needed was a religious stooge of their own: they wanted Archbishop Szepticky to collaborate. Everyone in the Ukraine, even the Orthodox clergy, loved the saintly old leader of the Uniate Catholics. The Nazis wanted to portray themselves as 'protectors of religion' by having Szepticky unite all the Ukrainian Christians into one pro-Nazi, anti-Communist Church.[12]

A united Eastern Church had been the Vatican's dream since the great Orthodox schism tore Christianity apart in 1024 AD. The hybrid Uniate Church was a compromise devised in the sixteenth century by the Jesuits and encouraged by the Habsburg dynasty of Austria as a political counterweight to Orthodox Russia. In 1942 the Nazis were offering the Pope a solution to the Ukrainian question. The Pope knew it was a cruel and cynical propaganda manoeuvre, but the Nazis were eagerly awaiting his answer. Would Pope Pius XII permit Archbishop Szepticky to fulfill the Church's ancient dream to unite the Orthodox and Uniate Sees of the Ukraine?[13]

In the darkness of those autumn nights, the Pope weighed his moral and political alternatives. If he accepted the Nazi offer in the Ukraine, there would be more demands, more requests, more deals. Soon the Vatican would be emasculated like the German Protestant Church. On the other hand, there were other considerations. Pius XII reread Szepticky's heartrending letter and considered his options.

Word of the Pope's secret decision reached American-born Bishop Ivan (John) Bučko, one of the Vatican's experts for Ukrainian issues. Bučko was a porcine figure with a receding hairline and close-set eyes that peered out from behind round-rimmed glasses. Bishop Bučko was also a fanatical Ukrainian nationalist. He was one of the first to find out that the Pope was planning to walk a delicate and dangerous tightrope between public collaboration and token resistance. The first step was to accept the Nazi offer to open negotiations in the Ukraine. An accommodation might be reached, the Bishop thought, if the discussions were approached carefully. Bučko smiled. His dream of an independent Ukraine might yet come true.

For Turkul's masters in the Soviet GRU, Ukrainian unity was a nightmare. The Soviets had encouraged division and splinter groups among the Ukrainian nationalists. It was no coincidence that Turkul's NTS agents in the Melnyk faction had denounced the Bandera group to the Gestapo. Before Admiral Canaris knew what had happened, his hand-picked Ukrainians were ousted, and Melnyk loyalists were running auxiliary police units for the SS. Even some of Bandera's followers, like Mykola Lebed and Father Ivan Grynioch, the Catholic Chaplain of the murderous Nachtigall Battalion, had deserted Bandera for the SS.[14]

Those Ukrainians who survived the purge of Bandera's followers served Soviet interests admirably by instituting a reign of terror that drove more and more of their country men into the hands of the Red Partisans. The last thing the GRU wanted was for the Vatican to negotiate peace among the Ukrainian religious factions and work with the Germans for a united Ukraine.

For the US War Department, the vision of a Nazi–Vatican accord was not a dream but a nightmare. At the end of September 1942, word of the impending deal exploded in the pro-Axis press in Catholic Spain and then in Italy. At first, no one believed the rumours of negotiations. Only a few months earlier, the Nazis had given orders that officials in the occupied Eastern countries were not even to meet with Vatican representatives.[15] But by the beginning of October 1942, the press was reporting an enormous change in Church–Reich relations. The teletype clattered out the news that the Vatican was starting to negotiate with Nazi Germany:

> Lisbon – Catholic circles in Italy confirm the report that Pius XII has sent a mission, headed by Cardinal Lavitrano, Archbishop of Palermo, to investigate the ecclesiastical situation in Nazi-occupied Russia. Catholic papers outside Rome have stated that this mission was sent at the invitation of the German government with the aim of studying the possible unification of the Roman Catholic Church and the Orthodox Church.[16]

US intelligence knew that this hinted at a propaganda coup for the Nazis, and tried to downplay its significance in a series of background briefings for the press, claiming that the Germans were only trying 'to play on the religious sentiments of the

Ukrainian people in restoring to the cult several churches which had been closed under the Soviet regime'.[17] But if that were so, why would the Pope send a Prince of the Church, a Cardinal, to discuss the Ukraine? It was evident that a change of tactics could be under way.

US intelligence feared that the Nazis might succeed with these new tactics, especially 'in the Ruthenian diocese of Lwow (Lemberg, Poland) of which metropolitan Mgr Szeptycki is the head . . . Mgr believed this means a real opportunity for the revival of faith and when overtures were made by Orthodox Bishops for the union of Christian churches, he has believed that a cherished project might come to execution . . . The Nazi authorities expressed their desires that Mgr Szeptycki should be appointed as metropolitan of Kiev, capital of Ukraine.'[18]

The Allies knew that Hitler did not share the Catholic Church's ambitions in the Ukraine. The War Department speculated that the Nazis had something else in mind than 'Christan Charity' for Archbishop Szepticky. The War Department Intelligence Division was worried that 'the Nazis wanted to use the influence of the extremely popular prelate to further political plans of a Ukrainian puppet state in which a nationalized church would cultivate hate against Russia'.[19]

British intelligence also sensed the explosive potential of a Catholic–Nazi alliance in the Ukraine. A report on the Uniate issue was prepared at Oxford University for the British Foreign Office:

> Mgr Szepticky's early policies were Ukrainophil; he supported the idea, which the Austrian Government encouraged for anti-Russian political reasons, of an independent Ukraine. It would appear that he still pursues this idea (which Germany has revived since her attack on Russia), if a recent report is true that he has issued an appeal to the Ukrainian Orthodox clergy . . . to unite with the Ruthenians . . . for the sake of national unity . . . The prestige of this Bishop, who is the Grand Old Man of this region, and is probably revered by Orthodox as well as his own flock, should be remembered in all propaganda to this part of the world . . . The policy of the Vatican in regard to this region is hard to predict.[20]

Suddenly it appeared to the Allies as if the Vatican's policy was beginning to tilt towards the Nazis. A confidential American report gave the War Department Intelligence Division reason to expect the worst:

A private information (sic) states that the most Rev. John Bučko who was up to the end of 1941 Auxiliary Bishop ... of the Ukrainian Greek Catholic dioceses in the United States, has accompanied the mission of Cardinal Lavitrano to the Ukraine ... Bishop Bučko ... is considered a friend of Msgr Szeptycki who was in this country repeatedly between 1916 and 1924 and it is not impossible that [Bučko] went to Rome with the intention of advocating the creation of an Ukraine (sic) ecclesiastical province under the leadership of Msgr Szeptycki.[21]

The War Department's confidential informant was probably the Most Reverend Constantine Bohachevsky, who had been Bishop Bučko's immediate superior when he was living in Pittsburgh. As the War Department noted: 'It is said that Mgr Bučko had in his last years of office dissented with Bishop Bohachevsky in stressing that the Catholic Ukrainians living around Pittsburgh had to be favored in their anti-Russian national sentiments.'[22]

News of Bishop Bučko's anti-Russian sentiments must have greatly disturbed the War Department, which was having problems enough with its temperamental Soviet ally. For Pius XII to select Bučko to be part of the Lavitrano Mission was a possible indication that the Vatican was considering a shift towards the Nazis. Equally alarming, official Vatican channels were providing no advance information on the Lavitrano Mission.[23]

Turkul knew because he had inside sources who were well informed about the negotiations. Metropolitan Anastasius of Yugoslavia was head of the Synodal or Karlowac Church, representing the right wing of Russian Orthodoxy which was ardently pro-German. The head of his German diocese was Metropolitan Seraphim of Berlin who called Hitler 'the great Leader of the German people who has raised the sword against the foes of the Lord'.[24] According to American intelligence files, the Orthodox cleric Anastasius was Turkul's direct collaborator in his anti-Communist centre. Metropolitan Seraphim is identified in British files as another member of the Turkul network.[26]

Their agent in the Ukraine was fully prepared to resist the Vatican's offer of unification. Instead of joining the Catholic Uniates:

A splinter group of the [Autonomous] Russian clergy, under Bishop Panteleimon of the ancient Lavra monastery at Kiev, was prepared to place itself under the émigré church of Metropolitan Seraphim in Berlin.[27]

The number of clerics who belonged to Turkul's network is amazing, among them Archbishop Vitalie in the United States,

Father George Leonidov Romanov, a 'Greek Orthodox' (possibly Uniate) priest who worked on the MAX network, and a number of minor luminaries, including Father Alexei Ionov and the Russian Priests Grabbe and Kisiliew, who later worked for Turkul in Munich.[28]

With so many potential sources of agitation, it would not have taken much effort for Turkul to inflame the existing tensions among the various Orthodox sects in the Ukraine, although he may have had some help. At least one of the Orthodox leaders, Archbishop Alexis Gromadskii, has been accused of being an NKVD agent.[29] The Orthodox could not agree to unite among themselves, let alone with Szepticky's Uniates:

> Szepticky made a series of attempts to bring about an alliance between the Uniates and the Autocephalous adherents, the two nationalist churches. However, Ohienko, who conducted the negotiations for the UAPTs, [Orthodox group] refused unification under the authority of the Pope.[30]

Despite Bishop Bučko's strident anti-Russian sentiments, Cardinal Lavitrano had apparently brought a sharp message from the Pope which disappointed Nazi expectations. When word got back to America, the War Department's Intelligence Division breathed a sigh of relief and prepared its own press report:

> Szeptycki has now declared officially that as an old and ailing man of 80 years, he cannot accept the See of Kiev ... To put it bluntly Msgr Szeptycki says that a religious union of Churches cannot be made under the political domination of the Nazis and that he does not desire to be their tool in accepting to be metropolitan of the Ukraine ... the investigations of Cardinal Lavitrano, confirm the fact that the Vatican will not accept to make any new division of dioceses as long as the Germans are occupying eastern Europe.[31]

However, within a few weeks, US intelligence dropped its fulsome praise of the Vatican's steadfastness. It was beginning to appear that Bishop Bučko's anti-Russian outlook may have won at least a partial victory. By the end of October 1942, US intelligence recognised that the Nazis' alternating promises of religious tolerance and threats of greater persecution, had achieved the desired result: 'the Nazis have avoided open protests from the Vatican in the last few months.'[32]

Evidence was trickling in that the Lavitrano Mission had struck a deal after all. On the eve of the Final Solution of the Jewish question, the Lavitrano Mission had agreed to compromise with the Nazis. In return for easing religious persecution in the East, the Vatican would become neutral in favour of the Germans. For the rest of the war, the Pope never discussed Nazi atrocities against the Russians, nor was the word 'Jew' ever mentioned in any Papal pronouncement.[33]

The terms of the Pope's bargain in Eastern Europe quickly became apparent to the American War Department, which noted that although 'the Vatican does not . . . allow any Bishops in those countries to make open collaborationist statements, it [does] not favor all too outspoken protests. A certain modus vivendi seems to have been established in this sense as the result of the Commission of Cardinal Lavitrano.'[34]

In a confidential comment, American intelligence cited as proof the fact that the Pope permitted Dr Werhun of Berlin to remain the official Apostolic Administrator for the Ukraine. For the rest of the war, while the local Jews were being exterminated, the Vatican's chief delegate for Ukrainian affairs was conveniently absent in Berlin. The War Department described Dr Werhun as 'just the man who will not go in for outspoken protests, and will try to make the best of an evil situation'.[35] Amid such silences, Auschwitz was built.

Soviet intelligence had other things to worry about: the subsequent German response to the Lavitrano mission was a direct threat to the Red Army. Within a year, the SS had reversed its anti-Slavic policy toward the Ukrainians and allowed them to form their own SS Division, the 'Galician'. After heavy losses on the Eastern front, the Germans were pleased that 40,000 young Ukrainians volunteered for SS service. Only half that number, the cream of the crop were accepted, usually from among those Ukrainians who had already proved their total devotion to the Nazis by service in the brutal auxiliary police battalions that had massacred Jews, Poles and even fellow Ukrainians.[36]

By the beginning of 1943, nearly all of the 800,000 Ukrainian Jews had been murdered and their police executioners needed new assignments. There were so many ex-police volunteers that the Ukrainian unit was originally named the 'Galician Police Division' before it was formally accepted by the SS. For the rest of his life, Simon Wiesenthal had a special hatred for Gustav Otto Wächter, the Nazi Governor of Galicia, who had directed the Jewish massacre and then rewarded his Ukrainian henchmen with the 'honour' of becoming SS volunteers.[37]

Unlike most senior German officials, Wächter recognised that a loyal Ukrainian SS force was a significant asset to the Nazis. The Soviet partisan underground was seriously threatening the German supply lines. As the war turned against them, Wächter recognised that it was essential to win the hearts and minds of the civilian population who were assisting the partisans. The centrepiece of Wächter's strategy was the five million Catholic Uniates, of which three and a half million were concentrated in the Galician region.[38]

Their religious leader, Archbishop Szepticky, pointed the way by blessing the Galician SS Division. Finally, the Ukraine had its own fighting force to smash the Soviet partisans. The Galician SS, complete with Uniate chaplains, would soon be a Catholic army in a crusade against the 'Godless Bolsheviks'.[39] Bishop Bučko must have been especially pleased that the 'anti-Russian nationalism' of his people had been preserved. The seeds of co-operation sown by the Lavitrano Mission were beginning to bear fruit.

The Uniate victory in the Ukraine was only the first step in the struggle to contain the hated Communists. Only three months after the Lavitrano Mission had concluded its work, the Vatican floated a story in the *New York Herald Tribune* and the *Washington Post* about Pius XII's post-war hopes for Europe. The Pope was said to be in favour of an anti-Communist Central European Confederation of Catholic states, 'which would stretch from the Baltic to the Black Seas'. Pius XI's dreams of a Catholic Intermarium were to be brought to fruition by Pius XII.[40]

Such a Catholic anti-communist bloc had also been the dream of the Pope's old friend, Archbishop Szepticky, who 'was in his younger days a personal friend of the Emperor Francis Joseph', last great ruler of the Austro-Hungarian Empire.[41] However, US intelligence did not view the Pope's post-war plans so favourably.

Most of the War Department's views on this sensitive topic are still censored, but their anger about the Pope's political attitude is quite clear from the report's conclusions:

... leading Catholics all over the world do not hold the view that it is in the interest of Christianity and the Church to have 'Catholic' States, but stress freedom for the Church everywhere, whether Catholics are in a majority in a particular country or not. There is definite tendency to avoid the repetition of the opposition between 'Catholic' and 'Protestant' States which did so much harm in the past. They can hardly favor the idea of a 'Catholic Slav Federation'.[42]

The Soviets certainly did not favour the idea and launched a religious propaganda exercise of their own in September 1943:

Stalin received the Metropolitan of Moscow, whereupon the restoration of the Synod was announced, with the Metropolitan as Patriarch. Moscow gave wide publicity to this event, contrasting it with reports of German atrocities ... In reply to the Moscow conclave, a special conference of eight Russian Orthodox Bishops, including Seraphim of Berlin, was convened in Vienna in October 1943 ...

Sergius of Riga expressed his displeasure in no uncertain terms. In general, he viewed Seraphim and the Karlowac church as decrepit reactionaries who had lost all touch with Soviet affairs and could only compromise the anti-Soviet cause by foisting themselves upon it. What he objected to most was the close and overt association between the monarchist *émigrés* and the Nazis.[43]

As one of the leaders of the 'monarchist émigrés', Turkul must have been amused. Seraphim and Anastasius had served their purpose, the Orthodox Church was hopelessly divided. Now it was time for the Catholic Uniates. His assistant, George Romanov, was sent to Switzerland to become ordained as a priest. It was a judicious move. Romanov had worked in Vienna on the MAX network and had written to Turkul that Klatt might be a Communist double agent. He had come close to the truth and had to be kept out of the way. Besides, Romanov might be useful in the future as a source on Orthodox–Uniate alliances. It was an area that had concerned Moscow for a long time.[44]

Since the time of the Bolshevik revolution, the Jesuits had revived their interest in playing the Uniate card. Uniate missionaries were trained in Rome for infiltration. Pius XI and his successor both foresaw that Jesuit-trained missionaries might reunite Orthodox Russia with the Catholic Church 'as soon as the way was open'.[45] Unfortunately, the Bolsheviks had blocked the way for three decades, and appeared to have no intention of stepping aside.

The heart of the anti-Communist crusade was a special unit of the Vatican which co-ordinated Eastern policy. During World War II, the secretary of this office, Congregatio pro Ecclesia Orientali, was 'the French Cardinal Tisserant, a well-known Orientalist', and a noted anti-Communist.[46] By 1942, this Congregation was actively preparing a missionary network of Uniates. Jesuits were sent in disguise into Soviet territory to provide intelligence reports on the prospects for religious reunification with the Orthodox.[47]

The extent to which Turkul assisted the Jesuit penetration missions may never be known (at least until the Vatican Secret Archives are opened). Yet it is interesting to note that of the three hundred volunteer 'Apostles' he admitted smuggling into the Soviet Union, only a handful ever came back out.[48] During the war, Turkul's assistant kept close watch on the Catholic Army of the Ukraine. It was not difficult for Klatt to follow the Galician SS since his network monitored all Soviet and German troop dispositions on the Eastern front:

> ... he conducted its activities in a manner that was unique. His office staff consisted of two persons – everything in the office was mechanized ... He was able to report large-scale strategic plans as well as details of troop movements in some important cases even down to divisional level; his reports usually came in two or three weeks ahead of events, so that our leaders could prepare suitable counter-measures – or, should I say, could have done so if Hitler paid more attention to the information.[49]

It was not Klatt's intelligence work, but his Jewish background that eventually drew Hitler's attention. The Führer ordered the dismissal of all Jews working for his intelligence services. Gehlen lamented: 'My most reliable agent, who had brought in the best information I have about Russia, I can't use anymore because he is half Jewish.'[50]

A temporary rescue was arranged by transferring Klatt on paper to the Hungarian intelligence staff. According to Farago, Klatt was in need of frequent rescue,

> not because his material was not satisfactory (it was uniformly excellent) but because his mystery continued to disturb his employers. Once, in 1945, only the personal intervention of General Heinz Guderian, then chief of the General Staff, saved his life; the Germans, totally exasperated by Klatt's impregnable secret, decided to get rid of him for good by sending him to a concentration camp. Guderian was scandalized; the information the man was supplying was so invaluable that the General Staff Chief gave orders to leave Klatt alone, or else, he said, the best source of information about the USSR would be lost.[51]

Despite his Catholicism, Klatt was still harassed about his Jewish racial status, but continued to provide information up to the last days of World War II. His mysterious sources never dried up.[52] Klatt had worked for Admiral Canaris of the Abwehr, then General Gehlen of FHO and finally, Walter Schellenberg of the SS. Every branch of Nazi intelligence, including General Guderian at Hitler's highest headquarters, depended on Klatt. It appears that he may have been the one mysterious Jew in the SS intelligence service who received Honorary Aryan status. It should be noted that those decrees were signed by Adolf Hitler personally. It would indeed be an irony if Klatt found his final rescuer at the top of the Third Reich.[53]

But the search for Klatt's intelligence source continued. According to the recently declassified files, Klatt's chief agent was 'Lang', yet another of General Turkul's spies who worked for the SS. His real name was 'Ira LONGIN aka IRA aka LANG, head of the "Dr LANG" Section [in] VIENNA which supplied amazingly accurate information to the Germans concerning top level Soviet strategy during the war'.[54]

If Klatt was getting his information from Lang, who was Lang getting his from? Lang supposedly had agents on Marshal Rokossovsky's Soviet General Staff, but how could he communicate with them? After all, one could not simply pick up a telephone in SS headquarters in Vienna and dial a traitor in the Kremlin. Heinz Höhne supplies the answer, although he misspells General Turkul's name:

> [The] line to the senior levels of the Red Army ran through the exiled Russian General Turgut. Living in Vienna and working for the Abwehr office there, he maintained radio stations in the Caucasus and Urals over which he communicated with anti-Stalinists among senior Red Army officers.[55]

Another author also misspelled Turkul's name, but confirms his direct involvement with radio espionage:

> After the outbreak of World War II, Turkhul disappeared ... General Turkhul showed up unexpectedly in Central Europe, having been traced through a secret transmitter which provided the Germans with intelligence on Soviet military formations and movements.[56]

In a recently declassified intelligence file, the US Army Counter Intelligence Corps filled in many of the blanks on Turkul's wartime movements:

1. Pius XI's Secretary of State Eugenio Pacelli, photographed after successfully concluding the Vatican's Concordat with Germany. Within a few years, Hitler was attacking the Catholic Church while Pacelli, as Pope Pius XII, tried to preserve his diplomatic neutrality on the eve of war.

2. After another triumph of Pacelli's diplomacy, the 1929 Concordat with Fascist Italy, Mussolini's cavalcade arrives at the Vatican for an official reception with Pope Pius XI. Unlike his successor Pacelli, Pius XI was willing to take a strong public stand against Hitler's policies.

3. After Hitler's defeat, Pacelli abandoned his controversial wartime neutrality towards Germany and spread the word that the Vatican would shelter Fascist fugitives. Fearing retribution for their wartime massacres, the Croatian Ustashi pack up for the flight to Austria, first stop on the Ratline to Rome.

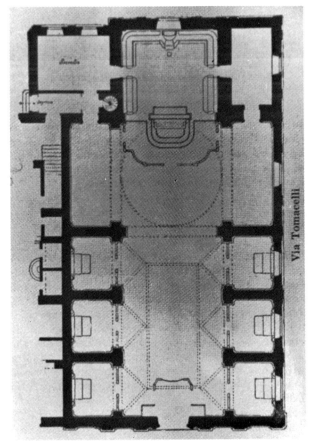

4. In the chaos of post-war Europe, the roads were clogged with refugees fleeing to the West away from the victorious Communists. Many infamous war criminals, including Croatian dictator Ante Pavelić, mingled with the throng to avoid capture by Marshal Tito's ruthless partisans.

5. All roads led to Rome and the charitable hands of Father Draganović at the Institute of San Girolamo at Via Tomacelli 132. After World War II Father Draganović turned this Croatian Institute into a sanctuary for Fascist fugitives going down the Vatican Ratline.

6. The drawing room in San Girolamo when it housed wanted war criminals in the late 1940s. After pro-Nazi Bishop Alois Hudal was exposed for smuggling German and Austrian war criminals such as Stangl and Eichmann, San Girolamo became the headquarters for a more discreet and far more efficient Vatican smuggling network.

7. The priests who ran San Girolamo in the early 1950s, posing with Church dignitaries. Father Draganović is in the second row, sixth from the left. Several of the priests who worked on Father Draganović's Ratlines gave tape-recorded interviews to the authors.

8. Father Draganović (left), and San Girolamo's Rector Monsignor Juraj Magjerec (right) celebrating a special mass in St John Lateran in Rome, 1953, on the occasion of the 500th anniversary of the Institute. Draganović and Magjerec were the key operatives in the Nazi-smuggling network run under the cover of San Girolamo's "charitable" work for refugees. Several religious orders, including the Franciscans and the Jesuits, supplied forged documents and other assistance to the Ratlines.

9. Draganović and Magjerec on one of their many visits to the largely Croatian Displaced Persons Camp of Bagnoli. After the war, many wanted Ustashi war criminals hid at Bagnoli and later used the camp as a centre for terrorist operations against the Communists. During the Cold War, Draganović was a secret Vatican liaison to the intelligence services of Italy, Britain and the United States. When Draganović retired behind the "Iron Curtain" in 1967, there were many who wondered whether his real loyalty lay with the Communists all along.

10. A large group of San Girolamo's priests together with well-wishers, posing on the steps of St Peter's during the celebrations of the Institute's 500th anniversary. Father Draganović is the second figure on the right of the bearded figure in the centre, and Monsignor Magjerec is the second on his left. By the time this picture was taken in 1953, Soviet intelligence had thoroughly infiltrated the Ratlines with their own agents, often posing as fugitive Nazis, and had even placed a spy, Miroslav Varoš, inside San Girolamo itself.

11. Pius XII's Under Secretary of State, Monsignor Giovanni Montini, with another dignitary on the terrace of San Girolamo. It was Montini who secretly supervised Draganović's Ratline and lobbied the Western powers for the release of war criminals. During this time Montini was recruited as a secret intelligence source for US counter-intelligence chief, James Jesus Angleton, a relationship which boosted Angleton's CIA career when Montini became Pope Paul VI.

12. Croatian war criminal Ante Pavelić in his office with Ustashi officials in Zagreb during the war. Under the direction of Adolf Hitler (whose picture hangs on Pavelić's office wall) the Poglavnik's government slaughtered over half a million Serbs, Jews and Gypsies in the most barbarous manner. After the war, the US Army staged a burglary at Father Draganović's office and discovered that Pavelić was living inside the Vatican along with other wanted war criminals.

13. A wartime picture of Croatian dictator Pavelić with a group of Franciscan priests. Many Croatian clerics supported Pavelić's Fascist Ustashi movement. After his post-war sanctuary in the Vatican was discovered by the American Army, Pavelić was allowed to quietly escape to South America in order to prevent a "staggering blow" to the Roman Catholic Church.

14. One of many villas in the grounds of the Pope's Summer Residence at Castelgandolfo outside of Rome. A number of important fugitives were in hiding at Castelgandolfo, including Ante Pavelić and Ferenc Vajta. Vajta worked for the Nazis in Hungary, was later recruited by French intelligence, then by the Vatican, and finally told all their secrets to the Americans.

15. Post-war Italian President Enrico de Nicola (centre) and Prime Minister Alcide de Gasperi (right) after an audience with Pope Pius XII in mid-1946. De Gasperi worked closely with Monsignor Montini of the Vatican Secretariat of State on anti-Communist plans, and his Government was heavily implicated in the Vatican's Ratline. Soon after this photograph was taken, de Gasperi became involved in running guns for the Vatican's "freedom fighters".

16 & 17. Unfortunately, many of the Vatican's "freedom fighters" were former Nazi collaborators. Here is a picture of an SS officer leading Bishop Gregory Rožman's "anti-Communist" army down the streets of Ljubljana in 1944. On the dais, Bishop Rožman himself reviews the troops with local SS commander and the Fascist president of Slovenia. The Bishop's wartime collaboration included a "Pastoral Letter" urging his flock to join the Nazi cause to "assure our existence and better future, in the fight against [the] Jewish conspiracy".

18. After the march-past Bishop Rožman extends his warm greetings to SS General Rösener. Although both the British and American Governments concluded that Rožman should be handed over to Tito as a Nazi collaborator, they permitted his "escape" to Switzerland in 1947. In Berne, Bishop Rožman laundered Fascist treasure to fund the Križari terrorist groups behind the "Iron Curtain".

19. Wanted war criminal Srečko Rover posing in his Ustashi uniform. After the war he was provided with false identity papers by Father Draganović, and rose to be a senior officer in the Križari terrorist network which launched a series of disastrous operations in 1946–48. After being denounced as a Communist agent, Rover finally settled in Australia and organised another equally disastrous terrorist network.

20 & 21. The Communist Yugoslav government accused Father Karlo Petranović of participating in the wartime massacres of Serbs around Ogulin. After the war he became one of many priests recruited by Draganović to run the Ratline, sending thousands of fugitives out of Genoa to North and South America and Australia. Here he is with some of his "passengers" on the waterfront in Genoa.

22. Bishop Ivan Bučko, the saviour of the Ukrainian SS Division 'Galicia'. Bučko worked closely with Father Draganović smuggling fugitive Nazis, and also had influential contacts with senior Vatican bureaucrats, including Pope Pius XII.

23. Ukrainian volunteers for the SS Division 'Galicia' on parade during the war. Although Archbishop Szepticky of the Uniate (Catholic) Church privately denounced the Nazis to Pope Pius XII, he blessed the SS volunteers, many of whom had previously committed war crimes while serving in auxiliary police units.

24. Ukrainian Nazi leader, Yaroslav Stetsko, whose Organisation of Ukrainian Nationalists conducted anti-Jewish pogroms following the Nazi invasion in 1941. Banned by the US State Department, Stetsko moved to Canada where he headed the British intelligence front, the Anti-Bolshevik Bloc of Nations. Stetsko's ABN was supervised by a British double agent named Kim Philby who used this Fascist-dominated organisation to crush legitimate anti-Communist resistance efforts behind the Iron Curtain.

25. Despite his cloudy past, Yaroslav Stetsko enjoyed a resurgence of popularity with the Reagan administration and was even received in the White House. Here Stetsko meets with former US Army General John Singlaub, one of the key figures named in the Iran–Contra scandal and former head of the World Anti-Communist League. WACL was formed by merging neo-Fascist and terrorist groups from many nations.

26. France's Ambassador to Italy, François Poncet (wearing a moustache and bow tie), was captured by the 'Butcher of Lyon', Klaus Barbie, and secretly collaborated against the Resistance. As the senior French official in occupied Germany, and later President of the International Red Cross, Poncet went on to play an important role in the Ratline. By the late 1940s, he had become Allen Dulles's conduit for Red Cross papers, so desperately needed by the Vatican's Nazi-smugglers.

27. Slovak Fascist leader, Jozef Kirschbaum, in his Hlinka Guard uniform during World War II. The CIA identified Kirschbaum's associate, Ferdinand Durčansky, as a class A war criminal and double agent whose intrigues with the Vatican helped bring about the Communist takeover of Czechoslovakia in 1948. Kirschbaum and Durčansky went to Canada along with other Slovak Fascists after American intelligence

28. General Prince Anton Vasilevich
Turkul, the greatest Communist agent of
them all. In addition to penetrating the
Holy See, General Turkul was a
Communist double agent in German,
Japanese, British, French and American
intelligence. It was Turkul who splintered
the anti-Bolshevik *émigré* groups after
World War I, sent Hitler false information
that crushed the Nazis on the Eastern
front, helped turn the Vatican Ratlines into
a vehicle for Soviet intelligence during
the Cold War, and culminated his career
by prematurely instigating the Hungarian
revolution of 1956.

In Rome subject succeeded in getting in contact with the Reichssicher-heitshauptamt (RSHA) for whom he allegedly worked as an agent in the winter of 1943. Subject was removed from Rome in 1943, primarily at the insistence of Richard KLATT aka KAUDER, who was one of [Turkul's] leading agents in the Balkans.

KLATT insisted that [Turkul] not be captured by the allies, fearing that then the organization would fall apart. [Turkul] was removed in an Abwehr plane. The Abwehr was helping Klatt. They believed that by establishing direct contact with [Turkul] and promising him financial support for his White Russian Organization they would keep the good will of . . . the 'Dr Lang' section [in] . . . Vienna which supplied amazingly good information to the Germans concerning top level Soviet strategy during the War, and other Turkul agents. Support of [Turkul] was the primary condition set by Lang for his service with the Abwehr.[57]

The incestuous trio of Turkul, Klatt and Lang was literally blackmailing German intelligence, by threatening to withhold its information on the Soviet Union unless Turkul's political pro-gramme was accepted. For decades, historians have puzzled over the German failure to adopt a cohesive strategy concerning the recruitment of Soviet *émigrés* for their Army. According to the recently declassified files, General Turkul was the principal obsta-cle to any unified volunteer force.

Wrecking the Vlasov Army was the key to Turkul's strategy. The Nazis were planning to use captured Soviet General Andrei Vlasov to recruit an army of Soviet volunteers from the POW camps, give them German arms and equipment, and send them against the Soviet Union. In order to infiltrate the Vlasov move-ment, Turkul ordered Klatt to make a counter proposition to Schellenberg of the SS.

Turkul ordered his NTS network to serve as 'political commi-sars' with Vlasov's units to ensure their loyalty to the Third Reich. The Germans quickly accepted, and Turkul's agents were soon in a position to denounce Soviet POW leaders.[58]

Turkul later suggested that it was Klatt who had penetrated and sabotaged the anti-Communist units. But the evidence showed that it was Turkul who was Vlasov's harshest critic.[59] Turkul's views carried great weight: in addition to Admiral Canaris, head of the Abwehr, he 'succeeded in gaining the trust of Himmler . . . and Alfred Rosenberg, who were both close to Hitler'.[60] Turkul's White Russian network was so valuable that only a handful of Third Reich officials even knew of its existence. None of them realised that Turkul's NTS had promoted its own agenda for the Soviets:

by placing members of its organization in stratgic positions (in the Reich as well as in the occupied areas) and seeking a monopoly of effective leadership among the *émigrés*, the influence of the Solidarists (NTS) was disproportionate. One of the top propagandists at the Wehrmacht propaganda compound ... was a leading NTS man. Kaminskii's Russian Nazi 'party' was guided by NTS officials. The Ostministerium's training camp for 'converted' prisoners at Wüstrau was in effect a fief of the NTS, where its ideas were propagated under the noses of the German mediocrities. In at least two-score towns and cities in the occupied areas there were Solidarist mayors, chiefs of police, or newspaper editors recruited by the proselytizers of the NTS; finally several of the top men within the Vlasov movement were likewise NTS members, although Vlasov himself refused to endorse their group.[61]

In hindsight, it is easy to see the trap that Turkul had set. Every detail of the new volunteer forces was passed to Soviet headquarters. The Vatican's dream of their Uniate missionaries marching into the Soviet Union on the heels of a Catholic army was severely dashed when the Galician SS was virtually destroyed in the Battle of Brody in 1944. To complete the débâcle, the survivors were reformed into various military units under KONR, a committee for the Liberation of the Peoples of Russia, led by General Vlasov.

The reaction of the minority groups was predictable. The Organisation of Ukrainian Nationalists under Bandera and Stetsko deeply resented being led by a Russian and had already established its own paramilitary force, the Ukrainian Insurgent Army, or UPA.[62] While the Wehrmacht was working to unite all the *émigrés* under Vlasov, Turkul and the SS were working in an entirely different direction.

The former Governor of Galicia and SS leader, Gustav Wächter, participated in sensitive and secret negotiations to gain the collaboration of Bandera's OUN/UPA forces. Bandera and Stetsko were quietly released from house arrest and eagerly rejoined the Nazi cause. It had been a long time since the Nazis had needed him, but now Bandera had conditions: the OUN/UPA would fight for Hitler, but not under the command of Vlasov, the renegade Soviet General who insisted on re-incorporating the Ukraine into a Great Russian Empire after the Nazi victory.[63]

Vlasov's scheme was anathema to the OUN separatists who wanted an independent Ukraine. Bandera joined with other anti-Russian nationalists to form a new bloc. Although there is little evidence to support it, OUN leaders claim that in 1944 Bandera formed the 'Anti-Bolshevik Bloc of Nations' (ABN), to unite all the non-Russian minorities working for the Third Reich.[64] It appears that Turkul's NTS may have overreached themselves with their divide and conquer strategy, and grown careless. The NTS headquarters in Warsaw was discovered to be in communication with the Soviets. In 1944 the Gestapo began a mass round-up of NTS members leaving the field open for a final German push to unite the *émigrés*. It was too little, too late.[65]

In view of the exigencies of the Nazi military situation, Bandera and the other anti-Vlasov separatists agreed to defer their squabbling in the interests of Nazi unity. At the urging of Wächter, Bandera agreed to have a moderate OUN spokesman, General Pavel Shandruk, conduct negotiations with the pan-Russian allies of the Third Reich. Soon General Vlasov had agreed that at least the Galician Ukraine would not be considered part of a Greater Russia after the Communists were defeated.[66]

In February 1945, as the Soviets swept across Eastern Europe, the last details of Slavic collaboration were still being ironed out in Berlin. The Nazis still refused to give any written guarantees of religious freedom, but at least no longer referred to the Slavs as 'sub-humans'.[67] Still, with the Nazi war machine in permanent retreat, the negotiations were completely futile.

In the spring of 1945 General Shandruk assumed command of the scattered Galician SS, which was simply renamed the First Ukrainian Division. At the end of the war, the unit took its place, on paper at least, as part of Vlasov's army. But instead of fighting the Soviets, the Catholic army of the Ukraine was fighting Tito's partisans in Yugoslavia before retreating into Austria.[68]

Turkul was hot on their heels. To show his good faith with the Nazis, he had assumed control of a Vlasov unit and also headed for Yugoslavia. 'A politically amorphous though distinctly tsarist group of Russian *émigrés* in Yugoslavia was authorized to form a Schützkorps, employed primarily against the partisans there.'[69] In an interesting bit of Stalinist duplicity, Turkul's mission was to crush Tito.[70]

Turkul's forces made contact with the Fascist commander Dimitrije Ljotić, and remnants of Draža Mihailović's Četniks, whose forces had also collaborated with the Nazis. When the war ended, Turkul established emissaries to the West through Ljotić and Mihailović who had already begun to negotiate sanctuary. Suddenly, all across Europe, the *émigré* armies of the Third Reich disappeared. Immediately, rumours about the Vatican's role began to spread.

9
Diplomacy and Deceit

The flight of the Ukrainian SS is a good example of a bad example. Many other Fascist groups, such as the Ustashi, followed in their path, imitating the Ukrainian strategies for post-war survival. The Vatican was not alone in protecting Nazi fugitives after the war. Nor was the Holy See solely behind the transformation of ex-Nazis into 'freedom fighters'. The termination of serious war crimes investigations was the result of official diplomatic decisions by several Western powers.

Intelligence front groups like the Ukrainian-dominated Anti-Bolshevik Bloc of Nations were not created in a vacuum. They were the product of a deliberate double standard and cynical secret policies. In many respects the Vatican was only a junior partner in a diplomatic shell game whose rules were largely shaped in London. It was a game that the fugitive Nazis learned quickly and well.

Even before the end of the war, word spread quickly throughout the Fascist forces of Eastern Europe: head for the British-occupied area of Austria to avoid capture by the Communists. Some of the fugitives, particularly those from the Ukraine, must have been a little apprehensive at surrendering to anyone. Many of the people in General Shandruk's Galician SS Division had previously earned a reputation for brutality during the gruesome police executions in the Ukraine. Some also allegedly participated in the bloody suppression of the Warsaw uprising, while others may have fought against the West at Monte Cassino. Some were reportedly involved in massacring French partisans.

Under Shandruk the unit had little chance to commit war crimes. To be fair, it appears that most of the real atrocities had already been committed prior to 1943, when the Ukrainian unit was still just an amalgam of auxiliary police battalions, and before it was formally absorbed into the SS.[1] Although the exact wartime role of the Galician SS is still hotly debated, one fact is certain: in

the spring of 1945 the Galicians headed westwards. The First
Ukrainian Division, Bishop Bučko's last great hope, surrendered
in May 1945 to the British Army at Klagenfurt, Austria.[2]

The arrival of Shandruk's Division, 90 per cent of whom were
Uniate Catholics, was not entirely unexpected by the British.
According to the Ukrainians, the British had a special interest in
them:

> ... contacts were established with the British forces ... On May 8th the
> entire unit was successful in crossing to join the British forces at Klagenfurt
> ... Arms were not removed from the unit; in fact, in many cases more
> arms were issued and the unit was instructed to cross over to Italy. The
> move beginning May 28th ended up ... at Rimini.[3]

According to their own detailed account, the Galician SS was
the only Axis unit to survive the war intact, under arms and with
their own officers. The British did not place the Ukrainians in a
POW cage, but in Camp 374, for 'Separated Enemy Personnel' at
Rimini, a distinction which, to the Ukrainians at least, denoted
their special status.[4] However, one unit of the Division had been
cut off, and fell into far less hospitable American hands.

On 5 July 1945 the President's Personal Representative to the
Pope received a diplomatic note from the Vatican Secretariat of
State:

> Several thousand Ukrainians are in Germany and fear they may be sent to
> Galicia. On their behalf, the Holy See has been requested to use its good
> offices in order that these poor refugees may soon be allowed to leave
> Germany and to take refuge in France, Belgium, the Netherlands, or any
> other country rather than being obliged to go to territories under Russian
> domination.[5]

The difficulty was that the 'poor refugees' were captured still
wearing German uniforms. The American Army lacked a sense of
humour about these prisoners. One of the Galician officers was
discovered to have the distinctive SS tattoo under his armpit,
listing his blood type in case he was wounded in battle. The
Americans promptly made arrangements to extradite him to the
Soviets. They had no intention of simply allowing an SS unit to
cross over to a friendly Catholic state as the Vatican had requested,
and continued their search for 'refugees' with SS tattoos.[6]

This must have been disquieting news: over 2,000 Galician SS
members had once undergone SS cadre training. A large number

of Shandruk's officers also bore the incriminating tattoo.[7] It was high time for the Vatican to intervene more directly on behalf of the Catholic Ukrainian army.

A few weeks later, on 11 August 1945, the Vatican Secretariat of State delivered a diplomatic note to the Americans 'on behalf of the spiritual and religious care of the displaced persons of Ruthenian Catholic Rite in Germany . . . whether the latter be within or outside concentration camps'.[8]

The Vatican specifically requested that its recently appointed Apostolic Visitor 'be authorized to visit . . . the concentration camps in Germany where there are Ruthenian Catholics'. It is not without coincidence that the man chosen for the Pope's emissary was none other than 'his excellence Monsignor Bučko'. Yet again, the Vatican had nominated a Fascist priest as its emissary to Catholic Nazi collaborators. They asked that he be given the assistance of priests 'whom he will find among the Ruthenian displaced persons'. This was apparently a reference to Uniate Chaplains like Ivan Grynioch who had served with the Galician SS.[9]

The Vatican also conveyed the opening shot in the amnesty barrage from the Oriental Congregation. Apparently, the Vatican's lawyers had been working overtime and had found a loophole to keep the Galician SS out of Soviet hands:

> . . . those Ukrainians . . . who are classified as prisoners of war . . . should not be considered as deserters from the Red Army; for their nationality in 1939 was Polish and not Russian. For the same reason their custody cannot be requested by the Soviet Authorities on the basis of the agreements of Yalta [which promised repatriation for] only those Russian citizens who departed from Soviet territory after 1927 or those individuals who were formerly members of the Red Army.[10]

The British Foreign Office understood this extremely clever argument. The Galician SS could not go back to the Soviets because they had once been Poles. On the other hand, they could not be sent to Poland because Galicia was now part of the Soviet Union. Under the Vatican's version of 'Catch 22', all Galician war criminals would simply have to be released into the benevolent hands of Bishop Bučko. But the Americans would not budge.[11] Under the Yalta agreement, these Nazis had to be returned to Soviet custody.

A week later the pressure was increased a notch when Bučko's old superior, Bishop Bohachevsky of Pittsburgh, sent a letter on 25 August to General George Marshall, Chief of Staff of the War Department. He insisted that all Ukrainians in the US zone be given asylum, Red Cross assistance and the right to organise their own 'charitable committees':

> These Ukrainians, who are classified as Russians or Poles, live in deathly fear and dread the thought of being sent to Soviet Russia or Poland. Reports from semi-official and private sources revealing tales of relentless, horrible, barbaric religious, social, and political persecutions, imprisonments, and executions of Ukrainians, especially the intellectuals, clergymen, etc., by the Soviet authorities give the Ukrainians good cause for fear and anxiety.[12]

Undoubtedly most Ukrainian refugees in Germany had good reason to fear those consequences. Stalin treated even slave labourers and POWs as Nazi collaborators. Many of those returned to him were summarily murdered and the rest shipped off to Siberia. But among the Galician SS were many who had previously served with the SS mobile killing units at places like Babi Yar, where over 100,000 Jews had been shot in just three days. These killers had real cause for fear and anxiety.[13]

The War Department dumped Bishop Bohachevsky's letter on the State Department, which sent him a cursory reply a few months later, saying simply that 'the situation of those who remain is receiving every appropriate consideration to avoiding undue hardship'.[14] Throughout the autumn of 1945 the American Army continued to round up fugitive Ukrainians and ship them off to the Soviet Union. As it turned out, they were among the last to be sent back. The Nazis were going to get a Christmas present.

On 30 November 1945 the Vatican sent a formal Diplomatic Note 'on behalf of 2,000 Ukrainian refugees residing in Stuttgart ... these refugees maintain that their repatriation would almost certainly expose them to deportation, physical and mental torture, and even death by shooting ... In view of the assurances recently given that Hungarian refugees would not be repatriated against their will, it is believed that there are grounds for hoping that the Ukrainians ... will likewise not be treated differently.'[15] Yet again the Americans gave the Vatican a polite brush-off. The men in question were suspected of being Nazi collaborators.[16]

Two weeks later, the Vatican was back with another Diplomatic Note marked URGENT. Bishop Bučko had issued an appeal directly to Pius XII. The Vatican stated that, contrary to all assurances, the Americans were still transferring Ukrainian prisoners to the Soviets at Stuttgart. They quoted Bučko's appeal to both Pius XII and the Americans for a temporary stay of transfer so that, 'as Bishop Bučko writes, "They could prepare themselves for a Christian death"'. Bučko also related 'that in the Displaced Persons Camp at Hannei some refugees committed suicide rather than permit themselves to be transferred'.[17]

Bučko's propaganda campaign was effective. Five weeks later, on 23 January 1946, the State Department issued a 'new directive' that altered the rules in favour of Ukrainians. From now on only those Ukrainians who were both residents and citizens of the Soviet Union after 1939 were liable for forcible hand-over. This exempted most of the 'Polish' Ukrainians from Galicia. In addition, the State Department would only hand over those 'non-Polish' Ukrainians who were actually captured in German uniform, or against whom there was 'reasonable evidence' that they had voluntarily rendered aid and comfort to the Nazis.[18]

The Americans were not alone in feeling Catholic pressure. The Canadian government reluctantly allowed Reverend Kushnir to visit imprisoned Ukrainians in the Western-occupied zones of Germany, allegedly on a charitable mission. Soon after, the British Foreign Office was chagrined to receive a broadside from Reverend Kushnir as 'Chairman of the Board' of a political group strongly protesting the policy of forcible repatriation of Ukrainians.[19]

The Vatican had obtained a signficant compromise on the Ukrainians, but pushed its luck in intervening for members of Vlasov's army.[20] The American decision was to treat all Russians under the Ukrainian rules which guaranteed that they would be handed over. It was a mistake that the West bitterly regretted, for it cost them dearly throughout the Cold War. At least Vlasov's army was largely untainted by war crimes. That could not be said for the Galician SS, some of whom had committed spectacular atrocities.

It is one of the tragedies of the post-war era that the American and British governments rounded up tens of thousands of petty collaborators, prisoners of war and innocent political refugees and forcibly handed them over to certain death or imprisonment. For a short period, the West was an accomplice in Stalin's post-war massacres.[21] The irony is that the Vatican's protests only helped the guilty evade punishment. As a result, the Ukrainians believed themselves favoured protégés and began to apply for American visas.[22]

The shift in American policy did not go unnoticed. On 25 June 1946 the Ukrainian–American League wrote to the State Department to

> unequivocally protest plans to bring to our country people who cooperated with German fascists in terrorizing the Ukrainian, Polish and Jewish populations of Western Ukraine (formerly Poland), or who were soldiers in the SS Division 'Halychyna' [Galician] which fought against the American and British armies in Italy, or who belonged to the armed bands which helped the German fascists in terrorizing and persecuting the people of our allied countries. They aided the Germans in the death camps in destroying not only Ukrainians, Poles and Jews, but citizens of Britain, France, and the United States.[23]

The State Department replied that the 'screening of war criminals, quislings and collaborators is being pressed vigorously by the allied military authorities . . . with a view to the elimination of such persons from the displaced persons centers'.[24] The American government was still under the illusion that no Nazi collaborators would escape unpunished. The British had no such illusions.

Incredible as it seems, the entire Galician SS Division had been basking in the sun for the previous two years in the British camp at Rimini. It had suddenly dawned on the British that they had to at least make a token attempt at screening them before the camp was turned over to the new Italian government in September 1947. In January Brigadier General Fitzroy Maclean and his assistant arrived at Rimini to screen for undesirables[25]

The screening was scanty. They interviewed only 200 men out of 8,272. They used camp inmates as interpreters, conducted no cross-examinations and basically asked the Ukrainians to tell them where they had been during World War II. Brigadier Maclean's 'screening team' cheerfully admitted that 'the short history of the Division was supplied entirely by the Ukrainians themselves and we had no information of any kind against which they could be checked'.[26]

The Ukrainian officers conjured up a false order of battle, claiming that their unit was the First Ukrainian Division of the Wehrmacht, which had a relatively innocent ring to it. The screening team noted: 'Some of the real villains . . . if there are any, may be sheltering behind these innocuous-sounding units, but that is a risk we have to take.'[27] The British were already months behind in their screening. 'If, however, we are to get anywhere, we must, and in my opinon safely can, assume that by and large the men are what they say they are and did what they said they did,' Maclean wrote.[28]

Brigadier Maclean had a little problem when several of the prisoners started talking about their ranks in the Galician SS. Such confessions did not cause the British screeners much anxiety. Surely, the prisoners had made an innocent mistake. 'I do not see anything suspicious in some of the men not knowing exactly what unit they were in . . . it seems however to have had some SS training.'[29] The British preferred to stick with the fictional Wehrmacht cover story even when faced with contrary evidence supplied by the prisoners themselves.

It was a little more difficult for the screeners when, despite all the hints, the prisoners persisted in saying that 'the great majority of them voluntarily enlisted in the German armed forces and fought against our allies.' Since that would have qualified them for handover to the Soviets, the screeners surmised that the prisoners really had not meant that they 'volunteered' in that sense.[30]

Fortunately, none of the prisoners was stupid enough to confess to war crimes, and so none was discovered. Despite his assistant's recommendation that it would take many months to screen each person in the camp properly, Maclean informed the Foreign Office in February that his investigation in Rimini would be completed by the middle of March.[31]

This was 'good news' to the Foreign Office, which hoped to avoid the embarrassment that would naturally follow any rigorous investigation.[32] The news that many had confessed their voluntary service to the Reich was even more embarrassing. The British hoped that those problem prisoners would simply disappear into the night, cynically noting: '. . . it is unlikely that there will be a big bag of quislings owing to the lack of guards to prevent their escape.'[33] They need not have worried.

A Soviet team had made a quick visit to the Ukrainians in the summer of 1945 and indentified a 'small fascist minority' in leadership positions. Eleven 'were in fact removed at the request of the Soviet Mission but were subsequently allowed by the British authorities to return'.[34] This is one of the rare instances where fugitive Nazis wanted to break back into a 'prison camp'. Such was British internment in Italy. Rimini was notorious among American counter-intelligence officials for the ease with which prisoners seemed to come and go at will.[35]

The Ukrainians enjoyed British custody and had no plans to leave. Brigadier Maclean, who genuinely liked these fellows,[36] asked the Foreign Office how to protect the Ukrainians from falling into Soviet hands once the Italian government took over the camp. Despite all the self-serving explanations, the Ukrainians had been captured in German uniforms and had already admitted that they volunteered to fight for the Nazis. 'In the circumstances, the only possible solution appears to be to remove them from Italy before the ratification of the Treaty to a British controlled area where they could be further investigated should this be necessary,' wrote Maclean.[37]

The Foreign Office was divided over this suggestion. A small majority favoured bringing the entire Galician SS Division to Britain until the matter could be resolved.[38] Some of the bureaucrats dissented vigorously, claiming that the scheme was a 'flimsy' pretext to evade the Yalta obligations.[39] Others said that only those who fought on the British side should be helped, not those who fought for the Germans.[40] British sympathy by this time was on the side of everyone who claimed to be anti-Communist. Whatever the unsavoury truth about the Galician unit, it was decided that Ukrainians in British custody were to be brought to safety in Britain.[41]

However, there were still large numbers of Ukrainian collaborators in American hands. The attempt to portray the Galician SS as 'freedom fighters' became international in scope. In February 1947 Reverend Kushnir's Ukrainian Canadian Committee launched another broadside at the US Secretary of State, claiming that 'to deliver these boys into the hands of the Soviets is tantamount to condemning them to death without trial. We appeal to you and your government for intervention and justice.'[42]

In May Cardinal Spellman of New York became the object of supplication. A petition, signed on behalf of 5,000 Ukrainians living in Salzburg in the US zone of Austria, was promptly delivered by the Cardinal to the National Catholic Welfare Conference, an organisation with no small political clout, which passed it on to the State Department.[43]

The petition marked a significant change in propaganda tactics by the *émigré* Ukrainians. For the first time, they took the offensive to claim that the Soviets were falsely accusing many Ukrainians of war crimes because they supported Bandera's anti-Communist underground, which was still engaged in a guerrilla war behind the Iron Curtain:

By the press communicates [sic] of the agencies 'associated Press' and 'Dana-Reuter' from May 12, 1947, we were informed, that . . . USSR, Poland, and Czechoslovakia signed a treaty against the partisan group the so-called Ukrainian Insurgent Army [UPA] . . . we find almost daily more and more news in the press about the heavy battles on the borders of the mentioned countries with heavy armour, artillery, air-force and parachut-ists . . . All this is happening in the second anniversary of ceasing all military actions in Europe . . . the official press of the mentioned countries finds only one expression of these units; 'bandits.' We know, your Emin-ence, that in the lines of these so-called 'bandits' have been many priests . . . we know that the . . . bloody facts of persecution of the Greek-Catholic Church on the West Ukrainian territory, are well known to you, your Eminence. All the world knows, that our seven bishops were thrown into prisons, where they either died or are tormented in the dreadfullest conditions.[44]

By the summer of 1947, the British government had completed their first efforts to protect the Ukrainian 'freedom fighters'. The move did not escape the attention of the world press:

'Galician Division' in Britain . . . A dispatch from Rome comments on the statement made by Mr Hector McNeil, British Minister of State, about Hitler's so-called 'Galician Division,' 8,000 members of which have been brought to Britain from Italy. Mr McNeil claims that a Soviet Commission took part in the screening of these 8,000 men from the Western Ukraine and that no war criminals have been discovered among them.

This statement has occasioned considerable surprise in Rome press circles, since the 'Galician Division' was notorious for its cruelty and belonged to an SS formation. No Soviet representatives took part in any check-up of these 8,000 men, as the British military authorities invariably replied with a refusal when approached by Soviet representatives on this subject. Mr McNeil's statement is clearly intended to mislead public opinion.[45]

The Foreign Office received a more gentle criticism from Felix Wirth of the Foreign Press Association in Britain, who apparently recognised that very little screening had been done in the rush to evacuate the Ukrainians:

It would be ... interesting to determine by careful investigation if any of these people could be classed as war criminals ... Little is known, on the whole, of the Ukrainians' terrible role as Germany's faithful and active henchmen in the slaughter of the Jews in Lwow and other towns in that part of the world, as well as in the murder factories throughout Eastern Europe. The notorious Ukrainian SS Division 'Galizien' and other Ukrainian formations bear full responsibility for a good deal of the monstrous outrages perpetrated there.

Whatever may be our quarrel with the Russians, surely the conscience of civilization could not permit to classify those people as innocent political refugees unless we establish that they are definitely not guilty of crimes which cry to Heaven unretributed.[46]

Had McNeil misled the British parliament? Was there no effective screening? Forty years later, in November 1988, a British All-Party Parliamentary Committee determined that the Galician SS had not received even the minimal screening required for normal immigration to Britain, let alone the rigorous scrutiny promised in 1947.[47] At that time, official assurances were given that further exhaustive screening would be undertaken and that the Ukrainians had only been brought to Britain 'to make it more difficult for persons with dubious wartime records to escape'.[48]

William Wilkinson of the Foreign Office insisted that 'it is unlikely that any war criminals will be found'.[49] Perhaps he knew that no one was really looking. In his many memoranda Wilkinson insisted that the Ukrainians had already been screened by Brigadier Maclean at Rimini.[50] Unfortunately, both Maclean and Wilkinson were relying on the prisoners' own information. The 'never in the SS' cover story was soon rebutted by the Ukrainians themselves.

By 1947 there were so many Ukrainians in Britain that they started holding conventions. In February 1948 the fourth convention of the Ukrainian Union was held at Westminster Cathedral. In addition to Cardinal Griffin, Father Josephat Jean was present as the representative of the Uniate Catholics. According to the convention reports, the 'Union anticipates a large increase of membership in the near future when the men of the SS "Galizien" who have hitherto been prisoners of war become free workmen'.[51]

This not only destroyed the cover story that they had only been part of the Wehrmacht; the Ukrainians also let the cat out of the bag about the Foreign Office plan to release the prisoners quietly and give them civilian status. The ensuing outcry in the press should have compelled an honest investigation. Instead, Wilkinson wrote a chatty note to 'Dear Garelon', the head of the Ukrainian Union and signed it 'Willie'. He chided his friend for publicising the embarrassing truth:

I am sure that you will agree with me that it is most undesirable that public expression should be given to statements likely to give the impression that SS men are being allowed to settle down in the United Kingdom, as the question of the future disposal of these people is still under consideration. I should be grateful if this subject could be treated with discretion.[52]

Instead of keeping his mouth shut, Garelon sent Willie a memorandum containing an even more startling admission: every man had to 'sign an "application form" declaring that he "voluntarily applied to serve"' in the Galician Division.[53] This not only contradicted Maclean's pronouncement that they were draftees, but Garelon's confession also meant that they could not legally be considered refugees.[54]

Having thus disqualified his own people for Displaced Person status, Garelon argued that their voluntary service to the Reich was not important.[55] After all, it was not the first time the British had bent the rules:

The Jugoslavs who constituted a similar unit of about 12,000 were moved to the British Zone at the same time when the Ukrainians were moved to the UK a year ago. *They were all released in the British Zone as DPs.* [emphasis in original][56]

It appears that 'Dear Garelon' was embarrassing the Foreign Office. Evidently, the Ukrainians knew too much about British protection of other ex-Fascists and could create an even greater public scandal. However, the Foreign Office declined Garelon's invitation to become publicly 'associated with tributes to the Ukrainian Insurrectionary Army'.[57] Surreptitiously, they accelerated plans to resettle the Ukrainian SS elsewhere.

In May 1948 Wilkinson asked the British Cabinet to repudiate the Yalta Agreement concerning forcible repatriation of Soviets, which 'would also have the merit of bringing our policy regarding Soviet nationals into line with our policy regarding Yugoslavs and others'.[58] The Cold War was heating up, and any enemy of Britain's enemy was now a friend. Laudable as it may have been to refuse to hand over people for summary execution, the British government made no attempt to deal with the nagging problem of suspected war criminals on their own territory. Even after the Soviet Ambassador supplied a list of 124 officers of the Galician SS wanted for war crimes, Wilkinson wrote 'I do not think that a full-blooded screening is called for at this time'.[59] Instead, he suggested that the Foreign Office rely on the already unsatisfactory Maclean screening.[60]

Unfortunately, the Home Office was not so easily deceived. They had checked with US intelligence in Germany. The Americans had already arrested one man when they discovered his SS tattoo. Worse, American censors provided copies of his correspondence with his Galician SS comrades in Britain.[61] The Home Office was not amused:

> It would obviously be embarrassing to them if they civilianised these 124 officers and afterwards discovered that they were either war criminals in the most serious sense or had unpleasant SS records.[62]

To the Foreign Office's dismay, the Home Office was 'proposing to return all these men willy-nilly to Germany'.[63] That suggestion was promptly postponed, pending discussions with the Canadian government to absorb them as immigrants,[64] despite the British Home Office's suspicion that 'some of these men really might be war criminals'.[65] Apparently, it was one thing to dump SS men on Canada, quite another to give them British citizenship.

Only a privileged few in the Foreign Office realised that the Galician SS was already on the British side. A good part of the Ukrainian Nazi puppet government had already been recruited by the Secret Intelligence Service.[66] It was not such an outrageous idea. The leader of the Ukrainian nationalists, Stepan Bandera, had worked for the SIS before the war. In 1945, after the Nazis were defeated, the prodigal Bandera was taken back into the fold.

He was not alone. Less than a year afterwards, General Pavel Shandruk, the last commander of the Galician SS, was listed as one of the top leaders of Prometheus, a pre-war British operation which had been taken over by the Nazis and then resurrected by SIS.[67] The British wanted more than just a Ukrainian resistance force; they wanted to merge all the 'freedom fighters' into a massive Anti-Bolshevik Bloc of Nations. At first, the ABN was simply a merger of the friendly Fascists of OUN and their northern neighbours, the Byelorussian (White Russian) Nazis.[68]

They were a motley crew. Jaroslav Stetsko became the President, Mikolai Abramtchik was Vice President and Stanislav Stankievich was Secretary.[69] Stetsko had pledged his undying loyalty to the Führer in the middle of the OUN massacre of Jews at Lvov.[70] Abramtchik had been the Nazi Minister of Intelligence in the puppet government of Byelorussia.[71] Stankievich was the kind of war criminal who made Stetsko look good; a description of his heinous atrocities had been read into the Congressional Record of the United States.[72]

Shortly afterwards, his name resurfaced when the Soviet Delegate rose in the UN and accused America of hiding Stankievich, Bandera and other 'quislings and traitors' in the Allied zones of West Germany.[73] The State Department denied the charges, but the US Army Counter Intelligence Corps began their own investigation in Germany. Stankievich was arrested, but quickly released after he told the Americans what was going on. British intelligence had cleverly located ABN headquarters in the American zone, along with Bandera and other top Nazis denounced in the UN.

The CIC was furious at the British scheme. SIS had previously offered Bandera's services to the Americans, but the offer was refused.[74] It was one thing to help the British in secrecy, another to be publicly blamed for their recruitment of notorious war criminals. Instead of keeping their Nazi agents in their own zone, they had cynically dumped them in Munich, setting up the Americans as scapegoats in case of adverse publicity. In self-defence, and as a prelude to exposing the truth, the Americans downgraded the Bandera case from *Top Secret* to *Confidential*.[75]

The War Department asked the State Department for permission to issue a press release saying that the American Army was not protecting war criminals and would make every effort to arrest Bandera, if he was found in their zone of Germany.[76] The proposal was quickly squelched by Jack D. Neal, Chief of the State Department's Division of Foreign Activity Correlation, which handled intelligence liaison with the British. Neal thought it 'inadvisable to issue any press release on the subject', since it 'implied a willingness to arrest' Bandera if they ever found him.[77] Later, another State Department spy chief admitted the real reason why the British protection of Ukrainian Nazis was swept under the rug. The Americans had been trying to cut their own deal behind Britain's back. Since 1946 the Ukrainian Nazi leadership had been chronically unable to cooperate wholeheartedly with American intelligence representatives in Germany, primarily because the price set by Stephan Bandera for complete cooperation involved types of political recognition and commitments to his group which no American in Germany was in a position to make ... It first came to the attention of the American authorities when the Russians demanded the extradition of Bandera and many other anti-Soviet Ukrainian nationalists as war criminals. Luckily the attempt to locate these anti-Soviet Ukrainians was sabotaged by a few far-sighted Americans who warned the persons concerned to go into hiding.[78]

The report concluded that, although the Ukrainians were not working for the Americans, 'alienating such a group could ... have no particular advantage to the United States'. Consequently, the State Department admitted that 'no serious attempt has ever been made by American officials in Germany to disband [them]'.[79] The Americans quietly released their Galician SS prisoners and watched them happily track across the border to the British zone or quietly merge into the refugee population in their own zone. Across Germany the Ukrainian SS began drawing rations as 'victims of Nazi oppression'.[80]

The UN accusations were quickly forgotten. But Simon Wiesenthal could not forget the man who organised the Galician Nazis, SS Brigadeführer Dr Otto Gustav Wächter:

I saw him early in 1942, in Lwow ghetto. He was personally in charge on August 15, 1942, when four thousand elderly people in the ghetto were rounded up and sent to the railway station. My mother was among them.[81]

Apparently Wiesenthal was ignorant of the connection between the Vatican and British intelligence; he thought that

Wächter escaped after the war with the help of ODESSA and was given refuge in a religious college in Rome by Slovak priests who didn't know his identity ... In 1949, Wächter became very sick and wasn't expected to live long. He told the people in Rome who he was ... and asked to see a priest. He was given the sacraments by Bishop Hudal.[82]

In an interview, Wiesenthal recounted the rest of the story. The West German prosecutors called Hudal as a witness in a criminal case involving the Galician SS. Under oath, Hudal confessed that Wächter was the same man who had been living in the Vatican disguised as 'Father Otto Reinhardt'. Hudal was obviously embarrassed, but said that he did not make the Holy See's policy.[83]

However, Wiesenthal wrote in his memoirs that 'an Austrian

aristocrat who occasionally helped me asked Bishop Hudal to release Wächter's files. The Bishop refused.'[84] The archives of the Galician SS are presumably still in Vatican custody. What Wiesenthal never knew was that the Ukrainians had much more powerful protectors than Bishop Hudal. The Pope himself had a hand in the sanctuary negotiations for the Ukrainian SS. Just as the war was ending

> General Pavlo Shandruk, the leader of a Ukrainian liberation committee that had been founded under Nazi auspices, contacted Archbishop Ivan Buchko, a high ranking prelate in Rome specializing in Ukrainian matters for the Holy See . . . Shandruk hoped that Archbishop Buchko might reach the Pope himself with the general's plea for mercy on behalf of his men.
>
> 'Archbishop Ivan [Buchko] answered my letter very soon informing me that he had already visited the Division,' Shandruk recalled later. 'In a special audience (at night) the Archbishop had pleaded with His Holiness Pope Pius XII to intercede . . . as a result of the intercession by His Holiness, the soldiers of the Division were reclassified merely as confinees and Bolshevik agents were prohibited to visit . . . By the Spring of 1946 Shandruk, backed by Archbishop Buchko and the Ukrainian Relief Committee of Great Britain, had arranged with the British government to extend 'free settler' emigration status to the Ukrainian Waffen SS veterans at Rimini and to assist them in resettling in Canada, Australia, and other Commonwealth Countries.[85]

It would be misleading to state that the Pope was to blame for pressuring the British government. The truth is that Britain had its own agents of influence inside the Vatican, pressuring Pius XII to support its programme for the Ukrainians. In a declassified document, American intelligence listed the prominent leaders of Intermarium. As previously recounted, the Ukrainian delegate was none other than Bishop Bučko. The saviour of the Galician SS was an agent of the British SIS.[86]

Nor was Bučko the only prelate to serve two masters. Intermarium was replete with priests, monks and brothers from a wide range of orders including the Jesuits, Benedictines and Franciscans. They ran the printing press for false identity cards, coordinated the network of convents and monasteries that served as safe houses, laundered money and, perhaps most importantly, organised a very effective propaganda campaign that worked hand in glove with British interests. From the Križari to the OUN, from the Baltic to the Black Sea, Catholic clerics like Draganović and Bučko administered an espionage network that was vital to British intelligence. It was also something of a problem for British diplomacy.

The Foreign Office had more than a few embarrassing moments protecting the vital Vatican connection from exposure. On the one hand, His Majesty's Government had made very noble (later very inconvenient) public pronouncements concerning Britain's obligations to hunt for Nazi war criminals. On the other hand, the Vatican had the largest intelligence service in Eastern Europe, which could substantially assist the creation of a British sphere of influence, or at least revive ties to scores of nationalist organisations which fled to the Vatican after the Nazis' defeat. Noble ideals soon gave way to recruiting Eastern European Nazis.

The Ukrainian Nazis were the last large group to be smuggled directly through British territory. With the help of Bishop Bučko, Shandruk made arrangements to evacuate the Galician SS to Canada and Australia. Shandruk repaid the British by taking over the leadership of Prometheus. The group had been renamed 'the Prometheus League of the Atlantic Charter' to give it a more democratic flair. But it was still the same front group, run by SIS chief Sir Stewart Menzies, which had defected to the SS before returning to the British. By 1946, the Prometheus propaganda arm was almost fully geared up to battle the Communists.[87]

It was, however, a bit risky for Britain to undertake any more large-scale Nazi-smuggling, at least directly. Not only was Parliament concerned about the true nature of the Galician SS, but US intelligence was starting to realise that Prometheus was a thinly disguised British attempt to rearm Ukrainian Nazis under the cover of General Anders's Polish Army in Italy.[88]

Besides, the cover was a bit overworked. Anders's forces had taken in the fugitive Byelorussian SS Division Belarus as well as the Ukrainians and things were becoming crowded in their camps. The Vatican had been generous, but there was insufficient room in their convents and monasteries for all the new recruits. With the imminent withdrawal of the Allies from Italy, something had to be done with the remaining Nazis before R Day, 1947, when the Italians might have to extradite them as war criminals.

The reality of R Day, when the Italians resumed control of their own territory, had certainly stiffened the resolve of several faint-hearted British diplomats. Even Pavelić's Ustashi felt the benefit of the Ukrainian backwash. As late as May 1947 the Foreign Office was still reprimanding the Vatican about protecting the Ustashi:

> I should be glad if you would point out to the [Vatican] Secretariat of State that those persons who actively worked for the Pavelić Ustashi Government were giving their support and approval to a regime which flouted humanitarian principles, and which condoned atrocities unsurpassed in any period of human history.[89]

By November the Foreign Office had turned completely around. Instead of criticising the Vatican, they discreetly asked them to help smuggle the Ustashi out of Italy:

> His Majesty's Government have asked the Vatican to assist in getting the Greys to South America, although they are certainly wanted by the Yugoslav government.[90]

Despite the code word, there is no doubt that the fugitives were wanted Nazis. 'Grey' was a term used by the Western Allies to denote known Nazi collaborators. The term 'Black' indicated that they were war criminals, whose extradition had been requested. 'Whites' were victims of Nazi oppression – Jews, former slave labourers, inmates of concentration camps etc. 'Whites' need not be smuggled: the International Refugee Organisation provided them with papers and funds for legal resettlement. Only 'Blacks' and 'Greys' needed Vatican help to get out of the country. For them, immigration was illegal.

In order to help the Vatican, the British changed all the rules so that some 4,000 'Blacks' were redesignated as 'Greys', much to the fury of Brigadier Maclean, who had served in Yugoslavia during the war. As much as he liked the Ukrainians, he had a fanatical hatred for the Croatian Ustashi. Maclean was very thorough in screening Yugoslav Nazis. He had no need to rely on phony histories supplied by the prisoners. He knew – first-hand – what Pavelić's followers had done.

As head of the Screening Mission, Maclean's stubbornness could wreck the scheme for getting the Nazis out of Italy. Worse, he was beginning to realise that his own British superiors were leaking his top secret screening reports to Father Draganović, who tipped off the Ustashi before they could be arrested. The good Brigadier was beginning to suspect too much. The solution was simple: circumvent Maclean with a higher authority. There were always a few friendly Americans willing to lend a hand.

In June 1947 the US and British Governments issued the top secret document known as FAN 757. They agreed that all Nazi screening would henceforth be done by a Joint Review Committee. After all Italy was an Allied problem, and who could object to Americans participating in screening? It sounded so innocent.

The reality, as shown by State Department cables, was a cynical charade to disguise the Vatican's smuggling of the so-called 'Grey' Nazis to Argentina before they could be screened. By mid-1947, those Americans involved were sending their top secret messages back and forth through military channels to avoid detection of the British–Vatican deal. On 7 June 1947 the US Political Adviser in Leghorn, Italy, informed the State Department that:

> I have discussed FAN 757 ... with my British colleague ...
> Understand that ... screeners will notify Vatican names and particulars of unacceptables as they appear. It seems possible that this arrangement may result in out shipment to Argentina of many individuals [who may screen Black or Grey]. To avoid possible misunderstanding and confusion I believe it should be clearly stated whether unacceptables must all be screened ... or only those Argentines refuse [to] accept ... Latter alternative would greatly reduce work ... and would solve before it began problem ... of how to dispose of Greys.[91]

This 'work saving' suggestion exposed the reality of the Allied solution for Nazi emigration: those too notorious to be categorised as legal emigrants (Whites) would be dumped on the Vatican. But the US State Department, however much they wanted to help the British, would not stomach sending category 'Black' war criminals through the Vatican Ratline:

> Such action should be confined to Whites and Greys only and Greys preferably before they have been formally labelled as such in order [to] facilitate their departure.[92]

The complete FAN 757 correspondence (half located in London, the rest in Washington) discloses the diplomatic complicity behind the Vatican Ratlines. The screening was a complete farce. The Nazis were deliberately rushed to the Vatican before they could 'be formally labelled as such'. Although the Vatican was sometimes ignorant of the passengers' true backgrounds as war criminals, the files show that Holy See officials were conspiring to help the West smuggle known Nazi collaborators.

From Rome, the last Nazis began the long journey to freedom.

They were gone from Italy by R Day. An extremely embarrassing situation had been averted. The pool of anti-Communist 'freedom fighters' had been increased. The diplomats of London, Washington and the Vatican had done their jobs too well. They were all to blame for the coming disasters of the Cold War.

By R Day, British intelligence was well under way with the merger of all the ex-Nazi front groups. Intermarium, Prometheus, the Abramtchik Faction, and Bandera's OUN were formed into the SIS-sponsored Anti-Bolshevik Bloc of Nations.[93] Their members spread around the world and settled in friendly Western nations. The West would never really know for sure which were legitimate Nazis and which were double agents. By 1947, a few Communists had already popped up in Intermarium, as the Americans found out from Ferenc Vajta, William Gowen's Hungarian Nazi contact.[94] The Vatican did not know it, but there were a lot more double agents. The real master of the Ratlines was the Kremlin. While the Soviet GRU was working with Turkul, the KGB had been busy as well.

10

The Philby Connection

One of the first Soviet agents to penetrate British intelligence was a Catholic priest. Between 1932 and 1937 the top NKVD 'illegal' in England was Father Theodore Maly. He was indeed a brilliant agent. It was Father Maly who recruited Anthony Blunt and the rest of the Cambridge ring:

> One of the most remarkable non-Russian Comintern agents who ever served as undercover Soviet Intelligence officers, Maly was a newly ordained Hungarian Priest, who became a regimental chaplain with the Austro-Hungarian army when World War I broke out. Captured by the Tsar's army on the Carpathian front, he was horrified by the starvation and disease in the prisoner of war camps.
>
> 'I lost my faith in God, and when the revolution broke out, I joined the Bolsheviks,' Maly once told a friend, explaining how service with the Cheka and Red Army during the brutal civil war against the Whites had hardened him.[1]

When Father Maly came to London in 1932, the Kremlin was already aware of tentative British–German negotiations for an alliance against Communism. Two cipher clerks in the British Foreign Office had been on the Soviet payroll since 1929, reporting to Father Maly.[2] The leaked cables told Moscow that there was indeed high level support for an Anglo-German initiative against Stalin. It is not surprising that penetration of Fascist circles in Britain became a high priority for the Kremlin.

Many of Father Maly's best recruits were young men from upper class backgrounds who pretended to hold Fascist sympathies to hide their true Communist loyalties. The most famous KGB agent was Harold Adrian Russell Philby. As with all of Father Maly's agents, 'Kim' Philby's upper class British background was impeccable. His father had been briefly imprisoned as an ardent Nazi supporter. Kim pretended to share his father's sympathies. He joined pro-German organisations and was awarded a Fascist decoration by Franco for his services as a war correspondent in

Spain. Many of his fellow agents had similar Fascist credentials which, judging by the rate at which they were hired, was certainly no impediment to a career with British intelligence.

But British Fascism was not the only secret to Soviet success in espionage, nor was the KGB their only agency active in Britain. Long before Father Maly arrived in London, the GRU had planted members of Turkul's network in London:

> One was the ubiquitous Anatoli Baykolov. This supposedly White Russian journalist was an associate of Sabline, the Tsarist *chargé d'affaires* who had gone over to the Soviets in the twenties.[3]

Both Communist agents in London had a mutual friend, Guy Liddell, an enterprising young officer working in Special Branch, the police unit responsible for domestic security. No one knows how or why Liddell was recruited by Turkul's GRU network but there are several theories:

> While it is impossible to do anything more than speculate on what personal frustrations and subtle external political forces *might* have led Guy Liddell to cast his lot in with the Soviets, certain obvious possibilities such as his artistic temperament, his long-term connections with Baykolov and the penetrated Russian *émigré* community in London – as well as the scars of his marriage – can be considered factors . . . Then, too, other sources told me about Liddell's premarital love affair in the early twenties with a London University student (believed to still be alive), whose Marxism and links to the Communist party were well known to her contemporaries. This lead has so far proved impossible to corroborate, but if true, it could explain how one of the ranking officers in Special Branch might have become an early victim of a Soviet 'honeytrap'.[4]

There is some circumstantial evidence to place the date of Liddell's recruitment to the 1920s. At that time, every Soviet Embassy was assigned a 'Soviet Kolonii' (SK) Officer to monitor the loyalty of the local 'Soviet Colony'. The principal function of the SK Officer was to ensure that no Soviet Diplomat defected. The Embassy in London never had an SK officer. There may be a simple explanation: Guy Liddell was performing that function for them. He was in charge of anti-Soviet operations for Special Branch. Any information on potential Soviet defectors was passed to him. In 1931 Liddell joined MI5 and became head of the entire anti-Soviet section.[5]

As the British author John Costello notes, the Liddell–Baykolov connection could explain why MI5 failed on nearly two dozen occasions to take effective action against Soviet operations.[6] Certainly by 1933, there was ample warning that Baykolov was a Communist:

In 1933 a Ukrainian named Korostorets warned *émigré* leaders in Paris that Baykolov was really working for the Soviets and a warning to that effect appeared in the October 22 edition of *Zovrozhdenie*. His activities interviewing recent Russian escapees, supposedly for a study of the Soviet judicial system, appear to have been tied up with his mission for the OGPU [Soviet Intelligence Service]. He was an associate of Sabline, the former Tsarist *chargé d'affaires* in London, who was later found to have been an undercover OGPU agent monitoring the White Russian exiles in Britain. He had links to Skoblin, the OGPU operative in Paris, who was involved in the 1932 kidnapping of General Miller, the Paris-based chairman of the Russian Military Union [ROWS] ... Baykolov was a longtime MI5 and Foreign Office source of Soviet intelligence; his contact was Guy Liddell.[7]

Baykolov was regarded as totally trustworthy because he and his GRU accomplice in the German Embassy, Putlitz, had helped protect one of the most embarrassing secrets of the British government:

Moscow did not hesitate to activate the Baykolov back channel when it believed Moscow's interests could be served.

This appears to have been the case on January 30, 1936, the day King George V died. There was a widespread concern about the pro-German sympathies of the new King, Edward VIII ... It was feared that Edward's coronation would accelerate a rapprochement between London and Berlin. There is evidence that the Soviets activated the Baykolov connection to pass word of this danger ... The Soviets were getting their information from inside the German embassy via their mole Putlitz.[8]

The information was astounding: Wallis Simpson was a Nazi agent. Simpson was also Edward's mistress. Through her royal lover, she was in a position to pass on Cabinet minutes and top secret information. If Putlitz and Baykolov were correct, there was a Nazi spy in the King's bedroom. Liddell had MI5 place a wiretap on the telephone lines of the Ambassador's residence in London to see if Simpson was working for the Germans. The wiretap was a major shock to the British government. As we shall see, Mrs Simpson was the least of their problems.

Transcripts of the British wiretaps have never been publicly released. However, in the US National Archives we discovered a top secret American interrogation file of Joachim von Ribbentrop, who was Hitler's Ambassador to London before becoming German Foreign Minister. It was Ribbentrop's phone that was tapped. Shortly before he was hanged at Nuremberg, Ribbentrop confirmed that he almost concluded an alliance in the 1930s with the help of two British leaders who were secret Nazi sympathisers. One was a former Prime Minister, the other was the future King:

It was perhaps hard to believe in the light of events, that the Führer's fondest dream had been of an Anglo-German alliance in the service of which he had been prepared to maintain a force of twelve divisions for the defence of any part of the British Empire. Such were the Führer's sentiments that he was the more deeply hurt when Britain seemed to mistrust his motives and to obstruct his plans ... but his efforts to win sympathy among distinguished people, including Mr Ramsay MacDonald and King Edward VIII for National Socialist conceptions had not been altogether unsuccessful.[9]

The recently disclosed papers of the Duke of Coburg confirm Ribbentrop's confession. Soon after his father's death, Edward Windsor, the Prince of Wales, had told the Nazis that an alliance between Germany and Britain was an 'urgent necessity'. Based on assurances from Windsor that he would prevent British intervention, Hitler seized the Rhineland from the French. Edward had promised Hitler that Britain would never interfere with his plans 're Jews or re anything else'.[10]

The Foreign Office was alarmed over the King's 'increasing and disturbing intervention in foreign affairs'. A search was under way for 'ways and means of compelling him to abdicate'. The King's mistress, the pro-Nazi American Wallis Simpson, was used as the excuse.[11] No mention was made of the Nazi wiretaps. For many years the public has believed that Windsor abdicated the throne to marry the woman he loved.[12]

There is ample evidence that Windsor was merely a pompous dilettante who was used as a pawn by Mrs Simpson. But FBI Director J. Edgar Hoover was convinced that Windsor was himself a dangerous Nazi agent. He wanted the former King imprisoned, not just interned in the Bahamas.[13] The British thought the suggestion absurd, but made every effort to monitor the former King to determine whether in fact

Edward was in correspondence on political matters with Hitler ... Menzies made extraordinary efforts to intercept the letters but was largely unsuccessful, and it was not until immediately after World War II that they were found. Then they gave the Churchill government and its successor a severe shock when evidence was received that laid open Edward to charges of having committed treason.[14]

There is direct evidence from another source that after he abdicated, Windsor betrayed his country while it was at war with the Nazis:

By 1940 . . . Windsor had become a member of the British Military Mission with the French Army Command . . . according to German Foreign Office Records, Windsor actually disclosed to [a Nazi] emissary the details of a secret meeting of the Allied War Council. Windsor revealed that the Council had discussed in detail the situation that would arise if Germany invaded Belgium . . . The entire message was of such importance to the German government that it was shown to Hitler in person.[15]

British intelligence realised that the Windsor secret was a bombshell. If Edward were put on trial, then a small but significant part of the British Establishment would have to be put in the dock with him. In the 1930s Fascism (or corporatism as it was called in polite circles) was a popular philosophy among more right-wing members of the British upper class. Some were in the pro-Fascist Cliveden set; others were prominent businessmen connected to Windsor's schemes, including Lord McGowan of Imperial Chemicals Industries and Montagu Norman of the Bank of England, who were laundering money to Hitler through Swiss banks in the mistaken belief that a Nazi victory was inevitable.[16] Lord Rothermere of the London *Daily Mail* 'gave a total of $5 million in cash to assist in Hitler's rise to power'.[17]

After Hitler started to lose the war, Windsor's contacts tried to hide their Nazi connections in Canaris's Black Orchestra. In fact, Lord Halifax and others in Windsor's group had been trying to negotiate peace with Hitler behind Churchill's back.[18] When the extent of Windsor's treason was confirmed by MI5, Churchill and Robert Vansittart, who handled sensitive matters for the Foreign Office, scrambled frantically to hide the scandal.

The Soviets, who had already penetrated the real Black Orchestra through Turkul, decided to help protect the secret, if for no other reason than insurance in case their agents were ever discovered. A wise precaution as it happened, since the Windsor scandal was later used to blackmail the British to protect Turkul and other double agents.[19]

The British did not realise until the 1960s that the original guardians of the Royal secret were all connected to Turkul. It was later discovered that Baykolov, who passed on the original tip about Mrs Simpson, had worked for Turkul in Paris. It is no coincidence that Baykolov's MI5 contact, Guy Liddell (who later vouched for Turkul's bona fides to the OSS), used another Turkul contact from Paris, Dickie Ellis, to translate the Ribbentrop wiretaps.[20]

The more they kept silent about upper class Fascists, the safer the Communist moles became. Respected by the British establishment as the trusted guardians of Royalty's greatest scandal, the GRU agents were quickly promoted. Baykolov became an adviser to Churchill and Vansittart on Soviet affairs. Liddell became head of MI5's counter-espionage section. His associate, Roger Hollis (also a suspected GRU agent), took over the MI5 section monitoring Fascists in Britain.[21]

By the end of World War II, Windsor's 'protectors' occupied so many key positions in MI5 that the GRU had to borrow KGB agents to help monitor Britain's Fascist minority.[22] Although the KGB did not know who was helping them, Father Maly's 'Apostles' discovered that not only could they pass security clearances for sensitive government posts, but they even became the guardians of the Windsor scandal:

> It was extremely odd that the head of counter espionage in England at that time, Guy Liddell – who preferred homosexual company though it was claimed that he himself was not a homosexual – paid little if any attention to the politics of the Apostles.[23]

Liddell not only ignored them, he hired them. The notoriously homosexual Guy Burgess took over from Baykolov as Putlitz's MI5 handler from whom he learned a great deal, 'especially concerning the Duke and Duchess of Windsor's association with Ribbentrop'.[24] Liddell subsequently helped Burgess to leave MI5 and join SIS.[25] Burgess's one-time lover and fellow Apostle, Anthony Blunt, was recruited by MI5 to retrieve copies of the embarrassing Windsor correspondence with the Nazis. Blunt then received an appointment at the Palace from the grateful Royal Family.[26]

Kim Philby, who may have met Mrs Simpson at German Embassy parties given by the Anglo-German Friendship Society, was a most unlikely candidate for Soviet espionage. At Cambridge, Philby was identified as a Marxist and a homosexual. Before the

GRU intervened, he could not find three referees to sponsor him for a minor Foreign Office post. Yet suddenly he found that there was 'nothing recorded against' him when he applied for the British Secret Service.[27]

There is no direct evidence that Philby's early SIS duties brought him into direct contact with the Vatican, although he was well positioned to observe them. As head of the Spanish desk (later expanded to include Italy) he may have been privy to the Black Orchestra's British–Vatican negotiations. Before the war was over, Philby was no longer a peripheral observer, but a principal player with the Vatican. In 1944 he was promoted to head the new anti-Soviet section of SIS.

Behind his unassuming stutter and false Nazi sympathies, Philby was working for the Soviets when he headed Britain's anti-Soviet programme.[28] The new position provided ample opportunity for sabotage. On 13 November 1944, shortly after Philby's promotion, 'a German officer named Karl Marcus, alias Carlsen, arrived in France ... "he had been sent to get in touch with the British, particularly Lord Vansittart, and that he would disclose his mission only to a British Officer" ... Marcus described himself as the secretary to and emissary of Kurt Jahnke.'[29]

Marcus's message was simple: Jahnke wanted to re-open the Black Orchestra peace negotiations through the Vatican. After Canaris's arrest for the 20 July plot, Jahnke had become the leader of the German opposition. According to Marcus, Jahnke had found a new recruit: SS intelligence leader Walter Schellenberg, who had helped save Turkul and Klatt from the Gestapo. Instead of smashing the Vatican's Black Orchestra, Schellenberg had joined up to save his neck. Once again the Vatican was sending peace messages from the Germans.[30] All of the Ultra intercepts of Nazi–Vatican negotiations for this period remain highly classified.

Stalin was kept apprised of the Anglo-German negotiations 'by an agent somewhere in the Allied high command – his informant may well have been Philby making his first appearance as a Soviet spy on the grand scale'.[31] On 3 April 1945 Stalin sent the British 'his ugliest message of the war', accusing them of making a deal with the Nazis behind his back:

> ... do not have doubts that the negotiations have taken place and that they have ended in an agreement ... As a result of this at the present

moment the Germans on the western front in fact have ceased the war against England . . . and continue the war with Russia.[32]

The battle statistics for the following week suggest that Stalin was prophetic. There were more than 40,000 German casualties on the Eastern front versus 2,500 in the West. Even more suspicious, over a quarter of a million German soldiers were suddenly reported 'missing' in the West.[33]

Stalin suspected that the British would use the 'missing' Nazis against him. Churchill later admitted that he had given orders 'to Lord Montgomery directing him to be careful in collecting the German arms, to stack them so that they could easily be issued again to the German soldiers'. Montgomery agreed that he had obeyed the order. It was true that 'England had prepared for war with Russia using the defeated German army as an ally even before the war was over'.[34]

If Philby helped Stalin expose the Black Orchestra deal, it was not his only coup that year. In September he became the first KGB officer to learn that they had a secret benefactor. A GRU defector in Canada named Gouzenko told the British that there was a GRU spy code named ELLI inside 'five of MI'. Soon after, another Soviet defector, Volkov, gave an even more explicit identification: 'I know, for instance, that one of these agents is fulfilling the duties of a head of section of the British Counterintelligence Director-ate.'[35] On 18 and 19 September Philby cabled this news to KGB headquarters in Moscow under his code name 'Stanley'.[36]

At first Moscow refused to believe Philby's cable. No one in KGB headquarters had ever heard of 'ELLI' nor did they know of such a high level agent. Moscow's 1945 reply to Philby was decoded many years later by Peter Wright of British intelligence:

It read: 'Consent has been obtained from the Chiefs to consult with the neighbors about Stanley's material about their affairs in Canada. Stanley's data is correct.'

. . . Philby by the time this message was sent, had been a top-class KGB agent and head of Counterespionage in MI6 for the best part of ten years, yet it appeared as if they doubted his intelligence. Why did it need checking? What was it about Stanley's data that had thrown the KGB into such confusion?

Only one explanation could account for all these oddities. The KGB must have been ignorant of the spy in 'five of MI' controlled by the GRU. Thus, when Philby relayed to them the news of this spy, and the threat made to him by Gouzenko, the KGB had to obtain permission from the 'Chiefs', the

Politburo to consult with the 'neighbors', the GRU to ask if they did indeed have such an asset in London. Having received assurances from the GRU that they did have such a spy, the KGB realized that the heat was likely to come on in London, so they sent back the message confirming Stanley's data, and followed it up with urgent orders to increase security.[37]

Whether ELLI was Hollis (head of Section F) or Liddell (head of Section B) is still hotly debated. But there is no doubt that after September 1945, Lavrenty Beria, head of the KGB, was told the Politbureau's greatest secret: through the Turkul network, the GRU had slowly but thoroughly taken over MI5 while the KGB was struggling to place a few agents inside MI6.[38] From that day, Beria insisted that all top Soviet agents be co-ordinated to help each other. From 1945 until the mid-1950s, Soviet intelligence ran the most effective spy operation in history: no one else before or since has ever come close.

While American and British intelligence were hopelessly divided and restructured after World War II, Soviet intelligence executed a plan of smooth integration to protect and promote all their agents in the West. For example, when MI6 discovered German documents proving that Turkul's friend Ellis was a Nazi agent, Philby ordered that the investigation be closed. No top KGB agent would have risked the inevitable exposure, except under orders from Moscow. If Ellis had been exposed in 1945, it would have jeopardised Turkul, who was far more valuable than Philby. Because of Philby's cover-up, Turkul and Ellis were safe for several more years.

Apart from being a suspected GRU agent, Ellis later confessed that he was a Nazi double agent during the war. Despite his admitted treason, Ellis was not tried because of what he knew: after all, if he were a Nazi so was Edward VIII. Rather, Ellis was recruited by SIS's Colin Gubbins to purge British intelligence files, presumably of any other embarrassing evidence. As we shall see, there was quite a bit to be put into the shredder. Ellis claimed that it was Menzies who ordered him to keep up Turkul's Nazi contacts in the first place.[39]

Returning to London in 1945, Philby must have been pleased with himself. It had been a very good year. In Stockholm he had personally trained yet another Baltic agent to use British intelligence codes.[40] Another anti-Communist 'freedom fighter' was already on his way across the Black Sea. Philby passed the new agent's codes and identity to the Soviets in order to prepare a proper reception. Upon his arrival, he was placed under discreet surveillance, and not disturbed until he had recruited all the local anti-Communist dissidents. As soon as Philby's Judas goat had unwittingly identified all his contacts, the entire network was arrested.

More than forty years later, when the Latvian Nazi agent, Robert Osis, was released from the Gulag, he identified Philby as the man who recruited him and then betrayed his entire network to the Communists.[41] But there was an even darker side to Philby's Nazi recruiting. He was helping the KGB take over the Vatican's networks.

Even before World War II, Soviet intelligence had planted Communist double agents among each of the Eastern European Fascist groups. Having riddled the Fascist opposition with informers, after the war the Soviets were only too glad to help the Vatican smuggle the Nazis to every Western nation gullible enough to take them in.[42] As one British intelligence officer later lamented, there was no better disguise than posing as a fugitive war criminal. 'It was the perfect cover.'[43] Soon after La Vista's report, the Americans warned the Vatican that Communist agents were using the Ratlines, but no one believed such reports. The Vatican never knew what hit them.

By the time he left London in 1946, Philby had merged the hopelessly riddled Nazi networks like Intermarium and Prometheus into the Anti-Bolshevik Bloc of Nations. The Vatican was unaware that the Soviets, not the British, controlled ABN from its inception and had bent the Ratlines into a complete circle.[44] The KGB must have been amused that the Vatican was smuggling Soviet agents to Western countries.

In 1946 Philby was sent to Turkey where, as chief of station for anti-Soviet operations, he would have a bird's-eye view of British, Vatican and American operations in the Balkans and Central Europe.[45] More importantly, Philby launched his own Vatican operation. Shortly before he left London, arrangements were made to surface another of Intermarium's fugitive Nazis. Ferdinand Durčansky had been the Foreign Minister of the Slovak Nazi puppet government, and was tried *in absentia* as a war criminal by the democratic government of Czechoslovakia. After disappearing at the end of the war, he resurfaced in Rome. According to the Czech trial records:

> Dr Ferdinand Durčansky was in Rome in October 1946, and in a certain coffee house met the English woman ... This English woman disclosed that there is some club of Central European Nations the aim of which is to restore those states which existed under German rule in Central Europe. Croat Ustashi, Poles of the Anders brand, Hungarians, Serb Chetniks are members of this club, together with the accused Dr Durčansky, whose main aim is to restore the totalitarian Slovak Republic.
> Durčansky had also a conversation with Anders on this subject, who had allegedly given his consent to this plan ... Durčansky has interesting information concerning present conditions in Slovakia. He asserts that only approximately 10% are Communists, and that all of those are Lutherans. According to him the Catholics and their priests, and 80% of the Bishops would be in favor of a restoration of Slovak State independence. Even the Vatican allegedly sympathizes with his plans. Asked by the English woman from where his money would come, Durčansky said that he had many friends in the world.[46]

On 6 June 1947 the *New York Times* reported that Durčansky was in Italy 'where he broadcasts daily to Slovakia and is in constant contact with the underground'.[47] On 24 June the Czechoslovak government announced that leaflets were being distributed claiming that a new government would soon seize power in Slovakia with Durčansky as premier.[48] Most of the world dismissed this as *émigré* hyperbole. After all, Durčansky was listed by the UN as a Category A war criminal. Who would possibly support an ex-Nazi to overthrow the only non-Communist government in Eastern Europe?

According to his CIA file, Durčansky proceeded with his plot. Further inquiries disclosed his source of funding:

> Durčansky in no way denies that the Slovak populist emigration is supported by the Vatican, and that a part of the financial means is received by them from some church dignitaries, especially in Belgium and Argentina.[49]

Since the CIA also described Durčansky as one of Intermarium's leaders, it is likely that the Vatican was again laundering British intelligence money to Durčansky's Slovak Liberation Movement. Before Durčansky's plot, the Communists were a significant minority but lacked important posts in the government; his plot changed all of that.

In September 1947 a commission headed by General Ferjenčik

announced that they had uncovered a 'massive conspiracy' to overthrow the government. The Durčansky ring had been thoroughly infiltrated, and numerous documents were produced linking scores of Slovak politicians to Durčansky's ring. The minority Communists demanded that parliament be purged. They then gained several key ministries and soon spread the anti-Fascist purge into every corner of the government. Within a few months, they seized control of the entire country from the fragmented Democratic opposition. The Communist counter coup occurred so quickly that the British Consul wondered if Durčansky had staged the whole thing:

> [Durčansky's] subversive organisation ... appears undoubtedly to exist, though it does have a curious aspect. The evidence collected is so complete and well-documented that it is difficult to believe in the genuineness of the movement, and Dr Frastachy believes that the participants were inveigled into it by *Agents Provocateurs* ... The whole thing, I was told, smacked of elaborate stage management: but it seems to have been effective, whether or not that was its purpose, in giving a handle to the instigation of the purge.[50]

At the time, no one realised Durčansky's connection to Intermarium and Philby. Under Philby's direction, Intermarium had not overthrown a single Communist regime, but it had destroyed a freely elected government. After the *débâcle*, a cover story went out to move suspicion from British intelligence:

> The Czechoslovak Telegraph Agency quotes the Slovak Commissioner of Interior as stating that Durčansky had escaped from a prison in Rome, disguised as a nun. He is reported trying to get in touch with French Foreign Minister Bidault, whom he has known since the days when they were students together.[51]

It was a plausible story because Durčansky had worked for French intelligence before Britain took over Intermarium. In fact, Durčansky had not fled to France but had gone down the Vatican Ratline to Argentina. As head of the Balkan section of SIS, Philby probably got credit for shielding his superiors from blame for the Czech disaster. Both he and Durčansky were subsequently promoted, Philby becoming the SIS liaison to CIA, while Durčansky became Intermarium President.[52]

With Philby running field operations in Central Europe from 1947 to 1949, it was hardly surprising that the Czech government was overthrown, the Križari smashed in Yugoslavia, the Romanian infiltration suppressed, and the abortive Albanian invasion betrayed. Every British initiative was leaked to the Communists well in advance. In 1948 the British reluctantly concluded that they lacked sufficient finances to combat the Communists' growing success in Greece and the Balkans. They asked President Truman to take over SIS's anti-Communist groups.[53]

Menzies's biographer candidly admits that many of the SIS nets passed on to the Americans were Nazi collaborators. The rationale was that these extremist organisations

> existed as a major political irritant that, at critical times throughout the period from 1925 until the mid-1950's, nourished Soviet insecurity. During the period immediately before World War II, the [SIS] cells inside Russia – they were known by such code names as the Prometheus Network, the Inter-Marium Programme, the Abramtchik faction, and the Russian Army of Liberation . . . were taken over by the German military intelligence service of Admiral Wilhelm Canaris . . . After World War II, when Canaris's men were all in jail, Menzies reacquired interest in these organisations until, at last, he passed them to the American intelligence services. Such complex tangles were not uncommon . . . although they had not yet become the infinity of complication . . . where, as the good wizard said of the bad ones in J. R. R. Tolkien's epic, *The Lord of the Rings*, 'It is difficult with these evil folk to know when they are in league, and when they are cheating one another.'[54]

The real 'Lord of the Rings' was not Menzies but Lavrenty Beria. KGB headquarters must have congratulated themselves when in 1949, Menzies announced that Philby had been promoted to Senior United Kingdom Liaison Officer to America and Canada. Philby's mission was to transfer Britain's Nazi 'freedom fighters' to the Americans.[55] This was an important opportunity for the KGB as most American intelligence services had been reluctant to employ Nazis, although they occasionally bent the rules for rocket scientists.

However, Philby was about to realise his first significant failure. The newly formed CIA wanted no part of Durčansky, Intermarium or the ABN. They supported the moderate Czech Democrats, many of whom had fled to America after the Communist takeover. Durčansky was anathema to them, and Philby had to find another sanctuary for his Slovak Nazis.

Some of the most embarrassing Canadian secrets are revealed in Durčansky's massive CIA file. Before its release in 1987, the CIA blanked out all references which might embarrass a foreign government, as required by the US Freedom of Information Act. However, the CIA declassified the fact that Durčansky headed Intermarium,[56] not knowing that a few months later a British author would reveal that it was run by British intelligence.

Anthony Cave Brown, in his recent book on Sir Stewart Menzies,[57] describes Intermarium as one of many 'long and witty' British intelligence operations. As we have seen from Philby's penetration, the joke was really on SIS. Cave Brown correctly identifies Intermarium as having worked for the British, then the Nazis, then the British again, and finally the Americans.

What Cave Brown does not mention is that in 1949 the wealthy Americans at first refused Philby's offer to take over Intermarium. In fact, the CIA tried to screen out all known Nazis before they entered the country. Some were easy to spot. The CIA noted that in 1946 Durčansky had been listed by the UN as a Category A war criminal, and that in 1947 he was 'condemned to death by the Slovakian National Council after trial in absentia'.[58] This was before the Communist takeover was completed.

On 20 September 1950 the CIA sent a nasty report on Durčansky to the US immigration authorities.[59] After they closed their door, Philby had no alternative but to dump Durčansky and his Slovak Nazis elsewhere. On 15 December Durčansky left Argentina via London for Canada. The British blushingly admitted that Durčansky was a wanted war criminal, but apologised to the Canadians, claiming that Durčansky's UK visa was an 'administrative error'.[60]

Despite this confession, the Canadians made no move to arrest or expel Durčansky. It is no coincidence that Philby travelled back and forth from Washington to Ottawa to help Canadian intelligence 'vet the Nazis' who were settling there.[61] Where his Nazi agents were concerned, Philby ensured that 'administrative errors' occurred with clockwork regularity. Durčansky travelled freely in and out of Canada, despite the fact that the government was fully aware of his war crimes.[62]

In 1951 Durčansky sent a letter to the White House listing his address as 97 Crawford Street, Ontario.[63] Although he spent most of his later years working for ABN in London and Germany, he was still giving occasional anti-Semitic speeches in Canada well

into the 1970s.[64] He had a friendly audience, as thousands of
Fascists settled in Canada.[65]

Among other Nazi collaborators identified by CIA in Canada is
Durčansky's close wartime companion, Jozef Kirschbaum.[66] Both
are listed in a report received by the CIA as senior Fascists 'guilty
of the gruesome calvary of the Slovak Jews'.[67] In 1952 Kirschbaum
tried to obtain a US visa, but was quickly exposed in the media. A
photo of him in Fascist uniform was shown on TV, and he quickly
scuttled back to safety in Canada.[68] He is still on the State
Department's banned list.[69]

Durčansky met the same reception in 1959. The *New York Times*
accused him of being a Nazi. Durčansky denied that he was a
Fascist, and blurted out that his 1950 American visa application
'was rejected on the grounds that he was "a Communist"'.[70]
America was not alone in suspecting that Durčansky was a
Communist spy, as the CIA noted:

> During his tenure of the Ministry of Foreign Affairs (1939–1941), Durčansky
> allegedly attempted – prior to the German–Soviet conflict – to establish
> certain contacts with Soviet politics through the Soviet Legation in Buda-
> pest ... Hitler is said to have summoned Tiso to Germany and ordered
> Durčansky's removal from office ... The Germans are said to have made
> further representations as a result of which Durčansky left Slovakia and
> eventually went to Italy.[71]

What the CIA did not know in 1950 was the extent of Durčansky's 'support from the Vatican', or its involvement with the
Canadian government. The Vatican can hardly shirk responsibility
for the emigration of Nazis to Canada. They had unsuccessfully
requested on several occasions that Durčansky's associate, the
Fascist Slovak Ambassador to the Vatican, Karol Sidor, be allowed
to settle in America. Sidor had become an embarrassment in
Rome, so Pius XII personally asked the Canadian Privy Council
to shelter him.[72]

Ironically, the Deschenes Commission which investigated Nazis
in Canada, concluded that America was most responsible for
dumping Nazis there.[73] In fairness, the Canadian investigators
were not even permitted by their own lawyer to request Durčansky's CIA file. Moreover, all references to British intelligence were
purged from the Deschenes Commission's 1986 report. Not one
word of the embarrassing Philby connection was published. The

lawyer involved was recently appointed Canada's Ambassador to the UN.[74]

Canada continues to pay the price for its indifference. The CIA files are filled with examples of Communist propaganda discrediting the West as a haven for war criminals like Durčansky and Stetsko. For the next two decades, the Communists held ABN up to the world as an organization of war criminals, whose leaders were frequent visitors to Canada.

In January 1990 some of the American intelligence files on the ABN were declassified at the authors' request. From the moment Stetsko became ABN head in 1949, US officials were told to ignore his persistent approaches. He was not to have a single piece of paper that he could use to claim US support.[75] By 1953, all the 'moderate and democratic member groups' had quit ABN.[76] In 1955 a US Senator was confidentially told that:

> Many of the leaders of the A.B.N. were closely associated either with the Nazi government or with the totalitarian regimes of their respective states. Because of their records many have been unable to obtain an immigration or visitor's visa into the United States or to other countries. There is no question of their anti-Communist sentiments but 'neither was there a question of the anti-Communist sentiments of Hitler'. I permitted [the senator's aide] to read brief biographic sketches on Ferenc Farkas, Grigore Manoilescu, Dimitr Waltscheff, Yaroslav Stetsko, Radoslav Ostrovski, and Ferdinand Durčansky. The sketches listed the war-time posts of the A.B.N. leaders, a record which itself is indicative of the political complexion of the A.B.N.[77]

In 1958 the US Veterans of Foreign Wars were warned to have nothing to do with the ABN:

> Mr. Stetsko's ... organization is based on the Führer principle ... and has a long record of murder, terror and coercion perpetrated in the DP camps in Germany against those Ukrainians who do not share their views.[78]

The Veterans were told to deal with the CIA front group, the 'American Committee for Liberation'. Philby had utterly failed to convince the Americans to take over ABN, and had to settle for second best by dumping his networks in Canada.

For Philby, the worst was yet to come. By 1951, US intelligence had broken portions of the Soviet diplomatic code. Several Communist agents were in danger of exposure, and Guy Burgess and Donald Maclean fled to the Soviet Union. Philby was unofficially expelled from Washington in disgrace, and the CIA never trusted him or his agents again. They set out to remove any of Philby's Nazis who had any contact with US intelligence.[79]

American intelligence naively believed that it had defeated the KGB's best agent. They had refused to swallow Philby's Nazi bait and had even detected several Communist agents among his 'freedom fighters' before they could emigrate to America.[80]

What the CIA did not realise for years was that the Vatican's Nazis had a new home just across America's northern border. Of course, they had received a great deal of assistance on the way to Canada from the KGB networks in Britain:

> Agents of the 'Cambridge network' were ... remarkably well placed at the start of the Cold War to ensure that the MI5 and MI6 vetting slips carried the magic words 'no traces against' when it came to the penetration of the ABN by Moscow. This ensured that a slew of Soviet agents, including ... the Czech Intermarium chief Ferdinand Durčansky, the Ukrainian Stefan Bandera and the Byelorussian leader Mikolai Abramtchik, were either directly involved or had staff members who ended up running and recruiting other agents for covert operations against the Soviet Union.[81]

Before he left Washington in 1951, Philby had merged all of the Vatican's Nazi groups – Intermarium, Prometheus, the International of Liberty and several others – into one giant Soviet sewer. The CIC files even listed Jaroslav Stetsko as a suspected Communist agent. Of course, it was probably a false lead; the real Communists were harder to find.

Back in Moscow, the Politbureau was not in the least dismayed when the KGB's operation collapsed. It really did not matter that the Americans had shunned ABN. Behind the KGB's back, the Politbureau had supervised a GRU counter-operation that had succeeded where Philby had failed. The Americans were enthusiastically funding Turkul's 'resistance movement'. They had dodged the KGB's Nazis only to fall into the GRU's trap.

At the end of World War II, the remnants of the Vlasov army under Turkul's control established liaison with the anti-Tito forces in Yugoslavia.[82] Turkul knew that the Fascist anti-Communist forces were 'secretly supported' by British intelligence, and so he attached his staff to theirs.[83] He joined the various Fascist factions in their escape to Austria. On 3 May 1945 Turkul's intelligence chief, Max Klatt, was released from a Nazi prison and headed to Salzburg to link up with Turkul.[84] It was time to recycle the phony MAX network to the even more gullible Allies.

In rapid succession, Turkul and Klatt offered their 'anti-Communist' network to British intelligence, the US Office of Strategic Services, and General Patton's intelligence staff.[85] Captured Germans had already reported on the incredible MAX network. The British Army's counter-intelligence staff was working on a report about the miraculous Abwehr spy team of the Hungarian Jew and the 'notorious professional spy General aka Prince Turkul normally resident in Rome'.[86] But some British officers were rather sceptical about Turkul's 'extensive and infallible intelligence service which delivered information with equal speed from Leningrad, Kuibischev, Nororossik on the Western desert, [which] was suspiciously free from the administrative hitches to which most spy systems are liable'.[87]

Fortunately for Turkul, Klatt was not captured by the author of that report. On 24 May 1945 he was arrested in Austria by two US CIC men who turned him over to the OSS. He had fallen into friendly hands indeed. 'By November of 1945, Klatt had concluded an agreement with OSS in Salzburg to work against the Communists.'[88] At the same time, Turkul had established the 'Russian National Central Committee' in Salzburg and, of course, was appointed chairman.[89] The Committee screened refugees for the OSS, looking for Communist double agents. Once again, the Communist fox was guarding the *émigré* chicken coop.

Turkul's success in contacting the OSS was no suprise. His aide, Father George Romanov, had long standing relations with the OSS in Switzerland. In fact, the Turkul network's 'first contact with the allies' was with Paul Blum, Allen Dulles's assistant in the Berne OSS office. Dulles was hoping to become head of OSS, but instead, was transferred to the backwaters of occupied Germany.[90]

Having been passed over for promotion, the disgruntled Dulles probably saw the Turkul net as his route to stardom. He had undoubtedly heard the Turkul legend from the American born Jahnke, who had fled to Switzerland to escape the SS. While Marcus was conveying the Jahnke–Schellenberg terms to London, the Black Orchestra was also negotiating with the Americans. The Vatican was asked to open peace talks with Dulles, and conveyed a message through Dom Emanuele Caronti, Abbot General of the Benedictines:

In the sixth year of war, Germany finds herself alone in the fight against Bolshevist Russia. In the interests of saving mankind, Germany now looks to the highest ecclesiastical authority to intervene with the Anglo-Americans and guarantee absolute secrecy to any negotiations with the Vatican.[91]

Dulles was no stranger to Vatican secret negotiations, as he had subsequently used Church contacts to negotiate the surrender of German forces in Italy.[92] Unfortunately, Stalin had found out about these talks and put pressure on President Truman to call them off. That did not stop Dulles, who went ahead anyway, much to the President's anger. As it turned out, Dulles's German contacts had been stalling him, and only concluded the agreement when they learned of Hitler's suicide. An investigation showed that Dulles had been thoroughly taken in, and had made embarrassing promises to protect major war criminals, but received nothing in return.[93]

Dulles returned to Washington as an outsider, but through his old contacts, kept his hand in intelligence work. If Dulles thought that Turkul's network would restore his tarnished prestige, he was in for a rude shock. By June 1946, Turkul's propaganda antics against the Soviet Union had attracted the attention of the CIC, which learned that he was living in a villa near Parsch DP camp:

> An interview with Mr Malkievich, fnu, director of the UNRRA team at Camp Parsch, Salzburg, disclosed that Subject and his associates have been actively engaged in disrupting morale and contributing to unrest and apprehension in the camp ... [they] circulated wild rumors among the camp's inhabitants and have, on frequent occasions, slandered UNRRA and its efforts to run the DP camp on peaceful democratic lines. On one occasion, the Turkul group stated its dissatisfaction with [the UNRRA leaders], claiming that the former was a Jew and the latter was a Communist.[94]

The CIC concluded, however, that despite Turkul's claim to be a 'Vlasov Army Commander', he was 'a vain, not-too-clever opportunist seeking always to be at the head of an organization of power or influence':

> There is no evidence as yet to hand to indicate that Subject is anything other than an old-time anti-Bolshevik constantly dreaming of leading again the fight against the Soviets with any available means.[95]

Apparently, Dulles took Turkul rather more seriously than the CIC. The next document in the CIC file has been completely censored by the CIA, perhaps to protect the reputation of a man who became CIA Director in 1953.[96] However, the other Turkul files contain ample references to the developing scandal.

In January 1946 a joint British–American intelligence unit, (SCI/A) attempted to recruit one of Turkul's aides in Munich. These élite Allied 'Special Counter Intelligence' units were the only ones entrusted with code breaking secrets such as ULTRA. As we shall see, many of the SCI teams were extremely sympathetic to Menzies's and Dulles's anti-Soviet schemes. In mid-1946, the SCI team sent an unnamed source (probably Turkul) to Germany to recruit yet another anti-Communist operative, his old GRU sponsor, Claudius Voss.[97]

Not suprisingly, the Communist moles in British intelligence gave Voss a clean bill of health, revealing to the Americans 'in the utmost discretion', that Voss had been a British agent since 1923 when he was 'one of the leading men of the Inner Line' counter-intelligence service in Paris. In 1929 Voss had 'in effect become chief' of ROWS for the Balkans. For the next ten years, he and Turkul had collaborated on a 'project unknown', which Voss later admitted was the creation of the NTS.[98]

No mention was made of Turkul's wartime service for the Nazis, but British intelligence volunteered 'that since the end of the war both Voss and [Klatt's deputy, Ira Longin] have been building intelligence nets for source, allegedly for the western allies'.[99] This was a coy reference to Dulles's recruitment of Turkul. Indeed, the files explicitly state that Voss's agents were working for British intelligence and a 'Colonel Dulles' in Washington.[100]

Armed with such impressive credentials, the SCI team should have quickly recruited Voss. There was only one minor obstacle: they discovered that he was a longstanding Communist agent.[101] The proof against Voss was never revealed, but he was suddenly placed under arrest.[102] In a desperate attempt to save himself, Voss tried to prove his anti-Communist bona fides by providing chapter and verse on the MAX reports and his longstanding association with Klatt, Longin and Turkul.[103] This only alarmed the SCI even more. If Voss was a Communist agent, maybe they all were; if so, Dulles's post-war work with Turkul's organisation had been hope-lessly compromised.

It was a potential catastrophe. Klatt and Turkul also worked for the same Colonel Lewis Perry who was co-ordinating the spectacu-larly unsuccessful Križari incursions into Yugoslavia.[104] Turkul's villa in Glasenbach was conveniently close to both the Križari bases and the starting point of Father Draganović's Ratline. Indeed, Turkul's intelligence reports were sent directly to the American officer co-ordinating the Ratline, Major Milano.[105] Apparently, Milano was relying on Turkul's information to determine which defectors were valuable enough to send down the Ratline. The code name for this programme was 'The Crown Project'.[106] As we shall see, this operation bears a striking similarity to another American programme involving Father Draganović.

Klatt was arrested in Salzburg in 1946 and held at a special Allied interrogation centre for preliminary questioning before being sent to London. He claimed that he had never collaborated with Voss, but this only aroused suspicion that he was lying. Since Klatt 'was unquestionably the brains of the Turkul operation, it would have made sense for him to deny any association with a known Soviet agent like Voss'. The more he talked, the more he contradicted the facts that Voss and others had already confirmed. It was beginning to look very bad. Orders were received from Washington to terminate the 'Crown Project' and bring Turkul in for interrogation.[107]

However, Turkul had skipped town: on 17 July 1946 he requested a Military Entry Permit and crossed the border into Bavaria just ahead of his pursuers. His reason for entry to Germany was listed as 'DP business'. Indeed it was, as Turkul was trying to become a Displaced Person himself.[108] Shortly after he arrived in Uffing, Bavaria, he wrote to a friend in South America, asking for some Chilean visas.[109] Unfortunately, Turkul's letter was intercepted. Even then, there were still those who spoke in his defence:

> It is pointed out however that Subject's action to escape Europe, coupled with his absence of any overt activity, indicates that a Soviet penetration is not likely. It is to be mentioned, however, that Subject in Salzburg has allowed himself to be 'used' by known or suspected Soviet agents due to his own stupidity, blind vanity, or his non-evaluation of personalities around him.[110]

The CIC arrested Turkul on 16 September 1946, and although he tried everything to talk his way out of it, the combined interrogation team of Mr Ryle of the CIC, and Mr Johnson of British intelligence wore him down. With Klatt's and Voss's interrogations behind them, they caught Turkul in lie after lie.[111]

In order to deny that Klatt got his information from the Soviets, Turkul claimed that the MAX reports were invented so that he could build his own White Russian organisation under the noses of the Germans.[112] However, he had to retract when confronted with proof that the Germans had corroborated the MAX reports down to the smallest detail.[113] Turkul also denied that he was anti-Tito, until told that his links to Fascist Yugoslavs had already been exposed.[114]

Still, Turkul did not break down completely but kept up a stubborn resistance. He did admit that he had penetrated numerous Nazi-controlled *émigré* organisations, and that his anti-Vlasov activities might have sabotaged German attempts to raise anti-Communist forces.[115] But he refused to admit that he deliberately wrecked the Axis recruitment effort, because that would have been a tacit admission that he was really a Soviet agent. Turkul fudged and said that he would never betray the White Russians, of whom he was the most trusted leader.[116]

Turkul's followers in the DP camps were outraged that their beloved leader had been imprisoned, and a chorus of protests erupted across Bavaria. The Americans had to do something quickly to quieten things down. Lieutenant Colonel Richard Stevens described Turkul as a Communist 'double agent in whom the British and [US] had consecutive interests'. Despite this, Stevens approved the creation of a cover story for Turkul's arrest to 'help prevent antipathy for the US' among the refugee population.[117]

On 8 November 1946 the Americans agreed to disseminate the story that Turkul was not being extradited in order to reassure the refugees.[118] The protest movement collapsed, confident that their beloved leader was off on some secret mission. Turkul did not know it, but his arrest had a serious impact on other American intelligence operations as well.

For example, Turkul's arrest was impeding Project 113, the recruitment of Nazi scientists, and Operation Rusty, the recruitment of Nazi intelligence experts.[119] Operation Tobacco, the cover name for using ex-Nazis to smoke out untrustworthy refugees, was also in jeopardy.[120]

After the protests ended, things only got worse for Turkul. Voss's testimony had led the investigators to Klatt's deputy, Ira

Longin, who was arrested and sent to London for further interrogation. Slowly but surely, the investigators were tearing Turkul's network to pieces. In order to save himself, he denounced Klatt. He was fitted up with a tape recorder by the Americans and confronted Klatt in the prison courtyard. The transcript shows that Klatt caught on quickly, indicating that if Turkul denounced him as Soviet spy, he understood.[121] It was a sad ending for the courageous Jew who had single-handedly sabotaged Hitler's armies on the Eastern front. The wages of spies are often paid in the coin of betrayal.

The Americans were not altogether taken in, and continued to wonder if Turkul were really the head of a gigantic Communist network.[122] The investigation widened. No cover story in the world can stand up to protracted and detailed scrutiny. By the end of November, it was time for Turkul to play his trump card: the GRU agents inside British intelligence provided phoney background clearances for Turkul and the rest of his network. Suddenly, the US investigator, Mr Ryle, discovered that his British counterpart, Mr Johnson, was solidly on Turkul's side. In December the two investigators travelled to Geneva, where Paul Blum introduced his best source on Turkul: Father George Romanov.[123]

Ryle pressed Father Romanov on the means by which the Turkul network acquired its information for the Nazis, recalling the German who suspected that the MAX reports came from Turkul in Rome. Romanov was aghast, insisting that Turkul chose to spend the war in 'splendid isolation in Rome . . . a model of inertia', while Klatt did all the work. Turkul was a '*quantité negligible*' he claimed, and no one paid the slightest attention to him because 'the White Russian émigrés in Rome counted for nothing'. Johnson concurred: the British view was that 'Rome was of no importance'.[124]

Ryle was completely taken in: he was unaware of the British–Vatican peace negotiations, or Turkul's connection to the Black Orchestra, or his dinners with Mussolini. Johnson may have been a victim of deception by his superiors in British intelligence, although he and Romanov were surprisingly knowledgeable about Yugoslav Fascists. Father George described Ljotić as the 'most honest and true enemy of the Soviets' he ever met.[125]

Perhaps to whet Ryle's appetite, he revealed that Turkul was the head of an organisation in Belgrade that supported the return of King Zog to the Albanian throne.[126] Ryle's ears must have perked up at this. At that very moment British and US intelligence were conspiring with the Fascist Balli Kombëtar party to overthrow the Communists and restore King Zog. No one knew that Turkul was helping out. His name is absent from the histories of the abortive Albanian coup. If Turkul did indeed have a hand in it, it is not surprising that it was so disastrous.

Both Johnson and Romanov tried to convince Ryle that Klatt, not Turkul, was the Soviet agent. Romanov stated that he had warned Turkul towards the end of the war that Klatt was a Communist.[127] Ryle was led to believe that Turkul was a great anti-Communist leader, beloved by the Church. Even Father George offered to travel to the US to meet privately with senior officials.[128] After all, there was 'no better cover than a priest's frock'.[129] It was all very amusing until one recalls that the Turkul net was working for the GRU.

Ryle was stubborn and insisted on checking Romanov's information.[130] He also asked the successor to the OSS to check on Turkul's known associates. They asked the British for help, as one author discovered documents in the US Archives showing

the extent to which OSS and its successor organization(s) relied heavily on MI5 to weed out these Communists . . . For example No. KEL 3064, dated April 28, 1947, contains assessments requested by the OSS station in Austria for ten contacts of General Anton Turkul, a White Russian who had fought with the Germans, although it was thought his intelligence chief Klatt was a double agent for the Russians. Turkul was arrested in Salzburg [in 1945], then released and employed as the White Russian representative in the American zone of Austria. On the strength of the 1947 MI5 report . . . the Americans concluded . . . 'Investigation did not reveal any information that SUBJECT has been doubling as a Soviet Agent.'[131]

After this, even Ryle began to wonder if he was barking up the wrong tree. However, Schellenberg's interrogation in London revealed that several Nazi agencies, including the Gestapo and part of the SS, were convinced that Turkul's network was a Communist front. Yet not one of Turkul's agents was ever identified by MI5. After the negative MI5 report, Johnson insisted Turkul be exonerated. All Ryle could do was file his dissent. Under increasing British pressure, Turkul was freed, and promptly wrote a nasty letter to CIC demanding that his papers be returned.[132]

How did he convince British intelligence to defend him? The

answer may never be known for sure, but the Black Orchestra was apparently alive and well in London. Turkul was not the only one to have his past sanitised by British intelligence. Many SS men posed as members of the Vatican's Black Orchestra at the end of the war, and Marcus was no exception. Marcus claimed that he had been arrested for the anti-Hitler plot, but was saved by his old friend, Dr Hoffman, who vouched for him and arranged his release.[133]

In fact, Marcus was nowhere near the Hitler plot, he was in Byelorussia co-ordinating SS networks of Soviet collaborators.[134] He had served as Schellenberg's co-ordinator of V-Men, and knew the identity of every SS confidential agent ('Vertrauensmann') in Eastern Europe.[135]

Marcus was quickly hired by Vansittart's propaganda section. His real mission was to recruit SS fugitives for Philby's anti-Communist section of SIS. In order to increase his effectiveness, Marcus was appointed mayor of a small town in the British zone of Germany. He was therefore able to provide new identity cards and assistance to his old SS friends. Word spread quickly that the British were hiring anti-Communist experts. He quickly hired his old friend, Hoffman, and gave him a letter falsely certifying that he was active in the resistance.[136] By now, the Black Orchestra had many more members than it had while Hitler was alive.

Hoffman had contact with the Nazi Romanian Iron Guard during the war.[137] French intelligence had placed a priest in the British zone to co-ordinate Iron Guard recruitment.[138] It is possible that Marcus sent Hoffman out to find more Romanian Fascists, although the British had recruited quite a few already.[139]

But Hoffman came back with an even bigger catch: he had found Klaus Barbie. Marcus knew Barbie well, but despite his record of atrocities in France, he quickly recruited him. Barbie became something of an operational genius in supplying false papers and equipment to the growing roster of Britain's ex-Nazi agents.[140] Barbie's notebook contained the names of some of the Third Reich's leading strategists on the Eastern front.[141]

British intelligence did Barbie a major favour. During this time, all the American reports about Barbie's brutal war crimes disappeared. The authors have discovered that the Allied lists were sanitised while Barbie was in British employ:

While I was special agent in charge of the Delta Base CIC in Marseille 1944–45, the Lyons France office was one of our satellite offices which I visited with Major Clarence Read, our Commanding Officer. While there we not only heard of the 'Butcher of Lyons' Klaus Barbie but saw several folders in our files with his name. These were transmitted to our office and to G-2 Marseille. Surely they were sent to SHAEF [Supreme Allied Headquarters in Paris]. What happened after that I will never know.[142]

There is clear evidence that the now missing Barbie war crimes dossiers were widely circulated by the Americans. His name is listed in the 11 October 1944 US Navy *Who's Who of agents and suspects* under the following entry:

BARBIE(R), Obersturmfuhrer von
German: born c. 1909: Sipo & SD Lyons in 1943 . . . later report of January 1944 said that he had returned to Lyons and was head of Abt IV [Gestapo]: height 5′6″ (167 cm.): stout, grey eyes, rosy complexion: described as combining brutality with effusiveness.[143]

It should be noted that British intelligence had direct access to these files at this time. Long before Barbie arrived in the US zone, his wanted status was mysteriously downgraded to security suspect. Soon afterwards, things went seriously wrong for the Marcus network. In autumn 1946 Hoffman quit after Marcus accused him of trifling with his wife.[144] Hoffman promptly teamed up with SIS's rivals in British Military Intelligence and gained his revenge by exposing the giant network of ex-SS agents working for a 'fascist Foreign Office Expert'.[145] It is unclear whether this refers to Vansittart or Philby.

In any event, the British Army took Hoffman's claims seriously, and arrested Barbie. Despite the fact that his 'escape' was apparently arranged by SIS, Barbie later said that he lost faith in the British and their many promises. When Hoffman begged him to come back, Barbie turned him down flat.[146] He had a better idea.

Like Turkul, Barbie headed down the long road to Munich in the American zone. He did not know it, but it would take him to Dulles's private spy network. It was no accident that many Turkul supporters were living in the quiet little towns around Munich: Dulles had arranged for his 'freedom fighters' to be tucked away in this discreet corner of Bavaria.

In 1946 Dulles's men in Germany simply changed their OSS uniforms, and became the War Department's Strategic Services Unit (SSU). Dulles's chameleons went under various names:

sometimes they were the SSU, sometimes the War Department Detachment (WDD); often they used the innocuous sounding 'Document Disposal Unit' (DDU) for cover.[147]

In effect, there were two CIAs in Germany, one liberal (Department of Army Detachment), one conservative (DDU). The first took orders from the President. DDU took its from Dulles, who had joined Thomas Dewey's Campaign Staff, expecting Dewey to be the next President.[148]

Dulles's DDU men were the OSS 'Political Intelligence' experts. This ultra-conservative (and very secret) corps wore Army uniforms although the State Department (where Dulles still had considerable influence) actually paid them. They were waiting for Truman to be swept from office by a conservative, who would unleash their *émigré* armies on Stalin.[149]

In the meantime, while DAD (the CIA's predecessor) hunted Nazis like Bandera, Dulles's clique recruited them and kept them in cold storage pending the 1948 election. Dulles's men had a secret ally: Region IV of the CIC in Munich had been quietly helping the DDU recruit ex-Nazis. There were plenty to choose from: Prince Turkul's followers; Bishop Bučko's Ukrainians; General Gehlen's men; and Father Draganović's Intermarium network.[150]

Hiding them all was a risky business as the Munich CIC was technically committing mutiny by protecting Nazis who were wanted by CIC Headquarters in Frankfurt. Barbie's arrival in Region IV complicated an already precarious situation. Barbie did not know it, but he was about to ignite a scandal between the CIC and the DDU that would send him on his way to Rome. It was not a problem for Dulles. He had good connections at the Vatican.

11
Barbie and the American Ratlines

There was what Moscow calls a 'useful idiot' in the CIA, not a witting Communist agent, but a person who helps his enemy without realising it. His name was James Jesus Angleton. While he was nominally a member of the 'liberal' wing of the CIA, he was a secret supporter of Allen Dulles's arch-conservative DDU faction in the State Department. As we shall see, Angleton played a central role in supporting the DDU's chameleons, and was Dulles's most brilliant protégé.

Angleton was an Anglophile, having spent his early war years in London. After Dulles and the Vatican arranged the German surrender in Italy, he joined the British–American Special Counter Intelligence unit (SCI-Z) that descended on Rome. This unit soon recruited Nazis like SS intelligence chief Walter Rauff, who had worked with Dulles on the surrender negotiations. Rauff was quickly released by SCI-Z over the CIC's protest that he was a major war criminal. Rauff then went off to work for the Vatican Ratlines.[1]

Although he was not a Catholic, Angleton had a close relationship with Vatican intelligence. He warned the Vatican that one of its code clerks had been suborned by the Soviets.[2] Many such acts of kindness followed, endearing Angleton to Pius XII's closest adviser, Giovanni Montini, in the Vatican Secretariat of State.

Angleton's friendship could not have come at a better time for the Vatican. In July 1946, just as Turkul was arrested in Germany, Pius XII was confronted with a Communist propaganda campaign to secularise Italy, destroy the Vatican's privileges and seize political power. The Communists were on his doorstep, and his nightmares of the 1919 Munich uprising were coming back through the ballot box.

The Pope abandoned any pretence of neutrality and ordered a covert programme of political intervention.[3] The Americans soon learned of the secret plan, probably from Montini himself. From the spring of 1945, Angleton

> had been cultivating his source directly within the Vatican – later identified as Giovanni Battista Montini, then a Bishop and under-secretary of state at the Vatican and later Pope Paul VI. This contact may have developed further as a by-product of the negotiations then underway between Allen Dulles in Berne and the German high command in Northern Italy to arrange for a separate surrender, for Angleton's source appears to have been privy to all that the German Ambassador to the Vatican, Ernst von Weizsäcker, was reporting about Pope Pius XII.[4]

Almost all references to the Vatican's wartime role have been censored in both the ULTRA and OSS files. After the war, Angleton kept his Vatican source a secret even from the local CIA office.[5] Angleton always denied the rumours that he had recruited Montini. However, we discovered new evidence that this future Pope was a source for American intelligence.

Montini's recently declassified CIC file contains two reports of his private discussions with Pius XII. On 30 July 1946 the Pope told Montini of his growing alarm

> because of the information collected by the Vatican regarding the execution of the Soviet plan in Italy by Italian Communists.
> The plan is to render difficult the relationship between Italians and Anglo-Americans to the total advantage of the Soviet Union . . . a part of this plan is the provocation of incidents between Italians and Anglo-Americans in Italy to render more bitter the relations between Italy and the Western Allies, in order to oblige England and the United States to take severe measures.
> The Pope has given instructions that Italian Catholics react to this Soviet Plan through their organizations.[6]

The following evening, Montini had another private discussion with Pius XII, who elaborated plans for a secret counter offensive to preserve the Lateran pacts:

> the Pope gave instructions to . . . Montini, acting Secretary of State, to send directives to the Italian Catholic Action . . . to the Demo-Christian Party and all the Italian parishes . . . in order that millions of signatures of Italian men and women may be collected . . .
> This action on the part of the Pontifice derives from reliable information obtained by the Holy See on a vast program of propaganda promoted by the leftist parties for the revision of these pacts in regard to matrimony, religious education and the sovereignty of the Pontifice . . .

The Communists directed by the Soviet Union are the most active in spreading such propaganda.[7]

Since only Montini was present when Pius XII discussed his plans, only he could have delivered these reports to the Americans. The speed with which they were delivered indicates the meetings' importance. Even before the Pope decided to give covert support to the Italian Christian Democrats in July 1946, Angleton was already helping the Vatican's anti-Communist politicians:

Angleton's first major postwar assignment in Italy was to help make certain that when elections were held the Communists did not come into power . . . A coalition of parties . . . governed until there could be free elections in June of 1946. The preceding June Ferruccio Parri, the resistance leader brought back from Switzerland through Allen Dulles's mediation, had been designated prime minister, but had been forced to resign . . . and Alcide de Gasperi, whom Angleton knew well, had succeeded him.

Angleton and others are said to have fed substantial sums of money into the June Referendum; he emphatically denies this. The vote . . . demonstrated the strength of de Gasperi's Christian Democrats.[8]

De Gasperi was not only Christian Democrat head and Angleton's close friend. As discussed in Chapter One, he was also Montini's accomplice in the Vatican's political initiatives. His government ran guns to the Križari, and de Gasperi had personally protected fugitive Fascist, Ferenc Vajta.

Before Angleton left for Washington in 1947, the Vatican was promised continuing American financial support in the critical 1948 elections. Despite the CIA's objections, the cash continued to flow with help from Angleton's friends in the State Department's Special Projects Division, where Dulles still had considerable influence.[9] For the rest of his career with US intelligence, Angleton kept the Vatican as his exclusive client. As the Vatican and de Gasperi appreciated, the Americans were willing to back their anti-Communism with cold, hard cash.

But there was a price for Angleton's largesse. It was no coincidence that the Americans asked for a share of the Ratlines in mid-1947. The Vatican probably did not need much convincing to switch horses, in view of Vajta's comments that they were disgusted with the tepid strategies of the French and British.[10]

According to Vajta, the Vatican was extremely displeased with British intelligence's handling of Intermarium.[11] 'However in the sad years of 1945 and 1946, it was the only organization of international character ... for combatting the Russians.'[12] The Vatican was equally disappointed with the French, but did not blame de Gaulle. He was betrayed by his own general staff which:

> wished to continue collaboration with the British and did not believe in the efficiency of collaboration with the Vatican.
>
> After the fall of the General, the socialists sabotaged [his] policy, but finally, they were forced to admit that de Gaulle had been right and, toward the month of May 1946, they took up the idea with the General. But by this time, it was not only the officers of the General Staff, but the Parisian Free Masons who wished to fight with the British ... Their game was too childish and the Vatican retired from the circle of French interest.[13]

In autumn 1947 Vajta fled to Madrid with William Gowen's help. Once there, as already discussed, he lobbied the Spanish government to establish a new Continental Union with Vatican and American support. Unfortunately, no one had cleared these plans, and Vajta was arrested after he entered America. President Truman demanded an investigation of who was smuggling Nazis to America.[14] Truman was no Charles de Gaulle, and Dulles's plans to send his Nazis to America had to be shelved until Dulles's candidate could replace Truman in the 1948 election. Vajta must have been confident of Dewey's victory, for he filed a series of appeals to stall his deportation.

In the meantime, Dulles had a problem. Turkul's agents were piling up in the Austrian refugee camps and the Army, although sympathetic, was getting nervous because the Nazis' 'continued residence in Austria constituted a security threat at well as a source of possible embarrassment ... since the Soviet command had become aware of their presence in the US zone of Austria and in some cases had requested the return of these persons to Soviet custody'.[15]

But how could Dulles get the Nazis out? After R Day, 1947, Allied control of Italy ceased and the terms of FAN 757 expired. The British had enough problems with the Galician Division and after the Vajta scandal, Dulles could hardly ask his State Department friends to help. He needed some method to put his Nazi 'freedom fighters' into temporary cold storage. He needed the Vatican's Ratlines.

After Angleton's munificent support in 1947, how could the Vatican refuse? There is clear evidence that a deal was made.

Several years later, an American agent, Paul Lyon, wrote a 'History of the Italian Rat Line' for Major Milano:

1. ORIGINS
a. During the summer of 1947 the undersigned received instructions from G-2 [army intelligence], USFA ... to establish a means of disposition for visitors who had been in the custody of the 430th CIC ...
b. The undersigned, therefore, proceeded to Rome where, through a mutual acquaintance, he conferred with a former Slovakian diplomat [Kirschbaum, Sidor and Durčansky were all in Rome at that time] who in turn was able to recruit the services of a Croatian Roman Catholic Priest, Father Draganovich ... [who] ... had by this time developed several clandestine evacuation channels to the various South American countries for various types of European refugees.[16]

Lyon observed that if anything went wrong, the Vatican could take the blame:

Draganovich is known and recorded as a Fascist, war criminal, etc ... and his contacts with South American diplomats of a similar class are not generally approved by US State Department officials, plus the fact that in the light of security, it is better that we may be able to state, if forced, that the turning over of a DP to a [National Catholic] Welfare Organization falls in line with our democratic way of thinking and that we are not engaged in illegal disposition of war criminals, defectees and the like.[17]

Unfortunately, Father Draganović wanted something in return. If he smuggled the Americans' Nazis, they would have to help him smuggle his. A subsequent memo revealed the terms of this distinctly immoral partnership:

Through the Vatican connections of Father Draganović, Croat, DP Resettlement Chief of the Vatican Circle, a tentative agreement was reached to assist in this operation. The agreement consists of simply mutual assistance, i.e. these agents assist persons of interest to Father Draganović to leave Germany and, in turn, Father Draganović will assist these agents in obtaining the necessary visas to Argentina, South America, for persons of interest to this Command ...
It may be stated that some of the persons of interest to Father Draganović may be of interest to the Denazification policy of the Allies; however, the persons assisted by Father Draganović are also of interest to our Russian ally. Therefore this operation cannot receive any official approval and must be handled with minimum amount of delay and with a minimum amount of general knowledge.[18]

It was probably Dulles or Angleton who resurrected the old OSS term for an escape and evasion network:

Early in 1944 Welles ... was a member of an OSS team being dropped
from Brindisi by parachute into Croatia ... [The OSS] played the Yugoslav
circuit for six months ... brought in supplies to the partisans ... and
helped man the rat line (or escape line) that got perhaps forty American
Air Force men, shot down in Austria or northern Yugoslavia, back behind
Allied lines in Italy.[19]

As previously explained, a ratline is the rope ladder reaching to
the top of the mast, the last place of safety when the ship is going
down. Thus Ratline became a generic intelligence term for an
evacuation network. But the Pentagon was hardly likely to spend
the large sums of money demanded by Father Draganović ($1,000
minimum per passenger) merely to establish a standby rescue
network in the event of World War III.

Colonel Lewis Perry, who was the Americans' secret liaison to
Pavelić's Križari, came up with a good cover story. The Vatican
was helping relocate Soviet defectors of interest to US intelligence.
If they remained in Austria, they would be a headache because of
Soviet surveillance and kidnapping teams. The best solution was
to have the Vatican put them on a boat and send them over the
hill to South America. Colonel Perry transformed Major Milano's
Operation Ratline into Operation Headache/Boathill and had it
quickly approved at the highest Pentagon levels. Here is an
example from the Top Secret Allied Forces Headquarters Message
Center of 13 December 1949:

> 13 travelers awaiting shipment follow (real names, aliases and shipping
> names listed . . .)
>
> Subsequent to debriefing subjects turned over to organization of Croa-
> tian Catholic Priest Father Draganović, K, Vatican DP Resettlement Chief,
> through contact Bosiliewicz, Vladimir in Salzburg Austria. [International
> Red Cross] passports carried by subjects procured by Bosiliewicz in
> Geneva Switzerland unassisted by CIC. Subjects departed separately
> from Salzburg, Austria current by train for Naples, Genoa and Rome.
> Subjects now in vicinity of Rome awaiting shipment to Paraguay, Argen-
> tina, Bolivia or Venezuela, depending on country from which visa can be
> procured. Effective control by CIC over subject ceases when subjects
> depart Austrian territory.[20]

'Bosiliewicz' was in fact Vladimir Bosiljević, a key member of
Father Draganović's network. It was no coincidence that he could
procure IRC passworks, as he had been working on the Ratline in
Salzburg since May 1945. US intelligence established that Bosiljević had been appointed to the position of Secretary General of

the Croatian Red Cross by no less a person than Father Vilim Cecelja, Draganović's Austrian representative. Colonel Perry had probably met Bosiljević during the spectacularly unsuccessful Križari operations, since the Croatian was also a senior Križari officer, working closely with Srećko Rover on maintaining radio contact with the terrorist groups in Yugoslavia.[21]

This was another reason why it was important to keep the CIC from knowing too much about the Ratlines' real purpose. Colonel Perry was probably one of Dulles's DDU chameleons, but he had to rely on the CIC for legmen. Even Major Milano was not told the source of the Red Cross passports, nor was he informed of the actual war crimes backgrounds of Perry's recruits. Many years later the bewildered CIC agents who manned the Austrian–Vatican Ratlines said that as far as they knew, only one Nazi had gone out through that route; they thought the rest were legitimate Soviet defectors.

They were telling the truth as far as they knew it. By the time the 430th CIC took over in 1947, most of the well known Nazis had already been sent down the Ratline; the remainder were little known collaborators who easily convinced the gullible Austrian CIC that they were really 'anti-Communist refugees'.

Most of the Austrian CIC agents were new recruits, fresh out of Fort Holabird. They had no bitter memories of World War II to cloud their perceptions of the Slavic refugees, who seemed like rather nice people. The Austrian CIC had the kind of dim but daring thinkers that Dulles wanted. Their mission was simple: the Nazis were defeated and the Communists were the new enemy.

The 430th CIC quickly got the message. In 1947 virtually all Nazi-hunting in their area came to a complete stop. CIC agents in Rome, Trieste and Salzburg started recruiting Nazis for their anti-Communist expertise. William Gowen's reports on Ante Pavelić reflect the winds of change that swept through sections of the CIC in 1947. The reports suddenly changed focus. While their counterparts in Germany were still keeping lists of wanted war criminals and devoting at least some resources to locating them, the 430th CIC was making lists of which Nazis worked for which foreign intelligence service as a guide for eventual recruitment by Dulles's DDU.[22]

There was, however, one CIC unit in Germany, which was considerably less co-operative with Dulles's plans. The 970th

Detachment had a nucleus of professional intelligence agents who had stayed on after the war. Both the anti-Nazi and anti-Communist desks in Germany were staffed by CIC veterans who hated war criminals, and suspected that the DDU's recruits were hopelessly penetrated by the Soviets.[23]

The CIC and CIA agents in Germany swapped stories about the DDU's latest idiocy. The 970th CIC was hard to fool: they maintained a massive Central Registry that all too frequently exposed the true backgrounds of the DDU's 'freedom fighters'. To put it bluntly, they were giving Allen Dulles fits.

One of the 970th CIC's most brilliant anti-Communist experts absolutely forbade hiring Nazis to spy on the Soviets. He later played a key role in closing down Klaus Barbie's network. President Truman had ordered the 970th Detachment to hunt Nazis and they obeyed him with quiet professionalism.[24] Despite the opprobrium that has recently been heaped on them, the 970th CIC was one of the few intelligence services that did a competent, dedicated job of Nazi-hunting.

The 430th CIC in Austria was another matter. For example, both Detachments were ordered to submit reports on Stanislaw Stankievich. The 970th correctly identified Stankievich as a former official of the Nazi puppet government in Byelorussia. The 430th reported that he was a prominent anti-Communist _émigré_. The State Department picked the Austrian CIC's version.[25]

Although Stankievich had confessed that he was a senior Nazi, he was released through State Department intercession.[26] The 970th were told to keep their hands off Nazis who worked for the British or French, but lived in the US zone.[27] The CIC reluctantly complied, but kept embarrassing lists of these 'freedom fighters' indexed by their previous war crimes and atrocities, to prevent them obtaining US visas.[28] As long as these existed, the 970th had closed off the US zone as an emigration route.

By and large, Austria was a much safer transit point for Dulles's growing army of agents. The 430th knew the true names of the passengers using the Ratline, but not their war crimes background. The 970th had the latter information, but was unaware that the 430th was running the Ratline. The two CIC units had virtually no contact, and Dulles wanted it that way. If they could be kept apart, the Ratlines would function smoothly.

Whether by design or coincidence, the Pentagon solved the

problem. As part of the massive reorganisation of the Defense Department between 1947 and 1949, Germany and Austria were placed under separate command headquarters. The military meddlers' most significant accomplishment seems to have been their bewildering array of acronyms. The bottom line for Dulles was that the two CIC Detachments were permanently divided under different commands.

After the reorganisation, the 430th in Austria was not really part of the CIC any more; it effectively ceased to exist. All intelligence units in Austria, Italy and Trieste were detached from their own agencies and placed under the direct command of US military intelligence headquarters in Salzburg, where Colonel Perry could keep an eye on the 430th. Their records were purged every three years for unexplained security reasons, and only a few reels of microfilm survive.[29]

As far as Major Milano knew, the 430th was supporting a legitimate anti-Communist programme that had been approved by higher headquarters. Perry knew better, but kept his mouth shut. Part of the Ratlines deal was to assist Draganović's Nazis to leave Germany and enter Austria. Perry had to contact the Nazis and get them across the border without the 970th learning about it. The Ratlines needed someone in Germany who was immune from arrest. Dulles had the perfect answer: he recruited Turkul's old boss, General Gehlen.[30]

Gehlen was a consummate con artist. He had built his reputation under the Nazis by claiming credit for the Abwehr's MAX reports. After the war, he used the same scam on the gullible Americans. In 1946, after a year of negotiations with Dulles and senior Pentagon commanders in Washington, Gehlen was flown to a secret base in Munich to establish a new US espionage network. Unfortunately, just as he arrived, Voss and Klatt were identified as Soviet agents and even Turkul was under suspicion. Where could Gehlen get the secrets he had promised the Americans?

Ignoring his instructions not to hire any tainted agents, Gehlen recruited Dr Franz Six and Emil Augsburg to head his anti-Communist desk. Both were infamous war criminals, but had encyclopaedic knowledge of Nazi intelligence operations in Eastern Europe. To stall for time, they interviewed German prisoners returning from the Soviet Union. It was not enough. The Americans pressed Gehlen to produce results by July 1947 or his funds would be cut. The truth was that Gehlen's only forte was rewriting other people's work and claiming the credit for himself. He did not have the faintest idea how to penetrate the 'Iron Curtain' on his own.[31]

The secret of Gehlen's success was timing. Just as the US connection to the Vatican Ratline was established in mid-1947, Turkul was cleared by the British and released in the US zone of Germany. He resumed leadership of the 'new' NTS,[32] which had penetrated every level of Soviet *émigrés* in Germany, and offered Gehlen

> a literally inexhaustible source of information. However impenetrable the Iron Curtain might seem, into the houses, the camps and the association offices of these émigrés ran the secret channels of communication; Red Army deserters found refuge with friends; Russians received letters from relatives in the Soviet Union; exiled politicians were in radio communication with the Ukraine.[33]

Virtually all the *émigré* organisations publicly identified as Gehlen fronts, including the NTS, and many other exotic groups like the Saint Andrew's Flag, were secretly controlled by Turkul. A comparison, for example, of the list of Gehlen front groups cited in E. H. Cookridge's biography of Gehlen with the recently declassified US intelligence files, shows the extent of Turkul's secret dominance of Operation Rusty and the Gehlen Organisation.[34]

Turkul located his headquarters in Munich, near Gehlen's own offices in the comparative safety of Region IV. Of course, Turkul's recruits did not stay in Germany, but he had connections in Salzburg. Here the 430th worked with, not against, him to evacuate Nazis under the nose of the 970th.[35] It was just the kind of connection Father Draganović needed.

Turkul was the link between Germany and the Austrian Ratlines. His network's reports were sent directly to Major Milano in Austria, who was working closely with Colonel Perry on Operation Headache/Boathill.[36] If anything went wrong, Perry could vouch for Turkul.[37] If the Americans wanted 'freedom fighters', Turkul knew just the men. His NTS reached into every *émigré* organisation in Europe.

First he took NTS away from the British and delivered it to Gehlen; then he took control of Gehlen's contacts with other *émigré* groups. According to Turkul's recently declassified files, he moved very quickly when he was released. 'For a short time Turkul was a member of General Peter von Glasenap's Russian Monarchist Organization, the League of Saint Andrew's Flag.'[38] Glasenap had been working for Gehlen, but was quickly dropped after Turkul took over the Saint Andrew's Flag. Neither Gehlen nor Glasenap resented Turkul as long as he got the job done.

Glasenap stayed 'in direct contact with Turkul' and passed information to Region IV's agents.[39] Perry vouched for Turkul as 'a close friend of General Glasenap . . . who has excellent contacts with a US intelligence agency in Germany'.[40] There was one little problem: wherever Turkul took over, security went to pieces:

> One of [Gehlen's] investigators came to the conclusion that in a certain émigré organization known as 'NTS, people working directly for the Soviet Union are recklessly given cover and support.' In another émigré society, the 'league of Andreas Flag', an informer detected an ex-Lieutenant Colonel Solomin of the Soviet Secret Police who 'when in his cups, would tell stories of his prowess in shooting Russian colonels and generals for attempted desertion to the Germans.' Vigilant though they were, Gehlen's men could never be sure whether they were dealing with figments of the imagination of some harum-scarum intelligence-peddler, or with doctored material fed to them by the Russians.[41]

Gehlen had fallen for the same game that Turkul had played on him during the war. Although his own people suspected that 90 per cent of the information they passed to the Americans was false, Gehlen had no other sources and continued to use NTS:

> Initially he had no alternative but to try the old methods once more. He therefore turned to the more reliable among the anti-Communist émigrés in the hope that they might assist him to penetrate the Soviet Union . . . In particular, with Gehlen's help, the Nationalist 'NTS' despatched parachutists as far away as Moscow; most of them, however, were discovered and arrested by the Soviet counter-espionage authorities.[42]

No one suspected that it was Turkul who leaked information to the GRU. It was always someone else, like Klatt or Voss, who was blamed. To plug the leaks, Gehlen hired Turkul's own Security Chief Tenzerov, whose real name was Puzanov. He seemed to be a reliable watchdog because he had himself been betrayed by some NTS leaders at war's end. But Tenzerov, who had been a leading Nazi propagandist for the Vlasov Army, still had good contacts with Turkul. He supported Gehlen's attempts to unite the Vlasov groups under the command of his old friend, Turkul.

It appears that Dulles's clique knew very little about Soviet infiltration of the NTS in 1947, and believed that it was just another Fascist organisation working for the British. Perry should have paid more attention to the note in Turkul's file: the Gestapo had arrested several NTS leaders in 1944 when they discovered a radio connection between their Warsaw headquarters and the Soviets.[43] Perhaps Perry overlooked things in the rush to find a secure way to get Draganović's friends out of Germany. Besides, Turkul had already been cleared by the British.

Gehlen was less picky about his agents' backgrounds. Soon there was a trickle, and then a flood of ex-Nazis moving south into Region IV. Why work for the British when the Americans were allowing the Germans to build their own espionage agency? Klaus Barbie was certainly impressed and in January 1947, went to work for Gehlen along with several of his SS friends who had worked on Ukrainian affairs. Unfortunately, Gehlen was no more adept at protecting war criminals than the British.

A few months after Barbie arrived, the CIA 'liberals' discovered that Gehlen had broken his promise and was hiring SS war criminals. They yanked Dr Six away from Gehlen and put him on trial at Nuremberg. Six was convicted of running an SS mobile killing unit, but was subsequently pardoned after Vatican intercession.[44]

But a small faction within US intelligence thought the CIA's morality misplaced. Dulles later said of his use of Gehlen's people: 'There are few Archbishops in Intelligence, and besides, one need not invite them to one's club.' Before the CIA could discover the other Nazis in Gehlen's club, Dulles's DDU smuggled Augsburg, Tenzerov, Barbie and others to a safehouse, and then resettled them in Augsburg, Bavaria, where the SS recruiting continued on the sly.[45]

Region IV was run by a series of temporary commanders like Aaron Banks, a former OSS agent (who later became 'Godfather to the Green Berets'), and Elliot Golden (who worked on 'special operations' for the Air Force). Their CIC employees were supposed to be hunting Nazis, but under their noses, Region IV became a haven for Dulles's recruits.

The fugitives were disguised as sub-agents for the innocuous

Abwehr Captain Peterson. In this corner of Bavaria, the DDU built a network of war criminals. It was several years before CIC Headquarters in Frankfurt discovered the DDU's double game in Region IV, but by then it was much too late to expose anyone. They were too deeply involved. Barbie, Augsburg and Tenzerov were working for Gehlen and had close contacts with Turkul's growing network.[46]

When the Barbie affair finally emerged into the glare of publicity thirty-five years later, the Americans launched an official inquiry. Although the US Justice Department's report on the Barbie affair discreetly censored most references to Barbie's previous work for British intelligence, enough references have been declassified to show the true reason for his recruitment by Gehlen. In addition to identifying SS officers working for the British,[47] Barbie had information on their Ukrainian operations.[48] In fact, he lured an entire faction of Ukrainian Fascists away from the British ABN and brought them over to Gehlen and Dulles.

Barbie submitted written reports on two men who played key roles in the Cold War. The reports no longer exist, but we know from Barbie's payment list that his subjects were Mykola Lebed and Ivan Grynioch. Both were subsequently recruited by DDU and moved to Bavaria. Barbie was small fry compared with them.

Grynioch, as previously discussed, was a Ukrainian Catholic priest who had joined Nazi intelligence before the war. He was chaplain to Bandera's Nachtigall Battalion when the Germans invaded the Ukraine, and remained in favour even after Stetsko and Bandera were unceremoniously dumped by the Nazis. Father Grynioch was Lebed's deputy.[49]

Like Bandera, Lebed had been convicted of political assassination in pre-war Poland, and was subsequently hired by the Abwehr. He was given special training at the Gestapo's security academy and became head of Bandera's security service, the SB. According to his intelligence file, Lebed consolidated OUN power by murdering the leaders of several rival Ukrainian nationalist groups during the war. Lebed successfully played the German factions against each other, and ended the war as Bandera's right-hand man and an SS favourite. Even pro-Ukrainian historians admit that Lebed's record was bloody indeed.[50]

In 1945 Lebed fled to Rome where he had high level contacts in the Vatican.[51] He called himself the Foreign Minister of the OUN, and downplayed his murderous past. Bishop Bučko was the Ukrainian contact for Intermarium at this time, and an avid OUN supporter. Unlike Bandera, who worked only for Philby and the British, Lebed was attracted by an offer to work with Turkul and his wealthy American friends.[52]

It was not the first offer. In autumn 1944 the Vlasovites offered to work with the OUN, but Bandera's attitude prevented this.[53] As we shall see, Turkul's connections to Region IV and the DDU allowed him to bring about a merger. It is ironic that the Soviets' strategy to divide and conquer the OUN finally succeeded with Barbie's help.

By the end of 1947, Region IV's commander was in the hot seat. CIC Headquarters had discovered the Nazi network and ordered Barbie's arrest. But DDU's operation was saved by an astounding stroke of luck. Judging from the dates of his reports it was probably Barbie who first alerted the Americans about Lebed's change of heart. Lebed was afraid that his Italian government and Vatican contacts would be unable to protect him after R day. Barbie's network offered him sanctuary in Augsburg.

In November 1947 Region IV asked permission to smuggle Lebed from Rome. Camile Hadju, Barbie's case handler, personally drafted the plan which was submitted up the chain of command.[54] The proposal to hire a known Ukrainian war criminal must have raised a few eyebrows at higher levels, but the chance to interview Lebed was too tempting. There were intriguing references to his 'connections with de Gaulle and French Intelligence'. Here was an opportunity to get to the bottom of Intermarium, not to mention the inside story on Bandera's work for the British.[55]

Captain Hale, who had co-ordinated CIC's hunt for Bandera, arranged for Lebed to be airlifted to Region IV. Barbie, who apparently provided the original contacts to Grynioch and Lebed, was not turned over to the French as a war criminal. Instead, he returned to work after a few months with instructions not to tell the British what had transpired.[56]

Only a few people at CIC Headquarters in Germany knew what had happened. Decisions about Region IV's Nazis were made at a much higher level. The Vatican was helping the DDU steal the OUN away from the British. According to William Gowen:

Early in April [1948] Monsignor Bučko, the only surviving Ukrainian Roman Catholic Bishop on the European Continent, left Rome for Salzburg Austria . . . and other cities in Western Europe. Bučko is sometimes described as the 'spiritual leader' of the Ukrainian resistance. He is the key man in Vatican affairs and to him go a proportion of the Ukrainian-American and Ukrainian-Canadian donations to the Ukrainian nationalist cause.[57]

According to Gowen, Bučko was impatient with Bandera's refusal to co-operate with other Ukrainian factions. His source claimed that 'Bandera is an overrated extremist. In the latter respect this agent was informed by Casimir Papée, Polish London Government Ambassador to the Vatican, that today Bandera's Army is largely dispersed and lacking all types of necessary equipment.'[58]

Like Bučko, Papée was a leading Intermarium member. The Vatican was laundering funds, but not to Bandera. Bučko later met with the Bavarian Culture Minister to discuss Vatican funding for the Ukrainian Red Cross, the Ukrainian Free University and other 'cultural groups'.[59] One of the most prominent 'cultural' leaders in Germany was Father Grynioch. Bučko's tour apparently had an energising effect on the anti-Bandera faction. The switch from British intelligence to Dulles was under way.

Lebed and Grynioch went to a secret showdown with Bandera in Munich in August 1948. They told him they were setting up their own Ukrainian organisation in Augsburg, the UHWR.[60] Bandera was furious:

. . . attacks were made against one Iwan Hrinioch (sic) and one Mikola Lebed, who were accused of being opportunists . . . [and splitting] the UHWR and OUN-R in order to weaken the position of Stephen Bandera.

In a rebuttal, Mikola Lebed, confirmed and reiterated statements made by Dr Hrinioch, to the effect that the UHWR . . . hoped, some day, to set up a free democratic government which is divorced from all dictatorial pressure.[61]

As a parting shot, Grynioch and Lebed 'stated that the latest events in the OUN indicated a trend toward Fascism, and in a demonstration, quit the session'.[62] Since they had been active Nazis themselves during the war, this quip was for the benefit of the gullible Americans. Bandera fired them and warned his organisation to avoid contact with the new Ukrainian centre in Augsburg.[63] All the Vatican's prodigal sons were coming home to Germany. There was just one problem: Dulles's friend Dewey lost the 1948 election, Truman was re-elected and Dulles's agents were out on a long, long limb.

Barbie's reports on Lebed and Grynioch could not have come at a better time. In March 1948 orders had been given to Region IV to break up the Barbie net, as he was of no further use. However, after the August split in the OUN, Barbie's position temporarily improved. The dissolution of Region IV's net was halted, but CIC Headquarters brooked no further delays when they discovered in November that Barbie and his friends were really running underground SS networks for Gehlen. Instead of working for the CIC, Region IV's net was working for Gehlen.[64]

Payments to Gehlen's fugitives in Augsburg had been handled by the DDU under cover of the War Department Detachment (WDD).[65] This was too much, as most senior agents at CIC Headquarters believed that Gehlen's operation was heavily penetrated by Soviet double agents. Their estimate was correct, as shown by the Felfe trial in the 1960s. Heinz Felfe was Gehlen's right-hand man, and had access to NATO's secrets, which he gave to Moscow.[66]

But in early 1949 Gehlen still had many protectors. In May a meeting was held at European Command Headquarters where Captain Vidal of CIC was told the facts of life, up to a point. Barbie would stay on the payroll, but Vidal was not told why. One reason was that Barbie's knowledge could compromise the DDU's Ukrainian operations. If Barbie was fired, he might talk about an even bigger scandal. DDU agents in Germany had learned that Tenzerov was on the Soviets' list of most wanted traitors and war criminals. The demand for his arrest had arrived only a few days earlier, on 13 May. Curiously, the Soviets did not mention Tenzerov's work for NTS, although they mentioned everything else:

PUZANOV, Nikolai Vasilievich, also known as TENZEROV Yevgeni Vasilievich ... a former officer in the Soviet Army. Collaborated with the enemy. After having been taken prisoner in 1942, he attended a school of the German 'Eastern Ministry' for training propagandists to be sent to the USSR. From the beginning of 1943 he worked as senior instructor and leader of studies in the Russian section of the propagandists school. Was editor of the anti-Soviet magazine 'Our Days'. In November 1944, he was brought into the German-sponsored Committee for the Liberation of Russian Nationalities [KONR]. From December of that year, he was Chief of the Security Branch of KONR. In February 1945, he was the authorized representative of KONR at Berlin. Has received German awards and the title of Lieutenant Colonel in [Vlasov's Army]. Is residing in the US Zone of occupation in Germany.[67]

Tenzerov was in the US zone all right; he was on Gehlen's payroll. Dulles's DDU had made a big mistake in putting Tenzerov in the same network with Augsburg and Barbie. If Barbie went down, he could take both the Gehlen and Turkul organisations with him. The State Department had to protect another war criminal. As with Pavelić, the orders were 'Hands Off'. The CIC was ordered to babysit Barbie for the State Department.[68]

Captain Vidal made hand-written notations in Barbie's file: his status was officially changed from a CIC asset ('Administratively dropped'), but his relations with Region IV were continued until CIC was 'notified by the State Department'. In short, Barbie was fired by CIC on paper, but was not told. Vidal was disgruntled, but orders were orders.[69] In occupied Germany, the State Department called the shots.

Other members of the Barbie net were taken off CIC's books. Augsburg was apparently more trustworthy than Barbie. He was allowed to quit CIC and go to work for a 'positive US intelligence agency', identified in Heinz Höhne's book as the Gehlen organisation. Barbie's other colleagues, like Kurt Merck, were regarded by CIC as 'not effective', but a top secret shroud was thrown over the Merck case, 'due to his connection with another American intelligence agency'. Once again the DDU had protected its own. Everyone went back to work for Gehlen, except Barbie.[70]

The DDU had good reason for keeping Barbie at arm's length. Most of the DDU officers were under cover as full or part-time State Department officers. They knew what CIC did not: the Barbie case was about to explode. Shortly after Vidal agreed to babysit Barbie for the State Department, he learned that Barbie was a major war criminal, wanted by the French Government.[71]

Vidal, no friend of DDU's Nazis, promptly arranged for French Military Intelligence to interview Barbie as a defence witness for René Hardy.[72] The Deuxième Bureau was content to take a written statement, but the rival Sûreté was livid. Barbie must be turned over for trial for his own war crimes. Vidal had no objection, and made the arrangements. Once again, the State Department had to tell Vidal the facts of life.[73]

They were better informed than CIC: the French conservatives really did not want Barbie back, because he could expose several prominent French politicians as Gestapo informers and create a scandal that might give the Communists a greater share of power. The Sûreté, which was heavily penetrated by Moscow,[74] wanted Barbie as a pawn to discredit François Poncet, the French High Commissioner for Germany. It was an ugly story. France's highest ranking official in occupied Germany had been an informant for Klaus Barbie and the Gestapo.[75]

By July 1949, Vidal knew that whatever Poncet had told Barbie during the war had caused the State Department to believe that France would never officially request Barbie's extradition. Indeed, Poncet ensured that the French paperwork never crossed his own desk to reach McCloy, his American counterpart.[76]

The DDU agents in Germany were quite amused at Poncet's game, until the French got wise and submitted the paperwork directly to Washington, bypassing Poncet and their operatives around McCloy. State Department channels buzzed with secret messages about Barbie's 'highly embarrassing' potential.[77]

That was an understatement. Barbie knew about the Tenzerov–Turkul–Gehlen connection and the relocation of Grynioch and Lebed. Worse, Poncet's wartime indiscretions to the Gestapo could hand the French Communists a major propaganda victory.

In May 1950 Vidal received instructions from Colonel Eckmann, the CIC 'special squad' liaison to DDU. Barbie was not to be turned over to the French, contrary to the State Department's public statements. There was more to the Barbie connection than CIC knew: 'there are ramifications at higher headquarters of which this region has no knowledge.'[78]

Indeed there were. CIC never knew it, but François Poncet was the secret source of the Vatican's Red Cross passports. According to a source in a Western intelligence service, whose information was confirmed by another Western agency, Poncet was de Gaulle's connection to Intermarium.[79] Before the war, he was the French Ambassador to the Third Reich and then to Italy. After war broke out, he was interned by Mussolini until he was kidnapped by Barbie and taken to France. Poncet confirmed this in his diaries.[80]

As early as 1946, US intelligence in Austria knew that the 'International Red Cross were issuing temporary identity documents under assumed names . . . to persons operating under the protection of the Vatican', including war criminals,[81] and that Red Cross couriers were being used to evade Allied mail censorship. Before his death in 1989, Father Cecelja confirmed that he had access to blank Red Cross papers, which he gave to fugitives in Austria *en route* to Draganović. Poncet was the source.

In pursuit of Intermarium, de Gaulle permitted Poncet to wear two hats. He was both French High Commissioner for Germany (which controlled the distribution of HICOG travel documents), and French representative to the International Red Cross (which distributed the passports that Father Draganović so desperately needed). Poncet became Vice President of the Red Cross International Committee, and later President.[82] The CIC later discovered that Poncet was meeting Dr Joseph Müller in a Munich safehouse, but did not realise that Müller had been the Black Orchestra's emissary to the Vatican.[83]

The State Department stumbled on the Red Cross connection because of La Vista's report on Vatican Nazi smuggling. His report was quickly removed from normal channels and passed to the super secret Special Projects Division in Washington (DDU's predecessor) where it was quietly shelved. The Red Cross was discreetly advised to tighten security before anyone else found out.[84]

When the Barbie case exploded, Dulles himself came to Poncet's rescue. They were old friends from the diplomatic service. In return for keeping Barbie out of harm's way, Poncet promised Dulles a share of the Red Cross passports. Their deal was reluctantly but absolutely confirmed by several sources in Western intelligence.[85] As we shall see, Poncet's recruitment was the culmination of DDU's plan to take over the Vatican's Ratlines from the British and the French.

Keeping Barbie out of harm's way was no easy matter. As late as June 1950, the State Department hoped the French would not press the case. They publicly told the French they could not find Barbie in the US zone. Simultaneously, they told the Army not to look.[86] Orders were orders, so the Army never *officially* asked CIC if they knew Barbie's whereabouts.

But the problem would not go away. The British suddenly chimed in with an arrest warrant for Barbie. The affidavit was signed by Hoffman, Barbie's old comrade-in-arms. Worse, the French extradition request would soon be officially delivered to the

American High Commissioner. The DDU feared that the case would blow up in their faces, and decided to make scapegoats of the CIC.[87]

To his utter shock, Vidal received an official State Department order to report whether CIC objected to Barbie's extradition. Vidal scrawled across the memo 'a foul one!' Indeed it was. Apparently, DDU was hoping that Barbie's side job with CIC was so sensitive that Vidal would conceal him, and let them off the hook for hiding him.[88]

But Barbie's actual work for CIC was so inconsequential that they had nothing to fear. The popular view, that the CIC protected him because he infiltrated the German Communists is a fraud. CIC Headquarters had already covertly photocopied the entire Communist party registry. Barbie's trivial bits of information were superfluous. The only operation he could expose was the dirty tricks shop of DDU.[89]

Vidal ensured the scapegoat plan backfired. Both CIC and CIA cheerfully informed the High Commissioner they had no objections to handing Barbie over for trial. In October 1950 DDU struck back with a last ditch effort to force CIC to take the blame for the Barbie fiasco. Cunningham of DDU (who was under cover as local HICOG representative) complained to McCloy's intelligence chief that CIC was *refusing* to look for Barbie, and that the Army should be forced to investigate his whereabouts.[90]

This bit of whining was ineffectual, as the CIC would not be bluffed. Vidal had previously agreed to turn Barbie over to the French and would have done so had it not been for DDU's counter order in May 1950. What happened next is difficult to document. The following fourteen files have been removed from the State Department's archives, but it appears that the High Commissioner's Office issued Barbie with Allied Control Board travel documents, and sent him down the Vatican Ratline.[91]

Draganović promptly shipped him off to South America under the name of Klaus Altmann. In Bolivia, Barbie was received by Draganović's local representative, Father Rocque Romac, another Fascist Croatian priest and wanted war criminal, whose real identity was Father Stjepan Osvaldi-Toth.[92] Vidal's obstinacy really did not matter in the end: the DDU arranged for Major Milano to staff the Ratlines, and CIC got the blame after all.

However, a close examination of the badly copied Barbie documents reveals that the State Department co-ordinated his passage down the Ratline.[93]

Indeed, almost all of the early passengers on the American Ratlines were handled by the State Department's Office of Policy Co-ordination (OPC) through their contact man in Rome:

> In fact, many of Draganović's phoney exit papers were arranged through Robert Bishop, an American ex-OSS agent who was then in charge of the eligibility office of the International Refugee Organization (IRO) in Rome, according to CIC records. Bishop was one of the . . . OPC's most important assets in that city. He had worked . . . on a variety of clandestine projects in Istanbul, Bucharest and Rome since at least 1944.[94]

Bishop, not surprisingly, had also been a member of Angleton's operation.[95] Unfortunately, he had a nervous breakdown due to alcoholism and started to babble stories about underground armies and covert financing of the Italian elections, claiming that he was 'the saviour of Italy'.[96] Like Barbie, he knew too much and was quietly removed before he could further embarrass the Vatican and his superiors.

In 1950, just as the Barbie case was threatening to explode, Dulles stepped out of the woodwork to take over briefly from Frank Wisner as head of OPC. Within a few months, Wisner was back in command when Dulles became Deputy Director of CIA. Bringing Dulles in to smooth relations between OPC and CIA was one of Truman's biggest mistakes, for he brought the Ratlines with him. Shortly after Barbie reached Bolivia, and Dulles joined CIA, the pretence was dropped. Perry's office told the Austrian CIC that their services were no longer required:

> In closing, 430th stated that they are not 'budgeted' beyond 30 June 1951, and implied that they may have to cease this [Ratline] operation after that date. They further stated that a directive received through G2, USFA, indicated that some time in the undetermined future CIA will assume all responsibility for evacuations. Although it is not certain, it appears to 430th that end of the budget and assumption of control by CIA roughly coincide.[97]

To this day, the Justice Department, the CIC and the CIA do not know how the State Department pulled off the Barbie affair, or what was really at stake. It was Dulles's very survival. While the CIA was booting out ABN's Nazis and Philby was sending them to Canada, DDU had brought them back in with phony (and very illegal) visas issued in Germany.[98] Although smuggling Nazis was a felony, the State Department brought Mykola Lebed to America in October 1949, using a false name and background.[99]

Barbie knew too much about Lebed, and Lebed knew too much about Turkul. By the time Barbie went down the Ratline in March 1951,[100] the Augsburg connection had passed the point of no return. Shortly after the OUN split, the 'Ukrainian Vlasov Committee' (Bučko's Galician SS) agreed to work with Turkul.[101] Barbie's Ukrainian contacts had solidified Turkul's base as the rising *émigré* force. With his ties to Lebed, Gehlen and Dulles, Turkul campaigned to 'unify' all the *émigré* groups. It was the same infiltration and co-option strategy he had used to split the Third Reich's *émigrés*.[102]

Turkul had an uncanny knack; he belonged to every faction simultaneously and through his interlocking membership on their executives, advanced his position as the *eminence grise* of the *émigré* anti-Communist movement. Turkul charmed his way through the alphabet soup of *émigré* groups and swallowed them one after another.

By March 1948, Turkul was a leading member of Saint Andrew's Flag, AZODNR, and the paramilitary youth wing of the Vlasov Army. In December 1948, as soon as he had formed a coalition of these groups, Turkul tried to dissolve them and form a new organisation, the KOW, or 'Committee of United Vlasovites'. Eighteen months later, KOW sponsored a conference with other Vlasov organisations, which formed the 'combat union for the liberation of the Peoples of Russia', with its own military centre called SWOD.[103]

To increase his influence, Turkul went international. In September 1950 he tried to merge with the US Kerensky Committee and the Russian monarchists in Paris, but Turkul's organisation was rejected for being too far on the totalitarian right. Turkul then downplayed his Nazi past, and joined the Supreme Council of Russian Exiles.[104] Finally, he proposed that all groups merge into the 'Russian Committee of Liberation'.

There was one ethnic group excluded from Turkul's new committee, as US censors discovered when they opened his mail: 'Our movement will never agree to have Jews on the Russian Committee of Liberation . . . Jews are responsible for 50 million people shot.'[105]

Turkul's shifting alliances were meant to confuse. He downplayed his Nazi affiliations to please the Americans, yet at the same time he joined the British-sponsored ABN. His contradictory loyalties did not trouble Colonel Perry. He vouched for Turkul as an ABN leader and close friend of General Glasenap, who had 'excellent contacts with a US Intelligence Agency in Germany'. As of 14 September 1950, Perry knew of no derogatory information on Turkul.[106] Even Region IV's renegades knew better, listing him as a 'Notorious double agent . . . heading NTS'.[107]

Turkul's post-war network included his old Ukrainian friend Kowalewsky and Vuković of the Serbian movement.[108] NTS leaders were a diverse group: Russian priest Alexiew Kisiliew, who ran a 'Russian School' in Munich along with Father Grabbe and Engineer Marmulkow; Baranowsky ran 'a considerable net for the Americans'; Victor Bajdalakow was NTS Chief, and his assistant, Boldyreff was the liaison in Washington.[109] Boris Ovseenko ran the Australian wing out of the Fairbane Hostel in Canberra, where many Ukrainian Nazis were housed after migrating under the DP scheme.[110]

Major Milano's agreement with the State Department in Germany, which barred NTS members from entry or exit from the US zone, was abandoned.[111] But NTS was still on CIC's banned list in Germany. They rejected Turkul's visa application in 1951, as it 'was felt that his previous intelligence activities could be a security risk to the country', and because he 'was considered [as] having totalitarian rightist leanings'.[112]

Turkul's liaison in Washington, Boldyreff, made things worse when he launched a propaganda offensive. This caused former SS leader, Werner Ohletz, to approach the Americans to warn them against Boldyreff:

BOLDYREFF portrays the ideologies of the NTS and emphasizes its fight against Nazism and Bolshevism. To this I say the following: As long as it seemed that Germany would win the war, the NTS was very eager to co-operate with the German authories and Intelligence Service. But when it became clear that the Allies would probably be victorious, the NTS began to work for both sides and thus became even more dangerous to the German cause . . .

[Ohletz] states that it is dangerous to co-operate with the NTS and that German Intelligence determined from experience long ago that it was more successful to collaborate with a Democratic Anti-Great Russian Organization and to back their political aims.[113]

As the officer in charge of the SS section which took over military intelligence from Canaris, Ohletz had long and bitter experience with Soviet *émigré* organisations. He described Vlasov's plan to 'liquidate a few million' in order to take over Russia, and added that 'a similar reply was also received from the White Russian General Turkul'.[114] Ohletz warned that 'the German Counter Intelligence Service found that all Émigré Organizations were infiltrated by the NKVD with such effectiveness that it was impossible to discover the connecting lines from top ranking people to the common follower'.[115]

Ohletz insisted that it was 'futile to attempt a co-ordination of Russian Émigré Groups toward a single political direction'.[116] Army intelligence agreed:

> As source emphasized in his conclusions, Émigré Groups have been infiltrated by Russian intelligence Agencies to the extent that the degree of penetration is not always discernible. *It is significant that neither OHLETZ or SCHELLENBERG, who were charged with the obtaining of positive intelligence in the RSHA, failed to discern the extent and ease with which the Turkul organization penetrated the German Intelligence Service and the Vlasov movement.* [emphasis in original]
> For the purposes of illustrating the danger of employing émigré organizations as intelligence collection agencies, Turkul's organization has been selected as a vehicle to illustrate the following:
> **a.** Penetration of émigré organizations by Russian agents;
> **b.** The elusiveness of the Soviet Intelligence deception measures;
> **c.** The unreliability and irresponsibility of these oganizations for intelligence purposes;
> **d.** The unsuspiciousness and failure of the German intelligence service to realize that this organization was working for the Soviets.[117]

It is ironic that Army intelligence selected NTS as an example of Soviet penetration, while ignoring Turkul himself. Still, the report was scathing. NTS was denounced for inciting premature rebellion with its propaganda. It was also believed that NTS had no partisans of its own behind the 'Iron Curtain', and was simply trying to wreck the fragile unity of pro-US groups.[118] Indeed, the CIC had also pegged Turkul's agents as saboteurs, citing their intrigues in the Saint Andrew's Flag.[119] The Soviets consistently helped their agents by denouncing them as war criminals.[120]

Dulles and Gehlen fell for the trap. Anyone condemned by the Soviets was all right in their book. They ignored the Army's warnings and expanded support for NTS. Without CIA knowing,

Dulles's clique poured millions of dollars into Turkul's networks. Dulles's determination to hide his Nazis from the 'liberals' fooled the CIA; they thought their money was going to democratic groups. As Philby himself recalls:

> The American attack on the alliance between Bandera and SIS gathered strength in 1950, and much of my time in the United States was spent in transmitting acrimonious exchanges between Washington and London on the rival merits of obscure émigré factions. The CIA proferred three objections to Bandera as an ally. His extreme nationalism, with its fascist overtones, was a handicap which would prejudice Western dealings with other groups inside the Soviet Union; for example, the Great Russians. He was alleged to have his roots in the old emigration and to lack all contact with the new 'more realistic' emigration which the Americans were busy cultivating. Finally, he was accused flatly of being anti-American. The British plea that Bandera was being used solely for the purpose of gathering intelligence, and that such a use could have no political significance, was brushed aside by the Americans, who argued that, whatever the nature of the connection, its very existence must inflate Bandera's prestige in the Ukraine. They professed fears that any reinforcement of Bandera's following must risk splitting the 'resistance movement' in the Ukraine with whom they were themselves working.[121]

Philby must have giggled when the Americans complained that SIS support for Bandera undermined their work with moderate Ukrainian and Russian *émigrés*. While the CIA chased Bandera's Nazis, Dulles brought the Turkul and Lebed network into the CIA through Gehlen's back door. Angleton made sure that the CIA kept their hands off Dulles's empire, regaling Philby with tales of Gehlen's prowess. Philby recalled that Angleton knew that French intelligence was hopelessly penetrated by Soviet double agents, however:

> Angleton had fewer fears about Germany. That country concerned him chiefly as a base of operations against the Soviet bloc and the socialist states of Eastern Europe. The CIA lost no time in taking over the anti-Soviet section of the German Abwehr, under von Gehlen ... Angleton [defended] with chapter and verse, the past record and current activities of the von Gehlen organization.[122]

The former Abwehr section hired by Angleton turned out to be Turkul's phoney MAX network. If Angleton knew that the Army believed NTS was riddled, he certainly kept it to himself. There are curious holes in the CIA files which suggest that Angleton 'compartmentalised' any information that might embarrass Dulles,

Gehlen or Turkul. For example, when Lebed's Nazi past was uncovered by the Immigration Service, CIA's head agreed to sponsor him for permanent citizenship under the special provisions of the 100 Persons Act (which allowed 100 US agents to surreptitiously enter the country each year).

Yet, the CIA's own analysts could not even find Lebed's first name when they compiled files on Nazi Ukrainian agents.[123] In the late 1970s, CIA reported to Congress that no 'war criminals, assassins, or persons of that type' had ever been brought in under the 100 Persons Act.

The popular view is that CIA deliberately lied. The truth is more tragic. The DDU became a pseudo-CIA inside CIA that hid information instead of centralising it. The CIA does not realise to this day that a trio of 'useful idiots' – Dulles, Wisner and Angleton – sabotaged their filing system to protect the State Department's Nazis. Much derogatory information was never passed by Angleton to the responsible CIA analysts.[124] Former British intelligence officer, Peter Wright, claimed that Angleton even hid files from the President.[125]

After Eisenhower became President in January 1953, Dulles's agency-within-the-Agency received official sanction. Dulles became CIA head, Wisner was placed in charge of covert operations, and Angleton kept the Vatican files to himself.[126] Even then the old DDU hands kept the rest of the CIA in the dark. All information on NTS was diverted to Wisner's Program Branch, where it was secure from the 'liberals'.[127]

Dulles told his staff that gloves were off. Lebed's SB assassinated suspected Soviet agents,[128] and Angleton and Wisner launched Operation Red Sox/Red Cap, the code name for the overthrow of Communist regimes behind the 'Iron Curtain'.[129] They were funding Turkul: his recently declassified CIC file contains several references to front groups 'financed by AMCOMLIB', the American Committee for the Liberation of the Peoples of Russia.[130] This committee, better known today as Radio Liberty, has been publicly acknowledged as one of Dulles's funding conduits.[131]

The CIA and Radio Liberty were ignorant of Ukrainian assassins or Nazi smuggling. They needed access to the Immigration Service's top secret files on the OUN and the State Department's security investigation of Stanislav Stankievich; neither is in the CIA's filing index.[132] To put it bluntly, the DDU clique was laundering CIA money to finance an array of corrupt activities, including the GRU's creature, the NTS.

In February 1956 Turkul tried to leave Europe before the final curtain came down, and again applied for a US visa under the laxer rules of the 1953 Refugee Relief Act. The Kremlin should erect a statue to Senator Joseph McCarthy: his hysterical anti-Communism forced Congress to change the laws to permit entry of Nazis who had only fought against the Soviets. Turkul's wife and sister-in-law were already in America. Relying on British intelligence advice, the CIC again concluded in August 1956 that 'investigation did not reveal any information that SUBJECT had been doubling as a Soviet Agent'.[133]

Three months later, at the height of the bloody Hungarian rebellion, the NTS incited false hopes of Western assistance, enabling the Soviets to smash the revolt and discredit Dulles's 'freedom fighters' for ever:

> In the wake of the failed rebellion there was considerable controversy over whether or not the United States had misled street fighters in Budapest into believing that US military aid would be delivered to the rebels. Many anti-Communist Hungarian refugees bitterly charged that such promises – supposedly broadcast over Radio Free Europe – had resulted in considerable unnecessary bloodshed when rebels held out to the last man in the false hope that international help was on the way . . .
>
> In fact, however, misleading claims that American military aid was on the way *had* been broadcast by radio, though not by Radio Free Europe. According to a special investigation by the parliamentary Council of Europe, the Russian nationalist NTS organization was responsible for beaming ill-considered pledges into Hungary at the height of the rebellion. The NTS, as it turns out, sporadically operated a clandestine radio station named Radio Free Moscow, aimed at Soviet troops in East Germany, and they decided to send its signal into Hungary at the height of the fighting. As with other NTS projects of the period, Radio Free Moscow was staffed primarily by former Nazi collaborators – for it is they who made up most of the NTS leadership during the 1950s – and was almost entirely financed by the CIA.[134]

In one master stroke, Turkul had broken the anti-Soviet resistance. Subsequent investigations showed that it was Angleton's and Wisner's Red Sox/Red Cap NTS agents who had broadcast the misleading propaganda to the Hungarians. The remaining operations were scrapped. Operation Red Sox/Red Cap was the culmination of General Turkul's work for the Soviet Union. He died peacefully in 1959.[135]

Both the CIA and Gehlen belatedly agreed that Turkul was himself a Soviet agent.[136] In order to absolve themselves, Dulles and Angleton blamed the mole ridden British Intelligence Service for this 'slew of Soviet agents, including the White Russian general Anton Turkul'.[137] In hindsight, even Sir William Stephenson agreed that Turkul 'was in fact a Soviet agent sending chickenfeed to the Nazis to maintain his credibility', while he was really loyal to Moscow.[138] There was enough embarrassment to go around. By mutual Western agreement, an eery shroud of silence descended over the Turkul scandal; it lasted for over three decades.

It was exactly what the Kremlin wanted. Because of the deliberate Soviet silence, the West was lulled to sleep. No one re-investigated Turkul's 'unimportant' years in Rome. No one re-examined his role in the Ratline run by Perry and Milano. No one remembered the mail intercepts showing that Turkul was co-ordinating the 'Yugoslav emigration' networks. No one suspected a Soviet connection inside the Vatican.[139]

Even when Father Draganović retired behind the 'Iron Curtain', no one suspected that the Vatican Ratlines had been run by Moscow from the beginning. There is not one word in Turkul's US intelligence files of his connection to the Vatican's Black Orchestra. The Americans did not even open a file on the *Schwarze Kapelle* until seven years after World War II.

In 1952 the US European Command requested information about 'the Schwarze Kapelle' from its three major intelligence organisations: the CIA's 'Department of Army Detachment' (DAD); the State Department's 'Document Disposal Unit' (DDU); and the Headquarters of the 66th CIC Detachment (previously the 970th). They searched their files and found nothing. However, in Berlin, Region I of the CIC had a 'usually reliable source', who described the Soviet operation to control the Black Orchestra. The origins of Soviet penetration were laid out in one short paragraph:

> ... the Schwarze Kapelle was formerly comprised of high ranking Wehrmacht officers and had at one time been directed by Admiral Canaris. [Source] stated that the Schwarze Kapelle had been activated between the years 1930 and 1934, at which time the Rote Kapelle, an organization comprised mainly of MVD [Soviet Military Intelligence] members and sympathizers, was active as a resistance organization. Initially the two organizations were co-ordinated to form a united front, however, the Schwarze Kapelle activities subsided to the extent that those

individuals who remained active looked to the Rote Kapelle for guidance.[140]

Somehow one man had discovered the Soviets' best kept secret: their Red Orchestra controlled the Vatican's Black Orchestra. The US agent had no idea what his source was talking about. He closed the file and put it away. The Vatican never realised that it had fallen into a Soviet trap when it joined the Black Orchestra in 1939. The Ratlines were run from the Kremlin.

12

Conclusions

We do not claim that this history of the Vatican Ratlines is complete, nor that it is totally free from error. Analysing the declassified files is akin to pasting the leaves back on a tree after a violent storm has passed. It is hard enough to trace the branches of Cold War diplomacy, let alone its secret intelligence roots. The passing decades have scattered many pages, covered over a great deal, and much remains hidden in the vaults. Even the declassified files may have deceived us; disinformation may have blurred our vision of how these documents originally fitted into the tangled web.

But our purpose was not to chart a single tree but to map the wreckage of the forest. Where disaster cut a swath across the nations, the débris of previously classified files from every corner of the world reveals the track of the secret storm. The trail of wrecked operations and covert destruction leads inexorably back to Rome. The hurricane's centre was in the Vatican.

However, Pius XII and his closest advisers were surrounded by a whirlwind of forces: the Soviets had penetrated the Nazi nationalists; the French, British and Americans had recruited the Nazis for their anti-Communist crusade. Some may feel that the Vatican should be exonerated because it was deceived on all sides. The truth is that the Vatican knew exactly what it was doing at critical points, and adopted policies which led to its own disgrace.

However, while the focus of this book is the Vatican, we would be remiss if we failed to mention the involvement of other nations. It would take many volumes to fully outline the evidence against them. Moreover, in the course of researching this book, we have come across many additional issues that are too complex for current resolution. Before turning to the Vatican itself, we set forth our suggestions on how the pieces may fit together, so that future historians may eventually solve the puzzle. The reader is cautioned that, unlike the preceding chapters, this is simply the authors' opinion of the possible international scope of the Ratlines.

The Union of Soviet Socialist Republics

The Soviet Union's infiltration of the Ratlines was a stunning technical achievement in espionage. The twin virus of the GRU and KGB encircled the Vatican and infiltrated every pore of the Nazi networks. The Soviets ascertained the weak spot in the Western defensive system: a sad tendency on the part of our intelligence services to affiliate with extreme right-wing movements. Stalin's agents not only used the ultra-right as a camouflage, they manipulated these extremist groups to polarise and defeat the Western response to Communism. Instead of democracy, there was Durčansky; instead of truth, there was Turkul; instead of freedom there were Fascist spokesmen for the anti-Communist cause; instead of ending Stalin's tyranny, totalitarian agents were infiltrated among our own populations.

We wished to conduct one final interview to complete the history of the Ratlines. One of our researchers travelled to Moscow and requested permission to film an interview with Kim Philby. Philby reviewed the list of questions we had prepared, and agreed to participate. We suspected that it was the first time that anyone had asked him about his part in Nazi-smuggling operations run by the Vatican and the Western nations. Senior Soviet officials assured us that in the new era of *glasnost*, it was time for all the old scandals of the Stalin era to be exposed. However, after repeated delays, the Philby interview was postponed.

Our contact explained with some embrarrassment that our request was being reviewed at a higher level. Shortly afterwards, news of the Ligachev–Gorbachev struggle in the Politbureau was leaked to the press. Perhaps coincidentally, we were told that Philby had changed his mind and, as a free Soviet citizen could not be compelled to do the interview. It was suggested that perhaps things would change in a few months. Shortly afterwards, Philby's death was announced.

Apparently, there are limits to *glasnost*. From the declassified Western files, there can be no doubt that Soviet intelligence encouraged and assisted the emigration of Nazis. Nor is there any doubt that Philby himself helped build the smuggling network as a Trojan horse for Communist penetration of Western intelligence.

Perhaps there are older, deeper scandals. There have been rumours, never verified, that some of the top Nazi war criminals were Soviet double agents. Schellenberg, for example, insisted that Müller, the head of the Gestapo, was working for Moscow.[1] If he is right, that would explain why it took so long for Müller's Gestapo to detect the Western half of the Red Orchestra, and why Turkul's net continued to survive.

Even the admission that Turkul's MAX network was working for Soviet military intelligence could be a major source of embarrassment. The issue for future historians may not be why the Soviet Army did so well in World War II, but why they did so poorly. The more interesting explanation for modern Soviet silence is that some aspects of the Ratlines are still being run from the Kremlin.

Austria

The declassified US files confirm that the post-war Austrian government supported the Vatican's plans for the revival of Intermarium. According to one source, the Austrian liaison was Kurt Waldheim.[2] If true, this would explain a great many things. Waldheim says that he was not involved with war crimes in the bloody Kozara massacre of 1942, that he was many miles away, working for the German Quartermaster in western Yugoslavia. Collecting food is hardly a capital offence, but it does show that Waldheim may have had an opportunity to meet Father Draganović, who was in charge of forced requisitioning for the Ustashi in western Bosnia at the time of the Kozara offensive.[3] Waldheim certainly made an impression on Ante Pavelić, who awarded him a silver medal with oak leaf clusters for his services in the same region at the same time.

As was later acknowledged by Waldheim's former superior, Allied intelligence should have disqualified him from any position with the Austrian Foreign Service.[4] In 1945 it was Allen Dulles's son-in-law who provided the Austrian government with a wildly erroneous background check that ignored Waldheim's true military record.[5]

Whether by blunder or design, Waldheim was cleared to join

the Austrian diplomatic corps at the time his governemnt repeatedly turned a blind eye toward the Ustashi's terrorist network on
their soil, even letting them openly recruit in the DP camps.
Draganović himself later became an Austrian citizen before he
returned to Yugoslavia.

The Communist countries have been unusually silent about
Waldheim's past, providing the necessary votes to elect him UN
Secretary General against the Western-backed candidate. The
West German press has critically examined Waldheim's UN
record, and now questions who he was really working for. It should
be noted, however, that the Yugoslav rumours about Waldheim's
secret Nazi dossier have never been verified. Indeed, the Yugoslav
Communists have engaged in what is apparently a calculated
campaign of disinformation on the Waldheim affair, perhaps
because of Tito's close post-war relations with the Austrian
President.

When the allegations against Waldheim were made in 1986, a
respected American journalist with impeccable Yugoslav contacts
made a series of startling claims about Communist attempts to
blackmail the Austrian in the late 1940s. Based on interviews with
former Yugoslav secret police and government officials, it was
alleged that the Waldheim war crimes dossier was manufactured
and used to threaten him when he was secretary to the Austrian
Foreign Minister. This was before the Tito–Stalin split, and it was
claimed that the blackmail operation was eventually taken over by
the Soviets, and that 'Waldheim was recruited' by them.[6]

The story was vehemently denied by both Waldheim and
Belgrade, and some of the journalist's Communist sources
retracted important details. But according to US intelligence files,
someone in the Austrian Foreign Ministry was in fact assisting the
Vatican's intelligence operations after the war. That person's
identity will only be known if an independent examination of the
classified files is made by the Austrian government.

Italy

The evidence is overwhelming that the covert policy of the Italian
government was to subvert foreign governments and create the
political entity known as Intermarium. This policy was pursued
with the help of the Vatican, Britain and America. There is a

consistent pattern of evidence that Italian security, police and intelligence officials played a prominent part in the false identity chain for the fugitive Nazi war criminals. Indeed, the Ratlines could not have functioned without Prime Minister Alcide de Gasperi's official sanction and support, as in the case of gun running to the Križari.

While the extent of Soviet penetration of Italy is not clear, it appears that Mussolini's intelligence service was co-opted by the Turkul network, and that a significant number of agents of the Fascist intelligence service remained in their posts after World War II. The P2 scandal, involving an extreme right wing intelligence group that supported neo-Fascist terrorism in an attempted coup, follows the pattern of Soviet *agent provocateur* successes in other Western countries which harboured Fascist cliques.

France

It is certain that François Poncet and Henri Lebrun worked for Barbie as informants, but what did they tell him? An American CIC officer confirmed that the US Government mentioned something called TECHNICA when they asked him why Barbie was protected for so long. It is difficult to know exactly what TECHNICA involved, but the few references in declassified literature suggest that it was a rogue French operation controlled by British intelligence, without de Gaulle's knowledge. It eliminated post-war Communist rivals in the resistance by betraying their identities to the Nazis. If true, the TECHNICA connection could explain why the anti-Communist French Military was so reluctant to have Barbie back.

Whatever Poncet's mysterious involvement with Barbie, the Black Orchestra, or TECHNICA, the role of the French government in the post-war revival of Intermarium is clearly demonstrated by several independent sources. Charles de Gaulle was the man who led the Nazis on the road to the Vatican and freedom. French politician Paul Reynaud was the Vatican's front man in France, and the French General Staff were up to their epaulettes in smuggling war criminals.

United States of America

The spectre of the Vatican Ratlines continues to haunt American politicians. In anticipation of certain victory by his candidate in the impending November 1948 American elections, Allen Dulles told his friend, Frank Wisner, to go ahead with smuggling the Ratlines' recruits. Much of the false paperwork was already in the visa pipeline when word came of Truman's stunning re-election. Dulles must have been crushed. It would be four more years before he would become head of the CIA. Wisner must have been terrified; he had transformed the Vatican Ratlines into an illegal immigration pipeline, codenamed Operation Bloodstone.

In 1949 Intermarium's first Nazi agents finished their long journey and arrived in America. They were welcomed by 'Carmel Offie, the OPC officer working under State Department cover who was responsible for the care and feeding of a number of Bloodstone *émigrés*'.[7] Offie had been promoted as Wisner's assistant for 'émigré affairs' and managed to find some of the Nazis jobs as broadcasters for Radio Liberty and the Voice of America.

Offie knew how the game was played. He had previously helped the Vatican get travel passes for their 'religious missions' (Hudal and Draganović) to the prison camps, and later served as Political Adviser in Germany. There was only one little problem: Carmel Offie was accused of being a Communist spy.

To this day, Offie's friends continue to deny that he was a Soviet mole. 'How could the Soviets blackmail him? Everyone in Washington knew he was a homosexual!'[8] Both Philby and Offie were widely regarded as victims of McCarthyism who were hounded out of public service. Like Philby, Offie received a sinecure position doing intelligence work on the side.[9]

What no one realised at the time was that Offie had succeeded where Philby had failed: he had transplanted the Vatican Virus to America where it would flourish undetected within US intelligence for the next several decades. While the CIA was booting out the Nazi Anti-Bolshevik Bloc of Nations, Offie was bringing them in the back door through DDU. The case of Carmel Offie deserves a long second look. It was another scandal that Dulles swept under the rug.

When Allen Dulles finally became head of the CIA in 1953, he and Wisner were too embarrassed or too stupid to realise what the Soviets had done. According to one former intelligence officer 'the final sting' was that a number of these infiltrated networks were taken on by Wisner, and later incorporated into the CIA.[10] According to one estimate, some 10,000 Nazi war criminals entered the United States after World War II.[11] Dulles could not risk investigating Communist infiltration among the Nazis without exposing his own involvement with illegal immigration.

In 1959 the NATO intelligence services reviewed their anti-Soviet failures and concluded that support for the *émigrés* should be abandoned, as these 'exile organizations were hopelessly riddled with Communist spies'.[12] Ironically, NATO's West German intelligence liaison was Hans Felfe, the top Communist mole in the Gehlen Organisation.

Soviet penetration of the Nazi networks were not only a threat to Allen Dulles's reputation, their exposure would have ruined the political career of Richard Nixon, the Republican candidate for President in 1959. Nixon authorised Dulles's covert projects during Eisenhower's illnesses in 1956 and 1957.[13] After Nixon was defeated and Dulles was fired by President Kennedy, a large number of OPC files were ordered 'routinely destroyed'. Wisner had already committed suicide; Dulles betrayed his country by taking the Vatican secret with him. The CIA discovered too late that Dulles's political cover-up had cost them a decade:

> But it was not until after Philby defected to Moscow [1963] and the Blunt investigations revealed the true extent of the 'Cambridge network' that James Angleton ordered a major reassessment of the CIA's European underground networks. This involved reviewing thousands of previous checks for agents and sources who had earlier been cleared by MI5 and MI6.[14]

Putting Angleton in charge of the investigation was like putting the fox in charge of the hen house. Angleton knew full well what had gone wrong. He was the CIA's principal expert on World War II Nazi intelligence, as well as its Vatican liaison. As Chief of CIA Counter Intelligence, Angleton was in a perfect position to see that politically embarrassing dossiers never made it out of his office.

Of course, there were always a few insiders who knew the dirty little Nazi secret. During the subsequent Nixon administration, the US States Department secretly informed the Australian government that they were ignoring Ustashi fugitives in America because they were useful in turning out the ethnic vote 'in several federal, state and municipal elections'.[15]

The only thing Nixon's State Department did about the Nazis

was to quietly warn a few American politicians not to attend any Croation functions on 10 April, as that is the occasion when the Ustashi celebrate the day Hitler set up Pavelić's puppet government. Apparently the warning did not reach Governor Ronald Reagan. He proclaimed 10 April as 'Croatian Independence Day' in California and later, as President, had his picture taken in the White house with prominent ex-Fascists and war criminals of the ABN. Despite the previous condemnation by the State Department and CIA, Jaroslav Stetsko was treated as an honoured guest by Reagan and the leaders of several other Western nations.

It is difficult to believe that George Bush knows absolutely nothing about the Croatian terrorists, since they hijacked an American airliner while he was head of the CIA. Yet President Bush made the same 'mistakes' as Reagan: his campaign staff published a calendar celebrating 10 April as 'Croatian Independence Day' and permitted known Fascists to work on his 'ethnic outreach' programme during the 1988 election campaign. Perhaps Bush heeded the cynical advice of the Nixon administration that the Eastern European Nazis can deliver the ethnic vote.

Many politicians, including Ronald Reagan, have embarrassing ties to the Ratlines. In the US Archives is a newsreel of Reagan in 1950, innocently raising money for one of Dulles's front groups that laundered money to Fascist 'freedom fighters'. Reagan's intelligence chief, William Casey, headed another front group, the International Rescue Committee, that helped the fugitives with their immigration problems. Perhaps Oliver North did not invent the money laundering system for Contragate; he may have simply copied the one that Casey and Reagan had previously worked on.

It seems certain that the Ratlines are alive and well in America. The Nazis from Intermarium and ABN have found a new home: the World Anti-Communist League, formerly headed by retired US General John Singlaub. This is the same organisation suspected by the US Congress of complicity in running guns for Contragate. Some of WACL's leaders were the same Nazis recruited by Kim Philby. The heads of the Western intelligence services may be afraid to open the Cold War files documenting their own leaders' involvement with Nazis for fear that they will hear Stalin laughing from his grave.

Germany

There is substantial evidence in US intelligence files that a portion of the Red Orchestra survived World War II. Soviet intelligence had a special section in Hitler's Germany: the 'BB Apparat', which focused on German technical and scientific advances in warfare. The BB Apparat was kept separate from the run-of-the-mill Communist informants in Germany, and if American intelligence's suspicions are correct, is still at work among the German military industrial complex. Such penetration would explain Stalin's fascination with Hitler's secret weapons development.[16]

Among the dubious achievements of Nazi science was the invention of Sarin, Tabun and Soman. These nerve gases, later called the G-series by NATO, were so effective that the same formulae are still in use today by both the Soviets and the West. According to British records, a man named Mengele was in their custody in 1945 for interrogation concerning chemical weapons, but whether this is a reference to Joseph Mengele or his brother, Karl, is not known. It should be noted that by agreement with the Americans, all German experts on bacteriological and chemical warfare were handed over to British custody.[17]

There is some circumstantial evidence that the British made a deal with Mengele for his nerve gas records. Joseph Mengele suddenly left his hiding place, and despite the fact that he was a wanted war criminal, crossed into the Soviet zone to bring back a trunkful of records that he had buried just before the end of the war. Soon afterwards, Mengele's brother, father and co-researcher at the Kaiser Wilhelm Institute were all released from custody and allowed to resume their civilian employment without regard to their Nazi pasts.[18]

Mengele himself proceeded to Italy for emigration to Argentina. According to Ivo Omrčanin, Draganović's assistant on the Ratlines, they processed 'thousands' of German scientists and technicians who wished to emigrate to South America. When the Americans realised the extent of Stalin's nerve gas production, they hired a few German experts of their own. Even the head of I. G. Farben was brought to America to work on the death gas plants, along with several of the more knowledgeable designers. When their task was finished, they were all allowed to return to West Germany and go back into business.[19]

During the 1970s, US codebreakers found dramatic evidence that West German companies were selling the Sarin secret to several Arab nations in the Middle East. Fifty years after *Kristallnacht*, Hitler's final solution may be coming to Israel.[20]

According to John McIntyre, an American intelligence agent who worked briefly on the Gehlen end of the Ratlines before he quit in disgust, the Third Reich's most ingenious weapon was the prussic acid gas gun for assassins.[22] Soviet intelligence obtained a copy of the device and issued it to its own assassins in order to make it look like a Gehlen hit. Two of Turkul's rivals, Stephan Bandera and an NTS leader were killed with these devices. Perhaps to protect the surviving members of the BB Apparat, Soviet intelligence has always attributed the proliferation of illegal weapons to the Americans and the Israelis. No one has ever examined the role of West German intelligence as a merchant of death for GRU clients such as Libya and Iraq. The greatest scandal may involve the German bankers, as discussed below.

Even more alarming are reports that West Germany is behind the secret proliferation of nuclear weapons. According to a former Argentine diplomat, a secret nuclear protocol was attached to a West German–Argentine Trade Treaty during the 1960s. The rationale was that West Germany was afraid that some day the Americans would pull out of NATO or withdraw their nuclear shield. Because of Soviet antipathy to German possession of the atomic bomb, it was decided to develop the nuclear weapons secretly by utilising the large *émigré* communities of German scientists in Argentina and South Africa.[21]

Great Britain

The lion's share of the blame for the Ratlines undoubtedly belongs to the government of Great Britain. In 1990 Lord Shawcross led the fight in the House of Lords to stop belated prosecutions of war criminals. Among the unsatisfactory reasons given was that British soldiers had been assassinated in Palestine after the war, which caused a change in attitude towards the Jews.[23] Despite the ineffective protests of Lord Shawcross, it was under his post-war leadership that British prosecution of Nazi war criminals utterly collapsed, as described in Tom Bower's work, *The Pledge Betrayed*.[24]

We believe there was another reason. In 1948 the British government had already secretly cabled the Commonwealth countries to stop all investigations of Nazi war criminals.[25] Even before the prosecutions collapsed, the evidence is overwhelming that British intelligence was recruiting Nazi war criminals for several covert projects including Intermarium, Prometheus and NTS. British intelligence sheltered Pavelić, smuggled the Ustashi gold and arranged the mass escapes from Rimini and other camps. His Majesty's Government asked the Vatican for assistance to resettle 'Grey' Nazis, and asked America to help sabotage the screening process. British intelligence maintained contact with their Nazi protégés in Canada and Australia under the guise of ABN. Finally, British intelligence vouched for the Communist-riddled Nazi networks and peddled them around the world as 'freedom fighters'.[26]

The American cover-up was not unique. The British also have methods of dealing with their embarrassing scandals caused by Philby, Ellis and Turkul. As a result of Philby's intervention in 1945, British intelligence did not discover until the mid-1960s that 'Dickie' Ellis was a Nazi agent with ties to General Turkul's Soviet net. Only a handful of people in British intelligence were told Ellis's secret, and they decided that it was so shocking that neither the FBI nor the CIA should know: the White Russian General who was Ellis's 'Nazi' contact had turned NTS into the most deadly weapon of Soviet espionage. British intelligence had sold a Communist net to the gullible Americans. It was better to lie and claim that Ellis was not prosecuted in order to protect the Windsor scandal. That sorry excuse has been used to death. In fact, it was SIS's Colin Gubbins (the Prometheus liaison) who put Ellis to work on the document shredder *after* Ellis had confessed to treason. It was SIS's reputation, not Windsor's, that was being salvaged.

For the last half century, Britain has been the only Western nation to refuse any access to its intelligence archives. There is good reason. Time after time, American records were withhheld from the authors on the grounds that it would embarrass a foreign government. When the authors asked who was withholding Nazi documents, we were provided with a copy of a letter from the British Embassy in Washington. The British government is sitting on the last secret of the Cold War, and is desperately pressuring its allies to keep the lid on.

The authors' documentary series on Nazis living 'down under' has been credited by the Australian government as the impetus for re-opening war crimes cases. When one of the authors requested CIA permission to inform Australia of certain classified details of Nazi-smuggling to that country, the letter came back with so many deletions that it looked like Swiss cheese. When the authors offered to provide declassified information on the role of British intelligence in protecting these Nazis for the last forty years, the Australian investigator reacted as if he had been bitten by a snake.

The Australian, British and Canadian war crimes investigators limit their inquiries to identifying Nazis living in their particular jurisdiction. No one investigates who helped the Nazis emigrate in the first place. In 1985 one of the authors testified before the US Congress about British sponsorship of Nazi emigration. The US General Accounting Office issued a report confirming our charges that American intelligence agencies had protected Nazis who had previously been employed by another Allied nation, but deleted all references to Britain. The only thing the British did well was the cover-up.

But we live in an age of documents, there are no more secrets, only deferred disclosures. Piece by piece, the archivists in Washington, Rome, Ottawa, London and Canberra have declassified seemingly innocuous documents, and the Ratlines' outlines have emerged. Behind the Nazis were the Vatican, behind the Vatican were the British, behind the British were the Communists.

'Forget about the Communists,' one of the old spies told us. He explained that we should ignore all the ideologies as a smokescreen and follow the one common denominator that made sense. 'Trace the money,' he said. And so we did. As the last layer of the onion peeled away, we found out who was at the centre of the Ratlines.

The Bankers

During World War II, the Swedish corporation SKF controlled 80 per cent of all the ball bearing production in Europe, and held the patents for most of the world:

> ... the power behind their production and distribution as SKF Chairman was Sven Winquist, a dashing playboy friend of Goering and the Duke and Duchess of Windsor. He was a prominent partner in Jacob Wallenberg's Stockholm Enskilda, the largest private bank in Sweden – a correspondent of Hitler's Reichsbank.[27]

While Raoul Wallenberg was heroically rescuing Hungary's Jews, his relative, Jacob, was the most important Nazi banker in history. Sixty per cent of SKF's world-wide production went to Germany.[28] By 1943, the Americans had had enough. But when the US Ambassador to Stockholm demanded an embargo, the Swedish Foreign Minister coolly threatened to publish the full correspondence which would show that 'trade between Sweden and Germany was on a contract basis known to the allied governments and based on prior agreements with them'.

British Chancellor of the Exchequer, Sir Kingsley Wood, described pre-war Western deals with Nazi bankers: 'This country has various rights and interests . . . under our international trust agreements between the various governments. It would not be in our interest to sever connection.'[29] The British Minister of Economic Warfare, Lord Selbourne, begged the Americans not to put SKF on the embargo blacklist, and instead outbid the Nazis for Wallenberg's ball bearings.[30]

According to Anthony Cave Brown, Wallenberg had high British connections indeed. He was working both sides of the fence as a go-between for the Black Orchestra. Apparently, British intelligence used Jacob Wallenberg for shuttle diplomacy with the Nazis at the same time that Raoul Wallenberg was aiding the Jews. The Soviets captured Raoul and tortured him for several weeks before they realised they had the wrong Wallenberg. They killed him to cover up their British connection. Of course, Jacob Wallenberg had an American intelligence connection as well. SKF's American lawyer was Allen Dulles. In fact, the Dulles brothers had represented most of the Nazi banks prior to the outbreak of the war.

Allen Dulles was also connected to the Swiss Bank of International Settlements (BIS) through a German correspondent bank headed by Kurt von Schroeder. Somehow the bankers learned of the secret American plan to invade North Africa in 1942, for immediately the

German bankers, along with their French correspondents, transferred 9 billion gold francs via the BIS to Algiers. Anticipating German defeat, they were seeking a killing in dollar exchange. The collaborationists boosted their holdings from $350 to $525 million almost overnight . . . Another collaborator in the scheme was one of the Vatican's espionage group who leaked the secret to others in Hitler's high command.[31]

Apparently the Holy See was not above making a profit out of its intelligence operations. Still the spectacle of Nazi, French, British, Japanese and Vatican bankers all swapping information to make a profit on the currency exchange is one that would have chilled the blood of the soldiers on whose lives they were betting.

From the bankers' point of view, the Vatican's peace negotiations with Germany were a convenient cover for continuing business as usual with the Nazis. At the same time, bankers like Wallenberg had protected themselves just in case the Allies won or the bumbling Black Orchestra ever succeeded in assassinating Hitler. The Vatican's role in the Black Orchestra takes on a whole new light.

State Department records for South America confirm that the Ustashi Minister for Finance and the French Under Secretary of State of the Vichy Government, went to Argentina via the Vatican Ratline.[32] According to Paul Manning, there were rumours of others. He cites the FBI's copy of a surveillance file forwarded by the Central de Intelligencia of Argentina's Ministry of the Interior:

> ... in 1948, Martin Bormann received the bulk of the treasure that had made up the financial reserve of the Deutsche Bank ... Like other fugitives, he entered Argentina in 1948, coming from Genoa on a second-class ticket, with forged Vatican documentation.[33]

The 'Bormann connection' may be nothing more than a clever hoax to discredit the underlying charges that stolen Nazi money was laundered to South America and injected back into West Germany for the 'great economic miracle' of 1948 to 1951. Most of these financial allegations have been dismissed out of hand, perhaps prematurely.

In 1945 the US Treasury Department accused Allen Dulles of laundering funds from the Nazi bank of Hungary into Switzerland. Similar charges were made against Dulles's agent, Hans Bernd Gisevius, who had worked for Dulles as an OSS agent while serving at the Reichsbank.[34] The State Department quickly took over the Treasury Department's money laundering allegations, and the Dulles–Gisevius investigation was quietly dropped.[35]

Gisevius may have had some involvement with the Ratlines. He was a senior member of the Black Orchestra during World War II and was considered to be 'Allen Dulles's pipeline to Admiral

Canaris'.[36] After the war, Gisevius personally briefed the Australian government on American efforts to resettle the surplus population of Europe in other countries, citing the support of the 'Committee for a Free Europe', later acknowledged as a clandestine front for Dulles's Cold War programmes. This was also the organisation which served as the American end of the Vatican Ratlines.[37]

The most important front group was an entity called the World Commerce Corporation established after World War II to rebuild German–South American trade networks.[38] The directors of this corporation were Sir William Stephenson, formerly of British intelligence and General William Donovan, formerly of the OSS. One of the attorneys for World Commerce was Allen Dulles, whose assistant, Frank Wisner, was the State Department's deputy for currency and economic reform in the American zone of West Germany. Many of the staff members for the economic reconstruction of occupied Germany came from the same international financial firms which had invested heavily in the pre-war German economy.

According to sworn testimony before the US Senate by a representative of the German banking industry, an organisation did exist in 1950 which was 'formed by Lord Shawcross of England and Mr Hermann Abs of Germany to bring about a Magna Carta for the protection of foreign investments of World War II'.[39] This is the same Lord Shawcross who led the recent campaign in the British House of Lords to prevent the re-opening of war crimes investigations in Britain. Despite allegations by Manning, it is difficult to believe that Shawcross would have lent his good name to Abs's organisation if he had known its real purpose. In a 1966 hearing before the Select Committee on Standards and Conduct of the US Senate, Abs was identified as the common denominator of a group seeking return of vested enemy properties of World War II.[40]

When the United States entered the war in 1941, all of the branches of American banks in France under German control were closed, except two which had ties to Abs: Morgan et Cie and Chase of New York:

> both received this special treatment through the intercession of Dr Hermann Josef Abs of Deutsche Bank, financial adviser to the German

government. According to US Treasury agent reports, the favorable treatment was due to ... an 'old school tie', an unspoken understanding among international bankers that wars may come and may go but the flux of wealth goes on forever.[41]

According to Nuremberg records, Abs's Deutsche Bank was the principal conduit for laundering Nazi money into Argentina during the war under the supervision of Martin Bormann.[42] The American war crimes investigation of Abs, former head of the Deutsche Bank, was quietly dropped and Abs was appointed economic adviser for the British zone of Germany.[43] It should also be noted that Abs became a financial adviser to the Vatican.[44]

According to Penny Lernoux, the financial collapse of Vatican-supported banks during the 1970s involved the same group of people connected to Dulles's and Angleton's network of money launderers.[45] Prior to World War II, Angleton's father had financial interests in Milan, and may have met both Montini and a Sicilian banker named Michele Sindona at this earlier time.

According to Lernoux, Sindona 'wangled an introduction to the powerful Giovanni Montini in Milan, who would later become Pope Paul VI'. Montini introduced Sindona to the leader of the Christian Democrats. Sindona served the younger Angleton for many years as a CIA 'funnel for supporting funds' to friendly Italian politicians.[46] In 1969 Sindona became the financial adviser to the Vatican while Montini was the Pope. Sindona and his cohort, Roberto Calvi, created a financial scandal that cost the Vatican Bank hundreds of millions of dollars.[47]

The laundering of Nazi war profits after World War II may be the most embarrassing secret of all. There is a pattern of Western silence on this topic which cannot be ignored. We believe such reticence stems from a desire to prevent their own citizens from learning the embarrassing truth, and not from any consideration of national security interests.

The Holy See

And so we turn now to the Vatican's scorecard. When we use the word 'Vatican', we mean only that tiny cabal of priests and diplomats who actively participated in the Ratlines. In the preceding chapters, we have endeavoured to set forth the facts in a straightforward manner. Now we wish to state our own opinions and conclusions. Our charges are sometimes harsh; we reiterate that they involve only those unworthy and unrepresentative bureaucrats who ran Vatican policy.

It is our opinion that Pius XII and Giovanni Montini (later Pope Paul VI) were not always swept up by forces beyond their control. In many cases, they were the architects of their own folly, or active accomplices to others' crimes. Sooner or later, the head of every state stands before the bar of history, and the Pontiff is no exception. When the Pope assumed the temporal powers of his third crown, he was held to temporal standards of accountability. There is one difference: the only tribunal is public opinion.

We do not claim that the evidence is sufficient to convict, only enough to warrant a belief among reasonable people that crimes were committed. We leave it to the reader, and history, to judge if there is cause for indictment and further inquiry, or whether it is time to put false accusations to rest . . .

COUNT ONE: *Crimes Against Peace.* We find no evidence that the Vatican encouraged Nazi Germany in any war of aggression. Contrary to popular belief, the evidence is fairly clear that the Holy See repeatedly attempted to resist Hitler's predatory policies. By means of the Church's intelligence services advance warning was given of Nazi plans to invade Belgium and Holland.

Far from being pro-Hitler, Pius XII personally assisted the German opposition in secret attempts to overthrow his regime. Although unsuccessful, the Black Orchestra risked their lives to end Nazism. Some will say that the Vatican's secret anti-Hitler negotiations are the finest hour of the Catholic Church. We submit it is also evidence of the Vatican's double standard.

In its Concordat with Mussolini, the Holy See undertook to stand above politics, to be a purely moral force, only intervening if requested by all parties to resolve a dispute. The Black Orchestra was hardly a case of international mediation; it was covert assistance to an attempted coup. Hitler's opponents received substantial assistance from the Vatican; does that not justify the Ratlines' support for Stalin's opposition? If the Vatican endorses covert diplomatic assistance to overthrow dictators, where does it draw the line? If combatting Hitler justifies breaking the rules, what about Quaddafi, Suharto or Saddam Hussein?

At the very least, the Black Orchestra precedent exposes the

Holy See to charges of selective moral involvement. The Vatican cannot privately support some causes while publicly ignoring others. The present Pope actively and successfully supported Poland's anti-Communists, but yet he remains silent about East Timor, although Indonesian occupation there has brought about another Holocaust. If the Vatican wishes to exert moral authority, it must be unequivocal and truly neutral. Only in that way can it remain above temporal affairs. The world has need of diplomats whose agenda is peace on earth and goodwill to all humanity. There are enough plotters.

The Vatican's defenders believe that it has been unjustly attacked for supporting Hitler's policies. Yet, in order to preserve confidence in its trustworthiness as a secret intermediary in time of war, the Vatican has remained silent about its role in the Black Orchestra. We do not believe that such silence is warranted, or such trust deserved.

According to Anthony Cave Brown, the Allies had so little hope in the Black Orchestra that they sacrificed it to deceive Hitler. In spring 1942 Nicholas Kallay became Prime Minister of Hungary. After Stalingrad, 'Kallay began to lobby the West for a separate peace through the Department of Extraordinary Affairs at the Vatican'. The Allies sent a known Soviet agent as their negotiator. Word of the Hungarian peace initiative was quickly leaked to Hitler. 'There was every reason to suppose the British had deliberately tipped Kallay's hand, and their revelations had the desired effect in provoking the Führer's wrath.'[48]

Similarly, 'there were indications from the Vatican that Romania could expect favorable terms' if it switched from the Axis to the Allies. But when the Romanian emissary met British negotiators in Cairo, 'both his whereabouts and his mission were revealed on Allied Newscasts'. Exposing the Vatican's peace efforts was part of an Allied deception programme co-ordinated with Moscow.[49] This had the desired effect: Hitler stripped his three best divisions from France and sent them to the Balkans to stop the Black Orchestra's uprisings. Shortly afterwards, Allied troops landed in Normandy.[50]

For the last half of the war, the Allies used the Vatican's Black Orchestra to mislead Hitler about D-Day. Pius XII wanted to be a major player on the international chessboard, but he was just a pawn. Pius XII's first mistake was to get involved with the Black

Orchestra; his second was to rely on the West, because the Soviets had outwitted them at every turn. The Vatican is not guilty of supporting Hitler, but guilty of hypocrisy, incompetence and stupidity in risking the lives of his opponents.

Naivety is the cardinal sin of diplomacy, and of that the Vatican was unquestionably guilty. The unintended result was the betrayal and execution of most Black Orchestra members, whom the Allies had judged, like the Jews, to be expendable to the war effort. In hindsight, the Vatican accomplished nothing.

COUNT TWO: *Obstruction of Justice*. What the Pope did after the war was worse than nothing. Instead of smuggling homeless Jews to Argentina, the Ratlines smuggled Eichmann, Pavelić and Stangl, among many others. Instead of denouncing Bishop Hudal, the Vatican replaced him with a less conspicuous, but far more efficient and effective operative in the form of Father Draganović. Instead of international justice, there was Intermarium and a host of *émigré* Nazi fronts. The world has paid a heavy price for that decision.

What the Vatican did after World War II was a crime. The evidence is unequivocal: the Holy See aided the flight of fugitives from international justice. The Ratlines were intentionally created to aid and abet the escape of wanted Nazi war criminals. Hudal was known for his Nazi affinities long before 1945, yet retained his influential position long after he was publicly exposed. His successor, Father Draganović, was assisted by several religious orders which printed false identity cards, procured Red Cross passports under false pretences, and provided transport under false names. These were not acts of Christian charity. The clandestine Nazi-smuggling immorally misused the Church's legitimate charitable organisations.

We find no defence of ignorance: Pius XII was fully aware of Ante Pavelić's crimes. Nor was he the only case. The Ratlines operated with reckless disregard for the fugitives' crimes against humanity. If the Pope wanted to know their real names, he had only to ask Father Draganović. The burglary of his office revealed that he kept lists of the fugitives' true and false identities. The Pope's diplomatic messages reveal a pattern of protection and intercession for war criminals. There was virtually unanimous agreement among the surviving witnesses, both clerical and intelligence officials, that the Vatican knew they were sheltering Nazis.

We find no defence of unauthorised conduct: the Ratlines were an official extension of covert Vatican diplomacy. Both the US and British files confirm that the Vatican was asked to smuggle Nazi collaborators, so-called 'Greys', and co-operated in this programme. There was virtually unanimous agreement among the surviving witnesses that Draganović operated with the highest official sanction. One key witness testified that Montini asked Draganović to smuggle fugitives. The intelligence files of several nations confirm that the Vatican's top leaders authorised and directed the smuggling of fugitive war criminals.

We find no defence of coercion, rescue, or necessity. The West were Stalin's accomplices when they handed back tens of thousands of people who had fled Communist tyranny. Many were not Nazis, but innocent victims of the war, although many were murderers deserving little sympathy. There was no acceptable system of justice behind the 'Iron Curtain', and those forcibly returned were slaughtered or imprisoned without trial. The Allied leaders were guilty of criminal naivety in 1945.

But the forced repatriations came to a halt almost immediately, when the Allied leaders realised their mistake. Thereafter only a few Communist extradition requests were agreed. The Ratlines continued to smuggle war criminals well into the 1950s, years after the threat of repatriation had disappeared. But what of Eichmann, Stangl and Rauff, among many others? What of the many German and Austrian Nazis who were of no interest to the Soviets and their allies? What excuse can be made for them? Was the Vatican afraid of democratic justice? The Western tribunals were shamefully lenient; only a handful were punished.[51]

Fear of Communist persecution was not the criterion for those who utilised the Ratlines. In every case we examined, the Vatican's fugitives were previously in Western not Soviet custody. The Vatican sheltered Nazis who had been condemned by the democratic governments of Hungary and Czechoslovakia. Barbie was fleeing from French justice, not Stalin's. The mitigating factors which led the Vatican to shelter Stalin's victims in 1945 had long expired by 1951. The Ratlines did not exist to rescue the innocent, only the guilty. The innocent had no need of false identities. We find overwhelming reason to indict the Vatican for obstruction of Justice.

COUNT THREE: *Receiving Stolen Goods*. Agents of the Vatican were knowingly receiving passports which were stolen or fraudulently obtained from the Red Cross. The available evidence only implicates François Poncet and later, Allen Dulles, in the actual theft. But Draganović knew he was trafficking in stolen goods. Indeed, he was forging identity cards as part of the same fraudulent scheme.

We have found no *direct* evidence that the Vatican profited from the property stolen from the Nazis' victims. However, circumstantial evidence raises troubling questions of a peripheral involvement in Allied intelligence money laundering. Certainly, the Ratlines were subsidised by Western intelligence, as documented in the Barbie case. However, that does not explain where the Vatican got the rest of the money. The evidence shows that Bishop Rožman laundered money on the black market in Switzerland, and that some or all of those funds were the Ustashi's plundered treasure, smuggled out of Yugoslavia by the Church and British intelligence. Draganović admitted that he took some of this money to the Vatican.

The weight of the evidence is that the Ratlines' laundered money originated with gold bullion from Pavelić's war booty. It was not, as suggested by one intelligence file, the property of the Croatian Catholic Church. Pavelić's treasure was in the form of gold bars and Western currency, not jewelled vestments or chalices. Moreover, even after the gold was safely out of Communist territory, Draganović remained accountable to Ustashi officials. We find sufficient evidence to accuse the Vatican of receiving stolen property, and overwhelming evidence that they trafficked in stolen or fraudulently obtained documents.

COUNT FOUR: *Abuse of Diplomatic Privileges*. The evidence shows a clear pattern of violation of diplomatic norms by the Vatican. Fugitive war criminals were escorted in vehicles with diplomatic plates, protecting them from arrest. Senior Vatican diplomats intervened with the Allies to obtain official travel documents for Bishop Hudal, Father Draganović, Bishop Bučko and others, enabling them to organise the Ratlines under cover of official religious duties. Vatican facilities with official extra-territoriality or *de facto* immunity were used to house transient war criminals. False representations by Hudal, Draganović, Bučko and others were conveyed by Vatican diplomatic channels to obtain the release of Nazi murderers and collaborators.

We find no defence of ignorance for the reasons stated previously. The Ratlines could not have existed without the Vatican's diplomatic protection. Vatican diplomats knowingly shipped Nazi nationalists to other countries in violation of their immigration laws. Indeed, that was the very purpose of the Ratlines. By turning a blind eye towards the Nazis' crimes, covert Vatican diplomacy helped create the disasters of the Cold War. They interceded on behalf of Slovak Fascists before, during and after the Durčansky plot which led directly to the Communist takeover of Czechoslovakia.

Apart from a few successes in local Italian politics, Vatican diplomacy played a significant role in discrediting the legitimate anti-Communist movements of Central and Eastern Europe. Intermarium was an act of war, and the human losses caused by the Vatican in the Cold War were far greater than the Canaris group's in World War II. By repeating the Black Orchestra mistake, they unwittingly helped the Communists maintain control.

The Vatican was not innocent by reason of mistake, they knew what they were doing. Pius XII and Montini were experienced diplomats, and they pursued strategic and diplomatic initiatives that were intended to subvert hostile states. Their goals were armed revolution, not diplomacy. Intermarium was meant to foment insurrection. The Vatican advanced its own geo-political interests, like the other major players. It is no defence to say that the Communists were more clever at espionage than the Vatican. Pius XII played Machiavelli, and Stalin beat him at his own game.

In conclusion, we believe that the evidence clears the Vatican of actively assisting Hitler, but indicts it for aiding war criminals, dealing in stolen property, and violating the norms of international diplomacy.

We recognise that this book will re-open old wounds and place the Vatican's response to the Holocaust in a new perspective. How, it will be asked, could the Vatican do so much to help the Nazis in the Cold War and so little to help the victims? Why did Pius XII switch in 1945 from his policy of silence towards the Jews to advocacy for the Nazis? Where were the Ratlines for those who wished to escape from Auschwitz? Why would the Vatican give false passports to the Nazis when its officials rarely gave false baptismal certificates to the Jews? Are the Ratlines evidence of hypocrisy, or worse, anti-Semitic double standards? We recognise that our evidence of Vatican misconduct in the Cold War raises new and harder questions about its conduct during the Holocaust.

We do not have all the answers, but believe these issues must be addressed, for on their resolution may well depend the future direction of Vatican activism. And so we turn to the ugliest accusation of all: that the Vatican was guilty of crimes against humanity.

We find no evidence to support the charge that the Vatican supported the Holocaust or encouraged the destruction of any racial, political or religious group. It is true that it showed selective morality, placing a lesser importance on some atrocities. Pius XII himself demonstrated this when he remained silent about the slaughter of the Spartacists in 1919, while loudly condemning their crimes. The evidence shows that the Vatican attempted to rescue as many Jews as possible with quiet diplomacy. In countries like Italy, where the Pope had some influence, he used it well. Even in Berlin, Vatican diplomacy was the conduit for bribes to save lives. The Israeli government publicly credits them for secretly negotiating payments that ransomed thousands of Jews from Nazi custody.[52] Churchill and Roosevelt made speeches in public, but in private, their policy was to abandon the Jews to their fate. The Pope did the opposite; without making speeches, the Catholic Church probably saved more Jews than all the Allied governments combined. We believe it was nowhere near enough.

Perhaps the Pontiff is held to a double standard (or a higher one). No matter what he may have done in secret, there are those who still condemn Pius XII for not speaking out in public. In truth, there is little that can be said in his defence. It does not matter that Britain and America wanted the Holy See to remain silent when the last Jews of Hungary were about to be deported. The Pope has higher obligations than diplomacy; the Vatican is not Switzerland.

Nor does it matter that the Pope sent a private telegram pleading for the lives of Hungarian Jews instead of making a radio appeal. By his public silence, he was perceived to be neutral in favour of the Germans. Raoul Wallenberg was neutral, and a diplomat, but that did not stop him. He handed out false citizenship papers to every Jew he could. He was never touched by the Nazis. Cardinal Roncalli, later John XXIII, handed out false baptismal certificates. He was not harmed.

Before his death, Pius XI had already published one Encyclical condemning Nazi teachings. The Church did not suffer; in fact, its status was enhanced. At death's door, he had prepared another denunciation of the Nazis' anti-Christian doctrines. His successor, Pius XII, quietly buried it. Therein, we submit, lies his guilt: from the moment he assumed St Peter's mantle he chose diplomacy over truth, his temporal powers over his moral duty.

Acknowledgements

Numerous people have assisted us in writing this book, not all of whom can be credited here, partly for space reasons, but also because many wish to remain anonymous. We are especially grateful to the many former and present officials of both Western and Communist governments who have quietly provided information, documents, leads and advice. Their identities must remain confidential, but they have our gratitude.

We could not have even started our work without the patience and perseverance of official archivists around the world, particularly in the Public Record Office in London and the United States National Archives in Washington, where John Taylor of the Modern Military Section and Sally Marks of the Diplomatic Branch were of immense help.

Christopher Simpson was enormously generous in allowing us access to his personal records, compiled in preparing his book, *Blowback*. James Walston is also gratefully acknowledged for his diligent research in the Italian Archives in Rome, as are many officials of the Roman Catholic Church and the Vatican, who encouraged certain lines of investigation. Although they do not wish to be cited by name, their help is reflected in the text.

It should be noted that we went to considerable trouble to obtain access to the Vatican's own records of the events dealt with, but were denied access to all relevant files. The access policy of the Vatican Secret Archives bars researchers from seeing most files after 22 January 1922. We thank official Vatican historian, Father Robert Graham, for trying to fill in some of the resultant gaps, and for his prompt responses to our many queries.

A large number of people gave us invaluable assistance by translating into English hundreds of pages of documents from many languages. Their work allowed us to present a rich diversity of material from international sources. We particularly thank Paula Gruden for translating Serbo-Croat and Slovenian material, and

Claudia Taranto for Italian. Pierre Vicary, East European Correspondent of the Australian Broadcasting Corporation, convinced surviving priests who worked on the Ratline to give tape recorded interviews and obtained rare personal photographs, some of which appear in the book. Mr. Vicary, a British citizen fluent in several languages, lives in Zagreb and was also instrumental in negotiating the release of several key documents from Communist sources.

We would also like to thank Mr. William Gowen, whose criticisms and comments reached us only after this book was written. While Mr. Gowen states that he was not personally aware of Pius XII's involvement in the Ratlines and disagrees with us on a number of points, he does confirm the secret support given to the Vatican's Intermarium program by British intelligence.

Finally, we wish to record that, although we frequently took the advice of our many contacts, we alone are responsible for any errors, omissions or shortcomings.

Mark Aarons and John Loftus
October 1991

Endnotes

A Note on Abbreviations

Because of the number of times material from the Public Record
Office and the United States National Archives is cited in the text
we have adopted the following abbreviations:

   Public Record Office is cited as PRO
   United States National Archives is cited as USNA
   The Turkul Dossiers in the USNA are cited 'T' as further
explained on page 319, endnote 35

Epigraph

1 Letter from the British Legation to the Holy See, to the Foreign
  Office, of 7 March 1947, PRO FO 371 67917c
2 Airgram from Cabot, Belgrade, to Washington, 12 June 1947, USNA,
  RG 59, 740.00116EW/6–1147

1 A Spectre was Haunting Europe

1 Corrado Pallenberg, *The Vatican From Within*, George Harrap, London,
  1961, p. 19; and Carlo Falconi, *The Silence of Pius XII*, Faber & Faber,
  London, 1970, p. 86
2 Other accounts of these incidents can be found in Richard
  Grunberger, *Red Rising in Bavaria*, Arthur Barker, London, 1973,
  pp. 110, 141, 145; and Branko Bokun, *Spy in the Vatican*, Tom Stacey,
  London, 1973, p. 39
3 Falconi, *The Silence of Pius XII*, p. 86
4 Grunberger, *Red Rising in Bavaria*, pp. 157–8
5 Falconi, *The Silence of Pius XII*, p. 86
6 Handwritten cover note to letter from the British Legation to the
  Holy See, to the Foreign Office, of 31 December 1938, PRO FO 371
  23810; and Owen Chadwick, *Britain and the Vatican during the Second
  World War*, Cambridge University Press, Cambridge, 1986, p. 7
7 Nicholas Cheetham, *Keepers of the Keys: The Pope in History*,
  Macdonald & Co, London, 1982, p. 283

8 'Holy See Annual Report, 1925' from British Legation to the Holy
See to the Foreign Office, 21 April 1926, PRO FO 371 11399
9 *Ibid.*
10 Letter from British Legation to the Holy See to the Foreign Office, 30
June 1926, PRO FO 371 11775
11 'Holy See Annual Report, 1925' from British Legation to the Holy
See to the Foreign Office, 21 April 1926, PRO FO 371 11399; 'Holy
See Annual Report, 1926' from British Legation to the Holy See to
the Foreign Office, 31 May 1927, PRO FO 371 12206; 'Holy See
Annual Report, 1927' from British Legation to the Holy See to the
Foreign Office, 27 February 1928, PRO FO 371 15258
12 Letter from British Legation to the Holy See to the Foreign Office, 28
December 1926, PRO FO 371 12582
13 Cheetham, *Keepers of the Keys: The Pope in History*, p. 283
14 Father Joseph Lecler, as quoted in Paul Ormonde, *The Movement*,
Thomas Nelson (Australia), Melbourne, 1972, p. 131
15 'A Survey of Modern Trends in Papal Diplomacy', State Department
research paper, USNA, RG 59, 866A.00/3–2448
16 Letter from British Legation to the Holy See to the Foreign Office, 6
January 1932, PRO FO 371 16400
17 'The policy of the Catholic Church in the Danube Valley', Foreign
Research and Press Service, Balliol College, Oxford, 21 October 1942,
PRO FO 371 33434
18 *Ibid.*
19 Anne Fremantle (ed.), *The Social Teachings of the Catholic Church*,
Menton-Omega, New York, 1963, p. 80
20 As quoted in 'The policy of the Catholic Church in the Danube
Valley', Foreign Research and Press Service, Balliol College, Oxford,
21 October 1942, PRO FO 371 33434; and Falconi, *The Silence of Pius
XII*, p. 22
21 'Holy See Annual Report, 1930' from British Legation to the Holy
See to the Foreign Office, 13 February 1931, PRO FO 371 15258
22 'Holy See Annual Report, 1930' from British Legation to the Holy
See to the Foreign Office, 13 February 1931, PRO FO 371 15258;
"Holy See Annual Report, 1932' from British Legation to the Holy
See to the Foreign Office, 20 February 1933, PRO FO 371 11410
23 Chadwick, *Britain and the Vatican during the Second World War*, pp. 7–13,
28
24 As quoted in Chadwick, *Britain and the Vatican during the Second World
War*, p. 20; and Falconi, *The Silence of Pius XII*, p. 95. See also, letter
from the British Legation to the Holy See, to the Foreign Office, 12
June 1945, PRO FO 371 50062
25 Cheetham, *Keepers of the Keys: The Pope in History*, p. 283
26 'Holy See Annual Report, 1937' from British Legation to the Holy
See to the Foreign Office, 10 February 1938, PRO FO 371 15258
27 Letter from the British Legation to the Holy See, to the Foreign
Office, 31 December 1938, PRO FO 371 23810; Chadwick, *Britain and*

the Vatican during the Second World War, pp. 25–7; and Falconi, *The Silence of Pius XII*, p. 96

28 Chadwick, *Britain and the Vatican during the Second World War*, p. 30

29 For a detailed account of Pacelli's election, see Chadwick, *Britain and the Vatican during the Second World War*, Chapter Two, pp. 30–56

30 A good account of Pacelli's career is found in Pallenberg, *The Vatican From Within*

31 Pallenberg, *The Vatican From Within*, pp. 123–4; and Central Intelligence Group memo from an unknown (censored) source, to Jack D. Neal, Department of State, 24 October 1946, USNA, RG 59, 866A.404/10–2446

32 Reports from the British Legation to the Holy See to the Foreign Office, 'Holy See Personalities', 21 June 1938 and 3 July 1939, PRO FO 371 22441 and 23827; other details about Pacelli are found in 'Notes on Leading Personalities connected with the Holy See', and 'Holy See: Personalities, 1932', from the British Legation to the Holy See to the Foreign Office, 29 April 1927 and 5 January 1932, PRO FO 371 12206 and 15979

33 Falconi, *The Silence of Pius XII*, p. 95

34 See for example, Falconi, *The Silence of Pius XII*; Pierre Blet, Robert A. Graham, Angelo Martini and Burkhart Schneider (eds), *Les Actes et Documents du Saint Siège relatif à la Seconde Guerre Mondiale*, Libreria Editrice Vaticana, Vatican City, Vols 1–11, 1966–81. For somewhat biased versions of the attack against the Vatican see, for example, Edmond Paris, *The Vatican against Europe*, Macmillan, London, 1961, and Avro Manhattan, *Terror Over Yugoslavia*, Watts & Co, London, 1953. A good summary of the Vatican's position is contained in the lecture given by official Vatican historian, Father Robert Graham, 'The "Good Samaritan" in World War II. The Record of Relief and Rescue, Particularly by the Vatican, in Favour of the Victims of War', delivered at the Bethesda Regional Library, Bethesda, Maryland, 30 January 1989, under the auspices of the Catholic League for Religious and Civil Rights

35 David S. Wyman, *The Abandonment of the Jews*, Pantheon, New York, 1984, p. 342

36 For accounts of the official policies of various governments see Walter Laqueur, *The Terrible Secret*, Weidenfeld & Nicolson, London, 1981; and Martin Gilbert, *Auschwitz and the Allies*, Michael Joseph/Rainbird, London, 1981

37 Note from US President's Personal Representative to the Holy See, 24 June 1944, to Vatican Secretary of State, Myron Taylor Papers, USNA, Box 4

38 Cable from US State Department to US President's Personal Representative to the Holy See, 25 October 1944, Myron Taylor Papers, USNA, Box 4

39 Note to Ambassador, 7 November 1944, Myron Taylor Papers, USNA, Box 4

40 *Ibid.*
41 Alan Abrams, *Special Treatment*, Lyle Stewart, New York, 1985, p. 34
42 Solomon Grayzel, *A History of the Jews*, Mentor, New York, 1968, p. 675
43 'Summary of Considerations on Communism Expressed by H. E. Monsignor Tardini in Conversation with Mr Myron Taylor September 17 1941', one of the documents in 'Memoranda Concerning Vatican, Czechoslovakia, Germany, Hungary, Italy, Poland, Rumania, Russia, Yugoslavia, Austria, 1941 to 1946', from Myron Taylor to State Department, 4 September 1946, USNA, RG 59, 121.866A/9–446
44 'Informal Notes Concerning Communistic Peril After the War by H. E. Monsignor Tardini May 30 1943', one of the documents in 'Memoranda Concerning Vatican, Czechoslovakia, Germany, Hungary, Italy, Poland, Rumania, Russia, Yugoslavia, Austria, 1941 to 1946', from Myron Taylor to State Department, 4 September 1946, USNA, RG 59, 121.866A/9–446
45 Report of 12 February 1944, USNA, RG 226, Records of the Office of Strategic Services, 60701. For Moscow's view of this, see also 'Annual Report for 1945', from the Holy See to the Foreign Office, 22 February 1946, PRO FO 371 60803
46 Details of Hartl's career are found in Gitta Sereny, *Into that Darkness: 'the mind of a mass murderer'*, Picador, London, 1977, pp. 17, 64–71, 97, 295–6
47 Interrogation Report of Albert Hartl, 17 May 1946, USNA, RG 59
48 Reports of 31 August 1944, and 10 February 1945, USNA, RG 226, Records of the Office of Strategic Services, 92389 and 118384
49 Francis Murphy, 'A Brief Biography of Paul VI', in James Andrews (ed.), *Paul VI: Critical Appraisals*, Bruce Publishing, New York, 1970, pp. 132–9; and Pallenberg, *The Vatican From Within*, p. 128. For further details of Montini see 'Holy See Personalities', 21 June 1938 and 3 July 1939, from British Legation to the Holy See to the Foreign Office, PRO FO 371 22441 and 23827
50 Report of 31 August 1944, USNA, RG 226, Records of the Office of Strategic Services, 92389
51 Report of 12 February 1944, USNA, RG 226, Records of the Office of Strategic Services, 60701
52 Telegram from Holy See to Foreign Office, 25 August 1945, PRO FO 371 47606
53 'Confidential notes on the situation in the Russian-occupied zone of Berlin – (April, May, June 1945)', attached to letter from the Holy See to the State Department, 15 October 1945, USNA, RG 59, 740.00119 Control (Germany)/10–1545
54 'Memorandum on Political and Religious Situation in Hungary, July 27 1946', one of the documents in 'Memoranda Concerning Vatican, Czechoslovakia, Germany, Hungary, Italy, Poland, Rumania, Russia, Yugoslavia, Austria, 1941 to 1946', from Myron Taylor to State Department, 4 September 1946, USNA, RG 59, 121.866A/9–446

55 Detailed reports on the religious situation in Soviet-occupied Europe
are found in 'Alleged persecution of the Catholic Church in the
Russian Sub-Carpathian Province and the Ukraine', from the Holy
See to the State Department, 29 January 1947, USNA, Myron Taylor
Papers, Box 17; 'Annual Report for 1945', from the Holy See to the
Foreign Office, 22 February 1946, PRO FO 371 60803; 'Annual
Political Review for 1946', from the Holy See to the Foreign Office, 10
February 1947, PRO FO 371 67920A; 'Annual Review for 1949', from
the Holy See to the Foreign Office, 11 March 1950, PRO FO 371
89815; 'The Catholic Church in Eastern Europe', Foreign Office
Research Department paper of 5 December 1949, PRO FO 371
79904; and 'Memorandum on Political and Religious Situation in
Czechoslovakia, August 1 1946'; 'Memorandum on Political and
Religious Situation in Poland, July 30 1946'; 'Memorandum on
Religious Situation in Germany, August 20 1946', documents in
'Memoranda Concerning Vatican, Czechoslovakia, Germany,
Hungary, Italy, Poland, Rumania, Russia, Yugoslavia, Austria, 1941
to 1946', from Myron Taylor to State Department, 4 September 1946,
USNA, RG 59, 121.866A/9–446
56 Information provided by Tardini to an American diplomat at the
Holy See, in Airgram of 9 January 1947, USNA, Myron Taylor
Papers, Box 10
57 'Italy: Ideological Report From The Holy See', report of 1 May 1947,
from the Holy See to the Foreign Office, PRO FO 371 67918
58 'Annual Report for 1945', from the Holy See to the Foreign Office, 22
February 1946, PRO FO 371 60803; 'Italy: Ideological Report From
The Holy See', report of 1 May 1947, from the Holy See to the
Foreign Office, PRO FO 371 67918; 'The Vatican and the "Iron
Curtain" countries', Foreign Office Research Department paper of 13
December 1949; and 'The Catholic Church in Eastern Europe',
Foreign Office Research Department paper, 5 December 1949, PRO
FO 371 89817 and 79904
59 'The Vatican and the "Iron Curtain" countries', Foreign Office
Research Department paper, 13 December 1949, PRO FO 371 89817
60 Handwritten note on the cover of 'Italy: Ideological Report From The
Holy See', report of 1 May 1947, from the Holy See to the Foreign
Office, PRO FO 371 67918
61 Telegram from Holy See to State Department, 18 September 1946,
USNA, RG 59, 761.00/9–1846
62 Memos of 15 March and 16 October 1944, USNA RG 319, ABC, Box
73
63 Interrogation Report of Albert Hartl, 17 May 1946, USNA, RG 59
64 Report of October 1945, USNA, RG 226, Records of the Office of
Strategic Services, XL 24218
65 Memos of 18 December 1947 and 5 January 1948, USNA, RG 59,
866A.20200/12–1847
66 'Memorandum on Reported "Christian Front"', attached to memo of

29 April 1948, from the Holy See to the State Department, USNA, RG 59, 866A.20200/4–2948

2 Bishop Hudal and the First Wave

1 This account is based on Gitta Sereny's interviews with Stangl, in *Into that Darkness*, p. 289
2 *Ibid.*
3 *Ibid.*
4 *Ibid.*
5 *Ibid.*
6 *Ibid.*
7 Interview with Simon Wiesenthal, Vienna, 21 February 1985
8 Testimony of Frau Stangl at her husband's trial in Düsseldorf, quoted in Sereny, *Into that Darkness*, p. 357
9 Interview with Simon Wiesenthal, Vienna, 21 February 1985
10 *Ibid.*
11 *Ibid.*
12 Interview with Father Graham, 15 April 1985
13 For example, in a letter written during the war Hudal recalls 'speaking in the town of Trier in November 1934, during a tour of lectures in Germany'. USNA, RG 226, Records of the Office of Strategic Services, Report of 2 September 1944, 95157
14 Alois Hudal, *Die Gründlagen des Nationalsozialismus; eine ideengeschichtliche Untersuchung*, Johannes Günther, Leipzig, 1937, p. 9
15 Erika Weinzierl, 'Austria: Church, State, Politics' in Richard Wolff and Jorg Hönsch (eds), *Catholics, the State and the European Radical Right 1919–1945*, Columbia University Press, New York, 1987, p. 23
16 USNA, RG 226, Records of the Office of Strategic Services, Report of September 1944, 95157
17 *Ibid.*
18 Karlheinz Deschner, *Ein Jahrhundert Heilsgeschichte; Die Politik der Papste im Zeitalter der Weltkriege. Von Pius XII 1939 bis zu Johannes Paul I 1978*, Kiepenheuer und Witsch, Köln, 1983, pp. 135, 359
19 Letter from Central Intelligence Group, source unknown (censored) to Jack D. Neal, Department of State, 24 October 1946, USNA, RG 59, 866A.404/10–2446; letter from Father Robert Graham, 22 January 1990; and Pallenberg, *The Vatican from Within*, pp. 185–90
20 Alois Hudal, *Römische Tagebücher: Lebenberichte eines alten Bishofs*, Leopold Stocker, Graz/Stuttgart, 1976, p. 317; interview with Anima Rector Nedbal, Rome, 13 May 1989; letter from Father Robert Graham, January 1990; and Pallenberg, *The Vatican from Within* p. 186
21 Interview with Father Graham, 15 April 1985
22 See Blet *et al.*, *Les Actes et Documents du Saint Siège relatif à la Seconde Guerre Mondiale*; and Sereny, *Into that Darkness*, p. 303
23 Sereny, *Into that Darkness*, p. 305
24 Alfred Persche, 'Die Aktion Hudal; Das letzte Aufgebot des

Abendlandes', Unpublished Manuscript, p. 73, held by the
Dokumentationsarchiv des Österreichischen Widerstandes

25 Anton Szanya, 'Alois Hudal Zum 100 Geburtstag eines gern
vergessenen Österreichers', *Der Freidenker*, anno 15, issue 4, 1985,
p. 12; and letter from Father Robert Graham, January 1990

26 Persche, 'Die Aktion Hudal; Das letzte Aufgebot des Abendlandes',
Unpublished Manuscript, p. 73, held by the Dokumentationsarchiv
des Österreichischen Widerstandes

27 Interview with Rector Nedbal, Rome, 13 May 1989

28 *Ibid.*

29 Raul Hilberg, *The Destruction of the European Jews*, Homes & Meier,
New York, 1985, pp. 333–4

30 Werner Brockdorff (Alfred Jarschel), *Flucht vor Nürnberg*, Welsermuhl
Verlag, Wels/Munich, 1969, pp. 25–6. For details of Rauff's Italian
assignment, see Hilberg, *The Destruction of the European Jews*, p. 668

31 Sereny, *Into that Darkness*, p. 321

32 USNA, RG 226, Records of the Office of Strategic Services, Report
number 88819

33 Central Intelligence Group memo from an unknown (censored)
source, to Jack D. Neal, Department of State, 24 October 1946,
USNA, RG 59, 866A.404/10–2446; Ladislas Farago, *Aftermath*, Pan,
London, 1976, pp. 210–11

34 Farago, *Aftermath*, pp. 211–12; and Father Graham letter of 22
January 1990

35 For details of the Vatican's request, and Allied policy see the Vatican
Secretariat of State's memo of 23 August 1944; Carmel Offie's letter
to Tittman, 8 September 1944; Myron Taylor's Note Verbale to the
Vatican Secretariat of State of 19 September 1944; the Vatican
Secretariat of State's memo of 3 October 1944; Carmel Offie's letters
to Myron Taylor of 26 October 1944 and 7 November 1944; and
Myron Taylor's Note Verbale to the Vatican Secretariat of State of 10
November 1944, USNA, Myron Taylor Papers, Box 6

36 Memo of 7 December 1945, to Samuel Reber, Washington, USNA,
Myron Taylor Papers, Box 29

37 In early September 1944 Bishop Hudal had written a report in which
he attempted to show that his book *The Fundamentals of National
Socialism*, 'far from Nazi propaganda was [in fact] an honest, calm,
scientific criticism . . . measuring nazism by Christian morale and
state doctrine'. See report of 2 September 1944, USNA, RG 226,
Records of the Office of Strategic Services, 95157

38 Letter of 19 December 1944, from John Chapman to Allied
Commission Liaison Division, USNA, Myron Taylor Papers, Box 6

39 Hudal, *Römische Tagebücher*, p. 21

40 *Ibid.*

41 Karl Wolff, for example, had been a commander of a notorious SS
Einsatzgruppe in the Soviet Union. He was personally involved in the
murder of 300,000 people, yet was sentenced in 1949 to the derisory

term of four years' imprisonment of which he served only a week. He
was re-arrested in 1962 and sentenced in 1964 to fifteen years'
imprisonment. He served six years before being freed because of ill
health. See Christopher Simpson, *Blowback*, Weidenfeld & Nicolson,
New York, 1988, pp. 92–4 and 93–4n; Wolff obituary, *Daily Telegraph*,
London, 17 July 1984; and Hilberg, *The Destruction of the European
Jews*, pp. 1085, 1109

42 Simpson, *Blowback*, pp. 92–3
43 Jarschel, *Flucht vor Nürnberg*, pp. 77–9
44 'Interrogation of SD Officers', 1 May 1945, USAINSCOM File D-
216719, Ft. George V. Meade, Md.
45 David Martin, *Wilderness of Mirrors*, Harper & Row, New York, 1980,
p. 182
46 Department of State, Report from Vincent La Vista to Herbert J.
Cummings, 15 May 1947, USNA, RG 59, FW 800.0128/5-1547; the
cite for the French book, *Cercle Noir*, is taken from translated excerpts
which were graciously provided by Charles Kenney of the *Boston Globe*
47 Interview with Simon Wiesenthal, Vienna, 21 February 1985. See
also Werner Brockdorff (Jarschel), *Flucht vor Nürnberg*, pp. 55–6, 81.
Brockdorff, that is former Nazi youth leader Jarschel, also confirms
that Schwendt was closely collaborating with Rauff in Milan
48 Jarschel, *Flucht vor Nürnberg*, p. 79
49 Department of State, Report from Vincent La Vista to Herbert J.
Cummings, 15 May 1947, USNA, RG 59, FW 800.0128/5-1547,
Appendix C, p. 4, paragraph 16
50 Sereny, *Into that Darkness*, pp. 316–17
51 *Ibid.*
52 *Ibid.*, p. 317
53 Department of State, report fom Vincent La Vista to Herbert J.
Cummings, 15 May 1947, USNA, RG 59, FW 800.0128/5-1547. Some
details of La Vista's earlier work can be found in a telegram from the
State Department to the US Embassy in Rome, of 28 July 1945,
USNA, RG 59, 840.414/7-2845. See also, Charles R. Allen, Junior,
'The Vatican and the Nazis', in *Reform Judaism*, Spring/Summer 1983,
and 'Debate Rages: did Vatican help Nazis to escape from Europe?',
in the *National Catholic Reporter*, 2 March 1984
54 Interview with Father Robert Graham, 15 April 1985
55 Department of State, Report fom Vincent La Vista to Herbert J.
Cummings, 15 May 1947, USNA, RG 59, FW 800.0128/5-1547,
Appendix A
56 CIC report by Leo Pagnotta of 28 December 1946, released under US
FOIA, pp. 1–10. This report is also attached to Department of State
Report from Vincent La Vista to Herbert J. Cummings, 15 May
1947, USNA, RG 59, FW 800.0128/5-1547, as Appendix B
57 *Ibid.*
58 *Ibid.*
59 Department of State, Report from Vincent La Vista to Herbert J.
Cummings, 15 May 1947, USNA, RG 59, FW 800.0128/5-1547, p. 10

60 *Ibid.*, pp. 3–4
61 CIC report number D-3330 by Paul Lyon of 16 December 1946, released under US FOIA, pp. 7–9
62 *Ibid.*
63 *Ibid.*
64 Top Secret Office memorandum from Hamilton Robinson, Office of European Affairs, 26 June 1947, USNA, RG 59, 865.56/6-2647
65 See Division of Protective Services, Department of State to Leland Harrison, American Minister, Berne, 11 July 1947, USNA, RG 59, 800.142/5-1547; and letter from Leland Harrison, Minister, American Legation Berne to Secretary of State, 12 September 1947, USNA, RG 59, 800.142/9-1247
66 Top Secret Office memorandum from Hamilton Robinson, Office of European Affairs, 26 June 1947, USNA, RG 59, 865.56/6-2647
67 Letter of 28 July 1947, from Dowling at the State Department to Parsons at the Vatican, USNA, Myron Taylor Papers, Box 17
68 Letter and Oral Message from Parsons to Dowling, of 29 August 1947, USNA, Myron Taylor Papers, Box 17
69 USNA, Myron Taylor Papers, Box 17
70 Letter and Oral Message from Parsons to Dowling, of 29 August 1947, USNA, Myron Taylor Papers, Box 17; and Charles R. Allen, Junior, 'The Vatican and the Nazis', in *Reform Judaism*, Spring/Summer 1983
71 Enclosure Number 1 to despatch 603 of 13 August 1947 from J. Graham Parsons, Vatican City, USNA, RG 59, 866A.00/8-1347
72 Hudal, *Römische Tagebücher*, p. 21
73 Several of the Austrian Episcopate members who voted to remove him later expressed their regrets. Salzburg's Archbishop Rohracher wrote to Hudal on 24 January 1952 saying that he had only signed the resignation demand 'under pressure'. And on 22 June 1953, after Hudal had already left the Anima, the Bishop of Graz, Ferdinand Pawlikowski did the same. See Hudal, *Römische Tagebücher*, pp. 303, 306
74 Hudal, *Römische Tagebücher*, p. 21
75 See letter from the Secretariat of State to Tittman of 11 August 1945, USNA, Myron Taylor Papers, Box 8

3 A French Spy in the Vatican

1 Vincent La Vista, 'Illegal Emigration Movements in and Through Italy', 15 May 1947, USNA, RG 59, FW 800.0128/5-1547
2 *Ibid.*
3 Interview with Simon Wiesenthal, Vienna, 21 February 1985
4 *New York Times*, 30 January 1984
5 Gowen CIC report of 23 June 1947, Vajta file, obtained under the US FOIA, pp. 49–51
6 *Intermarium Bulletin*, number 5, January 1947, courtesy of Christopher

Simpson. Copies of this publication are found in the Library of Congress, Washington, and some in FBI files available under US FOIA

7 Anthony Cave Brown, *The Secret Servant*, Michael Joseph, London, 1988, pp. 143–4

8 'Annual Report, 1925' from the British Minister to the Holy See, Sir Odo Russell, to London, 21 April 1926, PRO FO 371 11399; and Foreign Office Research and Press Service report, 'The policy of the Catholic Church in the Danube Valley', 21 October 1942, PRO FO 371 33434

9 CIC report on 'The Croatian National Independence Movement', 9 April 1946, Ustashi file, obtained under the US FOIA, pp. 23–5

10 Appendix D to Vincent La Vista, 'Illegal Emigration Movements in and Through Italy', 15 May 1947, USNA, RG 59, FW 800.0128/5-1547

11 See Gowen CIC report pf 5 March 1948, Vajta file, pp. 30–3, obtained under the US FOIA, for an account of his early contacts with Vajta

12 An extremely detailed account of Vajta's claims to the Americans is contained in his Curriculum Vitae, and his paper 'The Struggle for the Domination of Central and South Eastern Europe', Rome 10 February 1947, both in French and enclosed in State Department memo of 10 April 1948 from Rome to Washington, USNA, RG 59, 111.20A/4-1048

13 Vajta's Curriculum Vitae provided to the US Embassy in Rome, Enclosure to State Department memo of 10 April 1948 from Rome to Washington, USNA, RG 59, 111.20A/4-1048

14 Gowen CIC report of 22 March 1948, Vajta file, obtained under the US FOIA, pp. 9–14

15 Gowen CIC report of 22 March 1948, Vajta file, obtained under the US FOIA, pp. 9–14; memo of 20 December 1947, from Wilford to Culbertson, enclosed in State Department memo of 31 December 1947 from Madrid to Washington, from Vajta's FBI file, released under US FOIA, document 0009

16 Gowen CIC report of 22 March 1948, Vajta file, obtained under the US FOIA, pp. 9–14

17 'The Struggle for the Domination of Central and South Eastern Europe', Rome 10 February 1947, Enclosure to the State Department memo of 10 April 1948 from Rome to Washington, USNA, RG 59, 111.20A/4-1048; memo of 20 December 1947, from Wilford to Culbertson, enclosed in State Department memo of 31 December 1947 from Madrid to Washington, from Vajta's FBI file, released under US FOIA, document 0009

18 Memo of 20 December 1947 from Wilford to Culbertson, enclosed in State Department memo of 31 December 1947 from Madrid to Washington, from Vajta's FBI file, released under US FOIA, document 0009

19 Gowen CIC report of 23 June 1947, Vajta file, obtained under the US FOIA, pp. 49–51

20 State Department telegrams of 24 February and 24 March 1948 from Washington to Rome, and Madrid to Washington, USNA, RG 59, 111.20A/2-2448, and 111.20A/3-2448

21 Memo of 20 December 1947 from Wilford to Culbertson, enclosed in State Department memo of 31 December 1947 from Madrid to Washington, from Vajta's FBI file, released under US FOIA, document 0009

22 Smofford CIC report of 19 January 1948, Vajta file, obtained under the US FOIA, pp. 40–1

23 Gowen CIC report of 22 March 1948, Vajta file, obtained under the US FOIA, pp. 9–14; and Vajta Curriculum Vitae, enclosed in State Department memo of 10 April 1948 from Rome to Washington, USNA, RG 59, 111.20A/4-1048

24 Memo of 20 December 1947, from Wilford to Culbertson, enclosed in State Department memo of 31 December 1947 from Madrid to Washington, from Vajta's FBI file, released under US FOIA, document 0009

25 *Ibid.*

26 'The Struggle for the Domination of Central and South Eastern Europe', Rome 10 February 1947, Enclosure to State Department memo of 10 April 1948 from Rome to Washington, USNA, RG 59, 111.20A/4-1048

27 *Ibid.*

28 See 'The Ideological Basis of the Confederation of Central-Eastern Europe', in the *Intermarium Bulletin*, number five, January 1947 for the organisation's account of its aims, Library of Congress, Washington

29 Gowen CIC report of 23 June 1947, Vajta file, obtained under the US FOIA, pp. 49–51

30 'The Struggle for the Domination of Central and South Eastern Europe', Rome, 10 February 1947, and Vajta Curriculum Vitae, enclosed in State Department memo of 10 April 1948 from Rome to Washington, USNA, RG 59, 111.20A/4-1048; memo of 20 December 1947, from Wilford to Culbertson, enclosed in State Department memo of 31 December 1947 from Madrid to Washington, from Vajta's FBI file, released under US FOIA, document 0009

31 Gowen CIC report of 23 June 1947, Vajta file, obtained under the US FOIA, pp. 49–51; and CIC memos of 21 August, 4 and 15 October, and 10 December 1946, Intermarium file, obtained under US FOIA, pp. 1–6

32 For the early history of San Girolamo, see Mons Dr Juraj Magjerec, *Hrvatski Zavod Sv. Jeronima u Rimu: Jubilejske Proslave (1453–1953),* Tiskara Papinskog Sveučilsta Gregoriane, Rome, 1953. This is a particularly interesting account, especially as it was largely prepared by Father Draganović.

33 These details of Draganović's early life are taken from his statement

to the Yugoslav authorities, 26 September 1967; on Bishop Šarić see
Harrington CIC memo of 9 March 1948, 'Activity of Bishops Rožman
and Šarić', released under US FOIA

34 CIC Index Card and Captain Davis, undated memo, 'Consolidated
Interrogation Report on Dr Krunoslav Stepano Draganović',
Draganović file, obtained under the US FOIA, pp. 2, 41–6;
unpublished manuscript by Stephen Clissold; interview with Milan
Simčić, Rome, 12 May 1989; undated Italian Secret Service report,
attached to Ministry of Foreign Affairs memo of 20 August 1944,
Ministry of Foreign Affairs Archives, 'Affari politici (Jugoslavia),
1948 Busta 33 fasciolo 3, Attivita' di jugoslavi contrari di Tito in
Italia; Draganović statement to the Yugoslav authorities, 26
September 1967; and Bogdan Križman, *Pavelić u bjekstvu*, Globus,
Zagreb, 1986, quoting *Hrvatska Revija*, Munich, 1975, Year 25, issue 4,
pp. 655–64

35 Memo of 20 December 1947, from Wilford to Culbertson, enclosed in
State Department memo of 31 December 1947 from Madrid to
Washington, from Vajta's FBI file, released under US FOIA,
document 0009. For a good account of Vajta's and Krek's relations
see the former's letters to the latter, Rome, 16 March 1947, and
Innsbruck, Paris, Rome, 12 December 1946, enclosed in State
Department memo of 10 April 1948 from Rome to Washington,
USNA, RG 59, 111.20A/4-1048. Also see, Draganović statement to
the Yugoslav authorities, 26 September 1967

36 Gowen CIC report of 23 June 1947, Vajta file, obtained under the US
FOIA, pp. 49–51. See also, undated Italian Secret Service report,
attached to Ministry of Foreign Affairs memo of 20 August 1944,
Ministry of Foreign Affairs Archives, 'Affari politici (Jugoslavia),
1948 Busta 33 fasciolo 3, Attivita' di jugoslavi contrari di Tito in
Italia

37 OSS report of 8 February 1945, USNA, RG 226, 113566; Italian
Secret Service report of 6 July 1945, and undated Italian Secret
Service report, attached to Ministry of Foreign Affairs memo of 20
August 1944, Ministry of Foreign Affairs Archives, 'Affari politici
(Jugoslavia), 1948 Busta 33, fasciolo 3, Attivita' di jugoslavi contrari
al regime di Tito in Italia; and Draganović statement to the Yugoslav
authorities, 26 September 1967

38 Gowen CIC report of 23 June 1947, and CIC List of Intermarium
Leaders, Vajta file, obtained under the US FOIA, pp. 49–51 and 55;
memo of 20 December 1947, from Wilford to Culbertson, enclosed in
State Department memo of 31 December 1947 from Madrid to
Washington, from Vajta's FBI file, released under US FOIA,
document 0009. For details of Durčansky, see CIA Biographic Report
of 18 November 1949, CIA file obtained under the US FOIA, p. 11

39 Memo of 20 December 1947, from Wilford to Culbertson, enclosed in
State Department memo of 31 December 1947 from Madrid to
Washington, from Vajta's FBI file, released under US FOIA,

document 0009; Italian Secret Service report of 6 July 1945, Ministry of Foreign Affairs Archives, 'Affari politici (Jugoslavia), 1948 Busta 33, fasciolo 3, Attivita' di jugoslavi contrari al regime di Tito in Italia

40 Appendix A to Vincent La Vista, 'Illegal Emigration Movements in and Through Italy', 15 May 1947, USNA, RG 59, FW 800.0128/5-1547

41 Gowen CIC report of 5 March 1948, Vajta file, obtained under the US FOIA, pp. 30–3

42 See report of October 1945, USNA, RG 226, Records of the Office of Strategic Services, XL 24218

43 Vajta Curriculum Vitae, enclosed in State Department memo of 10 April 1948 from Rome to Washington, USNA, RG 59, 111.20A/4-1048

44 Gowen CIC report of 22 March 1948, Vajta file, obtained under the US FOIA, pp. 9–14

45 State Department telegram of 24 March 1948 from Madrid to Washington, USNA, RG 59, 111.20A/3-2448

46 Vajta Curriculum Vitae, enclosed in State Department memo of 10 April 1948 from Rome to Washington, USNA, RG 59, 111.20A/4-1048. For the official American view of Vajta's arrest see State Department Confidential Telegram from Rome to Washington, USNA, RG 59, 16 April 1947, 740.00116EW/4-1647

47 Gowen CIC report of 12 May 1947, Vajta file, obtained under the US FOIA, pp. 52–3

48 *Ibid.*, pp. 49–51

49 State Department Confidential Telegram from Budapest to Washington, USNA, RG 59, 24 April 1947, 740.00116EW/4-2447

50 Gowen CIC report of 23 June 1947, Vajta file, obtained under the US FOIA, pp. 49–51. For details of Rupprecht's role as a Nazi propagandist, see Randolph Braham, *The Politics of Genocide: The Holocaust in Hungary*, Columbia University Press, New York, 1981, pp. 55–6, 160–1

51 List of Hungarian war criminals of 5 February 1946, enclosed in State Department memo of 23 June 1947 from Budapest to Washington, USNA, RG 59, 740.00116EW/6-2347; handwritten CIC note, undated, and Smofford CIC report of 19 January 1948, and Gowen CIC report of 22 March 1948, Vajta file, obtained under the US FOIA, pp. 56, 40–1, 9–14; Vajta Curriculum Vitae, enclosed in State Department memo of 10 April 1948 from Rome to Washington, USNA, RG 59, 111.20A/4-1048; and Simpson, *Blowback*, p. 183

52 'The Struggle for the Domination of Central and South Eastern Europe', Rome 10 February 1947, Enclosure to State Department memo of 10 April 1948 from Rome to Washington, USNA, RG 59, 111.20A/4-1048

53 Gowen CIC report of 22 March 1948, Vajta file, obtained under the US FOIA, pp. 9–14; Vajta's Curriculum Vitae provided to the US Embassy in Rome, Enclosure to State Department memo of 10 April

1948 from Rome to Washington, USNA, RG 59, 111.20A/4-1048; and State Department memo of 5 March 1948, 'Biographic Report on Ferenc Vajta', from Vienna to Washington, from Vatja's FBI file, released under US FOIA

54 Braham, *The Politics of Genocide*, pp. 55–6, 160–1. Many details of Vajta's history are taken from his Curriculum Vitae provided to the US Embassy in Rome, Enclosure to State Department memo of 10 April 1948 from Rome to Washington, USNA, RG 59, 111.20A/4-1048

55 Open Letter to Ferenc Nagy, leader of Small Proprietors Party, 26 June 1947, Enclosure to State Department memo of 10 April 1948 from Rome to Washington, USNA, RG 59, 111.20A/4-1048

56 State Department memo of 30 March 1948 from Budapest to Washington, USNA, RG 59, 111.20A/3-3048; State Department Telegram of 9 January 1948 from Budapest to Washington, from Vatja's FBI file, released under US FOIA, document 0008

57 State Department memo of 30 March 1948 from Budapest to Washington, USNA, RG 59, 111.20A/3-3048

58 Simpson, *Blowback*, p. 181

59 This conversation between Gowen and Vajta is based on the latter's detailed paper submitted to the US Embassy at around the same time the two met, 'The Struggle for the Domination of Central and South Eastern Europe', Rome, 10 February 1947, enclosed in State Department memo of 10 April 1948 from Rome to Washington, USNA, RG 59, 111.20A/4-1048, and on what material has been declassified from Gowen's own reports

60 Gowen CIC report of 6 July 1947, Vajta file, obtained under US FOIA, pp. 44–8

61 *Ibid.*

62 Gowen CIC report of 22 March 1948, Vajta file, obtained under US FOIA, pp. 9–14

63 Memo of 20 December 1947, from Wilford to Culbertson, enclosed in State Department memo of 31 December 1947 from Madrid to Washington, from Vajta's FBI file, released under US FOIA, document 0009

64 Falconi, *The Silence of Pius XII*, p. 158

65 Gowen CIC report of 5 March 1948, Vajta file, obtained under US FOIA, pp. 30–3; and Caniglia and Gowen CIC report of 9 September 1947, Vajta file, obtained under US FOIA, pp. 47–8

66 State Department Memo of 31 December 1947 from Madrid to Washington, and enclosed memo of 20 December 1947, from Wilford to Culbertson, from Vajta's FBI file, released under US FOIA, document 0009; and 'Holy See: Annual Review for 1949', from the British Legation to the Holy See, to the Foreign Office, of 11 March 1950, PRO FO 371 150738

67 Memo of 20 December 1947, from Wilford to Culbertson, enclosed in State Department memo of 31 December 1947 from Madrid to

Washington, from Vajta's FBI file, released under US FOIA, document 0009

68 *Ibid.*

69 HQ European Command Confidential incoming telegram from Intelligence Division of 11 February 1948, Vajta file, obtained under US FOIA, p. 36. See also HQ European Command Incoming Message from Army Intelligence Director of 2 March 1948, Vajta file, obtained under US FOIA, pp. 34–5

70 State Department Telegram of 8 January 1948 from Madrid to Washington, from Vajta's FBI file, released under US FOIA, document 0003; State Department Memo of 31 December 1947 from Madrid to Washington, from Vajta's FBI file, released under US FOIA, document 0009

71 'Open Letter to Ferenc Nagy, leader of Small Proprietors Party', 26 June 1947, Enclosure to State Department memo of 10 April 1948 from Rome to Washington, USNA, RG 59, 111.20A/4-1048; and State Department Memo of 31 December 1947 from Madrid to Washington, from Vajta's FBI file, released under US FOIA, document 0009

72 HQ European Command Internal Route Slip of 16 February 1948, and Colonel Lyster report of 20 January 1948 to Major General Floyd Parks, Army Public Information Division in Washington, Vajta file, obtained under US FOIA, pp. 37–9; State Department telegram of 24 March 1948 from Budapest to Washington, USNA, RG 59, 111.20A/3-2448; Hungarian Legation note to State Department of 3 February 1948, USNA, RG 59, 740.00116EW/2-348; State Department telegram of 24 January 1948 from Budapest to Washington, USNA, RG 59, 851.20263/1-2348, Microfilm, LM 108, Roll 15, frame 00442; State Department telegram of 24 February 1948 from Washington to Rome, USNA, RG 59, 111.20A/2-2448; memo of 27 August 1948 from Clark to Culbertson, enclosed in State Department memo of 8 September 1948 from Madrid to Washington, from Vajta's FBI file, released under US FOIA; and Simpson, *Blowback*, p. 183

73 Gowen CIC report of 5 March 1948, Vajta file, obtained under US FOIA, pp. 30–3. The Hungarian press investigated how Vajta escaped and discovered most of the details, including the Vatican's role. For an account of this see, State Department telegram of 3 March 1948 from Budapest to Washington, USNA, RG 59, 864.00/3-348

74 Charles Ashman and Robert Wagman, *The Nazi Hunters*, Pharos Books, New York, 1988, pp. 189–90

4 A Staggering Blow to the Holy See

1 Accounts of Pavelić's flight from Zagreb via Rogaska Slatina and Maribor to Austria can be found in Križman, *Pavelić u bjekstvu*; and

Vilim Cecelja, 'Četrdesetdodjisnjica Bleiburga', in *Vjesnik,* Journal of Croatian Workers and Migrants in Germany, year 14, number 51, Easter 1985. The former gives his account from a pro-Yugoslav point of view, while the latter was a senior Ustashi member and gives a sympathetic portrayal of Pavelić.

2 A detailed history of the growth of the Ustashi, its terrorist activities in the 1930s and the terrible atrocities committed during the war can be found in Mark Aarons, *Sanctuary! Nazi Fugitives in Australia,* Heinemann Australia, Melbourne, 1989, pp. 57–63. A somewhat biased, although largely accurate account can be found in Edmond Paris, *Genocide in Satellite Croatia, 1941–1945,* The Serbian Thought, Melbourne, 1981

3 Magjerec, *Hrvatski Zavod Sv. Jeronima u Rimu: Jubilejske Proslave (1453–1953),* pp. 177–80

4 Handwritten notes of 5 June and 26 May 1941, PRO FO 371 30174 and 30226; and memo from Apostolic Delegate to Foreign Office of 23 May 1941 and memo from Eden to Osborne, British Ambassador to the Holy See, 24 May 1941, PRO FO 371 30174

5 Report from Osborne to the Foreign Office, 13 June 1941, PRO FO 371 30174

6 Handwritten note of 10 July 1941 and memo from the Foreign Office to Osborne, 21 July 1941, PRO FO 371 30174

7 Falconi, *The Silence of Pius XII,* p. 307

8 Bokun, *Spy in the Vatican,* pp. 21–3

9 Falconi, *The Silence of Pius XII,* pp. 308, 335–6

10 *Ibid.,* pp. 330 and 350

11 Paris, *Genocide in Satellite Croatia, 1941–1945,* pp. 167, 221; Bokun, *Spy in the Vatican,* p. 46; and Falconi, *The Silence of Pius XII,* pp. 344–51

12 Curzio Malaparte, *Kaputt,* Harborough, London, 1960, p. 200

13 See the account in Hilberg, *The Destruction of the European Jews,* pp. 711–8

14 Note of 3 July 1945, PRO FO 371 48890; and Note from Yugoslav Embassy, London, to Foreign Office, 30 August 1945, PRO FO 371 48892

15 Note from the Foreign Office to the Yugoslav Embassy, London, 9 October 1945, PRO FO 371 48892; and Telegram from Vienna to Foreign Office, 28 October 1945, PRO FO 371 48893

16 Telegram from Foreign Office to Caserta, 12 September 1945, PRO FO 371 48892; Telegram from Belgrade to Caserta, 15 October 1945, PRO FO 371 48893; Telegram from Belgrade to Foreign Office, 27 August 1945, PRO FO 371 48892; Telegram from Caserta to Foreign Office, 10 October 1945, PRO FO 371 48893; letter to Vyshinski from Frank Roberts of the British Embassy, Moscow, 15 October 1945, PRO FO 371 48893; letter to the Foreign Office from Allied Commission for Austria (British Element), 2 December 1945, PRO FO 371 48894; and letter from Foreign Office to Yugoslav Embassy, London, 3 January 1946, PRO FO 371 48894

17 Telegram from Belgrade to Foreign Office, 14 December 1945, PRO FO 371 48894; Colville note of 22 December 1945, PRO FO 371 48894; Telegram from Belgrade to Foreign Office, 14 December 1945, PRO FO 371 48894; and letter from Foreign Office to Yugoslav Embassy, London, 19 December 1945, PRO FO 371 48894

18 Colville note of 10 January 1946, PRO FO 371 59399; Telegram from Foreign Office to Washington, 10 January 1946, PRO FO 371 59399; and Telegram from Washington to Foreign Office, 14 January 1946, PRO FO 371 59399

19 See telegram from Belgrade to Foreign Office, 9 June 1946, PRO FO 371 59408, for an example of the Yugoslav press complaints; for the continuing official campaign, see for example, the Yugoslav Embassy's note to the Foreign Office of 2 August 1946, PRO FO 371 59415

20 Letter from British Embassy, Belgrade, to Yugoslav Foreign Affairs Minister, 21 August 1946, PRO FO 371 59417; and letter from Walworth Barbour, Acting Chief of the US State Department's Division of Southern European Affairs, to J. C. Mance, 7 October 1946, USNA, RG 59, 740.00116EW/9-2546

21 Letter of 21 November 1946 to Foreign Office, PRO FO 371 59423

22 Letter from British Embassy, Washington, to State Department, 9 November 1946, and State Department reply, 20 November 1946, USNA, RG 59, 860H.00/11-946; and letter from Father Robert Graham, 22 January 1990

23 Note of 18 December 1946; and Telegram from Vienna to Foreign Office, 14 December 1946, PRO FO 371 59423

24 Draganović statement to the Yugoslav authorities, 26 September 1967

25 *Ibid.*

26 See for example the index card reporting the views of the Judge Advocate General's War Crimes Branch of 5 November 1945, USNA, Investigative Records Repository, RG 319, Pavelić Dossier, XE 001109

27 Gowen and Caniglia report of 29 August 1947, Pavelić CIC file, obtained under US FOIA, pp. 2–6

28 Note of 16 July 1947, and letter from Major Vivian Street, Rome, to Foreign Office, 5 June 1947, PRO FO 371 67380

29 Mudd memo of 30 January 1947, CIC report of Caniglia and Zappala of 15 March 1947, and index card of 14 April 1947, USNA, Investigative Records Repository, RG 319, Pavelić Dossier, XE 001109

30 Pro Memoria of 10 May 1946, reporting the views of Source P, USNA, Investigative Records Repository, RG 319, Pavelić Dossier, XE 001109

31 Hubert Butler, *Escape from the Anthill*, The Lilliput Press, Mullingar, 1985, p. 282; and Communist intelligence document, 'The Poglavnik's Stay in Rome and Departure for Argentina'

32 Pro Memoria of 10 May 1946, reporting the views of Source P,

USNA, Investigative Records Repository, RG 319, Pavelić Dossier, XE 001109

33 Telegram of 7 January 1947 from Rome to Colonel Smith, USNA, Investigative Records Repository, RG 319, Pavelić Dossier, XE 001109

34 Gowen memo of 22 January 1947, USNA, Investigative Records Repository, RG 319, Pavelić Dossier, XE 001109. Father Robert Graham confirms that these Church establishments are in fact located in this complex. Letter of 22 January 1990

35 Father Robert Graham told us that 'Old Romans I have talked to do not remember any tramline that went "under" the Aventine. Of course there was a street car line circling there.' Letter of 22 January 1990

36 Gowen memo of 22 January 1947, USNA, Investigative Records Repository, RG 319, Pavelić Dossier, XE 001109

37 Letter from the British Political Adviser, Caserta, to the Foreign Office, 26 February 1947, PRO FO 371 67372

38 See for example, CIC report, 'Pavelić, Ante and the "Legitimists" in the Ustaša Movement', Pavelić CIC file, obtained under US FOIA, pp. 3–4; and CIC reports of 10 October and 26 November 1946, Draganović files, obtained under US FOIA, pp. 49–54, 54

39 CIC report of Marion Scott, of 18 April 1947, USNA, Investigative Records Repository, RG 319, Pavelić Dossier, XE 001109

40 See Summary of Information, Pavelić CIC File, obtained under US FOIA, p. 9; and memo of Captain Robert Stuart, 20 June 1947, USNA, Investigative Records Repository, RG 319, Pavelić Dossier, XE 001109

41 Memo of 22 May 1947, USNA, Myron Taylor Papers, Box 17

42 Parsons memo of 26 July 1947, USNA, Myron Taylor Papers, Box 17

43 Warner note of 19 June 1947, PRO FO 371 67385

44 Telegrams from Rome to Leghorn, 17 July 1947, and from Foreign Office to Rome, 20 July 1947, PRO FO 371 67385. See also Telegram from Rome to Foreign Office, 22 July 1947, PRO FO 371 67386

45 Telegram from Foreign Office to Washington, 25 July 1947, PRO FO 371 67385

46 Telegram from Washington to Foreign Office, 25 July 1947, PRO FO 371 67387

47 Telegram of 28 July 1947 from Washington to Rome, USNA, RG 59, 740.00116EW/7-2847

48 Memos of 29 July and 2 August 1947, USNA, Investigative Records Repository, RG 319, Pavelić Dossier, XE 001109. See also the two Telegrams from Leghorn to Foreign Office, 30 July 1947, PRO FO 371 67387

49 Telegram from Foreign Office to Rome, 30 July 1947, PRO FO 371 67387

50 USNA, Investigative Records Repository, RG 319, Pavelić Dossier, XE 001109

51 Informal Routing Slip, 8 August 1947; 'Ante Pavelić and other Ustasha personalities'; and Gowen and Caniglia CIC memo of 9 June 1947, USNA, Investigative Records Repository, RG 319, Pavelić Dossier, XE 001109

52 Articles in *La Repubblica*, 23, 24, and 26 September 1948, Ministry of Foreign Affairs Archives, 1948 Busta 33, fasciolo 2, Processo di Zagrabia

53 Telegrams from Foreign Office to Rome, 27 August and 7 October 1947, PRO FO 371 67387; and Telegram from Headquarters Trieste United States troops, 10 September 1947, Pavelić CIC file, obtained under US FOIA, pp. 1–2

54 Memo of 7 July 1947, and Morena handwritten note of 14 July 1947, USNA, Investigative Records Repository, RG 319, Pavelić Dossier, XE 001109

55 Gowen memo of 6 July 1947, Vajta file, obtained under US FOIA, pp. 44–8

56 Gowen and Caniglia report of 29 August 1947, Pavelić CIC file, obtained under US FOIA, pp. 2–6

57 *Ibid.*

58 *Ibid.*

59 *Ibid.*

60 *Ibid.*

61 Gowen, Caniglia and Morena report of 12 September 1947, USNA, Investigative Records Repository, RG 319, Pavelić Dossier, XE 001109

62 Interviews with Simčić, Rome, 12 May 1989 and 16 February 1990

63 Avro Manhattan, *Terror over Yugoslavia*, pp. 117–8, and *Catholic Terror Today*, Paravision, London, 1969

64 Sarajevo's *Svijet*, series of articles on Draganović, by Siniša Ivanović and Kršto Leković, published weekly from 13 June to 19 September 1986

65 Communist intelligence document, 'The Poglavnik's Stay in Rome and Departure for Argentina'

66 Interviews with Simčić, Rome, 16 February 1990; Križman, *Pavelić u bjekstvu*, p. 225

67 CIC memo, 'Pavelić Ante and the "Legitimists" in the Ustaša Movement', Pavelić file, obtained under US FOIA, pp. 3–4

68 Details of the scope of the smuggling operation were given by Ivo Omrčanin in interviews with the *Religious News Service*, May 1986, and John Loftus, 1985

5 Ratline

1 See 'United States Policy Toward the Ustashi', Research Project No. 61, Division of Historical Policy Research, Department of State, April 1948, USNA, RG 59, 740.00116EW/4-148

2 Interview with Father Graham, 15 April 1985

3 Report of 25 November 1943, USNA, RG 226, Records of the Office of Strategic Services, OB 6362

4 Draganović statement to the Yugoslav authorities, 26 September 1967; and statement by Ljubo Miloš to the Yugoslav authorities

5 Draganović statement to the Yugoslav authorities, 26 September 1967

6 *Ibid.*

7 *Ibid.*

8 Interview with Vilim Cecelja, Maria Pline, 23 May 1989

9 Miss Jackson's note of 22 August 1946, PRO FO 371 59415; Yugoslav War Crimes Commission dossier number 7103, Yugoslav Archives, Belgrade; Stella Alexander, *The Triple Myth*, East European Monographs, Boulder, 1987, pp. 86, 157; Yugoslav extradition requests of 6 August 1946, PRO FO 371 59415, and 4 September 1946, USNA RG 59, 860H.00/9-446

10 Interview with Vilim Cecelja, Maria Pline, 23 May 1989; and Paris, *Genocide in Satellite Croatia*, p. 74

11 Yugoslav War Crimes Commission dossier number 7103, Yugoslav Archives, Belgrade

12 Interview with Vilim Cecelja, Maria Pline, 23 May 1989

13 Security check for non-immigrant visa, 18 September 1957, USNA RG 319, Investigative Records Repository, Cecelja Dossier, XE 006538

14 Telegram from Zagreb to Washington, of 29 May 1947, USNA, RG 59, 740.00116EW/5-2947; and Interview with Vilim Cecelja, Maria Pline, 23 May 1989

15 Interview with Vilim Cecelja, Maria Pline, 23 May 1989

16 Appendix A to Personal Questionnaire, and Security Arrest Report, both citing CIC report, 'Ustasha Activity in Land Salzburg', of 2 October 1945; Index Card; Memo of 14 February 1947; and Memo of 26 February 1947, USNA, RG 319, Investigative Records Repository, Cecelja Dossier, XE 006538

17 Notes of 6 August 1946, PRO FO 371 59415, and 4 September 1946, USNA, RG 59, 860H.00/9-446

18 Note by Jackson of 22 August 1946, and Letter of 31 August 1946, PRO FO 371 59415

19 As quoted in Memo from Zagreb to Washington, of 30 May 1947, USNA, RG 59, 740.00116EW/5-3047; and Alexander, *The Triple Myth*, pp. 157–8

20 See Memo from Zagreb to Washington, of 4 June 1947, USNA, RG 59, 740.00116EW/6-447

21 Telegram from Zagreb to Washington, of 29 May 1947, USNA, RG 59, 740.00116EW/5-2947

22 Telegram from Vienna to Washington, of 4 April 1947, USNA, RG 59, 740.00116EW/4-447; and Memo of 12 March 1947, USNA, RG 319, Investigative Records Repository, Cecelja Dossier, XE006538

23 Telegram from Vienna to Washington, of 6 June 1947, USNA, RG 59, 740.00116EW/5-2947

24 Security check for non-immigrant visa, 18 September 1957, USNA, RG 319, Investigative Records Repository, Cecelja Dossier, XE 006538; Index Card of 24 June 1953, USNA, RG 319, Investigative Records Repository, Pavelić Dossier, XE 001109; CIC report on 'Croatian Émigré Activities in Austria', of 28 August 1953, Ustashi CIC file, released under US FOIA, p. 8; and documents of the Australian Security Intelligence Organisation, tabled in the Australian Senate, 27 March 1973

25 Interview with Vilim Cecelja, Maria Pline, 23 May 1989

26 *Ibid.*

27 *Ibid.*

28 'Memorandum on the Ustaša Organisation in Italy', enclosure in letter from Maclean to Wallinger, 17 October 1947, PRO FO 371 67398

29 Yugoslav War Crimes Commission document, 29 March 1949, Zh. 9670/11547, Yugoslav Archives, Belgrade

30 Draganović's extradition was asked for in a Yugoslav note of 26 July 1947, PRO FO 371 67387; some details of the work of the Office for Colonisation can be found in another Yugoslav note of 26 March 1947, USNA, RG 59, 740.00116EW/3-2547

31 Draganović statement to Yugoslav authorities, 26 September 1967

32 *Ibid.*

33 Draganović statement to Yugoslav authorities, 26 September 1967; and statements by Moškov and Miloš to the Yugoslav authorities

34 Mudd memo of 12 February 1947, Draganović CIC file, released under US FOIA, pp. 311–13

35 Draganović statement to Yugoslav authorities, 26 September 1967

36 'Memorandum on the Ustaša Organisation in Italy', enclosure in letter from Maclean to Wallinger, of 17 October 1947, PRO FO 371 67398; and 'Consolidated Interrogation Report on Dr Krunoslav Stepano Draganović', and memo of 26 November 1946, Draganović/ Pečnikar CIC file, obtained under US FOIA, pp. 41–6, 49

37 'Memorandum on the Ustaša Organisation in Italy', enclosure in letter from Maclean to Wallinger, of 17 October 1947, PRO FO 371 67398

38 Yugoslav note of 23 April 1947, PRO FO 371 67376; see also Yugoslav note of 7 November 1947, PRO FO 371 67400; Magjerec, *Hrvatski Zavod Sv. Jeronima u Rimu: Jubilejske Proslave (1453–1953)*, p. 133; and Manhattan, *Terror Over Yugoslavia*, p. 76

39 Note by Miss Jackson of 15 May 1947, PRO FO 371 67376; and enclosure to letter from Special Refugee Commission to Foreign Office, of 23 October 1947, PRO FO 371 67398

40 See for example, 'Consolidated Interrogation Report on Dr Krunoslav Stepano Draganović', Draganović/Pečnikar CIC file, obtained under US FOIA, pp. 41–6

41 Memo of 26 November 1946, Draganović/Pečnikar CIC file, obtained under US FOIA, p. 49

42 CIC memo of 10 October 1946, Draganović file, obtained under US FOIA, p. 54

43 For some details of Mandić's role in this propaganda campaign, see Paris, *Genocide in Satellite Croatia*, p. 260; Draganović statement to the Yugoslav authorities, 26 September 1967; evidence of Mimo Rosandić enclosed with the dispatch from the US Consulate in Zagreb, of 4 August 1948, USNA, RG 59, 860H.00/8-448

44 Ministry of Foreign Affairs memo of 2 November 1945, Ministry of Foreign Affairs Archives, 'Affari politici (Jugoslavia), 1946 Busta 1, fasciolo 3, Esponenti del cessato regime ustascia in Italia; and Ministry of Interior (Rome Police) report of 9 July 1946, attached to Ministry of Foreign Affairs memo of 30 July 1946, Ministry of Foreign Affairs Archives, 'Affari politici (Jugoslavia), 1948 Busta 33, fasciolo 3, Attivita' di jugoslavi contrari al regime di Tito in Italia

45 'Memorandum on the Ustaša Organisation in Italy', enclosure in letter from Maclean to Wallinger, of 17 October 1947, PRO FO 371 67398

46 Undated Italian Secret Service report, attached to Ministry of Foreign Affairs memo of 20 August 1944, Ministry of Foreign Affairs Archives, 'Affari politici (Jugoslavia), 1948 Busta 33, fasciolo 3, Attivita' di jugoslavi contrari di Tito in Italia

47 Interview with Simčić, Rome, 16 February 1990

48 Memo of 12 February 1947, Draganović/Pečnikar CIC file, obtained under US FOIA, pp. 38–40

49 Interview with Simčić, Rome, 16 February 1990

50 Memo of 12 February 1947, Draganović/Pečnikar CIC file, obtained under US FOIA, pp. 38–40

51 Telegram of 10 September 1947, Pavelić CIC file, obtained under US FOIA, p. 2

52 See Yugoslav note to the Foreign Office of 25 July 1946, and Foreign Office reply of 15 August 1946, PRO FO 371 59415. Also see Yugoslav note to the State Department of 15 August 1946, USNA, RG 59, 860H.00/8-1546

53 'Yugoslav Quislings and Possible War Criminals at Terni', PRO FO 371 59400

54 See note from British Embassy, Washington, to Foreign Office, of 20 June 1946, and Foreign Office note to the Yugoslav Embassy, London, of 2 July 1946, PRO FO 371 59412. Also see the Yugoslavs' earlier note of 11 May 1946, PRO FO 371 59406, for further details, and for Colville's and Jackson's comments of 14 and 17 May 1946. Details of Toth's flight to Buenos Aires are found in the memo from Buenos Aires to Washington of 16 July 1947, USNA, RG 59, 860H.20235/7-2347, Microfilm, LM 76, Roll 12, Frames 3328–9. Colville's confession about allowing many Ustashi to avoid repatriation is in John Colville, *Footprints in Time*, Michael Russell, Salisbury, 1984, pp. 212–13

55 'Yugoslav Quislings and Possible War Criminals at Terni', PRO FO

371 59400; Telegrams of 8 and 11 September 1946 from A Branch GHQ CMF to rear 13 Corps, and from Caserta to Foreign Office, 13 September 1946, PRO FO 371 59418; and CIC memo of 3 November 1947, Vrančić file, obtained under US FOIA, p. 2

56 See Yugoslav note to the State Department of 19 August 1946, and State Department reply of 3 April 1947, USNA, RG 59, 860H.00/8-1946; letter from British Embassy, Washington, to State Department, of 18 September 1946, and State Department reply of 15 October 1946, USNA, RG 59, 740.00116EW/9-1846, and 860H.00/10-1546; Telegram from Washington to Leghorn of 3 June 1947, USNA, RG 59, 740.00116EW/5-2747; and letters from Foreign Office to Vienna and Caserta, 17 August 1946, PRO FO 371 59415

57 Memo of 5 November 1946, Draganović/Pečnikar CIC file, obtained under US FOIA, pp. 53–4

58 Memo of 5 September 1947, Draganović CIC file, obtained under US FOIA, pp. 307–10

59 *Ibid.*

60 *Ibid.*

61 Memo of 12 February 1947, Draganović/Pečnikar CIC file, obtained under US FOIA, pp. 38–40

62 Interview with Karlo Dragutin Petranović, Niagara Falls, Canada, 17 June 1989

63 *Ibid.*

64 Yugoslav note of 21 July 1947, PRO FO 371 67386

65 *Ibid.*

66 As quoted in Manhattan, *Terror Over Yugoslavia*, p. 77

67 Interview with Karlo Dragutin Petranović, Niagara Falls, Canada, 17 June 1989

68 *Ibid.*

69 Telegram from Rome to Caserta, of 25 February 1947, PRO FO 371 67372

70 Foreign Office letter to the Screening Mission, Klagenfurt, of 14 August 1947, PRO FO 371 67386; G-2 memo of 16 January 1947, Ustashi CIC file, obtained under US FOIA, p. 47; letter from Caserta to Foreign Office, 26 February 1947, PRO FO 371 67372; 'Memorandum on the Ustaša Organisation in Italy', attached to letter from Maclean to Foreign Office, 17 October 1947, PRO FO 371 67398; and telegram from Leghorn to the State Department, USNA, RG 319. For further examples of the Genoa operation, see letter from Maclean to Foreign Office of 16 May 1947, from Foreign Office to Klagenfurt of 30 July 1947, Yugoslav notes to the Foreign Office of 15 July and 3 September 1947, letter from Klagenfurt to Foreign Office of 29 September 1947, PRO FO 371 67378, 67384, 67385, 67392 and 67393; and telegram from Leghorn to State Department, of 22 May 1947, USNA, RG 59, 740.00116EW/5-2147

71 Central Intelligence Group report of 21 January 1947, USNA, RG 59, 840.5510/1-2447

72 Interview with Karlo Dragutin Petranović, Niagara Falls, Canada, 17 June 1989
73 Stephen Clissold, unpublished manuscript; and Telegram from Rome to Foreign Office of 22 February 1947, PRO FO 371 67372
74 Clissold, unpublished manuscript
75 Interview with Karlo Dragutin Petranović, Nigara Falls, Canada, 17 June 1989
76 Clissold, unpublished manuscript
77 For a few of the many documents dealing with this operation, see telegrams from Leghorn to State Department, of 7 June 1947, and State Department to Leghorn, of 12 June 1947, USNA, RG 319; and telegrams of 12 and 25 June 1947, from Belgrade to State Department, USNA, RG 59, 740.00116EW/6-1147 and 740.00116EW/6-2547
78 'The Legal Position of Croatian War Criminals in Italy', 19 May 1947, enclosed with letter from Rome to State Department, of 28 May 1947, USNA, RG 59, 740.00116EW/5-2847
79 *Ibid.*
80 One account of Miloš's crimes is found in Zdenko Löwenthal (ed.), *The Crimes of the Fascist Occupants and their Collaborators against Jews in Yugoslavia*, Federation of Jewish Communities of the Federative People's Republic of Yugoslavia, Belgrade, 1957, p. 17
81 Draganović statement to the Yugoslav authorities, 26 September 1967
82 *Ibid.*
83 See CIC memo of 10 October 1946, Draganović file, obtained under US FOIA, p. 54; and letter from Caserta to Foreign Office, of 2 November 1946, PRO FO 371 57729
84 'Memorandum on the Ustaša Organisation in Italy', enclosure in letter from Maclean to Wallinger, of 17 October 1947, PRO FO 371 67398; and statements of Mimo Rosandić, Branko Kuštro, Ivica Gržeta, Julijo Spalj and Vladko Hranilović to the Yugoslav authorities
85 Article in *La Repubblica*, 26 September 1948, Ministry of Foreign Affairs Archives, 1948 Busta 33, fasciolo 2, Processo di Zagrabia
86 Interview with Karlo Dragutin Petranović, Niagara Falls, Canada, 17 June 1989; and with Vilim Cecelja, Maria Pline, 23 May 1989
87 Interview with Simčić, Rome, 5 May 1989 and 16 February 1990
88 Interview with a former British military intelligence officer, recorded on the condition that it would not be attributed, London, 5 May 1989
89 Interview with Simčić, Rome, 16 February 1990
90 Interview with a former British military intelligence officer, recorded on the condition that it would not be attributed, London, 5 May 1989
91 Perowne letter of 18 November 1947, and Wallinger reply of 5 December 1947, PRO FO 371 67402
92 Interviews with Simčić, Rome, 12 May 1989 and 16 February 1990
93 Interview with Simčić, Rome, 16 February 1990
94 Interviews with Simčić, Rome 12 May 1989 and 16 February 1990

95 Interview with Vilim Cecelja, Maria Pline, 23 May 1989; interviews
with Simčić, Rome, 12 May 1989 and 16 February 1990; Telegram
from COMGENUSFA (Rear) Salzburg, Austria from PAGBI, to
Department of the Army for CSGID for DISC, of 13 December
1949, USNA, RG 319, Records of the Army Staff, Box 135; and
statement by Božidar Kavran to the Yugoslav authorities

96 See Draganović letter of 5 March 1946, and also the French version
of the same material, PRO FO 800 476

97 Note of 27 March 1946, USNA, Myron Taylor Papers, Box 21; and
PRO WO 204 11133

98 'Memorandum on the Ustaša Organisation in Italy', enclosure in
letter from Maclean to Wallinger, 17 October 1947, PRO FO 371
67398; Italian Foreign Affairs Ministry letter to US Ambassador,
Rome, 7 July 1945, and Memorandum for the Allied Commission 29
July 1945, USNA, RG 331, Allied Control Commission, Executive
Commissioners, 10000/109/319, Box 9; and Clissold, unpublished
manuscript

99 Interview with Simčić, Rome, 16 February 1990

100 CIC Index Card, of 7 February, Draganović file, obtained under
US FOIA, p. 66; and interviews with Omrčanin by the *Religious
News Service*, May 1986 and John Loftus, 1985

101 'Memorandum on the Ustaša Organisation in Italy', enclosure in
letter from Maclean to Wallinger, of 17 October 1947, PRO FO 371
67398

102 CIC memo of 10 October 1946, Draganović file, obtained under US
FOIA, p. 54. On Father Mandić see Alexander, *The Triple Myth*,
p. 94; and Paris, *Genocide in Satellite Croatia*, p. 260

6 The Golden Priest

1 Detailed accounts of the trial can be found in US State Department
telegrams and memos, 16 July 1948 from Zagreb to Washington,
USNA, RG 59, 860H.00/7-1648, 19 July 1948, from Zagreb to
Washington, USNA, RG 59, 860H.00/7-1948, 2 August 1948, from
Belgrade to Washington, USNA, RG 59, 860H.00/8-248, 30 July
and 4 August 1948, from Zagreb to Washington, USNA, RG 59,
860H.00/8-448, 30 September 1948, from Zagreb to Washington,
USNA, RG 59, 860H.00/9-3048; and British Foreign Office reports
and memo of 10 September 1948, PRO FO 371 72563E

2 'Annual Report for 1945', from the British Legation to the Holy See,
to the Foreign Office, of 22 February 1946, PRO FO 371 60803

3 Report of trial in the Communist newspaper, *Borba*, as recounted in
US State Department telegram of 2 August 1948, from Belgrade to
Washington, USNA, RG 59, 860H.00/8-248; and letters from British
Embassy, Belgrade, to Foreign Office, 2 January and 20 March
1946, PRO FO 371 59399 and 59403

4 See accounts of the evidence of Adam Miličević, Mimo Rosandić

and Božidar Petračić, in US State Department memo of 30 July, enclosed in despach of 4 August 1948, from Zagreb to Washington, USNA, RG 59, 860H.00/8-448

5 See attachments 2 and 6 to US State Department memo of 30 July, enclosed in despatch of 4 August 1948, from Zagreb to Washington, USNA, RG 59, 860H.00/8-448

6 British Foreign Office reports and memo of 10 September 1948, PRO FO 371 72563E

7 Gowen memo of 29 August 1947, Pavelić CIC file, released under US FOIA, pp. 2–6

8 Statement of Mimo Rosandić to the Yugoslav authorities; and Clissold, unpublished manuscript

9 Gowen memo of 29 August 1947, Pavelić CIC file, released under US FOIA, pp. 2–6

10 Statement by Draganović to Yugoslav authorities, 26 September 1967

11 *Ibid.*

12 Statement by Draganović to Yugoslav authorities, 26 September 1967. For some details of Pečnikar's role in the Križari network, see 'Memorandum on the Ustaša Organisation in Italy', enclosure in letter from Maclean to Wallinger, of 17 October 1947, PRO FO 371 67398; and memoranda on the Križari intelligence organisation, TISSO, especially the Browning memo of 11 June 1947, Ustashi CIC file, released under US FOIA, pp. 89–113

13 Interviews with Simčić, Rome, 12 May 1989 and 16 February 1990

14 Draganović statement to the Yugoslav authorities, 26 September 1967

15 *Ibid.*

16 As quoted in Alexander, *Church and State in Yugoslavia since 1945*, p. 28, and *The Triple Myth*, p. 76; and Draganović statement to the Yugoslav authorities, 26 September 1967

17 Draganović statement to the Yugoslav authorities, 26 September 1967; and Simčić interview, Rome, 16 February 1990

18 A comprehensive account of this is found in the US Military Intelligence Service in Austria 'Special Investigation and Interrogation' report of 9 April 1946, dealing with 'The Croatian National Independence Movement', CIC file on the Ustashi, released under US FOIA, pp. 10–30

19 Interview with a former British military intelligence officer, recorded on the condition that it would not be attributed, London, 5 May 1989

20 Radell report of 4 April 1950, CIC file on the Ustashi, released under US FOIA, pp. 1–5

21 Interrogation of Ljubo Miloš, as reported in Attachment number 6 to US State Department report of 4 August 1948, from Zagreb to Washington, USNA, RG 59, 860H.00/8-448; Harrington CIC memo of 9 March 1948, 'Activity of Bishops Rožman and Šarić', released under US FOIA

22 Italian Ministry of Foreign Affairs report of 28 June 1945, Ministry of Foreign Affairs Archives, 1946 Busta 1, fasciolo 3, Esponenti del cessato regime ustascia in Italia

23 Italian Ministry of Foreign Affairs report of 23 July 1945, Ministry of Foreign Affairs Archives, 1946 Busta 1, fasciolo 3, Esponenti del cessato regime ustascia in Italia; and Gowen memo of 29 August 1947, Pavelić CIC file, released under US FOIA, pp. 2–6

24 Murdoch report of 25 September 1947, Križari CIC file, released under US FOIA, p. 6

25 Madewski report of 12 September 1946, CIC file on the Križari, released under US FOIA, pp. 38–9

26 Radoulovitch report of 23 July 1947, Ustashi CIC file, released under US FOIA, pp. 12–13

27 Radell reports of 18 November 1949, and 4 April 1950, CIC files on the Ustashi, released under US FOIA, p. 2 and pp. 1–5

28 Radoulovitch report of 23 July 1947, CIC Ustashi file released under US FOIA, pp. 12–13

29 Undated Italian Secret Service report, attached to Ministry of Foreign Affairs memo of 20 August 1944, Ministry of Foreign Affairs Archives, 'Affari politici (Jugoslavia), 1948 Busta 33 fasciolo 3, Attivita' di jugoslavi contrari di Tito in Italia

30 Report on 'Yugoslav personalities in Rome', of 20 July 1945, USNA, RG 226, Records of the Office of Strategic Services, 139960

31 Italian Secret Service report of 18 April 1946, Ministry of Foreign Affairs Archives, 1946 Busta 1, fasciolo 1, Rapporti politici

32 See, for example, Gettigan report of 24 May 1947, CIC Križari file, released under US FOIA, pp. 23–4

33 Interrogation report of Franc Južina, Gettigan report of 15 June 1947, CIC Križari file, released under US FOIA, pp. 14–18

34 Interview with Yugoslavian historian, Franček Saje, 1 April 1979

35 For a contemporary report of the Homeguard's atrocities see American Military Intelligence Division report of 19 February 1944, USNA, RG 226, Records of the Office of Strategic Services, 63632

36 Note from Yugoslav Ambassador in London, to British Secretary of State for Foreign Affairs, of 15 November 1945, PRO FO 371 48893

37 Letter from London to UK Embassy, Washington, of 28 November 1945, PRO FO 371 48893

38 Report of 8 February 1945, USNA, RG 226, Records of the Office of Strategic Services, 113566

39 Letter from Vatican Secretariat of State to Franklin Gowen at the Vatican, of 19 February 1946, USNA, Myron Taylor Papers, Box 21; handwritten note of 16 July 1945, PRO FO 371 48890; and telegram from the British Legation to the Holy See, to the Foreign Office, of 23 February 1946, PRO FO 371 59401

40 Telegram from Carmel Offie at Caserta, to Tittman at the Vatican, of 22 July 1945, USNA, Myron Taylor Papers, Box 29; and statement by Draganović to Yugoslav authorities, 26 September 1967

41 Note by John Colville, of 27 February 1946, PRO FO 371 59401; and letter from Washington to Foreign Office, of 25 January 1946, PRO FO 371 59400

42 Handwritten note on the cover of memo to the Secretary of State, of 29 December 1945, USNA, RG 59, 740.00116 EW/12-2945; and telegram from Washington to Caserta, of 21 February 1946, USNA, RG 59, 740.00116 CONTROL/2-2146

43 Memo by Krek, attached to letter from Stokes to the Foreign Office, 5 August 1947, PRO FO 371 67388

44 Letter from Somerlocks to Foreign Office, 8 November 1947, PRO FO 371 67402

45 *Ibid.*

46 *Ibid.*

47 Handwritten note by Christopher Warner, of 11 December 1947, PRO FO 371 67406

48 Letter from the British Legation, Vienna, to the Foreign Office, 23 January 1948; and handwritten note on its cover, PRO FO 371 72559

49 Draganović statement to Yugoslav authorities, 26 September 1967; and article in *La Repubblica*, 24 September 1948, Ministry of Foreign Affairs Archives, 1948 Busta 33, fasciolo 2, Processo di Zagrabia

50 Harrington CIC memo of 9 March 1948, 'Activity of Bishops Rožman and Šarić', released under US FOIA

51 Harrington CIC memo of 9 March 1948, 'Activity of Bishops Rožman and Šarić', released under US FOIA; Airgram from Berne to State Department, USNA, Myron Taylor Papers, Box 21; letter from Washington to Foreign Office, 1 July 1948, PRO FO 371 72563C; and Magjerec, *Hrvatski Zavod Sv. Jeronima u Rimu*, p. 188

52 Thomas memo of 17 May 1947, Križari CIC file, released under US FOIA, pp. 29–30

53 *Ibid.*

54 Gettigan memo of 1 July 1947, Križari CIC file, released under US FOIA, pp. 8–10

55 *Ibid.*

56 Interview with a former British military intelligence officer, recorded on the condition that it would not be attributed, London, 5 May 1989

57 Alexander, *The Triple Myth*, pp. 40–5; and interview with a former British military intelligence officer, recorded on the condition that it would not be attributed, London, 5 May 1989

58 Interview with a former British military intelligence officer, recorded on the condition that it would not be attributed, London, 5 May 1989

59 Report of 25 April 1947, Križari CIC file, released under US FOIA, pp. 34–5

60 *Ibid.*

61 British Foreign Office reports and memo of 10 September 1948, PRO FO 371 72563E

62 For details of Rover's wartime career, see Aarons, *Sanctuary! Nazi Fugitives in Australia*, pp. 219–20

63 Most of the details of Rover's activities in the Križari are taken from the official Yugoslav interrogation reports of Božidar Kavran and related documents, held at the High Court in Zagreb. See also, Aarons, *Sanctuary!*, pp. 220–4 for further details

64 Milovanovich *et al.* report of 11 December 1947, Ustashi CIC file, released under US FOIA, pp. 32–3
65 Radell report of 18 November 1949, CIC file on the Ustashi, released under US FOIA, p. 2. A further US intelligence account of continuing military operations is contained in a 12 January 1951 Biddle report, Ustashi CIC file, released under US FOIA, pp. 81–2. Reports of trials mentioning Draganović and the Križari can be found in a 25 February 1960 State Department Intelligence Report, USNA, RG 59; and translation of *Borba* article of 19 March 1960, Draganović CIC file, released under US FOIA, pp. 37–43
66 Golden report of 9 February 1948, Ustashi CIC file, released under US FOIA, p. 97; and report of 17 October 1947, USNA, RG 319, Investigative Records Repository, Pavelić dossier, XE 001109

7 The Vatican's Black Orchestra

1 *Oslobodjenje*, 16 November 1967; and Sarajevo's *Svijet*, series of articles on Draganović, by Siniša Ivanović and Kršto Leković, published weekly from 13 June to 19 September 1986
2 *Vjesnik*, 12 November 1967
3 *Oslobodjenje*, 16 November 1967
4 Interview with Milan Simčić, Rome, 2 February 1990
5 *Ibid.*
6 Sarajevo's *Svijet*, series of articles on Draganović, by Siniša Ivanović and Kršto Leković, published weekly from 13 June to 19 September 1986
7 *Ibid.*
8 *Ibid.*
9 Interview with a former British intelligence officer, given on the understanding that it would not be attributed, London, 5 May 1989
10 Interview with Milan Simčić, Rome, 2 February 1990
11 Ibid.; some details on Varoš can be found in Magjerec, *Hrvatski Zavod Sv. Jeronima u Rimu*, pp. 174, 211
12 Sarajevo's *Svijet*, series of articles on Draganović, by Siniša Ivanović and Kršto Leković, published weekly from 13 June to 19 September 1986
13 Interview with Milan Simčić, Rome, 2 February 1990
14 Interview with a former British intelligence officer, given on the understanding that it would not be attributed, London, 5 May 1989
15 Interview with Milan Simčić, Rome, 2 February 1990
16 *Oslobodjenje*, 16 November 1967
17 *Vjesnik*, 12 and 21 November 1967
18 *Ibid.*, 21 November 1967
19 Alexander, *Church and State in Yugoslavia since 1945*, footnote, pp. 238–9
20 Interview with Milan Simčić, Rome, 2 February 1990
21 Accounts of these trials can be found in State Department 'Intelligence Report', number 8230, of 25 February 1960, USNA, RG

59; Yugoslav press digest, reporting *Politika*, 17, 18 and 19 March 1960, Draganović CIC file, declassified under US FOIA, pp. 37–43; and Alexander, *Church and State in Yugoslavia since 1945*, pp. 239–40

22 Alexander, *Church and State in Yugoslavia since 1945*, p. 239

23 Interview with Vilim Cecelja, Maria Pline, 23 May 1989

24 Sarajevo's *Svijet*, series of articles on Draganović, by Siniša Ivanović and Kršto Leković, published weekly from 13 June to 19 September 1986

25 A detailed account of these developments is found in Alexander, *Church and State in Yugoslavia since 1945*, pp. 226–48

26 *Vjesnik*, 12 November 1967

27 Sarajevo's *Svijet*, series of aricles on Draganović, by Siniša Ivanović and Kršto Leković, published weekly from 13 June to 19 September 1986

28 Draganović statement to Yugoslav authorities, Sarajevo, 26 September 1967

29 Sarajevo's Svijet series of articles on Draganović, by Siniša Ivanović and Kršto Leković, published weekly from 13 June to 19 September 1986

30 Draganović statement to Yugoslav authorities, Sarajevo, 26 September 1967

31 Sarajevo's *Svijet*, series of articles on Draganović, by Siniša Ivanović and Kršto Leković, published weekly from 13 June to 19 September 1986

32 Richard Deacon, *A History of British Secret Service*, Granada, London, 1969, p. 297 (Czarist *agent provocateur* tactics copied by Bolsheviks); David Dallin, *Soviet Espionage*, Yale University. Press, New Haven, 1956, pp. 1–9; David Wise and Thomas B. Ross, *The Espionage Establishment*, Bantam, London/New York, 1968, pp. 35–64; John Barron, *KGB*, Bantam, London/New York, 1979, pp. 457–65 (on origins of Soviet intelligence services). For a comparison of Czarist and Communist organs see Ronald Hingley, *The Russian Secret Police: Muscovite Imperial Russian and Soviet Political Security Operations 1556–1970*, Simon & Schuster, New York, 1970

33 Deacon, *A History of British Secret Service*, pp. 297–304

34 Thomas Powers, *The Man Who Kept the Secrets: Richard Helms and the CIA*, Pocket Books, New York, 1981, pp. 48–52

35 CIC Agent Report, Refugee Relief Act, 'Turkul, Anton', dated 22 August 1956, found in USNA, RG 319, Box 303, Investigative Records Repository, CIC File XE 001758, TURKUL, Anton, hereinafter cited as 'T/1249'. Because of the fragility of the Turkul files in the US National Archives, the three voluminous dossiers in which this document appears were not yet available for photocopying, and cites are given to our tape recorder serial numbers in order to provide a relative guide to the sequence in which the Turkul documents appear. For example, 'Military Entry Permit, 17 July 1946, T/001,' indicates that this document can be found among the

earlier 1946 documents while the Refugee Relief Act Report of 22
August 1956, T/1249, can be found among the later entries in the file.
Since the three volumes of Turkul dossiers appear to be arranged in
reverse chronological order, researchers are cautioned to begin with
what is labeled as Box III, and proceed through Box II to Box I in
order to preserve the chronological sequence of our tape-recorded
index

36 In addition to the Turkul files in the US National Archives, the
authors received additional pages which were previously withheld
from declassification. Undated CIC index card 'Turkul, Anton; Born:
Bessarabia 2/12/1892' found on p. 3 of the INSCOM, USAIRR
dossier for 'Anton Turkel', released under US FOIA 16 April 1990.
The very next card on the same page lists Turkul's birthdate as '11
Dec 92 – Odessa, Russia'. Nineteenth-century Russian birthdates are
often misleading because of the subsequent change of calendar
systems. It is also possible that Turkul himself gave different
birthdates in order to hinder Western background checks.

37 CIC Agent Report, Refugee Relief Act, dated 22 August 1956, p. 1,
T/1249

38 Special Interrogation Report on Kauder, aka Klatt, MISC-USFET
Counter Intelligence, undated, circa 1947, T/363, continuing at T/
1000-60

39 Anthony Cave Brown, *'C': The Secret Life of Sir Stewart Menzies,
Spymaster to Winston Churchill*, Macmillan, New York, 1987, pp. 143–4.
Turkul's CIC file equates General Wrangel's 'Russian Officers
Committee' with 'ROWS'. Depending on the transliteration method
used ROWS stands for 'Ruski Obtshe Wojennyi Sojuz' or 'Ruski
Obtshe Vojenski Soiuz' (Russian Common Military Union). General
Kutepov's 'Combat Organization' of front line veterans is described
in Turkul's CIC file as the 'Verbander Frontksemper' or the
'Verband der Frontkaempfer' (Union of Front Line Fighters). CIC
Agent Report, Refugee Relief Act, dated 22 August 1956, p. 1, T/
1249; MISC USFET CI Special Interrogation Report on Kauder, aka
Klatt, undated series of reports, circa 1947, T/369

40 Cave Brown, *'C': The Secret Life of Sir Stewart Menzies*, pp. 142–3; Top
Secret Interrogation of Claudius Voss, alias Alexandrov, 20 March
1947, T/1167-78

41 Top Secret Interrogation of Claudius Voss, alias Alexandrov, 20
March 1947 (unsourced, apparently prepared by SCI-A), T/1178

42 CIC Index Card, undated, T/039; Special Interrogation Report on
Kauder, Richard, aka Klatt, MISC-USFET CI, undated, T/369-70

43 Top Secret Interrogation of Claudius Voss, alias Alexandrov, 20
March 1947, T/1167-84 (unsourced, apparently prepared by SCI-A)

44 Professor Ryle and Mr Johnson, 'The Turkul Organization and the
MAX/Moritz Messages', hereinafter cited as the 'Ryle-Johnson
Report', undated, T/178-88, 218

45 Ryle-Johnson Report, undated, T/218-29; Interrogation of Claudius
Alexandrovich Voss, 30 December 1947, T/1113–23

46 Interrogation of Claudius Alexandrovich Voss, 30 December 1947, T/
1110-36
47 Agent Report, Refugee Relief Act, dated 22 August 1956, p. 2, T/1249
48 For example, the Communists had clearly penetrated ROWS even
before NTS was formed. Ryle-Johnson Report, undated, at T/164-94
and T/200-28; note also the Communist agent Voss's admission that
he was an 'active participant' in the founding of NTS which then
denounced its parent group, ROWS, as a 'Bolshevist Front
Organization'. Interrogation of Claudius Alexandrovich Voss, 30
December 1947, T/1110-24
49 Jonathan Bloch and Patrick Fitzgerald, *British Intelligence and Covert
Action*, Brandon, Dublin, 1983, p. 33
50 External Research Paper, Series 3, No. 76, *NTS – The Russian Solidarist
Movement*, Office of Intelligence and Research, US State Department,
10 December 1951, released under US FOIA
51 Cave Brown, *'C': The Secret Life of Sir Stewart Menzies*, p. 143; for
Russian *émigré* politics in the pre-World War II period see Geoffrey
Bailey, *The Conspirators*, Harper, New York, 1960
52 CIC Agent Report, Refugee Relief Act, dated 22 August 1956, with
biographical appendix, T/1249
53 CIC Report, Rome Detachment, 23 June 1947, Subject Intermarium,
released under US FOIA
54 *Ibid.*
55 Ryle-Johnson Report, T/222–8, surmising that Voss arranged for
Turkul to come to Paris and take over the anti-Communist leadership
'without the mud of ROWS'.
56 The best work on such ethnographic distinctions is Nicholas Vakar,
Belorussia: The Making of a Nation, Harvard University Press, Harvard,
Cambridge, 1956
57 CIC Consolidated Orientation and Guidance Report, 1948, Par.
184g, 189, cited in Loftus, *The Belarus Secret*, Ch. 4, n. 11
58 The details of Turkul's liaisons wih other *émigré* factions are set forth
throughout his voluminous CIC dossier such as the Ryle-Johnson
Report's discussion of the Ljotić and Mihailović contacts at T/145–8.
However, we wish to acknowledge the assistance of a former CIC
officer who helped place these convoluted issues in perspective.
Confidential Interviews, 1988–90. For background on the
Abramtchik Faction, see Loftus, *The Belarus Secret*, pp. 37–44
59 Cave Brown, *'C': The Secret Life of Sir Stewart Menzies*, pp. 142–3,
quoting CIA estimate; see also CIC File 'Operation Circle' on the
origins of Intermarium, and Loftus, *The Belarus Secret*, pp. 49, on
French involvement with Prometheus
60 Turkul's CIC Index Cards contain an original of a German card file
showing Turkul's Paris address in 1927, T/046
61 Anthony Cave Brown, *Bodyguard of Lies*, Star, London, 1977,
pp. 145–6
62 *Ibid.*, p. 140

63 William Stevenson, *Intrepid's Last Case*, Villard, New York, 1983, p. 281

64 Compare Cave Brown's and Stevenson's accounts on this point

65 John Costello, *Mask of Treachery*, Morrow, New York, 1988, pp. 351, 384

66 Undated summary of previous CIC reports, T1/1017

67 Ryle-Johnson Report, undated, T1/164-78

68 Ladislas Farago, *Burn After Reading*, Walker & Co., New York, 1961, pp. 116–17

69 Farago, *Burn After Reading*, pp. 114–16

70 CIC Agent Report, Refugee Relief Act, dated 22 August 1956, T/1249

71 Walter Schellenberg, *The Labyrinth*, Harper, New York, 1956, p. 237

72 *Ibid.*, pp. 237–9

73 Schellenberg Interrogation by British Intelligence, circa 1945, declassified copy provided courtesy John Taylor, Modern Military Branch, USNA. Schellenberg's memoirs were published in 1956 but Turkul's NTS continued to work for British Intelligence until the 1960s. Bloch and Fitzgerald, *British Intelligence and Covert Action*, p. 33

74 Cave Brown, *Bodyguard of Lies*, p. 263

75 MISC USFET Interrogation, circa 1946, Turkul, Anton, T/1234

76 Schellenberg, *The Labyrinth*, p. 160

77 Compare Farago, *Burn After Reading*, p. 117 (identifying Sorge as Klatt's Japanese contact) with CIC Summary of Previous Reports, undated (Turkul suspected Soviet agent working for the Japanese), T/1017

78 Schellenberg, *The Labyrinth*, p. 263

79 Cave Brown, *Bodyguard of Lies*, p. 175

80 Cave Brown, *'C': The Secret Life of Sir Stewart Menzies*, pp. 211–12

81 Cave Brown, *Bodyguard of Lies*, p. 178

82 Special Interrogation Report on Kauder, aka Klatt, undated, circa 1946, MISC-USFET Counter Intelligence, T/363–80 (Turkul moved to Rome in 1939)

83 Cave Brown, *Bodyguard of Lies*, p. 181

84 *Ibid.*, p. 182

85 It has been suggested that Stalin himself wished to keep Hitler alive during 1939–41 in the vain hope that his Western opponents might destroy themselves in a bloody repetition of World War I. Stalin's pre-war support of Hitler might also explain the ruthless post-war persecution of those Soviet Red Orchestra agents who had warned Stalin of Hitler's betrayal. See for example, Leopold Trepper, *The Great Game*, McGraw-Hill, New York, 1977, p. 378

86 Cave Brown, *Bodyguard of Lies*, p. 148; Schellenberg, *The Labyrinth*, p. 277

87 Cave Brown, *Bodyguard of Lies*, pp. 184–5

88 *Ibid.*, p. 184

89 Chadwick, *Britain and the Vatican during the Second World War*, p. 87

90 Schellenberg, *The Labyrinth*, pp. 68–80

91 Cave Brown, *Bodyguard of Lies*, p. 192

92 *Ibid.*, pp. 192–4

93 Schellenberg, *The Labyrinth*, pp. 349–51; Cave Brown, *Bodyguard of Lies*, pp. 195–8

94 Cave Brown, *Bodyguard of Lies*, p. 206

95 CIC Agent Report, Refugee Relief Act, dated 22 August 1956, p. 1, T/1249

96 Special Interrogation Report on Kauder, aka Klatt, MISC-USFET Counter Intelligence, undated, T/363

97 This is the famous 'Russicum' recently depicted in the espionage film *The Third Solution*. The origins of the missionary work into Russia are described in Chapter One

98 Schellenberg, *The Labyrinth*, pp. 125–30

99 *Ibid.*, pp. 134–5

100 Chadwick, *Britain and the Vatican during the Second World War*, pp. 88–9

101 Cave Brown, *'C': The Secret Life of Sir Stewart Menzies*, pp. 284–5

102 Farago, *Burn After Reading*, p. 117

103 Special Interrogation Report on Kauder, aka Klatt, MISC-USFET Counter Intelligence, undated, T/1005

104 Schellenberg, *The Labyrinth*, pp. 158, 193, 355, 359

105 *Ibid.*, pp. 235, 241

106 *Ibid.*, pp. 239–44

107 Edwin Layton, Roger Pineau and John Costello, *And I was There*, Quill, New York, 1985, p. 178

108 'towers of the Kremlin . . .' Cave Brown, *Bodyguard of Lies*, p. 229. The Vatican–Black Orchestra connection indeed cost Hitler dearly. Shortly before D Day, he transferred his three best divisions from Normandy to the Balkans to put down a phantom invasion. Cave Brown, *Bodyguard of Lies*, pp. 443–54

109 CIC IRS, 'Die Schwarze Kapelle', 24 April 1952, declassified under US FOIA

110 Heinz Höhne and Hermann Zolling, *The General was a Spy*, Bantam, New York, 1972, p. 23 (Baun's Walli I network was incorporated directly into Gehlen's FHO)

111 *Ibid.*, p. 24

112 *Ibid.*, pp. 22–5

113 The Ryle-Johnson Report concluded that there was 'no doubt' that the network acted as a Soviet Trojan horse, T/105

114 Ryle-Johnson Report citing Summary of Wahl Interrogation, T/260–3

115 Schellenberg, *The Labyrinth*, p. 363

116 CIC Agent Report, Refugee Relief Act, dated 22 August 1956, pp. 1–2, T/1249

117 Ryle-Johnson Report, T/101–38

118 Schellenberg, *The Labyrinth*, pp. 161–4, 239–40, 253–6, 258

119 There are several good sources on the mystery of the Red Orchestra, the best of which is Heinz Höhne's *Codeword: 'Direktor'*, Secker &

Warburg, London, 1971. The US intelligence files are only beginning to be declassified but they reveal a complete ignorance of how the Eastern European GRU networks passed information. USAIRR CIC File, Red Orchestra, declassified under FOIA, January 1990. However there are intriguing references to a possible Vatican connection in the earlier works, notably in Alexander Foote's recollection that the Lucy ring operated under a Catholic publishing house and seemed to receive detailed German plans via diplomatic pouch. A. Foote, *Story of a Russian Spy*, formerly *Handbook for Spies*, Doubleday, New York, 1949. See also Leopold Trepper, *The Great Game*, McGraw-Hill, New York, 1977 for an intriguing account of yet another deception scheme, the 'Brown Orchestra' in which the Gestapo attempted to feed disinformation to the Soviets. With Turkul's ability to check the actual German troop dispositions, it is not surprising that the GRU failed to be taken in

120 The Ryle-Johnson Report is based upon voluminous interrogations of the members of the MAX network and includes a diagram of their wireless net. T/229–96. The only missing element in the communication system was the secret Vatican burst transmitter which was not revealed until 1956. Schellenberg, *The Labyrinth*, p. 363

121 Höhne and Zolling, *The General was a Spy*, p. 22. The best account of the Third Reich's *Untermensch* recruitment strategy was written by the fugitive war criminal SS Obersturmbannführer Friedrich Buchardt, which manuscript became the basis for Alexander Dallin's seminal work, *German Rule in Russia*, St Martin's Press, New York, 1957

122 Ryle-Johnson Report (American assessment), T/248–58

8 The Catholic Army of the Ukraine

1 Franz von Papen, *Memoirs*, Deutsch, London, 1952, p. 278, cited in Dallin, *German Rule in Russia*, p. 475, n.2

2 English translation quoted by Sereny, *Into That Darkness*, pp. 279–80

3 The best overview of Uniate history is probably the September 1942 report to the Foreign Office, by Thomas M. Parker, Librarian of Pusey House, Oxford, PRO FO 371/33434, *The Uniat Roman Catholic Churches*

4 English translation quoted by Sereny, *Into That Darkness*, pp. 279–80

5 *Ibid.*

6 *Ibid.*

7 The OUN version of these events is presented in John Armstrong's *Ukrainian Nationalism 1939–45*, Columbia University Press, New York, 1955. For a somewhat less biased account, see Dallin, *German Rule in Russia*, Chs VI, XXII, XXVIII

8 Simon Wiesenthal, *The Murderers Among Us: The Wiesenthal Memoirs*, McGraw-Hill, New York, 1967, p. 28

9 SS Obersturmbannführer Friedrich Buchardt, Unpublished Memoirs, *Die Behandlung des russischen Problems während der Zeit des national-sozialistischen Regimes in Deutschland*, Top Secret Sensitive Documents – Confidential Informant's Index, Office of the Army Chief of Staff for Intelligence, Vault 2, USNA, Suitland, Md.; Simpson, *Blowback*, pp. 164–5; Dallin, *German Rule in Russia*, Chs VI, XXII, XXVIII

10 English translation quoted by Sereny, *Into That Darkness*, pp. 279–80

11 *Ibid.*

12 September 1942 report to the Foreign Office, by Thomas M. Parker, Librarian of Pusey House, Oxford, PRO FO 371/33434, *The Uniat Roman Catholic Churches*

13 *Ibid.*

14 Lebed's and Grynioch's secret work for the SS was known only to a handful of insiders. SS Obersturmbannführer Friedrich Buchardt, Unpublished Memoirs, *Die Behandlung des russischen Problems während der Zeit des national-sozialistischen Regimes in Deutschland*, Top Secret Sensitive Documents – Confidential Informant's Index, Office of the Army Chief of Staff for Intelligence, Vault 2, USNA, Suitland, Md.; Dallin, *German Rule in Russia*, p. xix

15 Dallin, *German Rule in Russia*, p. 475, n.2

16 War Department, Special Report IDS 52, 7 October 1942, USNA, RG 226, Box 179, 23570, p. 3

17 *Ibid.*, p. 3 (Summary of Previous Reports)

18 *Ibid.*, p. 1

19 *Ibid.*

20 September 1942 report to the Foreign Office, by Thomas M. Parker, Librarian of Pusey House, Oxford, PRO, FO 371/33434, *The Uniat Roman Catholic Churches*, pp. 19–20, n.1

21 War Department, Special Report IDS 52, 7 October 1942, USNA, RG 226, Box 179, 23570, p. 1

22 *Ibid.*, p. 2

23 *Ibid.*

24 Dallin, *Russia Under German Rule*, p. 474, n.1

25 'Metropolitan Anastasia, Lodgensky and Turkul were the center of anticommunism in the event of a future war with Soviet Russia'. Klatt Interrogation Continued, undated report, T/1022-4

26 MI5 'Kel' report submited to 7707 CIC, 6 May 1947, T/1154. According to the British, Father Seraphim Ivanovich Rodianov was the former Chairman of the Karlowac exarchy and may have travelled to Moscow after the war

27 Dallin, *Russia Under German Rule*, p. 482, n.3

28 Interrogation of Father George Leonidov Romanov, 19-20 December 1946, T1/1053 and T/1069; Klatt Interrogation Continued, undated, T/1023-4; Interrogation of Claudius Alexandrovich Voss, 30 December 1947, T/1133-9

29 Dallin, *Russia Under German Rule*, p. 485, n.1

30 *Ibid.*, n.2

31 War Department, Special Report IDS 52, 7 October 1942, USNA, RG 226, Box 179, 23570, p. 1

32 War Department, Special Report IDS 66, 27 October 1942, USNA, RG 226, Box 179, p. 1

33 Sereny, *Into That Darkness*, pp. 141–2, 283–4, 298–9

34 War Department, Special Report IDS 66, 27 October 1942, USNA, RG 226, Box 179, p. 1

35 *Ibid.*; War Department, Special Report IDS 52, USNA, RG 226, Box 154, 22067, p. 1

36 Raul Hilberg, *The Destruction of European Jewry*, Quadrangle Books, New York, 1961, pp. 329–30; SS Obersturmbannführer Friedrich Buchardt, Unpublished Memoirs, *Die Behandlung des russischen Problems während der Zeit des national-sozialistischen Regimes in Deutschland*, Top Secret Sensitive Documents – Confidential Informant's Index, Office of the Army Chief of Staff for Intelligence, Vault 2, USNA, Suitland, Md.; Simpson, *Blowback*, p. 164; Dallin, *German Rule in Russia*, Chs VI, XXII, XXVIII

37 Wiesenthal, *The Murderers Among Us*, p. 275; Scott and Jon Lee Anderson, *Inside the League*, Dodd, Mead, New York, 1986, p. 25

38 See SS Obersturmbannführer Friedrich Buchardt, Unpublished Memoirs, *Die Behandlung des russischen Problems während der Zeit des national-sozialistischen Regimes in Deutschland*, Top Secret Sensitive Documents – Confidential Informant's Index, Office of the Army Chief of Staff for Intelligence, Vault 2, USNA, Suitland, Md.; Simpson, *Blowback*, p. 164; Dallin, *German Rule in Russia*, Chs VI, XXII, XXVIII

39 Dallin, *German Rule in Russia*, Chs VI, XXII, XXVIII

40 Andre Visson, 'Federation of Catholic Slavs Seen As Vatican's Post-War Goal', *New York Herald Tribune*, 11 February 1945, cited in War Department Special Report IDS 142, USNA, RG 226, Box 0277, 30348, pp. 1–2

41 September 1942 report to the Foreign Office, by Thomas M. Parker, Librarian of Pusey House, Oxford, PRO FO 371/33434, *The Uniat Roman Catholic Churches*, p. 19, para. 90

42 Visson, 'Federation of Catholic Slavs Seen As Vatican's Post-War Goal', *New York Herald Tribune*, 11 February 1945 cited in War Department Special Report IDS 142, USNA, RG 226, Box 0277, 30348, pp. 1–2

43 Dallin, *Russia Under German Rule*, pp. 490–1

44 Interrogation of Father George Leonidov Romonov, 19–20 December 1946, T/1053-69

45 September 1942 report to the Foreign Office, by Thomas M. Parker, Librarian of Pusey House, Oxford, PRO FO 371/33434, *The Uniat Roman Catholic Churches*, p. 20

46 *Ibid.*

47 *Ibid.*

48 Ryle-Johnson Report, T/164-72

49 Schellenberg, *The Labyrinth*, p. 263
50 Charles Whiting, *Gehlen's Master Spy*, Ballantine, New York, 1972, p. 41
51 Farago, *Burn After Reading*, p. 118
52 *Ibid.*
53 For a reasonably accurate background history, see Special Interrogation Report on Kauder aka Klatt, undated, MISC-USFET Counter Intelligence, T/356-390, continued at T/1000-07. A somewhat conflicting version can be found in David Kahn, *Hitler's Spies*, Arrow, London, 1980, pp. 298–303. Kahn's work is intriguing as it connects 'Fritz Kauders' and the MAX network to an American consul in Zagreb as well as to a 'Miss Beloševic of the embassy of the newly founded Croatian state'. This early link to the Ustashi may well have been the forerunner of Soviet penetration of the post-war Ratlines. For the handling of Jewish *Mischlinge*, see Abrams, *Special Treatment*, pp. 148–9
54 CIC Agent Report, Refugee Relief Act, dated 22 August 1956, T/1249, p. 2
55 Höhne and Zolling, *The General Was a Spy*, pp. 23–4
56 Stevenson, *Intrepid's Last Case*, p. 281
57 CIC Agent Report, Refugee Relief Act, dated 22 August 1956, T/1249, pp. 2–3
58 Compare the Ryle-Johnson Report at T/131-45 with Interrogation of Richard Klatt, undated, p. 13, T/1040-2
59 Ryle-Johnson Report, T/133-45
60 Chapman Pincher, *Too Secret Too Long*, St Martin's Press, New York, 1984, p. 441
61 Dallin, *Russia Under German Rule*, p. 256
62 Anderson, *Inside the League*, p. 25; SS Obersturmbannführer Friedrich Buchardt, Unpublished Memoirs, *Die Behandlung des russischen Problems während der Zeit des national-sozialistischen Regimes in Deutschland*, Top Secret Sensitive Documents – Confidential Informant's Index, Office of the Army Chief of Staff for Intelligence, Vault 2, USNA, Suitland, Md.; Simpson, *Blowback*, p. 164; Dallin, *German Rule in Russia*, Chs VI, XXII, XXVIII
63 *Ibid.; Ibid.; Ibid.*
64 Peter Potichny, *et al.*, *Political Thought of the Ukrainian Underground*, University of Toronto Press, Toronto, 1986, pp. 224–5, n.34
65 Interrogation of Claudius Alexandrovich Voss, 30 December 1947, T/1110-1125
66 Dallin, *German Rule in Russia*, Chs VI, XXII, XXVIII, especially pp. 620–53
67 *Ibid.*
68 Memorandum, Ukrainian 'Divisia Halychyna', (Ukrainian POW in Great Britain), undated, PRO FO 371/71636, p. 3
69 Dallin, *Russia Under German Rule*, p. 525, n.4
70 Ryle-Johnson Report, T/340-5

9 Diplomacy and Deceit

1 Hilberg, *The Destruction of European Jewry*, pp. 329–30; SS Obersturmbannführer Friedrich Buchardt, Unpublished Memoirs, *Die Behandlung des russischen Problems während der Zeit des national- sozialistischen Regimes in Deutschland*, Top Secret Sensitive Documents – Confidential Informant's Index, Office of the Army Chief of Staff for Intelligence, Vault 2, USNA, Suitland, Md.; Simpson, *Blowback*, p. 164; Dallin, *German Rule in Russia*, Chs VI, XXII, XXVIII

2 Memorandum, Ukrainian 'Divisia Halychyna' (Ukrainian POW in Great Britain), PRO FO371/71636, p. 3

3 Refugee Screening Commission. Report on Ukrainians in SEP Camp No. 374 Italy, 21 February 1947, PRO FO 371/66605, p. 2; Memorandum, Ukrainian 'Divisia Halychyna', (Ukrainian POW in Great Britain), PRO FO 371/71636, p. 3

4 Simpson, *Blowback*, p. 180n

5 Airgram, Confidential Files, Secretary of State, 6 July 1945 USNA, RG 59, Box 291

6 Apparently, the Foreign Office was the only Allied institution not to recognise the incriminating character of this mark. See RAE Minute to N7588, 6 July 1948, PRO FO 371/71663

7 Letter, 3 July 1948, enclosure to N7588, 6 July 1948, PRO FO 371/ 71663

8 Note Verbale, 27 August 1945, USNA, Myron Taylor Papers, Box 8/ 800

9 *Ibid.*

10 *Ibid.*

11 'these men are really having the best of both worlds'. Report, Refugee Screening Commission, PRO, FO 371/66605, p. 6

12 Letter No. 1423, Bishop's Chancery Office, 25 August 1945, USNA, RG 59, Box 4112, p. 1

13 The best history of the Allied deportations is Nikolai Tolstoy, *The Secret Betrayal*, Charles Scribner, New York, 1978. For a discussion of the Babi Yar massacre, see Hilberg, *The Destruction of European Jewry*, pp. 329–30

14 Letter of 12 October 1945, USNA RG 59, 800.4016 DP/9-145

15 Tolstoy, *The Secret Betrayal*

16 Enclosure No. 3 to State Department Decimal File 840.48 REFUGEES/12-145 (0358), USNA, RG 59

17 Tolstoy, *The Secret Betrayal*

18 Vatican Correspondence of 19 December 1945, USNA, RG 59, 800.4016DP/12-2045

19 *Ibid.*

20 Letter, 5 March 1946, PRO FO 945/575

21 Vatican Correspondence, 30 March 1945, USNA, RG 59, 840.48 REFUGEES/3-3046, pp. 1061–2

22 Response to Vatican Correspondence, 30 March 1945, USNA, RG

59, 840.48 REFUGEES/3-3046, p. 1063. However, not all of the forces who fought with Vlasov were lily white. See Simpson, *Blowback*, p. 20

23 Letter, 25 June 1946, Ukrainian-American League, USNA, RG 59, 800.4010 DP/6-2546

24 8 July 1946 Response to Letter of 25 June 1946, Ukrainian-American League, USNA, RG 59, 88.4010 DP/6-2546

25 Refugee Screening Commission, Report on Ukrainians in SEP Camp No. 374 Italy, 21 February 1947, PRO FO 371/ 66605

26 *Ibid.*, p. 1, para. 3 and p. 5, para. 11

27 *Ibid.*, p. 3, para. 7

28 *Ibid.*, p. 5, para. 11

29 *Ibid.*, p. 2, para 5

30 *Ibid.*, p. 6, para. B

31 Compare Outgoing Cable No. 457, 22 February 1947, attached to Refugee Screening Commission, Report on Ukrainians in SEP Camp No. 374 Italy, 21 February 1947, PRO FO 371/66605 at para. 3, with Cypher/OTP No. 584, 9 March 1947, PRO FO 371/66605

32 Handwritten Minutes to WR858, 12 March 1947, PRO FO 371/ 66605

33 *Ibid.*

34 Refugee Screening Commission, Report on Ukrainians in SEP Camp No. 374 Italy, 21 February 1947, PRO FO 371/66605, p. 4, para. 8

35 See, for example, the incident of the German escapees described in Chapter Three which led the CIC to initiate Operation Circle

36 Refugee Screening Commission, LACAB/62/INT/WOSM, 1 March 1947, enclosure to Report on Ukrainians in SEP Camp No. 374 Italy, 21 February 1947, PRO, FO 371/66605 ('These men surrendered to us . . . They must therefore be regarded as a British responsibility. It is hard to see how H.M.G. could justify . . . [the likelihood of] forcible repatriation.') Note also his assistant's comments, p. 6, para. B, that 'We must however I think, take into account their motives . . . They probably were not, and certainly do not now seem to be at heart pro-German . . .'

37 *Ibid.*,p. 2

38 Minutes, WR 957, 7 March 1947, PRO FO 371/66606, para. 1 of Legal Officers Minutes

39 *Ibid.*, para. 2 of Brimelow Minutes. See also para: 2 of Hankey Minutes

40 *Ibid.*, para. 6 of Hankey Minutes

41 Armstrong, *Ukrainian Nationalism 1939–45*

42 Cable of 19 February 1947, Special Projects Division, USNA, RG 59, 740. 62114/2-1947

43 Correspondence of 16 September 1947, USNA, RG 59, 860E.00/9-1647

44 Petition of 21 June 1947, enclosure to Correspondence of 16 September 1947, USNA, RG 59, 860E. 00/9-1647

45 Press clipping enclosure to WR 2353, 19 June 1947, PRO FO 371/66712

46 Letter, 8 June 1947, enclosure to WR 2353, 19 June 1947, PRO FO 371/66712

47 Letter, 9 July 1947, enclosure to WR 2353, 19 June 1947, PRO FO 371/66712

48 *Ibid.*

49 Handwritten Minutes to WR 2353, 19 June 1947, PRO FO 371/66712

50 *Ibid.* At least Maclean's screeners recognized that 'the men may all be lying, even about their names'.

51 Letter, 24 February 1948, enclosure to N2193, PRO FO 371/71636

52 Letter, 8 April 1948, enclosure to N2193, PRO FO 371/71636

53 Memorandum, Ukrainian 'Divisia Halychyna' (Ukrainian POW in Great Britain), Enclosure to N2193, PRO FO 371/71636, para. 6

54 Refugee Screening Commission, LACAB/62/INT/WOSM, 1 March 1947, enclosure to Report on Ukrainians in SEP Camp No. 374 Italy, 21 February 1947, PRO FO 371/66605, pp. 2–3 (distinguishing those who were forced to volunteer)

55 Compare Panchuk's Memorandum, Ukrainian 'Divisia Halychyna' (Ukrainian POW in Great Britain), Enclosure to N2193, PRO FO 371/71636 with the British Screening Team's discussion of Displaced Person Status under the rules of the International Refugee Organization. Refugee Screening Commission, LACAB/62/INT/WOSM, 1 March 1947, enclosure to Report on Ukrainians in SEP Camp No. 374 Italy, 21 February 1947, PRO FO 371/66605, pp. 2–8

56 Memorandum, Ukrainian 'Divisia Halychyna' (Ukrainian POW in Great Britain), enclosure to N2193, PRO FO 371/71636, p. 8, Part V, para. 7

57 First Handwritten Minutes to N2193, 24 February 1948, PRO FO 371/71636

58 First Handwritten Minutes to Flag C of N2153, 26 February 1948, PRO FO 371/71661

59 Second Handwritten Minutes to N3730, 25 March 1948, PRO FO 371/71662

60 First Handwritten Minutes to N3730, 25 March 1948, PRO FO 371/71662

61 N7688, and enclosures, July 1948, PRO FO 371/71663

62 O'Grady Typewritten Minute to N7500, 30 June 1948, PRO FO 371/71663

63 RAE Typewritten Minute to N7500, 30 June 1948, PRO FO 371/71663

64 N7500, July 1948, Handwritten Minutes of Mr Stark, PRO FO 371/71663

65 'RMAH' Typewritten Minute to N7500, 30 June 1948, PRO FO 371/71663

66 Bruce Page *et al.*, *The Philby Conspiracy*, Ballantine, New York, 1988,

pp. 188–9; Kim Philby, *My Silent War*, Ballantine, New York, 1983, pp. 163–4, 208

67 USAINSCOM Dossier 'Prometheus', undated card index listing Shandruk as a leader, US Army Investigative Records Repository, Fort George V. Meade, Md., released under US FOIA; Stevenson, *Intrepid's Last Case*, p. 243, acknowledging Colin Gubbins as head of Prometheus; and Cave Brown, *'C': The Secret Life of Sir Stewart Menzies*, pp. 143–4, acknowledging Prometheus as a long-standing British intelligence operation before being taken over by German Intelligence; Dallin, *Russia Under German Rule*, pp. 111, 117–18, 258n, describing Prometheus's work with the Nazis

68 Costello, *Mask of Treachery*, pp. 535, 565–6; Anderson, *Inside the League*, pp. 35–7; Simpson, *Blowback*, pp. 269–73

69 Anderson, *Inside the League*, pp. 33–7

70 Dallin, *Russia Under German Rule*, citing original German reports, pp. 119–20, nn.2–4

71 Loftus, *The Belarus Secret*, pp. 48–9, 73–8, 106–19; Cave Brown, *'C': The Secret Life of Sir Stewart Menzies*, pp. 143–4

72 Loftus, *The Belarus Secret*, pp. 20–8, 65–6

73 Cable Number S 6496, 27 November 1946, enclosure to State Department Decimal File 860E.00/12-346, USNA, RG 59

74 Philby, *My Silent War*, pp. 163–6

75 Cable Number S 6496, 27 November 1946, enclosure to State Department Decimal File 860E.00/12-346, USNA, RG 59

76 *Ibid.*

77 Letter of 17 December 1946, enclosure to State Department Decimal File 860E.00/12-346, USNA, RG 59

78 OUN/SB Classified Files, US Immigration and Naturalization Service, Washington HQ, quoted in Loftus, *The Belarus Secret*, pp. 102–4

79 *Ibid.*

80 Without citation, Panchuk's history of the Galician Brigade alleges that the American forces kept 3,000 POWs for six months to a year, released them, and allowed them to acquire DP status

81 Wiesenthal, *The Murderers Among Us*, p. 275

82 *Ibid.*

83 Interview with Simon Wiesenthal, 21 February 1985

84 Wiesenthal, *The Murderers Among Us*, p. 275

85 Simpson, *Blowback*, pp. 180–1, n

86 USAINSCOM Dossier 'Intermarium', US Army Investigative Records Repository, Fort George V. Meade, Md., released under US FOIA

87 USAINSCOM Dossier 'Prometheus', undated card index listing Shandruk as a leader, US Army Investigative Records Repository, Fort George V. Meade, Md., released under US FOIA; Stevenson, *Intrepid's Last Case*, p. 243, acknowledging Colin Gubbins as head of Prometheus; and Cave Brown, *'C': The Secret Life of Sir Stewart*

Menzies, pp. 143–4, acknowledging Prometheus as a long-standing British intelligence operation before being taken over by German Intelligence; Dallin, *Russia Under German Rule*, pp. 111, 117–18, 258n, describing Prometheus's work with the Nazis

88 INSCOM Dossier, 'Polish-Ukrainian Military Staff', 970th CIC, US Army Investigative Records Repository, Fort George V. Meade, Md., released under US FOIA

89 Memo of 14 May 1947, from London to British Embassy at the Holy See, PRO FO 371 67376

90 Letter of 18 November 1947, from British Embassy at the Holy See to London, PRO FO 371 67402

91 War Department Top Secret INCOMING CLASSIFIED MESSAGE No. 89, 7 June 1947, AFHQ Declassified Files, USNA. (The AFHQ Cable Files are arranged chronologically in incoming and outgoing transmission sequence and are stored in Vault Six of the Suitland Annexe)

92 War Department Top Secret INCOMING CLASSIFIED MESSAGE No. 44, 12 June 1947, AFHQ Declassified Files, USNA

93 Costello, *Mask of Treachery*, p. 535

94 Memo of 20 December 1947, from Wilford to Culbertson, enclosed in State Department memo of 31 December 1947, from Madrid to Washington, from Vajta's FBI file, released under US FOIA, document 0009

10 The Philby Connection

1 Costello, *Mask of Treachery*, p. 279
2 *Ibid.*, p. 174
3 *Ibid.*, p. 602
4 *Ibid.*, p. 720, n.41
5 A serial of the incriminating evidence against Liddell is set forth in Costello, *Mask of Treachery*, pp. 602–3, including two occurrences in the late 1920s before he joined MI5. The peculiar omission of the Soviet Kolonii section in London was described in January 1989 by a former American Counter Intelligence officer, on the condition that it not be attributed
6 Costello, *Mask of Treachery*, pp. 602–3
7 *Ibid.*, p. 672, n.77
8 *Ibid.*, pp. 311–12
9 Ribbentrop, Joachim Von, CC HQ GP CC, 2 July 1945, Top Secret Interrogation Summaries, Vault 14W, USNA
10 Cave Brown, *'C': The Secret Life of Sir Stewart Menzies*, pp. 178–85
11 *Ibid.*, pp. 181–5
12 *Ibid.*
13 Memo from Director to US Attorney General, Justice Department Files, Washington, Attorney General's Eyes Only Records, Sixth Floor Vault, Main Justice Department, indexed under 'Windsor'

14 Cave Brown, *'C': The Secret Life of Sir Stewart Menzies*, p. 180
15 Charles Higham, *Trading with the Enemy*, Delacorte Press, New York, 1983, p. 182
16 *Ibid.*
17 *Ibid.*, p. 190
18 *Ibid.*, pp. 189–209
19 Pincher, *Too Secret Too Long*, p. 350 (regarding Anthony Blunt). The matter is alluded to again in Peter Wright, *Spycatcher*, Viking Penguin, New York, 1987, p. 223. The post-war MI5 cover-up of the Turkul network is discussed infra.
20 See Costello, *Mask of Treachery*, p. 602 (Liddell-Baykolov-Paris connection). For Ellis's connections to Turkul's network in Paris, see Pincher, *Too Secret Too Long*, pp. 440–1. According to Nigel West, *MI6*, Random House, New York, 1983, p. 123, Ellis 'as a German linguist, participated in a telephone tap placed on Ribbentrop's supposedly secure direct line to Berlin'.
21 Costello, *Mask of Treachery*, p. 672 notes 77–8
22 As head of B Division, Liddell was authorised to overrule negative MI5 reports at the time he hired KGB agents Blunt and Burgess. Costello, *Mask of Treachery*, p. 603
23 Cave Brown, *'C': The Secret Life of Sir Stewart Menzies*, p. 173
24 *Ibid.*, p. 198
25 *Ibid.*, p. 198
26 Pincher, *Too Secret Too Long*, p. 351
27 *Ibid.*, pp. 157–67
28 *Ibid.*, pp. 166–7
29 Cave Brown, *'C': The Secret Life of Sir Stewart Menzies*, pp. 651–4
30 *Ibid.*, pp. 652–5
31 *Ibid.*, p. 658
32 *Ibid.*, pp. 658–9
33 *Ibid.*, pp. 658–9, n.
34 *Ibid.*, p. 664
35 Wright, *Spycatcher*, p. 281
36 *Ibid.*, p. 284
37 *Ibid.*, p. 285
38 Compare Wright's treatment of the 'ELLI' cable in *Spycatcher*, pp. 281–5 with Costello's in *Mask of Treachery*, pp. 514–16
39 Stevenson, *Intrepid's Last Case*, pp. 243, 252, 254–6
40 Interview, *Reporting London*, 27 June 1988 subsequently seen as 1989 Thames Television Interview, *This Week*
41 *Ibid.*
42 See for example, the discussion of Stankievich's role as a Nazi/Communist double agent and his subsequent transfer to America from the British, in Loftus, *The Belarus Secret*, pp. 93–4
43 5 May 1989 interview with former British Intelligence Officer given on the condition that it remain unattributed.
44 For a discussion of Soviet agents in ABN, see Costello, *Mask of Treachery*, pp. 535, 595–6

334

45 Philby, *My Silent War*, pp. 163–5
46 CIA File Ferdinand Durčansky, translation of Czech Home Service, 5 March 1947, declassified under US FOIA, p. 49a (hereinafter cited as Durčansky CIA File)
47 *Ibid.*, p. 25a
48 *Ibid.*
49 *Ibid.*, p. 47a
50 Undated Memo, British PRO FO 371 65809
51 Durčansky CIA File, p. 27a, quoting *Kis Ujsag*, Budapest, 20 November 1947
52 Durčansky CIA File, Biographical Information, pp. 1–16a
53 Costello, *Mask of Treachery*, p. 596
54 Cave Brown, *'C': The Secret Life of Sir Stewart Menzies*, acknowledging long-standing British intelligence fronts, pp. 173–4
55 Costello, *Mask of Treachery*, pp. 535–6; Philby, *My Silent War*, pp. 163–5
56 Durčansky CIA File, Biographical Information, p. 16a, par. 5
57 Cave Brown, *'C': The Secret Life of Sir Stewart Menzies*, acknowledging long-standing British intelligence fronts, pp. 173–4
58 Durčansky CIA File, Biographical Information, pp. 2–3a
59 Durčansky CIA File, Letter of 20 September 1950, p. 15, para. 2
60 Secret Cypher Cable 'From: The High Commissioner for Canada, London, England To: The Secretary of State for External Affairs, Ottawa' forwarding reply from Mr Purvis of Northern Department, British Foreign Office, 13 December 1950, External Affairs File No. 7899-40, Canadian Archives, Ottawa, Canada
61 Remark attributed to Philby in Edward Jay Epstein, *Disinformation*, Simon & Schuster, New York, 1989, p. 35
62 Durčansky's war crimes background was apparently known to the Canadian Government two days *before* he arrived on 15 December 1950. Compare note 60 supra with Letter No. C. 593, 2 February 1951, From: The Under-Secretary of State for External Affairs, Ottawa File No. 7899-40. The February 1951 letter confirms that both the immigration service and the Royal Canadian Mounted Police had been informed of Durčansky's particulars
63 White House correspondence 20 March 1951, State Department Decimal File, USNA, RG 59, FV 700/42051, enclosing Letter of 5 March 1951 from Professor Dr Ferdinand Durčansky, 97 Crawford St, Toronto, Ontario, Canada
64 The text of Durčansky's speeches to conventions of the Slovak World Council in Canada were provided by a Jewish source in Canada who wishes to remain anonymous, but copies are freely available from the SWC in Toronto, which continues to revere Durčansky in its publications
65 The Galician Division is probably the largest of the surviving Fascist organisations in Canada, but the other ethnic factions of the ABN remain very active. The exact number of Fascists who entered

Canada is the subject of some dispute between the Deschenes
Commission and its critics in the Wiesenthal Centre. Interviews with
Alti Rodal, 1986–9

66 Durčansky CIA file, 'Wartime Card Index', apparently provided by
Czech *émigrés* in the US. Kirschbaum's photo is on p. 11a. The CIA
combined the Durčansky and Kirschbaum files in its response to our
Freedom of Information Act request

67 Card Index, Durčansky CIA File, pp. 9a–10a

68 Kirschbaum Biographical Information, Durčansky CIA File, p. 8a

69 1989 Conversations with US General Accounting Office Investigators
on the condition that their identities remain anonymous

70 Durčansky CIA File, p. 42a, citing *New York Times*, 16 March 1959

71 Durčansky CIA File, Biographical Information, pp. 14–16a

72 Alti Rodal, *Presence in Canada of other Nazi collaborators from Central and
Eastern Europe and their links with Western intelligence agencies and the
Vatican*, Chapter XII, Part 4, Historical Appendix to Deschenes
Commission Report, Ottawa, 1985, pp. 409–27. According to Rodal,
'Sidor was admitted to Canada only after the direct intervention of
Pope Pius XII with the Prime Minister, Louis St Laurent.' Rodal
Report, p. 414. The Vatican began interceding for Sidor soon after
the war. By the end of 1945, Monsignor Montini of the Secretariat of
State was dropping hints that Sidor should be allowed to settle in
America, and over the following four years several official requests
were sent. See Airgram of 13 December 1945 from Tittman to
Washington, USNA, Myron Taylor Papers, Box 29 and State
Department Decimal File 701.60F66A/12-1345; letter from US
Consulate, Naples to Gowen, 15 May 1947 and Note Verbale from
the Personal Representative of the US President to the Vatican, 20
May 1947, USNA, Myron Taylor Papers, Box 17; and letters from
the Vatican to Taylor, 28 June 1949, and from Gowen to Montini, 5
July 1949, USNA, Myron Taylor Papers, Box 25. The US State
Department concluded that 'Mr Sidor's entry into the United States
either as an immigrant or as a temporary visitor, would be prejudicial
to American interests.' US Embassy (Consular Section) memo, 18
July 1949, USNA, Myron Taylor Papers, Box 25

73 A cursory reading of the main report of the Deschenes Commission
contains numerous references to an American connection, but
virtually all references to British involvement were deleted from both
the main report and the Appendix. See Rodal Report, for example
pp. 415–20. Interview with Alti Rodal, 1990

74 Interview with Alti Rodal, 1990. Ms Rodal was the author of the
heavily censored Appendix to the Deschenes Report and confirms
that she indeed requested access to these files and was denied on the
grounds that they were beyond the Commission's scope of inquiry

75 Memo to File, State Department Decimal File 800.43 International of
Liberty/6-1549 and 1649, USNA, RG 59, Secret Files

76 Memo to File, State Department Decimal Files, 7618.00/6-1256,
USNA, RG 59

77 Memo to File, State Department Confidential File 700.001/1-1355 CS/LGS, USNA, RG 59

78 Memo to File, State Department Decimal File 811. 4613/4-1658, USNA, RG 59

79 See, e.g. FBI Dossier of Frantishek Kushel on shift of CIA [AMCOMLIB] funding from the Abramtchik Faction, discussed in Loftus, *The Belarus Secret*, pp. 110–13. The FBI's source was none other than Jan Stankievich, brother of the infamous war criminal

80 See, e.g. US Immigration and Naturalization Service, Stankievich visa file, rejecting immigration on grounds of suspected Communist affiliation, original documents now in the possession of OSI, US Justice Department, Washington, DC

81 Costello, *Mask of Treachery*, pp. 595–6

82 Ryle-Johnson Report, T/148

83 *Ibid.*, T/145–148

84 Special Interrogation Report on Kauder, aka Klatt, MISC-USFET Counter Intelligence, T/1001

85 *Ibid.*, T/1004

86 War Room London CI Report; 'German Intelligence Service and the War', 1 December 1945, T/1239

87 *Ibid.*

88 Ira Longin Interrogation, 16 September 1947, T/1141-44

89 Interrogation of Nikolai Singular, T/1071-1075

90 Interrogation of Father George Leonidov Romanov, 19–20 December 1946, T/1063; as to Allen Dulles's thwarted plans, see Leonard Mosley, *Dulles*, Dial Press, New York, 1968, pp. 222–4

91 Cave Brown, *'C': The Secret Life of Sir Stewart Menzies*, p. 655

92 Interrogation of Father George Leonidov Romanov, 19–20 December 1946, T1/063; Allen Dulles, *The Secret Surrender*, Harper & Row, New York, 1966, pp. 88–124

93 Top Secret No. 11265, 'Role of the Wolff Group in Operation Sunrise, US Political Adviser for Germany, Berlin, 10 November 1947, US State Department Decimal Files, 740.00116EW/11-1047 A/VS, pp. 1–2, USNA, RG 59

94 CIC Salzburg Det., Subject 'Turkul, Anton', MOIC 29 June 1946, Declassified under FOIA 16 April 1990

95 *Ibid.*

96 CIC Salzburg Det., Letter of 16 July 46, declassificaion refused May 1990, citing CIA

97 Top Secret Interrogation of Claudius Voss, aka Alexandrov, 20 March 1947, SCI/A, T/1167-1181

98 *Ibid.*

99 *Ibid.*

100 Interrogation of Claudius Alexandrovich Voss, 970th CIC Det., 30 December 1947, T/1107

101 Top Secret Interrogation of Claudius Voss, aka Alexandrov, 20 March 1947, SCI/A, T/1167-1181

102 *Ibid.*
103 *Ibid.*
104 Cable, 17 August 1950 from Lewis E. Perry, Col. GSC Dep Acof S, G-2 USFET, T/1400
105 Cover Letter, 4 January 1949, Subject: White Russian net intelligence reports: attn. Major Milano, T/1312
106 SCI/A Interrogation, Ira Longin, circa 1946, T/328
107 *Ibid.*
108 Allied Military Control Stamp issued 17 July 1946, T/001
109 Interrogation of Nikolai Singular, T1/113–115
110 CIC Salzburg, Letter of 21 July 1946, declassified in part under FOIA, 16 April 1990
111 Ryle-Johnson Report, T/115-48
112 *Ibid.*, T/128-131
113 *Ibid.*, T/133
114 *Ibid.*, T/150
115 *Ibid.*, T/138-142
116 *Ibid.*, T/150
117 Memo of 20 October 1946 to SSU, War Department Mission to Germany, USFET, T/1212-221
118 CI Report no. 53, Subject OPERATION RUSTY, to Asst. Chief of Staff G-2 Headquarters USFET by s/a Paul H. Marvin, CIC, Project 113, 8 November 1946, T/1190-1200. Among the interesting items in this series is a mention of a 'Mr Harry Hecksher' of the 'War Department Detachment', a predecessor of the CIA's covert operations section in Germany. Hecksher was later the CIA Chief of Station in Berlin under Dulles. Thomas Powers, *The Man Who Kept the Secrets*, Pocket Books, New York, 1979, pp. 56–7
119 CI Report no. 53, Subject OPERATION RUSTY, to Asst. Chief of Staff G-2 Headquarters USFET by s/a Paul H. Marvin, CIC, Project 113, 8 November 1946, T/1190-1200
120 Loftus, *The Belarus Secret*, pp. 59–60
121 Undated summary of Turkul/Kauder conversations, T/1404
122 *Ibid.*
123 Interrogation of Father George Leonidov Romanov, 19–20 December 1946, T/1050-69
124 *Ibid.*
125 *Ibid.*
126 *Ibid.*
127 *Ibid.*
128 *Ibid.*
129 *Ibid.*
130 Although it is not certain, it appears that Ryle was the American who requested the MI5 background checks discussed infra
131 Costello, *Mask of Treachery*, p. 595 and n.24, p. 720
132 Ryle-Johnson Report, Observation of Gilbert Riles [sic], T/235; Turkul Letter, 24 October 1947, T/1138

133 CI Special Interrogation Report 62, 15 April 1948, 7707 ECIC. App. 166. Documents reproduced in the Appendix to the US Justice Department's Report on Klaus Barbie are cited by numbering the Appendix pages in sequence, e.g., App. 166 is the forty-third page from the front of the Appendix

134 CIA biographical file for Radislav Ostrowsky, describing Marcus's recruitment of White Russian Nazis in 1944, released under US FOIA

135 British Interrogation Report of Walter Schellenberg, London, 1945, copy in USNA, Military Reference Branch

136 CI Special Interrogation Report 62, 15 April 1948, 7707 ECIC. App. 166

137 *Ibid.*

138 CIC Trust Report, 'Subject: IRON GUARD', INSCOM DOSSIER, US Army Intelligence Records Repository, Ft. George V. Meade, Md., released under US FOIA

139 *Ibid.*

140 Operation Selection Board, Master Target List, 970th CIC, App. 27–8

141 *Ibid.*

142 Letter from former CIC Agent to Isadore Zack, Military Intelligence Association of New England, 28 September 1983, copy in authors' possession

143 Volume One, p. B8, *The German Intelligence Services*, Secret Files, US Navy Archives, copy in authors' possession

144 CI Special Interrogation Report 62, 15 April 1948, 7707 ECIC, App. 167

145 Undated Document entitled 'Operation Selection Board', apparently prepared for the 970th CIC Historical Files, App. 10

146 CI Special Interrogation Report 62, 15 April 1948, 7707 ECIC. App. 167

147 CIC File, Subject 'Black Orchestra', containing 1951 correspondence to DDU and DAD, declassified under US FOIA May 1990; Letter of 23 August 1946 to Captain O'Neal SSU/War Department Detachment, T1/017. We gratefully acknowledge the background explanations by a former US Counter Intelligence Officer. The CIA has recently published a multi-volume history of the early disputes between the CIA and Dulles, the so-called 'Darlin Report' which is available behind the information desk of the Main Reading Room of the USNA. However, neither the Darlin Report nor any other CIA history has ever identified the DDU as the cover for Dulles's rival intelligence organisation in the State Department. To our knowledge, this is the first time the existence of this super-secret organisation has ever been discussed in print

148 Allen had been promised the directorate of the CIA after Dewey's victory. His brother, John Foster Dulles, was to become Dewey's Secretary of State. Mosley, *Dulles*, p. 245. Allen did not wait for the

election results before hiring his staff. John A. Bross, who later went
on to a distinguished career in the CIA, confirmed that he was
interviewed by Allen Dulles in the middle of the 1948 election
campaign. Bross Interview, 1988. Mr Bross insists however that his
own involvement as a legal officer in the Barbie case was prior to his
actual employment with Dulles and not in any way connected with
intelligence work. See for example, Bross's Office Memorandum of
13 June 1950, Office of the US High Commissioner for Germany,
App. 410–11, which does not reflect any knowledge of Barbie's
intelligence connection. Subsequently, Bross became Chief of the
East European Division where he supervised Harry Heckscher of
the old 'WDD'. See note 118, supra; Bowie interview, 1985

149 'Around the White House they were still smoldering over some of
the things Dulles and his political supporters had said about
Truman during the recent Senate Campaign.' Mosley, *Dulles*, p. 249

150 References to each can be found in the Barbie documents, discussed
in the next chapter

11 Barbie and the American Ratlines

1 Although Rauff's name is not mentioned in Dulles's memoirs of
Operation Sunrise, *The Secret Surrender*, Rauff certainly remembered
Dulles's name during his CIC interrogation. The sensitive Rauff-
Dulles connection undoubtedly came to Angleton's attention as he had
been 'transferred to Italy in November 1944, as the commanding
officer of the SCI Unit Z'. Robin W. Winks, *Cloak and Gown*,
Morrow, New York, 1987, p. 350. After March 1945, Angleton was
in charge of co-ordinating all OSS interrogation information,
especially concerning captured SD officers, such as Rauff. *Id.* p. 362.
The US Army's files confirm that after SD officer Walter Rauff was
interrogated by CIC he was released to the OSS unit 'S Force
Verona'. INSCOM DOSSIER, 'Subject: Walter Rauff', US Army
Investigative Records Repository, Ft. George V. Meade, Md.,
originally released under US FOIA to the Simon Wiesenthal Centre.
Shortly after the CIC turned Rauff over to the OSS, he escaped
under mysterious and controversial circumstances. See Chapter
Two, supra. Rauff's subsequent role in the Ratlines is discussed in
the French book, *Cercle Noir*, translated excerpts of which were
graciously provided by Charles Kenney of the *Boston Globe*

2 David Martin, *Wilderness of Mirrors*, Ballantine Books, New York,
1981, pp. 23–4

3 INSCOM DOSSIER, Subject: 'Giovanni Montini', Memo of 30
July 1946, US Army Investigative Records Repository, Ft. George
V. Meade, Md., declassified under US FOIA

4 Winks, *Cloak and Gown, p. 354*

5 Martin, *Wilderness of Mirrors*, p. 182

6 INSCOM DOSSIER, Subject: 'Giovanni Montini', Memo of 30 July

1946, Unattributed, US Army Investigative Records Repository, Ft. George V. Meade, Md., declassified under US FOIA

7 INSCOM DOSSIER, Subject: 'Giovannli Montini', Memo of 31 July 1946, Unattributed, US Army Investigative Records Repository, Ft. George V. Meade, Md., declassified under US FOIA

8 Winks, *Cloak and Gown*, pp. 380–1

9 A number of authors have correctly described the 'Special Procedures Group' as a component of CIA, without mentioning that SPG was an ad hoc joint operation between the CIA and the State Department's Special Projects Division. It was the latter which pushed the Italian election initiative over the reluctant CIA. SPD formally became OPC in 1948 as a permanent State Department mechanism for circumventing the CIA's scepticism for covert political action. Compare Winks, *Cloak and Gown*, p. 385, with Powers, *The Man Who Kept The Secrets*, pp. 36–7, and Loftus, *The Belarus Secret*, pp. 69–70. We use the term SPD to identify the non-CIA covert operations section run by the State Department prior to November 1948. Although Angleton was technically in the CIA, he was also one of the SPG co-ordinators for Italy and helped SPD run the election campaign through his assistant, Raymond Rocca in Rome. Winks, *Cloak and Gown*, p. 385, n. The recently released 'Darlin Report', discussed supra, explains many but not all of the bureaucratic tangles

10 Declassified US State Department Archives released under US FOIA: Enclosure to dispatch No. 4404 dated 31 December 1947, subject, 'Recent Developments in the Establishment of an Anti-Communist Eastern European Center in Madrid'.

11 *Ibid.*, pp. 3–5

12 *Ibid.*

13 *Ibid.*, pp. 3–4

14 *New York Times*, 10 January 1948, p. 6; 12 January 1948, p. 4; 15 January 1948, p. 11. On Vajta's plans to solicit US support, see Declassified US State Department Archives released under US FOIA; Enclosure to dispatch No. 4404 dated 31 December 1947, subject, 'Recent Developments in the Establishment of an Anti-Communist Eastern European Center in Madrid'.

15 Informal Routing Slip, Headquarters, United States Forces Austria, 'History of the Italian Ratlines', 10 April 1950, Paul Lyon, HQ 430th CIC Opns, Attn: Maj. Milano, p. 1, App. 474

16 *Ibid.*

17 *Ibid.*, p. 3, App. 476

18 Top Secret Informal Routing Slip, Headquarters, United States Forces Austria, 'Rat Line from Austria to South America', HQs 430th CIC, 12 July 1948; para. 2–3. App. 481

19 Winks, *Cloak and Gown*, p. 445

20 Top Secret Incoming Cable, Number P 4232, 13 December 1949, Department of the Army, Staff Message Center, AFHQ Record Group, USNA, p. 3

21 Details of Bosiljević's activities in the Križari are from the official Yugoslav interrogation reports of Božidar Kavran and related documents, held at the High Court in Zagreb. On Bosiljević's activities with Cecelja and the Croatian Red Cross, see Cecelja's 'Final Interrogation Report', USNA RG 319, Cecelja Dossier, XE 006538

22 See, e.g. CIC Trust Report, 'Subject: IRON GUARD', INSCOM Dossier, US Army Intelligence Records Repository, Ft. George V. Meade, Md., released under US FOIA, indexing Fascist Romanians working for British, French and American intelligence services in 1947

23 Interviews with former 970th CIC Officers, 1988–90

24 Only one 970th CIC agent, Henry Quarles, was found to be involved in illegal immigration activities. He was courtmartialed. Confidential File Index, Statement of Henry Quarles, US Army War College, Carlisle Barracks, Pennsylvania; Interview with former 970th CIC Officer, September 1990

25 Incoming Airgram, A-150, Nr 2337, 16 April 1948, US State Department decimal File Nr. 740.00116 EW/4-1648, citing 'security agencies in Austria', para. 1, USNA, RG 59; see Loftus, *The Belarus Secret*, pp. 65–6

26 Loftus, *The Belarus Secret*, p. 66

27 *Ibid.*, pp. 66, 73–4

28 *Ibid.*, pp. 74–5

29 After the separation of the commands, OPERATION HEADACHE BOATHILL preferred to recruit their personnel from the recent graduates at Fort Holabird rather than from their more experienced colleagues in Germany. Incoming Classified Message, P 4233, 14 December 1949, Department of the Army, Staff Message Center, USNA, AFHQ RG. Information concerning 430th records was given to John Loftus in 1979 on a briefing tour of classified microfilm room, US Army Investigative Records Repository, Ft. George V. Meade, Md

30 Interview with Major Milano, 1984; US Department of Justice, *Klaus Barbie and the United States Government*, August 1983, p. 136 [hereinafter the Ryan Report]

31 Höhne and Zolling, *The General was a Spy*, pp. 92–4 (July 1947 deadline, POW interrogations); p. 199 (Emil Augsburg); Loftus, *The Belarus Secret*, pp. 63, 78 (Dr Six)

32 CHISEL [secret operation] REPORT No. 563, 28 February 1947, T/1008

33 Höhne and Zolling, *The General was a Spy*, pp. 170

34 Compare E. H. Cookridge, *Gehlen: Spy of the Century* Hodder & Stoughton, London 1972; with Höhne and Zolling, *The General was a Spy*, p. 162 (Gehlen and SBONR organisation); p. 180 (Gehlen and League of the Andreas Flag); p. 187 (Gehlen and NTS). Each of these organisations is listed as controlled or infiltrated by Turkul. See, e.g.,

MISC-USFET, 'Answer of Brief for Interrogation to: SSU Rep USFET', 30 October 1946, T/1085. In addition, Turkul's aides were caught by CIC with Gehlen's paperwork on them. Interrogation of Claudius Alexandrovich Voss, 970th CIC, 30 December 1947, T/1105 (Voss file mentions 'Rusty' and 'TIB', both codenames for the Gehlen Organization). In addition, Peter von Glasenap, the leader of St Andrew's Flag, is listed both as a Gehlen informant (7021 Composite Group, a CIC code name for Gehlen) and as a contact for General Turkul. CIC Card Indexes, undated, T/1364-1370

35 CHISEL [secret operation] Report No. 563, 28 February 1947, T/1008

36 Compare Memorandum: Subject: White Russian Net Intelligence Reports, Attn: Major Milano, 4 January 1949, T/1308 with Informal Routing Slip, Headquarters, United States Forces Austria, 'History of the Italian Ratlines,' 10 April 1950, Paul Lyon, HQ 430th CIC Opns, Attn: Maj. Milano, App. 474

37 Cable from Lewis E. Perry, Col. GSC, to Deputy to the Assistant Chief of Staff G-2 USFET, 17 August 1950, T/1402 (advising his intelligence counterpart in Germany that Turkul 'has excellent contacts with US intell agy in Germ.' Apparently a reference to Gehlen or the DDU)

38 MISC-USFET, 'Answer of Brief for Interrogation to: SSU Rep USFET', 30 October 1946, T/1085

39 CIC Card Indexes, Undated, T/1364-1370

40 Cable from Lewis E. Perry, Col. GSC, to Deputy to the Assistant Chief of Staff G-2 USFET, 17 August 1950, T/1402

41 Höhne and Zolling, *The General was a Spy*, p. 180

42 *Ibid.*, pp. 186–7

43 Interrogation of Claudius Alexandrovich Voss, 970th CIC, 30 December 1947, T/1122-23

44 CI Special Interrogation Report NO. 65, File CI-SIR/66, 16 June 1948, p. 133, App. 190 (Barbie learns of Dr Six arrest from Emil Augsburg); Interviews with John Bross and John McCloy, 1983 (Vatican intercession among reasons for Six's pardon); see general discussion of Dr Six's career in Loftus, *The Belarus Secret*

45 Simpson, *Blowback*, pp. 224–5n (Tenzerov, Augsburg and Barbie worked for the Gehlen Organization). There is no doubt that this network was working part-time for Dulles's undercover 'War Department Detachment' as the CIC makes explicit mention of payments received by the WDD. Letter, 8 March 1948, 970th CIC Region IV, p. 2, para d, App. 159. Unfortunately, the subsequent Barbie investigation missed the Dulles connection entirely because they could find no trace of the term 'War Department Detachment'. Ryan Report, p. 159n. The Turkul file contains ample references to this unit, e.g., CI Report 53, Subject: Operation RUSTY, 8 November 1946 (mentioning a conference about Turkul with Mr Hecksher of the War Department Detachment), T/1190-1200.

Hecksher was Dulles's representative in Berlin. Powers, *The Man Who Kept the Secrets*, p. 56

46 Simpson, *Blowback*, pp. 224–5n (Tenzerov, Barbie and Augsburg work for Gehlen); a diagram of Barbie's and Augsburg's role in the Peterson Organization is contained in App. 213. The Peterson net's secret connection to the Gehlen Organization (codenamed TIB) is discussed in Letter, Subject: Merk, Kurt; Barbie, Klaus, 16 November 1948, CIC Region IV, App. 217, para. 4, p. 2. The Turkul-Tenzerov-DDU connection is discussed infra

47 See the references to Bandera and Ukrainian contacts in the British Zone in Letter, Subject: Operation Flowerbox, 20 March 1947, 970th CIC Region I, App. 61–2

48 *Ibid.*

49 Letter to HQ 970th CIC Det., Subj: Klaus Barbie, 11 December 1947, p. 4, App. 113 (note that Barbie's reports on Lebed and Grynioch were submitted to CIC on 18 November 1947, almost three weeks *before* Barbie's case handler, Camille Hadju, arranged to smuggle them from Rome and hide them in his house; compare INSCOM Dossier C8043982J, Mykola Lebed, US Army Investigative Records Repository, Ft. George V. Meade, Md., declassified under US FOIA, pp. 15–16 (report by Hadju on conduct of 5 December 1947 smuggling). The Barbie-Hadju-Ukrainian connection may have begun even earlier. Hadju's informal memorandum of 10 November 1947, unsourced (p. 142) was apparently based on oral reports from the Merck-Barbie network, as Hadju had no other network with contacts outside Germany. Barbie's information about Lebed and Grynioch had to have been typed up during the week of 10 November in order to be logged in for payment on 18 November. It is no coincidence that on 17 November 1947, Barbie's case handler, Hadju submitted his first official request (pp. 47–50), to smuggle Lebed from Rome to Germany, and then logged the Barbie reports in the following day as back-up. (App. 113)

The recently declassified Lebed file also contains a wealth of information on the wartime and post-war activities of Father Grynioch and the OUN, see e.g., p. 31 (Father Grynioch served as Lebed's deputy); p. 9 (Grynioch describes co-operative agreements with Germans), p. 19 (Galician training ground), p. 12 (Lebed's association with Abwehr intelligence); p. 146 (Father Grynioch was co-founder of the Ukrainian Army, UPA, along with Lebed)

50 INSCOM Dossier C8043982J, Mykola Lebed, US Army Investigative Records Repository, Ft. George V. Meade, Md., declassified under US FOIA, p. 36, described Lebed as 'a well known sadist and collaborator of the Germans'. Another source, listed as highly reliable by CIC, confirmed that Lebed, in order to dominate the anti-Soviet resistance movement, simply murdered several of his Ukrainian rivals and burned their villages to the ground. 'As a result, the Ukrainians now have difficulty forgetting the fact that Lebed

killed some Ukrainian partisans who were fighting for the same cause,' p. 39. For an overview of the SB's gruesome conduct, see generally, Armstrong, *Ukrainian Nationalism 1939–45*

51 INSCOM Dossier C8043982J, Mykola Lebed, US Army Investigative Records Repository, Ft. George V. Meade, Md., declassified under US FOIA, pp. 24, 149

52 INSCOM Dossier C8043982J, Mykola Lebed, US Army Investigative Records Repository, Ft. George V. Meade, Md., declassified under US FOIA, pp. 9, 24 (Lebed fled to Rome along with the Croatians in May 1945 and established himself as 'General Secretary for Foreign Affairs'). Bishop Bučko was not his only Church contact: Archbishop Szepticky had previously helped commute Lebed's sentence for political assassination in Poland, p. 7. Lebed's CIC File, p. 6, lists his 1955 occupation as 'Secretary General, Foreign Affairs, Supreme Ukrainian Liberation Council, 353 Fort Washington Avenue, New York 37, New York'. This was a subsidiary of Dulles's American Committee of Liberation (AMCOMLIB) in New York which was subsiding General Turkul at the same time. Agent's Report, Refugee Relief Act, 22 August 1956, T/1279. OPC sponsorship of Lebed's group is discussed in Loftus, *The Belarus Secret*, pp. 102–3. See also App. 158–60 (under Hadju, Barbie net was giving information of much value to the WDD which in turn subsidised this CIC net)

53 INSCOM Dossier, Jaroslav Stetsko, Extract from CI report, 5 September 1947, US Army Investigative Records Repository, Ft. George V. Meade, Md., released under US FOIA

54 INSCOM Dossier C8043982J, Mykola Lebed, US Army Investigative Records Repository, Ft. George V. Meade, Md., declassified under US FOIA, pp. 15, 44 (Lebed warned by Italian police that Soviets would kidnap him after American forces withdrew from Italy); pp. 13–20, 43–50 and 142 contain the paperwork approved by the chain of command; see note 49 for a discussion of Barbie's foreknowledge

55 INSCOM Dossier C8043982J, Mykola Lebed, US Army Investigative Records Repository, Ft. George V. Meade, Md., declassified under US FOIA, p. 11

56 INSCOM Dossier C8043982J, Mykola Lebed, US Army Investigative Records Repository, Ft. George V. Meade, Md., declassified under US FOIA, p. 21, 46 (Captain Hale's role); Top Secret Letter, Barbie, Klaus, 18 March 1948, para 3–4, App. 162–3 (superseding December 1947 instructions, now asking that Barbie be dissuaded from talking to the British by making co-operation a condition of his release). It should be noted that these new instructions were signed by Colonel Eckmann, one of the CIC liaisons to Dulles's group.

57 INSCOM Dossier, Subject: Ukrainian Nationalist Activities, Letter of 21 May 1948, US Army Investigative Records Repository, Ft. George V. Meade, Md., released under US FOIA

58 *Ibid.*
59 INSCOM Dossier, Subject: Ukrainian Nationalist Activities, Letter of 31 March 1950, US Army Investigative Records Repository, Ft. George V. Meade, Md., released under US FOIA
60 INSCOM Dossier C8043982J, Mykola Lebed, US Army Investigative Records Repository, Ft. George V. Meade, Md., released under US FOIA, pp. 4, 12
61 *Ibid.*, p. 3
62 *Ibid.*, p. 2
63 *Ibid.*, pp. 3–4
64 Letter, Subject: Informants Net, 9 March 1948, App. 154–6 (Hadju's summary of orders to close down net); Letter, Subject: Merk, Kurt and Barbie, Klaus, 25 October 1948, App. 222 (listing CIC Headquarters decision to drop the Barbie network, or ask the CIA (DAD) if they wished to run it); Letter, Subject Merk, Kurt and Barbie, Klaus, 16 November 1948, App. 217–219 (admitting Gehlen penetration: 'TIB'); B/L – CIC Region IV, Subject: Merk, Kurt and Barbie, Klaus, 16 November 1948, App. 215 (three months extension on closing down net). Apparently the CIA did not want Barbie either
65 See note 45 supra and previous discussions of WDD-DDU as Dulles's front groups
66 Höhne and Zolling, *The General was a Spy*, pp. 280–91
67 US POLAD, Berlin, 13 May 1949, State Department Decimal File 740.00116 EW/5-1349, USNA, RG 59
68 Letters, Subject: Barbie, Klaus, 12 January 1950, App. 250–1 (Vidal is listed as the action officer); the history of the 'drop him but don't tell him' charade is set forth in Vidal's 'Memorandum for Colonel Erskine', 3 May 1950, App. 332–6 (containing Vidal's hand-written comments)
69 It should be noted that the man who gave the bizarre drop-off orders described in the preceding footnote was Colonel Eckmann, the CIC liaison to DDU. IRS, Barbie, Klaus, 24 May 1949, App. 247
70 Agent Report, Merk, Kurt, 19 October 1949, App. 238–42
71 Memorandum for Colonel Erskine, 3 May 1950, p. 5, para. 23, App. 336 ('prior to May 1949, this headquarters had had no indication that Barbie was wanted by the French for war crimes')
72 Top Secret Cable No. 26, 15 May 1950, App. 328
73 Memorandum for Colonel Erskine, 3 May 1950, p. 5, para. 23, App. 336 ('decided by Col . . . Eckmann . . . that Barbie shall not be placed in hands of French contrary to opinion expressed before'. Colonel Johnson and Ligon of Intelligence Division concurred in decision); Letter, Subject: Extradition of Klaus Barbie, 30 August 1950, App. 440 (decision not to hand Barbie over was co-ordinated with Mr B. Shute, Director of Intelligence (State Department), High Commissioner for Germany and Colonel W. R. Philp, Intelligence Division). Vidal noted that the reasons for the May 1950 hands-off decision on Barbie was 'well known to the above mentioned persons'.

Shute was State's liaison for DDU, Colonel William R. 'Rusty' Philp was the red-headed Army liaison to Gehlen's 'Operation Rusty'. Interview with former State DDU (and later CIA) officer, John A. Bross, 1983–4; see also Höhne and Zolling, *The General was a Spy*, p. 68 (Col. Philp recruited Gehlen in 1945). It is not surprising that they ordered Vidal to keep the French from getting their hands on Barbie

74 Memorandum for Colonel Erskine, 3 May 1950, p. 4, para. 16, App. 335 ('French Sûreté has been thoroughly penetrated by Communistic elements'); Office Memorandum, 21 June 1950, HICOG to Shute, App. 421 (Several influential French officials would be embarrassed by extradition to France)

75 IRS, HQ EUCOM (contd), 20 July 1949 (Barbie interrogated some very high French officials including François Poncet and Lebrun)

76 IRS, HQ EUCOM (contd), 20 July 1949 (Barbie interrogated four times by French but 'no attempt has ever been made' to bring formal charges); Memorandum for Colonel Erskine, 3 May 1950, p. 5, para. 23, App. 336 (no written request for extradition ever received by our headquarters); Secret Telegram, 26 May 1950 ('Note summarizes unsuccessful attempts' to obtain extradition through HICOG channels, recalling earlier conversations with McCloy that the French were no longer interested in obtaining Barbie's presence); Letter (undated circa 1950) from Office of General Counsel to M Lebegue, App. 360–1 (reminds French HICOG that no formal paperwork, only informal requests, have been transmitted to American HICOG)

77 Incoming Telegram, Department of State, No. 2172, 8 May 1950, App. 365 (Barbie case has 'highly embarrassing possibilities to put it mildly')

78 See Vidal's handwritten memo discussed in note 73, supra, and 1st Ind., HQ, Region XII, 16 May 1950, App. 339

79 1984–5 Confidential Interview including John Bross (now deceased). Permission to write an unclassified version of Poncet's activities for *Stern* Magazine was obtained in a series of correspondence with CIA/PRC, copies in authors' possession

80 INSCOM Dossier, François Poncet, US Army Investigative Records Repository, Ft. George V. Meade, Md., released under US FOIA; Poncet's wartime background and diaries are discussed in John Loftus, *L'affreux secret*, Plon, Paris, 1985, pp. 172–222

81 430th CIC, Vienna City Section, Memo of 16 December 1946, INSCOM Dossier, 'RED CROSS CENSORSHIP', US Army Investigative Records Repository, Ft. George V. Meade, Md., p. 7, released under US FOIA

82 INSCOM Dossier, François Poncet, US Army Investigative Records Repository, Ft. George V. Meade, Md., released under US FOIA

83 *Ibid.*

84 Memo to Mr Robinson from Mr Clattenburg of SPD (Special Projects Division), 20 June 1947, USNA RG 59, FW800.142/5-1547, showing that the La Vista report was passed to the SPD for handling

85 1984–5 Confidential Interviews including John Bross (now deceased). Permission to write an unclassified version of Poncet's activities for *Stern* Magazine was obtained in a series of correspondence with CIA/PRC, copies in authors' possession; Bowie interview, 1985

86 Top Secret Office Memorandum, US HICOG, 21 June 1950, App. 421

87 Top Secret Letter, 20 June 1950, Lightner to Wallner, App. 416 ('Mr McCloy directed that we smoke out EUCOM on the matter to . . . get more details as to just how embarrassing it would be to them (CIC) if he were turned over to the French.')

88 Confidential S-3 Work Sheet, 23 August 1950, App. 442 and HQ Eucom SRI 732–50, 21 August 1950, App. 443; Vidal sent a typed memo recalling the earlier decision by several higher authorities, including Shute, of HICOG and queried if either they or the French had now changed their minds about denying extradition

89 Confidential Interview with former US Counter Intelligence Officer, 1988–90. According to this officer, the CIC already had the 'crown jewels' and had no need for Barbie's baubles of information about the Communists in Germany. On 14 September 1950, Vidal approved a cable telling HICOG that CIC had no objections to Barbie's extradition, and reminding them that Barbie was not under the control of any Army agency, especially CIC. Secret Cable from CIC Liaison Office Heidelberg, 9 September 1949. Vidal's handwritten instructions are at the bottom of the page, App. 445

90 Confidential Office Memorandum, US HICOG, 20 October 1950, App. 457

91 Letter, 20 April 1983, International Committee of the Red Cross, App. 521 confirms that Barbie travelled on documents issued by the Allied High Commission for Germany, but noted that the original documents were missing

92 Romac's role in Barbie's escape are discussed in Neal Ascherson, Magnus Linklater and Isabel Hilton, *The Fourth Reich*, Hodder & Stoughton, London, 1984, pp. 192, 219–20; and Aarons, *Sanctuary!*, pp. 222, 233, 239, 240–51. *Sanctuary!* also details Romac's subsequent emigration to Australia and his role in organising Ustashi terrorist cells which launched a wave of bombings, shootings and guerrilla incursions into Yugoslavia in the 1960s and 1970s

93 Top Secret Memo for Record, Subject: Informant Disposal, undated, p. 5, App. 488, notes that the 430th informs the Department of State of the informant's real name and 'shipping name' and then the State Department notifies the US consul in the 'receiving country' to expect his arrival; Undated Memorandum, 66th CIC Germany, App. 493–4 para. 3, n, notes that 'The 430th handles all 66th cases *via State Department communication* as though they were 66th cases; no further 66th involvement?' [emphasis added]

94 Simpson, *Blowback*, p. 195

95 Winks, *Cloak and Gown*, p. 140

348

96 IRS, HQ USFA, Subject, History of the Italian Rat Line, 10 April
   1950, App. 476–7
97 66th CIC Memorandum for the Record, Subject: Informant
   Disposal, undated, pp. 7–8, App. 490–1
98 See discussion in Loftus, *The Belarus Secret*, pp. 89n, 95–6, 103n,
   123–8
99 Classified Information provided by author to 1985 GAO Report to
   US Congress; Lebed has been publicly named as the subject of the
   report in Simpson, *Blowback*, p. 168
100 Barbie's Argentine Visa was stamped in Geneva on 19 March 1951,
   App. 533, but he did not actually depart from Genoa until 22 March
   1951, Steamship Ticket, No. 15659, App. 549
101 Blue Card, 28 August 1948, T/025 (Ukrainian Vlasov Division);
   War Department General Staff, Intelligence Report, 'Russian
   Émigré Organizations', para. 6.a., enclosure to Letter, 10 May 1949,
   US POLAD, State Department Decimal Files, USNA, RG 59,
   861.20262/5-1049 MM Secret File (post-war attempts by NTS to
   compromise Vlasov movement)
102 MOIC, 8 June 1948, CIC Sub-Region Landshut, Alleged
   Regrouping of Former ROA Members, USNA, RG 319, IRR index
   under AZODNR (controversial attempts by Turkul's aides to recruit
   Ukrainian Vlasovities); MOIC, 13 April 1948, CIC Region V, Re;
   Anti-Soviet Activities, USNA, RG 319, IRR index under AZODNR
   (policy differences causing lack of co-operation between General
   Shandruk's Ukrainians and General Turkul's factions)
103 Undated reports circa 1959 attached to MISC USFET, Answer of
   Brief for Interrogation, 30 October 1946, T/1085–1098 (reciting
   history of Turkul's affiliations)
104 SOURCE PICA, Letter to ODDI via USFA, Subject Turkul,
   Supreme Council of Russian exiles KROMIADI contra Glasenap;
   members of Supreme Council, Turkul, FNU, General; 10 May 1951,
   T/1315–17
105 Intercept Report, Civil Censorship Austria, 18 June 1951, T/1306-11
106 Cable, 14 September 1950 From Perry to Dep ACOS G-2 USFET,
   T/1402 (enclosed note Slip: no derogatory information as of 14
   September 1950)
107 Region IV File Check, 30 June 1951, T/1404
108 Interrogation of Richard Klatt (supplemental, undated), p. 13, T/
   1042-8
109 Interrogation of Claudius Alexandrovich Voss, 970th CIC, 30
   December 1947, T/1128-36
110 IRS, undated, Ovseenko source of Huntington reports recently
   emigrated, T/1322
111 Memo from Major Milano, 4 October 1949, T/1327
112 Secret Cable EUCOM, 10 May 1951, enclosure to CIC Agent
   Report, Refugee Relief Act, 22 August 1956, T/1249
113 War Department General Staff, Intelligence Report, No. R-E&A/81-
   49, 'Russian Émigré Organizations', enclosure to Letter, 10 May

1949, US POLAD, State Department Decimal Files, USNA, RG 59, 861.20262/5-1049 MM Secret File

114 *Ibid.*, para. 5a

115 *Ibid.*, para. 5b

116 *Ibid.*, para. 5f

117 *Ibid.*, para. 6

118 *Ibid.* (citing the Russian organization ATSONDR as an example), Para. 6a

119 MOIC, 13 April 1948, CIC Region V, Re; Anti-Soviet Activities, USNA, RG 319, IRR index under AZODNR, ANTI COMMUNIST CENTER LIBERATION MOVEMENT OF THE PEOPLES OF RUSSIA, VOL. I

120 Letter, 13 May 1949, US POLAD, USNA, RG 59, State Department Decimal File 740.00116 EW/5-1349

121 Philby, *My Silent War*, pp. 163–4

122 *Ibid.*, p. 157

123 Simpson, *Blowback*, pp. 166–7; CIA Declassified Report, German Intelligence Agents on The Eastern Front, Room 13W, USNA

124 One of the authors had access to the classified files of the 100 Persons Act during his employment with the US Justice Department and compared the CIA's information with the Army and State Department files. See Loftus, *The Belarus Secret*, p. 136

125 Wright, *Spycatcher*, pp. 346–7

126 Powers, *The Man Who Kept the Secrets*, pp. 59–61; Loftus, *The Belarus Secret*, pp. 116–17, 130

127 Confidential Interview with former intelligence officer familiar with NTS programmes under Wisner, 1981

128 Letter, Immigration and Nationalization Service, Top Secret Headquarters File, Indexed under OUN, quoted with permission in Loftus, *The Belarus Secret*, pp. 102–3 (alleging 35,000 Soviets killed by OUN inside the Soviet Union since the end of World War II)

129 William Corson, *The Armies of Ignorance*, Dial Press, New York, 1977, pp. 366–71

130 CIC Agent Report, Refugee Relief Act, 22 August 1956, T/1275-79 (Turkul cashier of organization Funded by AMCOMLIB, 6 East 45th St, New York)

131 Powers, *The Man Who Kept the Secrets*, p. 101; Loftus, *The Belarus Secret*, p. 107

132 Neither the report on OUN/SB assassinations, note 128 supra, nor the State Department's security investigation of Stankievich appear anywhere in the CIA files. See Loftus, *The Belarus Secret*, pp. 142–3

133 CIC Agent Report, Refugee Relief Act, 22 August 1956, p. 3, T/1250

134 Simpson, *Blowback*, p. 267

135 General Turkul's obituary appears in the December 1959 edition of 'ROA', Russian language newspaper collection, Hoover Institution, Palo Alto, California

136 Confidential Interview, 1981, former intelligence officer who worked

on NTS programmes in Germany. According to this rather defensive source, the OPC's attitude at the time was that they were merely writing cheques; if Turkul produced something good, fine, if he turned out to be a spy, all they had lost was money. In fact, Turkul helped them lose Hungary in 1956 and wrecked most of Gehlen's operations. See discussion of NTS failures in Höhne, *Gehlen: Spy of the Century*

137 Compare Costello, *Mask of Treachery*, p. 595; with Pincher, *Too Secret Too Long*, p. 441 (Ellis' contact, Prince Turkul, part of a major Soviet deception program) and p. 442 (indusputable evidence that Ellis's White Russian contacts worked for the Soviet GRU)

138 Stevenson, *Intrepid's Last Case*, p. 281

139 Notes to CBI Detachment 35 F, 358, Civil Censorship Group Austria, 11 April 1952, T/1290-5 (Turkul attempted to get in contact with General Miodrag Damjanović in the British Zone about co-ordinating the work of the Yugoslav emigration)

140 Internal Route Slip, European Command, Die Schwarze Kapelle, 24 April 1952, p. 6 of INSCOM Dossier, 'Schwarze Kapelle – Black Band', US Army Investigative Records Repository, Ft. George V. Meade, Suitland, Md.; partly declassified May 1990 under US FOIA

12 Conclusions

1 Schellenberg, *Labyrinth*, pp. 318–21

2 Confidential 1984 Interview, former Western intelligence officer. The person who named Waldheim also described extensive details of the Italian-Austrian leg of the Ratline which were subsequently corroborated by another source who admitted that the DDU unit was disguised as a medical team for the 351st Infantry Regimental Combat Team in Trieste, later the 349th regiment in Linz, Austria. Waldheim's own superior in the Austrian Foreign Ministry also confirmed that 'there may be a link between the US intelligence community and Waldheim'. Statement of Karl Gruber to the London Observer Service, quoted in *Quincy Patriot Ledger*, 29 April 1986

3 Waldheim was awarded the Ustashi silver medal of King Zvonimir with oak leaf clusters for bravery under fire for his services during July 1942. Waldheim admits that this was the period of the Kozara massacre, but claims that he was 200 miles away at the time. *New York Times*, 6 March 1986, 'Waldheim Says His Past Was Misrepresented'; see also *Der Spiegel*, 14 April 1986, 'The Waldheim Case: Austria's Quiet Fascism'. However, a check of the original Ustashi newspapers in the Yugoslav Archives showed that Pavelić awarded Waldheim the medal specifically for services in 'Western Bosnia' which was also the area assigned Father Draganović by the Ustashi Bureau of Colonisation

4 London Observer Service, Interview with Karl Gruber, reported in *Quincy Patriot Ledger*, 29 April 1986

5 *Ibid.* (Fritz Molden, Dulles's son-in-law recommended that Gruber hire Waldheim and performed Waldheim's background check. Molden had served as an OSS officer in Italy)

6 Duško Doder, 'Agents Say Waldheim Was Blackmail Target', *International Herald Tribune*, 31 October 1986

7 Simpson, *Blowback*, p. 121

8 1986 Interview with senior OPC official attached to HICOG; see also Powers, *The Man Who Kept the Secrets*, pp. 74–5

9 'after leaving the CIA, Offie went to work for the AFL-CIO in Europe. In 1972 he was killed in an air crash at London Airport.' Powers, *The Man Who Kept the Secrets*, p. 409, n.21

10 Costello, *Mask of Treachery*, p. 596

11 Estimate by Allan Ryan, author of *Quiet Neighbors*, and formerly director of the Office of Special Investigations at the US Justice Department. He is also the author of the Ryan Report on Klaus Barbie. However, Ryan continues to insist that the 10,000 Nazis entered America without any governmental assistance and that Barbie was the only war criminal to go through the Ratline. E.g., *Ryan Report*, p. 212

12 The 1959 report, which is still classified, was a belated admission from the Gehlen organisation. Some elements of the CIA had been saying the same thing openly since 1952. Lyman Kirkpatrick, *The Real CIA*, Macmillan, New York, 1968, p. 153

13 Corson, *Armies of Ignorance*, pp. 36–9

14 Costello, *Mask of Treachery*, p. 596

15 Memo, Australian Department of Foreign Affairs, reporting comments made by Mr Johnson of the US State Department. A copy of this document was tabled in the Senate by the Australian Attorney General, 27 March 1973

16 September 1990 Interview with former US Counter Intelligence officer. The Red Orchestra and BB Apparat files are only beginning to be declassified. INSCOM Dossier, Rote Kapelle, US Army Investigative Records Repository, Ft. George V. Meade, Md., partially declassified under US FOIA, 1990

17 Department of Army, Combined Intelligence Objective Summaries, 'Chemical Warfare Activities in the Munsterlager Area', July–August 1945, declassified under US FOIA. The document citing Mengele appears in the Appendix of German chemical warfare officers. An asterisk denotes that Mengele was in custody at the time of the British CIOS report

18 Gerald Posner and John Ware, *Mengele: The Complete Story*, McGraw-Hill, New York, 1986, pp. 66–9, 70

19 Nearly 20,000 pages on wartime and post-war recruitment of German chemical warfare scientists were recently released to the authors under the US FOIA. Among the more intriguing revelations are

detailed formulas and instructions for the manufacture of each type of nerve gas

20 Both Iraq and Syria possess pilot plants for Sarin, and both are on the verge of mass production. According to a chemical warfare expert for the United States, American monitoring of West German sales continued for a decade before Bonn could be pressured into taking any action. 1988–9 Confidential Interviews

21 The American author, Paul Manning, has obtained startlingly direct confirmation from a German nuclear scientist who worked on the programme, and graciously permitted the authors to review his material. Apparently both of us were working on the same investigation at the same time

22 1984–5 Interview with John McIntyre, who was also one of the DDU escorts from Gehlen's headquarters to the Ratlines. The remarkable story of McIntyre and his family is set forth in John Loftus and Emily McIntyre, *Valhalla's Wake*, Atlantic Monthly Press, New York, 1989

23 *Washington Post*, 6 June 1990, p. A20, 'British Lords Kill War Crimes Bill in Rare Display of Parliamentary Power'. Lord Shawcross stated that Jewish attacks on British troops created an atmosphere in which it would have been impossible to continue war crimes trials, and criticised the younger generation for their 'more simplistic ideas of right and wrong'

24 Title Doubleday, New York, 1981

25 Press statement of Deschenes Commission, 8 October 1985, releasing Top Secret cable from British Government, cited on p. 54; Testimony of John Loftus before the US House of Representatives, Committee on the Judiciary, Subcommittee on Immigration, Refugees, and International Law, 17 October 1985 (written submission)

26 Testimony of John Loftus before the US House of Representatives, Committee on the Judiciary, Subcommittee on Immigration, Refugees, and International Law, 17 October 1985 (written submission), pp. 32–7

27 Higham, *Trading With the Enemy*, p. 117

28 *Ibid.*

29 *Ibid.*, p. 10

30 *Ibid.*, p. 122

31 *Ibid.*, p. 11, citing sworn statement of Otto Abetz to American officials on 21 June 1946

32 Buenos Aires despatch of 23 July 1947, enclosure to Secret Letter No. 1563, Subject: Illegal Emigration from Italy to South America, Rome, 5 September 1947, USNA RG 59, 800.142/9-547

33 Paul Manning, *Martin Bormann*, Lyle Stuart, New York, 1981, pp. 205–6

34 US State Department Post Files, Switzerland, 1945, Folder for Operation Safehaven, Interrogation of Allen Dulles, USNA; Manning, *Martin Bormann*, p. 251

35 It should be recalled that about the same time, the Treasury

Department was alleged to have been infiltrated with Communists, the Morgenthau plan for dismembering the German cartels was overturned, and jurisdiction over the economy of occupied Germany was turned over to the far more conservative State Department

36 Manning, *Martin Bormann*, p. 251

37 Memos of meetings with Hans Gisevius and Australian government ministers and officials, Australian Archives, Canberra, AA CRS A445, Items 194/2/3 P3, and 194/2/4 (citing Rockefeller's assistance to the Committee for a Free Europe); Simpson, *Blowback*, pp. 202–3

38 Fortunately, World Commerce left behind a substantial paper trail of litigation. See, e.g., *Matter of Minerals Corp. and Panamerican Commodities*, Volume 15 New York State Appellate Division Reports, 2nd series, p. 432, 1st Department, 27 February 1962 (World Commerce Corp. represented by Donovan, Leisure, Newton & Irvine)

39 Manning, *Martin Bormann*, p. 268, citing Senate committee testimony of Julius Klein

40 *Ibid.*, pp. 268–9

41 *Ibid.*, pp. 71–2

42 Sworn statement of George Wilhelm Marty to investigators at Nuremberg Trial, document quoted without citation in Manning, *Martin Bormann*, p. 59

43 Statement of Walter Rockler, former US Prosecutor at Nuremberg Bankers' Trial, at 40th Anniversary Reunion of Nuremberg Prosecutors, Boston College Law School, Massachusetts

44 Penny Lernoux, *In Banks We Trust*, Doubleday, New York, 1984, p. 214

45 *Ibid.*, p. 189

46 *Ibid.*, pp. 181–2

47 *Ibid.*, pp. 188–214

48 Cave Brown, *Bodyguard of Lies*, pp. 450–1

49 *Ibid.*, p. 453

50 *Ibid.*, pp. 453–4

51 Bowers, *The Pledge Betrayed*, pp. 182–203, 236–8, 276–7

52 Grayzel, *A History of the Jews*, p. 676; Wyman, *The Abandonment of the Jews*, pp. 240–79; Interview with Father Robert Graham, 15 April 1985

Bibliography

Publications of brief extracts from copyrighted material is gratefully acknowledge for the following works *

*Mark Aarons, *Sanctuary! Nazi Fugitives in Australia*, Heinemann Australia, Melbourne, 1989
Alan Abrams, *Special Treatment*, Lyle Stewart, New York, 1985
Paul Addison, *Now the War is Over. A Social History of Britain 1945–51*, BBC and Jonathan Cape, London, 1985
Reuben Ainsztein, *Jewish Resistance in Nazi Occupied Eastern Europe*, Paul Elek, London 1964
Stella Alexander, *Church and State in Yugoslavia since 1945*, Cambridge University Press, Cambridge, 1979
Stella Alexander, *The Triple Myth. A Life of Archbishop Alojzije Stepinac*, East European Monographs, Boulder, 1987
All Party Parliamentary War Crimes Group, *Report on the Entry of Nazi War Criminals and Collaborators into the UK, 1945–1950*, House of Commons, London, 1988
Charles R. Allen, Junior, 'The Vatican and the Nazis', in *Reform Judaism*, Spring/Summer 1983, and 'Debate Rages: did Vatican help Nazis to escape from Europe?', in the *National Catholic Reporter*, 2 March 1984
Gennady Alov and Vassily Victorov, *Aggressive Broadcasting*, Novosti Press Agency Publishing House, Moscow, 1985
Julian Amery, *Approach March*, Hutchinson, London, 1973
Scott and Jon Lee Anderson, *Inside the League*, Dodd & Mead, New York, 1988
Christopher Andrew, *Secret Service*, Heinemann, London, 1985
Christopher Andrew and Oleg Gordievsky, *KGB: The Inside Story of its Foreign Operations from Lenin to Gorbachev*, Hodder & Stoughton, London, 1990
John Armstrong, *Ukrainian Nationalism 1939–45*, Columbia University Press, New York, 1955
Charles Ashman and Robert Wagman, *Nazi Hunters*, Pharos Books, New York, 1988
Gerald Astor, *The Last Nazi: The Life and Times of Joseph Mengele*, Donal Fine, New York, 1985
John Barron, *KGB*, Bantam, London/New York, 1979
John Beattie, *Klaus Barbie. His Life and Career*, Methuen, London, 1984

Nora Beloff, *Tito's Flawed Legacy: Yugoslavia and the West 1939–1984*, Victor
Gollancz, London, 1985
James Bentley, *Martin Niemüller*, Oxford University Press, Oxford, 1984
Nicholas Bethell, *The Last Secret. Forced Repatriation to Russia 1944–47*,
André Deutsch, London, 1974
Nicholas Bethell, *The Great Betrayal: The Untold Story of Kim Philby's
Biggest Coup*, Hodder & Stoughton, London, 1984
Pierre Blet, Robert A. Graham, Angelo Martini and Burkhart Schneider
(eds), *Les Actes et Documents du Saint Siège relatif à la Seconde Guerre
Mondiale*, Libreria Editrice Vaticana, Vatican City, Vols 1–11,
1966–81
*Jonathan Bloch and Patrick Fitzgerald, *British Intelligence and Covert
Action*, Brandon, Ireland, 1983
Howard Blum, *Wanted. The Search for Nazis in America*, Quadrangle/*New
York Times*, New York, 1977
*Branko Bokun, *Spy in the Vatican*, Tom Stacey, London, 1973
Joseph Borkin, *The Crime and Punishment of I. G. Farben*, The Free Press,
New York, 1978
Yury Boshyk (ed.), *Ukraine During World War II: History and its Aftermath*,
Canadian Institute of Ukrainian Studies, University of Alberta,
Edmonton, 1986
Douglas Botting, *In the Ruins of the Reich*, Allen & Unwin, London, 1985
Douglas Botting and Ian Sayer, *Nazi Gold*, Grove Press, New York, 1984
Douglas Botting and Ian Sayer, *America's Secret Army*, Fontana, 1989
Tom Bower, *Blind Eye to Murder*, Granada, London, 1983
Tom Bower, *Klaus Barbie*, Pantheon Books, New York, 1984
Tom Bower, *The Paperclip Conspiracy*, Michael Joseph, London, 1987
Randolph Braham, *The Politics of Genocide: The Holocaust in Hungary*,
Columbia University Press, New York, 1981
Werner Brockdorff, *Flucht vor Nürnberg. Plane und Organisation der
Fluchtwege der NS-Priminenz im 'Römischen Weg'*, Verlag Welsermühl,
Munich, 1969
*Anthony Cave Brown, *Bodyguard of Lies*, W. H. Allen (Star), London,
1977
Anthony Cave Brown, *The Secret Servant*, Michael Joseph, London, 1987
*Anthony Cave Brown, *'C': The Secret Life of Sir Stewart Menzies*,
Macmilian, New York, 1987
Friedrich Buchardt, *The Treatment of the Russian Problem during the Time of
the National Socialist Regime in Germany*, unpublished US intelligence
document
Hubert Butler, *Escape from the Anthill*, The Lilliput Press, Mullingar,
1985
Owen Chadwick, *Catholicism and History. The Opening of the Vatican
Archives*, Cambridge University Press, Cambridge, 1978
Owen Chadwick, 'The Pope and the Jews in 1942', in *Studies in Church
History*, Vol. 21, edited by W. J. Sheils, Basil Blackwell, Oxford, 1984
*Owen Chadwick, *Britain and the Vatican during the Second World War*,
Cambridge University Press, Cambridge, 1986

Nicolas Cheetham, *Keepers of the Keys: The Pope in History*, Macdonald, London, 1982

Yurij Chumatskyj (pseudonym), *Why Is One Holocaust Worth More Than Others?*, Veterans of the Ukrainian Insurgent Army, Sydney, 1986

Stephen Clissold, *Whirlwind*, Cresset Press, London, 1949

Stephen Clissold, *Croat Separatism: Nationalism, Dissidence and Terrorism*, Institute for the Study of Conflict, London, 1979

Stephen Clissold, unpublished autobiography

John Colville, *Footprints in Time*, Richard Russell, Salisbury, 1984

*E. H. Cookridge, *Gehlen. Spy of the Century*, Hodder & Stoughton, London, 1972

John Cooney, *The American Pope. The Life and Times of Francis Cardinal Spellman*, New York Times, New York, 1984

John Cornwell, *A Thief in the Night. The Death of Pope John Paul I*, Viking, London, 1989

Rupert Cornwall, *God's Banker. The Life and Death of Roberto Calvi*, Unwin, London, 1984

William Corson, *The Armies of Ignorance*, Dial Press, New York, 1977

*John Costello, *Mask of Treachery*, Morrow, New York, 1988

Geoffrey Cox, *The Race for Trieste*, Kimber, London, 1977

Tom Cullen, *Maundy Gregory*, Bodley Head, London, 1974

Erhard Dabringhaus, *Klaus Barbie*, Acropolis, Washington, 1984

*Alexander Dallin, *German Rule in Russia 1941–1945*, St Martin's Press, New York, 1957

Alexander Dallin, *Soviet Espionage*, Yale University Press, New Haven, 1956

Michael Davie (ed.), *The Diaries of Evelyn Waugh*, Penguin, Harmondsworth, 1979

Richard Deacon, *A History of British Secret Service*, Granada, London, 1969

Ladislas de Hoyas, *Klaus Barbie. The Untold Story*, W. H. Allen, London, 1985

Leon de Poncins, *Judaism and the Vatican*, Revisionist Press, Brooklyn, 1982

Leon de Poncins, *Vatican and Freemasons*, Revisionist Press, Brooklyn, 1982

Justice Jules Deschenes, *Report of the Commission of Inquiry on War Criminals*, Ottawa, 1986

Karlheinz Deschner, *Ein Jahrhundert Heilsgeschichte: Die Politik der Papste im Zeitalter der Weltkriege. Von Pius XII 1939 bis zu Johannes Paul I 1978*, Kiepenheuer und Witsch, Cologne, 1983

Luigi di Fonzo, *St Peter's Banker*, Watts, New York, 1983

Ahmet Donlagić, Žarko Atanacković and Dušan Plenča, *Yugoslavia in the Second World War*, Interpress, Belgrade, 1967

Madelaine Duke, *Top Secret Mission*, Evans Brothers, London, 1954

Allen Dulles, *The Secret Surrender*, Harper & Row, New York, 1966

John Dziak, *Chekisty. A History of the KGB*, Lexington Books, Massachusetts, 1988

Robert Erickson, *Theologians under Hitler*, Yale University Press, 1985
Carlo Falconi, *The Silence of Pius XII*, Faber & Faber, London, 1970
*Ladislas Farago, *Burn After Reading*, Walker, New York, 1961
*Ladislas Farago, *Aftermath*, Pan, London, 1976
Benjamin B. Ferencz, *Less than Slaves*, Harvard University Press, Cambridge, Massachusetts, 1979
Alexander Foote, *Story of a Russian Spy*, formerly *Handbook for Spies*, Doubleday, New York, 1949
Anne Fremantle (ed.), *The Social Teachings of the Catholic Church*, Menton-Omega, New York, 1963
Saul Friedlander, *Pius XII and the Third Reich*, Chatto & Windus; London, 1966
Jozef Garlinski, *Fighting Auschwitz. The Resistance Movement in the Concentration Camp*, Julien Friedmann, London, 1975
Peter Gay, *Weimar Culture*, Penguin, London, 1974
Reinhard Gehlen, *The Gehlen Memoirs*, Collins, London, 1972
Martin Gilbert, *Auschwitz and the Allies*, Michael Joseph, London, 1981
Martin Gilbert, *Atlas of the Holocaust*, Michael Joseph, London, 1982
Marin Gilbert, *The Holocaust*, Holt, Rinehart & Winston, New York, 1986
Martin Gilbert, *Final Journey*, Allen & Unwin, London, 1979
Father Robert Graham, The "Good Samaritan" in World War II. The Record of Relief and Rescue, Particularly by the Vatican, in Favour of the Victims of War', delivered at the Bethesda Regional Library, Bethesda, Maryland, 30 January 1989, under the auspices of the Catholic League for Religious and Civil Rights
*Solomon Grayzel, *A History of the Jews*, Mentor, New York, 1968
Andrew Greeley, *The Making of the Popes*, Futura Press, London, 1978
Richard Grunberger, *Red Rising in Bavaria*, Arthur Barker, London, 1973
Richard grunberger, *A Social History of the Third Reich*, Pelican, Harmondsworth, 1977
Larry Gurwin, *The Calvi Affair. Death of a Banker*, Macmillan, London, 1983
Michael Hanusiak, *Ukrainischer Nationalismus*, Globus Verlag, Vienna, 1979
Peter Hebblethwaite, *John XXIII. Pope of the Council*, Geoffrey Chapman, London, 1984
Stjepan Hefer, *Croatian Struggle for Freedom and Statehood*, Croatian Liberation Movement, USA, 1979
Robert Herzstein, *Waldheim, the Missing Years*, Grafton, London, 1988
Charles Higham, *American Swastika*, Doubleday, New York, 1985
*Charles Higham, *Trading with the Enemy*, Delacorte, New York, 1983
Raul Hilberg, *The Destruction of the European Jews*, Holmes & Meier, New York, 1985
Ronald Hingley, *The Russian Secret Police: Muscovite Imperial Russian and Soviet Political Security Operations 1556–1970*, Simon & Schuster, New York, 1970

Rolf Hochhuth, *The Representative*, Methuen, London, 1963
Heinz Höhne, *Codeword: 'Direktor'*, Secker & Warburg, London, 1971
Heinz Höhne, *Canaris*, Secker & Warburg, London, 1976
*Heinz Höhne and Hermann Zolling, *The General was a Spy*, Pan Books, London, 1973
Alois Hudal, *Die Grundlagen des Nationsozialismus; eine ideengeschichtliche Untersuchung*, Johannes Günther, Leipzig, 1937
Alois Hudal, *Römische Tagebücher: Lebensberichte eines alten Bischofs*, Leopold Stocker, Graz/Stuttgart, 1976
Siniša Ivanović, *Spijun u Mantiji*, Nova Knjiga, Belgrade, 1987
Fikreta Jelić-Butić, *Ustaše i NDH*, Skolska Knjiga, Zagreb, 1978
Peter Jordan, *Central Union of Europe*, Robert Marrick, New York, 1944
*David Kahn, *Hitler's Spies*, Macmillan, New York, 1978
Ihor Kamenetsky, *Hitler's Occupation of Ukraine*, Marquette University Press, Milwaukee, 1956
J. Kelly, *The Oxford Dictionary of Popes*, Oxford University Press, 1986
Stephen Knight, *The Brotherhood: The Secret World of the Freemasons*, Granada, London 1984
Lazo Kostich, *Holocaust in the Independent State of Croatia*, Liberty Press, Chicago, 1981
Bogdan Križman, *Ante Pavelić i Ustaše*, Globus, Zagreb, 1978
Bogdan Križman, *Pavelić izmedu Hitlera i Mussolinija*, Globus, Zagreb, 1980
Bogdan Križman, *Pavelić u Bjekstvu*, Globus, Zagreb, 1986
Walter Laqueur, *Weimar: A Cultural History 1918–1933*, Weidenfeld & Nicolson, London, 1974
Walter Laqueur, *The Terrible Secret*, Wedenfeld & Nicolson, London, 1981
George Leggett, *The Cheka: Lenin's Political Police*, Clarenden Press, Oxford, 1981
Penny Lernoux, *In Banks We Trust*, Doubleday, New York, 1984
Penny Lernoux, *People of God: The Struggle for World Catholicism*, Viking, New York, 1989
Djordje Ličina, *Dvadeseti Čovjek*, Centar za Informacije i Publicitet, Zagreb, 1985
Djordje Ličina, *Roverova Brača*, Centar za Informacije i Publicitet, Zagreb, 1987
Robert Jay Lifton, *The Nazi Doctors*, Basic Books, New York, 1986
Magnus Linklater, Isobel Hilton and Neal Ascherson, *The Fourth Reich*, Hodder & Stoughton, London, 1984
David Littlejohn, *The Patriotic Traitors*, Heinemann, London, 1972
*John Loftus, *The Belarus Secret*, Knopf, New York, 1982
Zdenko Löwenthal (ed.), *The Crimes of the Fascist Occupants and their Collaborators against Jews in Yugoslavia*, Federation of Jewish Communities of the Federative People's Republic of Yugoslavia, Belgrade, 1957
Fitzroy Maclean, *Eastern Approaches*, Jonathan Cape, London, 1949

Juraj Magjerec, *Hrvatski Zavod Sv. Jeronima u Rimu*, Tiskara Papinskog Sveučilista Gregoriane, Rome, 1953

Curzio Malaparte, *Kaputt*, Harborough, London, 1960

Avro Manhattan, *Terror Over Yugoslavia*, Watts, London, 1953

Avro Manhattan, *Catholic Terror Today*, Paravision, London, 1970

*Paul Manning, Martin Bormann: Nazi in Exile, Lyle Stuart, Seacaucus, 1981

Jovan Marjanović (ed.), *The Collaboration of D. Mihailović's Chetnik's with the Enemy Forces of Occupation*, Arhivski Pregled, Belgrade, 1976

David Martin, *Wilderness of Mirrors*, Harper & Row, New York, 1980

Malachi Martin, *The Vatican*, Secker & Warburg, London, 1986

Andjelko Maslić, *Terrorism by Fascist Emigration of Yugoslav Origin*, Socialist Thought and Practice, Belgrade, 1981

Mark Mason, *Christian Illusions and Papal Power*, Markwell Press, Hong Kong, 1981

Giuseppe Masucci, *Misija u Hrvatskoj*, Drina, Madrid, 1967

Andrew Menzies, *Review of Material Relating to the Entry of Suspected War Criminals into Australia*, Canberra, 1986

Leonard Mosley, *Dulles*, Dial Press, New York, 1978

Ewen Montagu, *Beyond Top Secret U*, Peter Davies, London, 1977

Brendan Murphy, *The Butcher of Lyon*, Empire Books, New York, 1983

Francis Murphy, *The Papacy Today*, Macmillan, New York, 1981

Francis Murphy, 'A Brief Biography of Paul VI', in James Andrews (ed.), *Paul VI: Critical Appraisals*, Bruce Publishing, New York, 1970

Ivo Omrčanin, *Dramatis Personae and Finis of the Independent State of Croatia*, Dorrance, Bryn Mawr, 1983

Ivo Omrčanin, *Enigma Tito*, Samizdat, Washington, 1984

Marcel Ophuls, *The Sorrow and the Pity*, Paladin, London, 1975

Paul Ormonde, *The Movement*, Nelson, Melbourne, 1972

Nazareno Padallaro, *Portrait of Pius XII*, J. M. Dent, London, 1956

Bruce Page, Phillip Knightley and David Leitch, *Philby*, André Deutsch, London, 1968

Michael Palumbo, *The Waldheim Files*, Faber & Faber, London, 1988

Corrado Pallenberg, *The Vatican From Within*, Harrap, London, 1961

Edmond Paris, *Genocide in Satellite Croatia 1941–45*, The Serbian Thought, Melbourne, 1981

Edmond Paris, *The Vatican Against Europe*, Macmillan, London, 1961

Edmond Paris, *The Secret History of the Jesuits*, Chick Publications, USA, 1982

Alfred Persche, 'Die Aktion Hudal; Das letzte Aufgebot des Abendlandes', Unpublished Manuscript, held by the Dokumentationsarchiv des Österreichischen Widerstandes

*Kim Philby, *My Silent War*, Ballantine, New York, 1983

*Chapman Pincher, *Too Secret Too Long*, St Martin's Press, New York, 1984

John Pollard, *The Vatican and Italian Fascism*, Cambridge University Press, 1988

James and Suzanne Poole, *Who Financed Hitler? The Secret Funding of Hitler's Rise to Power 1919–1933*, Dial Press, New York, 1978

Peter Potichnyi and Shtendera Yevhen (eds), *Political Thought of the Ukrainian Underground 1943–1951*, Canadian Institute of Ukrainian Studies, University of Alberta, Edmonton, 1986

Thomas Powers, *The Man Who Kept the Secrets*, Knopf, New York, 1979

John Prados, *Presidents' Secret Wars*, Morrow, New York, 1986

Prison Notes of Cardinal Wyszynski: A Freedom Within, Hodder & Stoughton, London, 1985

Alexander Ramati, *While the Pope Kept Silent*, Allen & Unwin, London, 1978

John Ranelagh, *The Agency*, Simon & Schuster, New York, 1986

Gerald Reitlinger, *The House Built on Sand*, Weidenfeld & Nicolson, London, 1960

Gerald Reitlinger, *The Final Solution*, Perpetua, New York, 1961

Gerald Reitlinger, *The SS. Alibi of a Nation 1922–1945*, Arms and Armour Press, London, 1981

Werner Rings, *L'or des Nazis: la Suisse, un relais discret*, Payot, Lausanne, 1985

Walter Roberts, *Tito, Mihailović and the Allies: 1941–1945*, Rutgers University Press, New Brunswick, 1973

Alti Rodal, *Nazi War Criminals in Canada: The Historical and Policy Setting from the 1940s to the Present*, prepared for Justice Jules Deschenes's Canadian Commission, Ottowa, 1986

Harry Rositzke, *Secret Operations*, Reader's Digest Press, New York, 1977

Barry Rubin, *Istanbul Intrigues*, McGraw Hill, New York, 1989

Allan Ryan, *Klaus Barbie and the United States Government*, report with appendices, to the US Attorney General, US Department of Justice, Washington, 1983

Allan Ryan, *Quiet Neighbors*, Harcourt Brace Jovanovich, New York, 1984

*Walter Schellenberg, *The Labyrinth*, Harper Bros, New York, 1956

Klaus Scholder, *The Churches and the Third Reich*, Vol. One 1918–34, Vol. Two 1934–, SCM Press, London, 1987 and 1988

Matthias Schmidt, *Albert Speer, the End of a Myth*, St Martin's Press, New York, 1985

Günther Schwarberg, *The Murders at Bullenhauser Damm*, Indiana University Press, Bloomingdale, 1984

*Gitta Sereny, *Into that Darkness . . . the Mind of a Mass Murderer*, Picador, London, 1977

Neal Sher, Aron Goldberg and Elizabeth White, *Robert Jan Verbelen and the United States Government*, report to the US Assistant Attorney General, Washington, 1988

William Shirer, *The Rise and Fall of the Third Reich*, Pan, London, 1968

William Shirer, *The Nightmare Years 1930–1940*, Little Brown, Boston, 1984

Paul Shoup, *Communism and the Yugoslav National Question*, Columbia University Press, New York, 1968

*Christopher Simpson, *Blowback*, Weidenfeld & Nicolson, New York, 1988

Dušar Sindik (ed.), Secaija Jevreja na Logor Jasenovac, Čačanski Glas, Beograd, 1972

David Smiley, *Albanian Assignement*, Chatto & Windus, London, 1984

Branimir Stanojević, *Under the Wing of Fascism. Andrija Artuković and the Ustaša Regime*, Tanjug, Belgrade, 1985

Branimir Stanojević, *Tunel Pačova*, Eksportpres, Belgrade, 1988

Hansjacob Stehle, *Die Ospolitik des Vatikans 1917–1975*, Piper Verlag, Munich, 1975

Stewart Stehling, *Weimar and the Vatican 1919–1933*, Princeton University Press, 1983

*William Stevenson, *Intrepid's Last Case*, Villard Books, New York, 1983

Drago Šudar, *Coming of Age in Tito's Prisons*, Mosor, Los Angeles, 1987

Anton Szanya, *Alois Hudal Zum 100 Geburtstag eines gern vergessenen Österreichers*, Der Freidenker, anno 15, issue 4, 1985

James Taylor and Warren Shaw, *A Dictionary of the Third Reich*, Grafton Books, London, 1987

Tajni Documenti od Odnosima Vatikana i Ustaške NDH, Biblioteka Društva Novinara Hrvatska, Zagreb, 1952

Nikolai Tolstoy, *The Great Betrayal*, Charles Scribner, New York, 1978

Nikolai Tolstoy, *Victims of Yalta*, Corgi, London, 1979

Nikolai Tolstoy, *The Minister and the Massacres*, Century Hutchinson, London, 1986

Jozo Tomasevich, *The Chetniks*, Stanford University Press, Stanford, 1975

Leopold Trepper, *The Great Game*, McGraw-Hill, New York, 1977

Henry Turner, *German Big Business and the Rise of Hitler*, Oxford University Press, New York, 1987

Ann and John Tusa, *The Nuremberg Trial*, Papermac, London, 1984

United States, Comptroller General, *Nazis and Axis Collaborators Were Used to Further US Anti-Communist Objectives in Europe – Some Immigrated to the United States*, General Accounting Office, Washington, 1985

Bela Vago, *The Shadow of the Swastika*, Saxon House, Farnborough, 1975

Nicholas Vakar, *Belorussia: The Making of a Nation*, Harvard University Press, Harvard, 1956

Jochen von Lang (ed.), *Eichmann Interrogated*, Farrar, Strauss & Giroux, New York, 1983

Fritz von Papen, *Memoirs*, André Deutsch, London, 1952

Bernard Wasserstein, *Britain and the Jews of Europe 1939–1945*, Clarendon, London, 1979

Peter Watson, *The Nazi's Wife*, Grafton, London, 1986

Erika Weinzierl, 'Austria: Church, State, Politics' in Richard Wolff and Jorg Hönsch (eds), *Catholics, the State and the European Radical Right 1919–1945*, Columbia University Press, New York, 1987

Charles Whiting, *Gehlen's Master Spy*, Ballantine, New York 1972

*Simon Wiesenthal, *The Murderers Among Us*, Heinemann, London, 1967

*Robin Winks, *Cloak and Gown*, Morrow, New York, 1987

David Wise and Thomas B. Ross, *The Espionage Establishment*, Bantam, London/New York, 1968

Robert Wistrich, *Who's Who in Nazi Germany*, Weidenfeld & Nicolson, London, 1982

*Peter Wright, *Spycatcher*, Viking Penguin, New York, 1987

David S. Wyman, *The Abandonment of the Jews*, Pantheon, New York, 1984

David Yallop, *In God's Name*, Jonathan Cape, London, 1984

Dragoljub Zivojinović and Dejan Lučić, *Varvarstvo u ime Hristovo. Priloži za Magnum Crimen*, Nova Knjiga, Belgrade, 1988

Susan Zucotti, *The Italians and the Holocaust*, Halban, London, 1988

Index